CONFLICTING WOR

New Dimensions of the American

T. Michael Parrish, Editor

D1553628

While in the Hands of the Enemy

MILITARY PRISONS OF THE CIVIL WAR

Charles W. Sanders, Jr.

LOUISIANA STATE UNIVERSITY PRESS

BATON ROUGE

Published by Louisiana State University Press
Copyright © 2005 by Louisiana State University Press
All rights reserved
Manufactured in the United States of America
LOUISIANA PAPERBACK EDITION, 2017

DESIGNER: *Andrew Shurtz*
TYPEFACE: *Adobe Caslon*

LIBRARY OF CONGRESS CATALOGING-IN-PUBLICATION DATA

Sanders, Charles W., 1947–
    While in the hands of the enemy : military prisons of the Civil War / Charles W. Sanders, Jr.
      p. cm. — (Conflicting worlds)
    Includes bibliographical references (p.) and index.
    ISBN 978-0-8071-6663-5 (pbk. : alk. paper)
    1. United States—History—Civil War, 1861–1865—Prisoners and prisons. 2. Military prisons—
United States—History—19th century. 3. Military prisons—Confederate States of America—History—19th century. 4. Prisoners of war—United States—History—19th century. 5. Prisoners of
war—Confederate States of America—History. I. Title. II. Series.
E615.S218 2005
973.7'71–dc22

           2005003407

The paper in this book meets the guidelines for permanence
and durability of the Committee on Production
Guidelines for Book Longevity of the
Council on Library Resources.

FOR JCSS
My Love, My Partner, My Pal

Contents

Acknowledgments

BRINGING THIS STORY of the Civil War prison systems to print would have
been impossible without the help and contributions of many people. For years
Lynda Laswell Crist, editor of the Jefferson Davis papers, has sustained my study
with her encyclopedic knowledge and enthusiastic encouragement. I am also
indebted to Professor Carol Reardon of Pennsylvania State University for taking time from her hectic schedule to offer an invaluable critique of my musings
on the afterlife of Civil War prisons and prisoners. T. Michael Parrish, scholar,
professor, author, and series editor at Louisiana State University Press, has long
been a dear friend and exacting advisor, and without his unflagging interest this
project would never have been published.

Of all the trips I made to research various collections of prison archives, none
was as fascinating or as useful as my visit to the Andersonville National Historical Site. The trip was made possible by a generous grant from the Magnolia
Chapter of the American Ex-Prisoners of War, and the enthusiasm and courtesy
extended to me by Park Superintendent Fred Boyles and Cultural Resources
Specialist Alan Marsh went far beyond the call of duty. Although I visited Andersonville at its very busiest season, Fred and Alan eagerly took time to answer
my questions and directed me to the most important archives and other available
resources. For their immense knowledge and willingness to share their precious
time with a bothersome scholar, I will be eternally grateful.

At Kansas State University, I was and am blessed with the most capable and
helpful group of mentors and colleagues one could ever desire. Sue Zschoche,
chair of the Department of History, has been unflinching in her support and
encouragement, and Louise Breen, John Fliter, Mark Parillo, and Lou Falkner
Williams have supplied not only guidance in the preparation of this work, but
years of patient teaching and training as well. Peter B. Knupfer, now on the fac-

ulty of the University of Michigan, was "present at the creation" of this project, and at every stage he was a steady source of precise direction and penetrating criticism. He never accepted less than my best, but his door was always open and his patience was infinite. I am deeply indebted to Michael Ramsay for the long talks and exchanges of ideas and humor, and a special thanks to librarians Kathy, Lori, and Sharon for filling my unending requests for arcane tomes from obscure collections with cheerfulness and dispatch.

Finally, the completion of this book would have been impossible without the love and encouragement of my family. I was blessed with a mother and father who taught me to value learning and to honor the past, and the example they provided with their lives set the compass of mine. My greatest obligation of all, however, is to my wife, Jo, and my son, Chad. They endured each day of the "prison experience" right along with me, accepting untold sacrifices without a murmur while supplying boundless love and inspiration. Scooter and Josie—for the help, for the humor, for the happiness, and for the hope, I am thankful beyond words.

WHILE IN THE HANDS
OF THE ENEMY

Introduction

OF ALL THE CONTROVERSIES generated by the American Civil War, few have been as acrimonious or enduring as those that arose over the treatment of prisoners of war. The first accusations of cruel and barbarous treatment of captives were leveled soon after the initial prisoners were taken. As the war dragged on, charges of incompetence, neglect, and even criminal intent on the part of the Union and Confederate governments became more frequent and venomous. The animosity spawned by the mistreatment of prisoners was so deep that it continued even after the termination of hostilities. A series of carefully staged "investigations" by the U.S. Congress and War Department into the operation of Confederate camps culminated with the only execution of a Civil War soldier for war crimes, and for the remaining decades of the nineteenth century, bookstores in both North and South were flooded with accounts penned by scores of former captives who sought to highlight the beastly cruelty of their captors while lauding the humane and enlightened policies that guided the prisoner-of-war policies of their own governments.

The motives and hyperbole of these competing narratives are readily apparent, as is the fact that the history of Civil War prisons was not a happy one. In the four years of the American Civil War, 409,608 soldiers—one out of every seven who served in the Union or Confederate armies—became prisoners of war, and a great many did not survive that experience. Of the 194,743 Yankees who were confined in Confederate prisons, 30,218 died; of the 214,865 Rebels who entered Union camps, 25,976 never left them alive. Given the vast scope of the war and the close and brutal nature of the fighting, the fact that one of every seven Civil War soldiers became a prisoner of war comes as no surprise. Much more difficult to understand is why 56,194 of these men—one in seven, again—perished at the hands of their captors.

Explanations and justifications aplenty have been offered in answer to this question, and they all share one common characteristic. While conceding that the loss of life in the camps was indeed terrible, historians have argued that the suffering and death resulted from factors beyond the control of the belligerents and that neither the North nor the South was guilty of systematically mistreating prisoners.

This book will challenge that conclusion. It will argue that although difficulties such as organizational incompetence, inexperience, and chronic shortages of essential resources certainly contributed to the horrors in the camps, these factors pale to insignificance when compared to the devastation wrought by Union and Confederate leaders who knew full well the horrific toll of misery and death their decisions and actions would exact in the camps. The most telling evidence in support of this assertion is found in the official and personal correspondence of the national leaders who devised the prisoner-of-war policies and directed the prison operations, and in this study those men will be allowed to speak for themselves. What emerges is a chilling chronicle of military and civilian leaders who increasingly came to regard prisoners not as men, but as mere pawns to be used and then callously discarded in pursuit of national objectives.

Although the Civil War was not the first time the nation faced the challenge of managing large numbers of prisoners, the adequacy of Union and Confederate prisoner-of-war plans in 1861 might most charitably be characterized as limited. The lessons learned from short-term confinements and the operation of parole and exchange cartels during the Revolution, the War of 1812, and the Mexican War were often ignored; even when followed, they were insufficient to guide Civil War planners, who were compelled to establish a sprawling network of prisons that swiftly filled with thousands of captives. Because of this inadequate planning, prisoner management was chaotic during the first year of the Civil War. The establishment of an exchange cartel permitting the immediate release of captives on parole was delayed due to President Abraham Lincoln's refusal to enter into any formal agreement that might have implied a de facto recognition of the Confederacy. As a result, the number of prisoners retained by each side mounted rapidly. Soldiers held by the North were confined primarily in expedient sites such as old forts and unoccupied military training camps. Because few such facilities existed in the South, Union prisoners were interned in existing jails, vacant warehouses, or hastily constructed open stockades.

Both governments quickly realized that such arrangements were inadequate, and by the fall of 1861 each was taking steps to establish an effective system of prisoner management. In the North, leadership of this initiative fell to Brigadier

General Montgomery C. Meigs, the quartermaster general of the army. Fully appreciating the immensity of the task he faced, Meigs appointed Lieutenant Colonel William Hoffman to the position of commissary general of prisoners with primary responsibility for directing the northern system of prisons. Southern leaders opted not to appoint a single officer to superintend prisoner operations. Because the most important Confederate prisons of the first year of the war were established in and around Richmond, direction of the system fell by default to General John H. Winder, provost marshal of the city. Both Hoffman and Winder initiated policies intended to enhance and extend their degree of control over the existing prisons and speed the establishment of additional facilities, but new arrivals in the camps far outpaced these efforts.

As historian Bell I. Wiley noted years ago, the life of the Civil War soldier was difficult even in the best of circumstances; for every "Billy Yank" or "Johnny Reb" killed in battle, two would succumb to sickness and disease. Confinement in a Civil War prison increased those odds exponentially. Reports from prison commanders and medical inspectors confirmed that overcrowding, exposure, inadequate medical care, and shortages of rations and basic supplies were exacting a terrible toll in the camps. As newspapers and magazines filled their pages with lurid descriptions of helpless prisoners suffering under heinous keepers, public pressure for repatriation rose in both the North and the South.[1]

Relief finally came in July 1862, when the Union and Confederate governments signed a cartel mandating the swift and complete exchange of all prisoners. Most were rapidly repatriated, and soldiers captured while the cartel was in operation were promptly released on parole. The number of prisoners in northern and southern camps dropped to a manageable level, and conditions in all installations improved dramatically.

This respite proved brief, however. Both governments began to violate the terms of the cartel almost immediately, and in July 1863 Union secretary of war Edwin M. Stanton ordered that the agreement be modified to allow man-for-man exchanges only. By Stanton's order, immediate paroles on the battlefield were also discontinued, and the parole of "excess" prisoners (beyond the number actually held by each side) was prohibited. The Confederacy refused to accept Stanton's modifications, and by the fall of 1863 general exchanges had ceased.

It was at this point that officials charged with the direction of the two prisoner-of-war systems began to adopt increasingly harsh measures. In the North, Stanton used allegations that Union prisoners were being mistreated to justify successive rounds of retaliation against Confederate prisoners. In the South, Secretary of War James Seddon transferred responsibility for provisioning Union captives to Commissary General of Subsistence Lucius B. Northrop, an obstreperous and pitiless officer who had clearly and repeatedly demonstrated his opposition to supplying food to prisoners at the rate required by Confederate army regulations. As these new, harsher attitudes took hold, the quantity and the quality of food, clothing, blankets, and medical care provided to prisoners in Union and Confederate camps was slashed dramatically; with the onset of winter, conditions in the prisons of both nations plummeted.

By January 1864, hundreds were dying each day in the sprawling networks of Union and Confederate prisons. In an effort to relieve the desperate overcrowding, both sides opened even more facilities. But rather than alleviating the crisis, these hastily established prisons would prove to be the most lethal of the war. In dozens of reports, camp commanders and medical inspectors alerted their superiors in Washington and Richmond to the alarming rates of sickness and death among captives, but neither government took decisive action to reverse this appalling trend. By August 1864 conditions in Confederate camps had become so desperate that the Davis administration was compelled to agree to Stanton's revision of the terms of the cartel, but hopes that this concession would stem the suffering and dying were dashed when General Ulysses S. Grant prohibited the resumption of general exchanges.

Although Grant publicly proclaimed that his decision was prompted by the South's refusal to exchange black soldiers under the same terms as whites, the general's refusal was actually based on simple, ghastly arithmetic. The surest way to deplete Confederate combat strength, he explained to Stanton and Secretary of State William Seward, was to slam shut the prison gates and retain all the Rebel prisoners then held by the North. Although Grant acknowledged that refusing to permit general exchanges was tantamount to a death sentence for the thousands of Union boys wasting away in southern camps, he was convinced that this strategy would ultimately yield victory at the least cost in Union blood and treasure.

With exchanges terminated, the camps became more overcrowded than ever, and it was during this period that conditions in all the prisons reached their nadir. In southern pens such as Andersonville, Cahaba, Florence, and Danville, the strains produced by overcrowding were compounded by neglect and poor administration, while in northern installations like Camp Douglas, Elmira, Camp Chase, and Rock Island, the suffering of prisoners was heightened with each round of ration reductions. Freedom for most soldiers captured during this period came only in the closing months of the war.

Much of this history is well known and available to readers through prisoner narratives and the histories of individual camps. Although this study incorporates scholarship from these earlier works, it is not intended to provide a comprehensive history of all the camps established during the war. Although Camp Ford and Camp Groce were major installations in the trans-Mississippi theater, for example, facilities in that theater did not fall under the control of the prison systems of the two governments and are therefore addressed only in passing. The focus of this work, rather, is to provide a comprehensive examination of the manner in which the scores of Union and Confederate prisons were administered as a system over the course of the war. It will detail the establishment and operation of the major camps and supply an explanation of how and why the policies that controlled operations within them were shaped by the two governments to achieve national objectives.

Most importantly, this study will confront one of the last bastions of revisionist Civil War historiography—the stubborn refusal of scholars and the lay public to trace the responsibility for the darkest chapter of that conflict to its source, the leadership of the Union and the Confederacy. Both of the belligerent powers deliberately and systematically mistreated the captives they held, and the depth of their guilt was such that that even before the guns fell silent each was furiously constructing elaborate explanations for and justifications of their actions. As the victor, the Union compiled "official histories" of the prisons; these histories consistently portrayed the Federal system as efficient and humane while casting the Rebel installations as death camps in which helpless Union boys were systematically tortured, starved, and murdered by their maniacal keepers. In the South, defeat neither delayed nor diminished the weaving of an intricate tapestry of rationalization, half-truths, and outright lies to justify the actions of the Confederate government. The authors of this southern defense did their work well, and their creation has become one of the most important and enduring components of the myth of the "Lost Cause."

In the last analysis, however, these national fabrications spun by Union and Confederate apologists fail to conceal or justify the horrific human cost of their actions. The simple and inescapable fact is that at Elmira, Andersonville, Salisbury, Fort Delaware, and dozens of other Civil War prisons, it was common for young men in blue and gray who were perfectly healthy when they entered the stockades to sicken and die within the space of a few weeks—victims of overcrowding, exposure, poor sanitation, inadequate medical care, and starvation. While it is impossible to know precisely how many deaths could have been prevented, it is quite clear that tens of thousands of Union and Confederate captives would not have perished as they did had the men who directed the prison systems cared for them as their own regulations and basic humanity dictated. But this they very deliberately chose not to do; and that choice, as one young girl who witnessed firsthand the brutal mistreatment of prisoners warned, surely constituted "a most horrible national sin."[2]

CHAPTER I

A People Unprepared

NO ONE SAW it coming. As incredible as it seems in retrospect, not a single leader, North or South, military or civilian, anticipated that the fighting in the American Civil War would result in hundreds of thousands of soldiers becoming prisoners of war. No one on either side had any idea of the extraordinary efforts that would be required to house, feed, and clothe these prisoners or to protect them from the ravages of a grisly array of diseases.

Americans, in truth, were naive about many of the requirements that civil war would impose upon them. Before Fort Sumter, most believed that war, if it came at all, would be a heroic affair consisting of one or two glorious battles and almost devoid of bloodshed.[1] This notion was buried along with the bodies at Manassas in 1861, but there was no such revelation in the planning for prisoners of war. Although each of the belligerents eventually developed complex and comprehensive systems to manage their far-flung network of prisons, the policies that regulated operations in the scores of Union and Confederate camps and determined the living conditions for the soldiers within them seldom derived from comprehensive plans that were formulated to secure long-term objectives. Rather, they were reactive measures, promulgated in response to an endless series of crises or instituted in an effort to satisfy a constantly shifting set of military requirements and political agendas. This perpetual lack of strategic focus and preparedness was one of the primary contributors to the deplorable conditions routinely found in Civil War prisons, and it was one of the principal reasons why over fifty thousand prisoners died.[2]

One possible explanation for this absence of adequate planning is that Americans had little experience in managing large numbers of prisoners and that military and civilian leaders were therefore taken by surprise when presented with such challenges in the Civil War. In fact, just the opposite was true. The United

States had fought three major wars prior to 1860, and in each it had been forced to address the complex problems of securing and providing for enemy prisoners while simultaneously endeavoring to secure the best possible treatment for Americans held captive. A review of the way in which the nation responded to such challenges in the Revolution, the War of 1812, and the Mexican War clearly reveals that Americans had not only dealt with such problems before the Civil War, but also that earlier plans and policies decisively shaped the prisoner-of-war systems developed by the Union and Confederate governments.

America's initial experience with prisoners came with its first war, the Revolution. Although no single body of rules and regulations existed to govern the treatment of prisoners in the last quarter of the eighteenth century, most western nations adhered to the statutes of the Treaty of Westphalia (1648) and the dictates of custom and international law. Without exception, these provisions called for humane treatment of prisoners, routine exchanges of captives by belligerent powers, and the timely release of all those interned at war's end.[3]

Although both the British and the Americans professed compliance with these conventions, questions concerning the legal status of American prisoners complicated all negotiations concerning prisoners. At the center of the dispute was the British decision to classify captured Americans not simply as enemies, but as traitors. As such, the British reasoned, the colonials taken under arms were entitled neither to the legal status of prisoners of war nor to the protection afforded by accepted conventions. Americans countered that Continental regulars and militia were bona fide soldiers fighting in a war for independence and were therefore fully deserving of all the commonly accepted rights accorded prisoners. Intense wrangling over such fine points of law persisted until the last months of the war, and while the debate dragged on, neither the British nor the Americans were establishing an enviable record of humane prisoner treatment.[4]

Ashore, the British most often confined their captives in existing jails or makeshift facilities. Installations in the latter category included abandoned or commandeered factory buildings, warehouses, and—much to the disgust of pious colonials—churches. The treatment received by prisoners confined in such facilities was, in the main, not considered particularly brutal or inhumane by eighteenth-century standards, and the greatest single source of their suffering was simple neglect.[5]

Such was not the case for their comrades interned in the prison ships that rode at anchor in American harbors from New York to Charleston. Beneath the decks of these floating abominations, hundreds of men were confined in dark, dank spaces that were so overcrowded the captives could only lie in their own filth. Rations, when furnished at all, were both unappetizing and nutritionally insufficient. Virtually all of the prisoners suffered from chronic dysentery, and diseases such as smallpox and scurvy were rampant. "The air was so foul," one survivor recalled, "that a lamp could not be kept burning, by reason of which three boys were not missed until they had been dead ten days." The death toll on these hulks was appalling. On a single prison ship—the infamous *Jersey*—almost seven thousand prisoners died.[6]

Reports of British mistreatment of Continental prisoners reached American leaders soon after the war began. On 11 August 1775 General George Washington, recently appointed to command the American forces, protested to the British commander, General Thomas Gage, that colonial prisoners were being "cast into jail for felons" and denied the most basic "Rights of Humanity." Gage disputed this claim, arguing that although colonials captured while bearing arms against the king were no more than common traitors who, by law and custom, deserved the gallows, they were in fact being treated with "care and kindness" in conditions much more favorable than those afforded the Crown prisoners in Washington's hands.[7]

Washington's protests did little to alter British policies. By the winter of 1777, reports of British mistreatment of captives had become so common that the Continental Congress directed the general to demand an explanation of the alleged misconduct from Gage's replacement, General Sir William Howe. "Such treatment of American prisoners," Congress ordered Washington to convey to Howe, "is not only inconsistent with the practice of civilized nations, but totally the reverse of that humane treatment which the British prisoners have uniformly received in these united states." Howe responded rather vaguely that while conditions for American prisoners might indeed be harsh, they were suffering no "mistreatment." Congress judged the response to be "by no means explicit and satisfactory"; it continued to lodge similar complaints throughout the war. Such protests had little effect, however, and the mistreatment of prisoners by the British continued to pose a problem for American authorities.[8]

Along with attempting to secure humane treatment for their own soldiers held by the Crown, colonial leaders were also faced with the daunting challenge of maintaining the thousands of British soldiers and sailors who became American prisoners. While conditions in Yankee prisons were certainly better than those found on Royal Navy prison ships, the nascent Continental government had made no preparations for caring for large numbers of enemy captives. As a result, British prisoners were frequently ill-fed and poorly housed. Moreover, due to chronic shortages of supplies and rapidly shifting colonial military fortunes, they were often compelled to endure long forced marches to locations deemed secure by their captors.[9] Soldiers captured at the battle of Saratoga, for example, were first confined in Massachusetts, but when it appeared that advancing British soldiers might overrun the prison, the captives were moved by forced marches almost six hundred miles south, to barracks in Charlottesville, Virginia. Medical care for prisoners during this and other such movements was virtually nonexistent, and many of those who fell ill en route died.[10]

Although the logistical and security problems of providing for thousands of British prisoners were daunting, the legal status of these captives was never in doubt. When taken in battle, they were immediately accorded the status of prisoners of war and were treated as such by the Americans. Loyalists captured while bearing arms in support of the Crown, however, presented the Continental Congress with a special problem. Were these combatants to be considered British subjects in the lawful service of their king, or were they to be regarded as Americans and therefore traitors to the United States and the states in which they resided?

The question, ironically, was much the same as that faced by the British when classifying American captives, and in the end, Congress opted for the same solution: loyalists captured under arms would be considered traitors and treated accordingly. But here the similarities between the British and American policies ended. Although the Crown officially classified colonial captives as rebels and confined them under horrible conditions, such treatment was in actuality no different than that meted out to the soldiers of any enemy nation unfortunate enough to fall into British hands during this period. The Americans, however, were determined to make good their threat of harsh treatment for loyalists, and on 30 December 1777, the Continental Congress resolved that colonials captured in the voluntary service of the Crown would be held in close confinement until transferred to the jurisdiction of the state in which they resided. They would then be liable to the laws of that state—a dark prospect indeed, given that each of the states had enacted severe statutes under which loyalists who refused to swear an oath of allegiance to the new American government could expect incarceration with little hope of exchange, confiscation of their property, whippings, brandings, and, in some cases, execution.[11]

As the war dragged on and the number of British and American prisoners continued to rise, both governments wrestled with the problem of securing the repatriation of their own soldiers and improving prison conditions for those who remained in the hands of the enemy. A partial solution was effected in late 1776, when the belligerents initiated programs permitting limited paroles and exchanges of prisoners. Under these agreements, commanders in the field were granted the authority to negotiate special arrangements for the release of designated prisoners in accordance with specific terms. Those released might find their movements restricted to certain regions, for instance, and officers granted parole were usually required to pledge on their honor that they would not again take up arms until formally exchanged. The army provost marshal and civilian law-enforcement officers monitored the movements and activities of parolees, and those found in violation of the terms under which they had been freed were subject to reincarceration without the hope of future release.[12]

But such arrangements did not free all soldiers and sailors held captive, and whenever allegations of mistreatment of those who remained prisoners arose, both belligerents quickly turned to threats of retaliation unless conditions improved. This course of action, however, was not without risks. Absent an agreement for regular prisoner exchanges, the threat of retaliation might provoke the opposing government into allowing prison conditions to become even worse or instituting even harsher retaliatory measures. With this possibility in mind, Congress was very circumspect in ordering acts of retaliation; but when legislators judged that there was no other course of action open to them, they turned to the threat of "due retaliation" unless His Majesty's forces improved conditions in British prisons and aboard prison ships. And when such improvements were not forthcoming, Congress acted.[13]

Acts of retaliation implemented by Americans during the war usually mandated close confinement and reductions in the quantity of rations provided British captives. In December 1775, for example, Washington notified Gage that the conditions under which British prisoners were held would be patterned "exactly by the Rule you shall observe," and that Gage's response would determine whether the Americans followed a policy of "Kindness and Humanity" or "Severity and Hardship."[14] In late 1776 Congress followed through on this threat by ordering six British officers to be held in close confinement until conditions for their Continental counterparts improved. Among the group of His Majesty's soldiers selected to endure this retribution was Lieutenant Colonel Archibald Campbell of the 71st Regiment of Highlanders. Following his capture in June 1776, Campbell had been paroled near Boston and had lived in that city in relative comfort with his servants. His life of ease ended in December, when he was transported to the city jail in Concord, Massachusetts. There, as Campbell recalled, he was confined "in a dungeon of twelve or thirteen feet square," the walls of which were "black with the grease and litter of successive criminals." He was held in these conditions until again paroled almost one year later.[15]

On 21 January 1778 Congress initiated its broadest application of retaliation of the war, directing the commissary general of prisoners to reduce the daily rations of all British prisoners and ensure that they were confined under conditions equal to those borne by Americans in captivity. For the next three years, acts of retaliation were instituted under this order whenever Congress deemed necessary. This retaliation usually assumed the form of ration reductions or maintaining specified prisoners in close confinement, and the restrictions were usually relaxed after a few weeks or as soon as credible evidence of an improvement in the treatment of American prisoners was received. In 1781 Congress toughened its 1778 directive by reserving to itself the authority to terminate retaliatory reductions or restrictions once they had been imposed.[16] There is scant evidence to suggest that any of these retaliatory measures actually mitigated the misery of American prisoners, but leaders in Congress soon discovered that stern threats of retribution (such as those issued in 1778 and 1781) were of excellent propaganda value and went far to assure anxious citizens that their representatives were doing everything possible to relieve the suffering of Americans held captive.[17]

Members of the Continental Congress nonetheless understood that limited grants of parole would do little to reduce the total number of men in captivity, while threats of retaliation, even when executed, were fraught with risk and effective only in response to very specific situations. Eager to speed the repatriation of its own soldiers and diminish the financial and administrative burdens associated with managing thousands of enemy captives, Congress repeatedly proposed a full exchange of prisoners, "citizen for citizen, officer for officer of equal rank, and soldier for soldier."[18] Under normal circumstances, the British, like other traditional European armies of the late eighteenth century, would have been eager to approve any agreement that would have returned their soldiers to the ranks, but here again the thorny question of the legal status of American prisoners presented the Crown with circumstances that were far from normal. King George III's ministers, mindful of their official characterization of the conflict as a rebellion of traitorous subjects rather than a war between two sovereign nations, were loath to enter into any negotiations that might imply de facto recognition of the rebels or increase the risk that unfriendly powers like Spain and France might intervene as allies of the Americans.[19] As a result, each of the numerous conferences convened for the purpose of negotiating a general exchange ultimately foundered, and the number of men held by each side continued to climb.

Still, British and American negotiators were able to expand the scope of the limited exchanges initiated early in the war. In the closing months of 1781 they agreed to exchange prisoners by "composition," a program that assigned captives an exchange value based on their rank. A lieutenant general, for example, was assigned a value of 1,044, and he might be exchanged for one prisoner of equal rank or for 1,044 privates, a rank holding a value of one.[20]

It was not until 25 March 1782, almost six months after the surrender of Lord Cornwallis and his entire army at Yorktown, that the British parliament at last voted to recognize American captives as prisoners of war. In August of that year, ships bearing Americans released from prisons in Great Britain began arriving in Boston and Philadelphia. Finally, in 1783, after more than eight years of fighting, the British at last agreed to a full exchange of all remaining prisoners.[21]

The Revolution was the first time that the United States was compelled to resolve the issues attendant in managing large numbers of enemy prisoners while working simultaneously to ensure humane treatment for American captives, and the experience gained in solving these problems shaped the nation's thought on the subject in a number of important ways. First, it fostered the expectation that soldiers, if captured, would face a grim existence in which the absence of adequate food, clothing, billeting, and medical care would simply be daily facts of life. Second, it reinforced the conviction that the only reliable strategy for ending the suffering of prisoners was the negotiation of general exchange cartels that would provide for the swiftest possible repatriation. Lastly, it strengthened the belief that retaliation against prisoners of war afforded a completely acceptable means of influencing enemy behavior, and that while such acts often did little to ameliorate the suffering of captives, they were of immense propaganda value to government leaders seeking to assure anxious constituents that their loved ones held by the enemy had not been forgotten.

These lessons were still fresh in the minds of Americans when war with England came again. Although there were many differences between the circumstances that shaped the conduct of the Revolution and the War of 1812, one of the most important was the fact that the later conflict was not a war between a nation and its rebellious colonies, but a war fought by two equally sovereign states. This distinction would influence all deliberations concerning prisoners of war, for it removed the major impediment that had thwarted efforts to resolve prisoner issues during the Revolution. In the War of 1812, the British could no longer refuse to treat with their enemy based on the legal technicality that the Americans were no more than an armed rabble engaged in treason against the king. Americans now held the same legal status as their British opponents—a fact that would significantly expedite negotiations concerning prisoners.

Although the United States had been drifting toward war with Great Britain for years, the commencement of hostilities in summer of 1812 found the new nation unprepared to cope with the problem of enemy prisoners. No government bureaus or other administrative agencies had been established for that purpose, and the existing army and navy regulations contained no regulations for the management of large numbers of captured enemy combatants. With the experience of the Revolution still fresh, Congress moved to correct this deficiency; on 26 June 1812 it enacted legislation directing that all enemy personnel captured at sea were to be reported to the Federal authorities at the port where they were delivered and then transferred to the jurisdiction of Federal marshals, who would be responsible for confining them until they were released. In the early months of the war it quickly became apparent that both sides were disposed to effect prisoner releases as swiftly as possible.

The British, aware that the war was extremely unpopular among Americans in New England, hoped that combining the lenient treatment of prisoners with a generous policy of early releases would encourage the development of an opposition movement that would challenge the administration of President James Madison. American leaders, aware that their nation was completely unprepared to resolve satisfactorily the problems inherent in maintaining large numbers of British prisoners, shared this preference for the expedient release of prisoners. In August 1812, this mutual desire for speedy repatriation led the warring governments to agree on a general parole of all captured seamen. A similar arrangement in November freed all prisoners who had been captured in engagements ashore. By the end of the year both sides had divested themselves of most of the prisoners captured during the first six months of the war.[22]

This initial success held out the promise that a more extensive and formal accord—regulating not only the exchange of prisoners but their treatment while confined—might be formalized. Both governments were eager to conclude such an arrangement, for under the existing rules of warfare, freed prisoners retained the legal status of parolees who could not resume full military duties until officially exchanged. As a consequence, hundreds of soldiers and sailors were milling about in the Canadian and American ports where they had been transported following their release, and both governments sought to return them to full duty as quickly as possible.[23]

The opportunity to resolve this issue surfaced when John Mitchell, the American agent charged with the disposition of American prisoners paroled in Halifax, Nova Scotia, arrived at his post in October 1812. British officials immediately pressed Mitchell to conclude an agreement whereby paroled prisoners might be officially exchanged. Although not formally authorized to engage in such discussions, Mitchell agreed to explore the possibility of establishing such an accord.

The talks proceeded with amazing speed, and on 28 November, Mitchell and his British counterpart signed a proposed agreement that prescribed the terms of paroles and exchanges, prohibited certain forms of punishments for prisoners, and specified the procedures the governments were to follow in registering complaints and redressing grievances.[24]

As soon as the documents were signed, Mitchell dispatched a copy to Washington. Not surprisingly, the Madison administration was a bit taken aback by the degree of authority assumed by its representative, and upon review found a number of the provisions unacceptable. But the Americans were as desperate as their enemies for an agreement codifying the treatment and exchange of prisoners, and Madison therefore directed Secretary of State James Monroe to meet with the British agent for prisoners, Thomas Barclay, for the purpose of resolving the American objections. This Monroe did, and on 12 May 1813 the Cartel for the Exchange of Prisoners of War between Great Britain and the United States of America was signed. The U.S. Congress quickly ratified the cartel; although objections by the Lords of the Admiralty precluded official Crown approval, Barclay assured Monroe that as the king's representative, he would consider the terms of the cartel in force.[25] For the first time in its history, the United States had concluded a formal agreement governing the care and exchange of prisoners of war with a belligerent power.

Although exchanges, when possible, were to proceed rank for equivalent rank, article one of the cartel assigned relative values to combatants of various ranks and positions, much like the composition system introduced in the Revolutionary War. By applying these relative values, combatants of unequal rank might be exchanged when required. An admiral or general could be exchanged "for forty men each," while lieutenants could be traded for only six men. All exchanges were to be effected "without delay and as speedily as circumstances will admit." This article also stipulated that "prisoners taken at sea, or on land, on both sides, shall be treated with humanity, conformable to the usage and practice of the most civilized nations during war." Article seven assigned the responsibility for providing captives with "a subsistence of sound and wholesome provisions" to the detaining government, but allowed each nation the option of providing "clothing and such other small allowances as may be deemed reasonable" for its prisoners in enemy hands. This article also specified that no prisoner was to be "struck with the hand, whip, stick or any other weapon whatever," and that "the complaints of prisoners shall be attended to, and real grievances redressed." To ensure that these provisions were maintained, the respective governments were afforded the right to "inspect at all times the quality and quantity of subsistence provided for the prisoners," as well as the conditions under which they were being maintained.[26]

The Madison administration soon realized that successful implementation of the sweeping provisions of the cartel would require the creation of a new Federal post. On 6 July 1812 Congress had granted the president the authority to "make such regulations and arrangements for the safe keeping, support and exchange of prisoners of war as he may deem expedient," and in the spring of 1813 Madison exercised this authority to create the Office of the Commissary General of Prisoners. The office had first been established during the Revolution, but in that conflict the authority and responsibility for managing and exchanging prisoners of war had continued to reside primarily with individual states. During the War of 1812, however, the Office of the Commissary General of Prisoners became a fully institutionalized agency within the Department of State, assuming sole authority in all matters concerning prisoners. To fill the post of commissary general, the president selected John Mason, a prominent District of Columbia resident with extensive experience in government service.[27]

Mason's duties did not include developing policy. He was to implement the directives of the secretary of state and, in special instances, those of the president. Still, his responsibilities were vast. As commissary general he was charged with coordinating the actions of all Federal departments on issues concerning prisoners, and to his office also fell the responsibility for directing the activities of commissary agents who monitored the treatment of American captives held by the British in Halifax, Quebec, the West Indies, and England. In addition, he served as the principal U.S. liaison in negotiations with the primary British agent for prisoners, and quite often he was required to respond to inquiries and complaints from private citizens and individual British and American prisoners.[28]

Mason was also charged with the supervision of the marshals and collectors of customs responsible for the actual incarceration of enemy soldiers and sailors, as well as the conditions under which these prisoners were held. As in the Revolution, Americans confined enemy captives in a variety of facilities. Most were existing jails, but for the first time in the nation's history the government also established depots, or cantonments, that were specifically designed for the incarceration of enemy prisoners. The largest and most famous of these was established in the fall of 1813 at an abandoned military training facility in Pittsfield, Massachusetts. The Pittsfield cantonment, as the site came to be known, consisted of about eighteen acres enclosed by a board fence, along which were posted seven sentry boxes. The cantonment was originally expected to house three hundred inmates, but when that number was quickly exceeded, other buildings—including the site's granary and two large barns—were appropriated and converted to prison use. By the end of the war, the capacity at Pittsfield had been expanded to 1,500, and the facility housed the largest concentration of prisoners in the United States.[29]

The procedures for prisoner exchanges were established in the sessions between Mason and Barclay. The two men would examine lists of prisoners held by their respective governments, agree on exchange ratios in accordance with the provisions of the cartel, designate by name the prisoners who were to be exchanged, and arrange for the transport of those men to locations where they would again come under the control of their country of origin. Once under friendly control, soldiers and sailors who had been officially exchanged would return to full military duty; those who had been released on parole had to await formal exchange before again taking up arms. Under this system Mason and Barclay negotiated five major exchanges during the war, and in the main, the transfers went smoothly. Two problems snarled the exchange process significantly, however, and each would also complicate the exchange of prisoners during the Civil War.[30]

The first problem arose from American indecision over how to deal with "prisoners of color"—black sailors who were captured while serving aboard Royal Navy vessels in the Caribbean. As historian Steven A. Channing notes, southerners were perpetually wary of the threat of slave insurrections like the bloody uprising that had engulfed Santo Domingo in the 1790s. The fear that blacks from the West Indies might incite American slaves to similar revolts was so great that care was taken to preclude the importation of blacks who had previously labored on the plantations of those islands. This fear of an influx of "barbarians" from the Caribbean islands largely abated when the United States terminated its international slave trade in 1807, but it swiftly returned when American ships began to offload their cargoes of black prisoners in southern ports.[31]

These captives were deemed particularly dangerous, for along with being residents of the Indies, they had served aboard British vessels as free men. Such men, slaveowners were convinced, were carriers of the dreaded virus of black revolution, and southern leaders went to extraordinary lengths to prevent its spread among American slaves. In 1813, for example, the mayor of Savannah appealed directly to Secretary of State Monroe for the removal of blacks who had been incarcerated in that city. These captives, the mayor warned, were sure to hold "principles inconsistent with subordination," which "may be imbibed" by slaves with whom they came into contact. To avoid such contamination, he called on the secretary to prevent the landing of such prisoners in southern ports in the future.[32]

The Madison government knew full well that requiring Yankee captains to sail hundreds of additional miles just so they could deposit captured blacks in northern ports would seriously diminish the time these vessels might be at sea engaging the enemy. The request to prohibit the landing of black prisoners in southern ports was therefore denied. At the same time, the president and his advisors took advantage of the situation to craft a policy they hoped would remove the troublesome issues raised by prisoners of color, even as it resolved another problem that was plaguing the administration.

Hundreds of runaway American slaves had found sanctuary within British lines, and slaveowners were angrily petitioning the Madison administration for action to secure the return of their property.[33] In response to these demands, Commissary General of Prisoners Mason was directed to have the marshals who held black prisoners determine which of the captives were slaves and which were free men. The latter were to be treated as ordinary prisoners of war subject to exchange, while the former were to be confined without hope of release under the terms of the 1813 cartel. Men in this second group, Mason was charged to inform his British counterpart, would be released only if the Crown agreed to an in-kind exchange for the American slaves who had fled within British lines. The British refused, and black prisoners who had been designated as slaves accordingly languished in American prisons until their release in 1816.[34]

Although the question of the disposition of prisoners of color complicated exchanges under the cartel, it did not halt them. Such was not the case with the second problem. The dispute it engendered proved so disruptive that it completely derailed the entire exchange process. That problem centered on the old issue of the legal status of prisoners. In the vast majority of cases, both the United States and Great Britain accepted prisoners' claims of citizenship without question. Trouble arose in October 1812, however, when twenty-three American soldiers captured by the British at the battle of Queenstown were designated Crown subjects and transported to England to stand trial for treason. The British claim was based on a provision of English common law, which held that the men, most of whom were Irish, had been born subjects of the king and would remain British subjects until their deaths, despite their claim to be naturalized citizens of the United States.[35] When appeals to royal officials failed to obtain the release of the prisoners or an adjustment of their legal status, Madison secured authority from Congress to retaliate. In May 1813, he directed Secretary of War John Armstrong to order Major General John Dearborn, commander of the U.S. forces on the Niagara frontier, to "put into close confinement twenty-three British soldiers, to be kept as hostages" until the Americans were returned and exchanged. When informed of this action, the British responded by placing into close confinement double that number of American officers, and they then upped the stakes by notifying Dearborn that "if any of the said British soldiers shall suffer death" due to the execution of the Irish-American prisoners for treason, the commander of British forces in Canada would select from the forty-six officers "as many as would double the number of British soldiers who shall have been so unwarrantably put to death, and cause such officers . . . to suffer death immediately."[36]

Realizing that the basic question in this dispute was nothing less than the recognition of American citizenship, Madison was determined not to be bested by the British. He ordered Commissary General Mason to place into close confinement all the British commissioned officers then held in Massachusetts, Kentucky, and Ohio to ensure that the United States held "a sufficient number of hostages to answer in their persons for the proper treatment of a certain number of American officers now in possession of the enemy." The officers selected by Mason, the British were told, would immediately be put to death should the American hostages be executed. Successive rounds of British and American threats followed by retaliatory confinement ensued, with the net result that by the spring of 1814, every officer interred by either side in North America was being held in close confinement and subject to execution.[37] But in the end, no hostages on either side were harmed, the rounds of retaliation ceased, and all prisoners who had been closely confined were released. Regular exchanges under the cartel, however, had been terminated by the controversy. It was not until May 1814 that large-scale repatriations resumed.[38]

Although the daily treatment of prisoners by both the British and the Americans during the War of 1812 was markedly more humane than that provided by either of the two governments during the Revolution, the exact letter of the cartel was not always observed. One point of contention was the stipulation that prisoners were to be issued "sound and wholesome" rations by the "government in whose possession they may be."[39] Americans insisted that the provision required that American prisoners be issued the same rations provided Continental soldiers, while the British maintained that the lower level of subsistence they habitually provided captives was adequate. Hoping to persuade the Crown to increase food allowances, Commissary General Mason continued to provide British prisoners subsistence at the higher level, but by July 1814 he was convinced that the English government would not change its policy, and he ordered the rations reduced to the level being furnished American captives. Still, the quality of the rations provided by each side was deemed sufficient, and successive rounds of retaliatory reductions were avoided.[40]

Although the cartel stipulated that the provision of rations was the responsibility of the detaining nation, it retained the accepted practice of requiring that prisoners' clothing be furnished by the nation of origin. The rules under which standard items (such as shirts, trousers, shoes, and blankets) and amenities (such as tobacco, razors, and soap) were to be supplied to captives were negotiated by Mason and Barclay, and the actual issuing of these items at the detention points was supervised by their agents. Again, this procedure generated no significant controversies, and the prisoners of both governments were adequately supplied.[41]

As in the Revolution, the United States' experience with prisoners in the War of 1812 yielded important lessons that would decisively shape American ideas and opinions in the Civil War. The expectation that captives would be forced to endure conditions that would be difficult at best was confirmed, as was the belief that the only strategy certain to secure swift relief for these men was one that resulted in repatriation. The degree to which the cartel of 1813 and subsequent agreements facilitated prisoner treatment and exchange negotiations clearly demonstrated the benefits of such accords, and the able and energetic performance of John Mason and his staff plainly indicated that when adequately manned and provided the requisite authority, the Office of Commissary General of Prisoners was invaluable in resolving the complex challenges of managing large numbers of prisoners. Administration and congressional leaders again found that although acts of retaliation did little to shape Crown policies regarding the treatment of American prisoners, they were of immense value in placating constituent demands for action to counter alleged British injustices.

Finally, the prisoner-of-war experience in the War of 1812 illustrated that disputes concerning the legal status of captives could quickly render even the most carefully crafted exchange agreements moot. The case of the American soldiers of Irish origin had much in common with similar instances that arose during the Revolution. The American decision to deny former slaves captured under arms the accepted rights and privileges of prisoners of war, however, established a completely new precedent—and one that would become a major obstacle in the exchange negotiations of the Civil War.

America's final conflict prior to 1860 presented the nation with a number of circumstances quite different from those that characterized the two wars with Great Britain. The Mexican War was fought almost entirely in a foreign country against an enemy with a language and culture different from that of the United States. Communications between Washington, D.C., and the armies of Generals Winfield Scott and Zachary Taylor were uncertain at best, and directives from the capital, when they were delivered, were often rendered irrelevant by events in the field. These difficulties were compounded by the fact that once more the United States had entered a war completely unprepared to cope with the problem of managing enemy captives, and decisions concerning the treatment of enemy prisoners were usually left to the commanders in the field. This was also the first war in which American military commanders were faced with the challenge of disposing of hundreds—in some cases thousands—of enemy prisoners following each major battle. Finally, in this war U.S. forces were compelled, for the first time, to occupy major enemy cities and install military governments to direct an occupation.

Not surprisingly, these unique factors had a significant impact on the manner in which American leaders resolved prisoner-of-war issues. In the Mexican War, the U.S. government made no attempt to reestablish the Office of Commissary General of Prisoners, which had served the nation so well during the War of 1812. Nor did the administration of President James K. Polk attempt to establish a formal cartel governing the treatment and exchange of prisoners. Rather, the resolution of questions concerning friendly and enemy prisoners of war remained the responsibility of American commanders in the field, and the solution most commonly implemented was swift and complete parole.

Throughout the war, both Scott and Taylor maintained that the conditions under which they were conducting their campaigns precluded the adoption of any option other than the immediate parole of enemy prisoners. Advances into the interior of Mexico pulled the American armies far from secure bases of supply, and in virtually every battle they were opposed by an enemy force of superior numbers. They possessed neither the manpower to constitute an adequate guard nor the rations and other provisions required to supply a large prisoner population over an extended period of time. In the battle of Cerro Gordo, for example, the Mexican defenders numbered between 12,000 and 18,000 men, against whom Scott could muster a force of only 8,500 regulars and poorly trained volunteers.[42] Scott routed the Mexicans, but he soon found that even victory yielded problems. As the general later recalled, he was "quite embarrassed with the results of victory—prisoners of war, heavy ordnance, field batteries, small arms, and accouterments. About 3,000 men laid down their arms, with the usual proportion of field and company grade officers, besides five generals, several of them of great distinction."[43] In his official report of the action, Scott notified Washington that he had "determined to parole the prisoners," for he did not have "the means of feeding them here beyond today, and cannot afford to detach a heavy body of horse and foot with wagons, to accompany them to Vera Cruz." When presented with the same problem following the battles of Palo Alto and Resaca de la Palma, Taylor opted for the same solution.[44]

This policy of liberal and speedy parole was not without its critics. Many of Scott's own officers argued that the Mexicans would not honor the terms of their parole and would again take up arms before official exchanges could be effected. The Polk administration was also concerned that such releases would prove harmful to the American effort. When informed of the policy through reports, it ordered that Mexican officers be denied parole unless special circumstances dictated otherwise.[45]

In those rare instances where Americans or Mexicans captured in battle were confined, there appears to have been mutual satisfaction regarding their treatment. Americans, mindful of the Mexican atrocities committed against prisoners at the Alamo and Goliad during the Texas Revolution, were justifiably worried that such brutalities would be repeated, but their fears proved groundless. In fact, U.S. prisoners were treated so well that in 1847 the commander in chief of American naval forces wrote (with Polk's approval) to the Mexican minister of foreign relations, applauding the "kind and liberal treatment" granted American captives and hastening to assure the minister that such treatment had been "fully reciprocated by us towards those Mexicans who have fallen into our hands."[46]

Most Mexican soldiers were treated very well by the Americans for the short periods of time they were held, but there was one glaring exception to this rule. As in the Revolution, Americans in the Mexican War were compelled to decide the fate of U.S. citizens who bore arms in support of the enemy, and, as in that earlier conflict, their decision was draconian indeed. On 20 August 1847 the San Patricio Battalion, composed primarily of American Catholics who had deserted the U.S. army to take up arms with the Mexicans, was captured during the battle of Churubusco. The prisoners were charged with desertion and tried by courts-martial. Seventy were convicted and sentenced to be hanged, and fifty were executed. Scott pardoned five of the convicted soldiers and reduced the sentences of the remaining fifteen to a punishment of fifty lashes—to be laid on not by an army bandsman, as was the custom, but by experienced Mexican muleteers. The general in charge of executing the punishments promised the floggers large bonuses should the leaders of the San Patricios happen to die under their whips. None did, although one witness remembered that the lashings reduced the backs of the men to "the appearance of a pounded piece of raw beef, the blood oozing from every stripe as given." The deserters were then branded on the cheek with the letter *D* and drummed out of the army.[47]

This grisly episode aside, the good treatment afforded prisoners by the belligerents during the Mexican War obviated the need for acts of retaliation like those seen in both the Revolution and the War of 1812. Following the conclusion of the general armistice in 1847, however, Americans who remained in Mexico as part of the army of occupation were routinely menaced by acts of sabotage and other guerrilla activities perpetrated by Mexicans who refused to accept the terms of the agreement. The American response to such attacks was swift, and when the lives of U.S. soldiers were threatened, retribution was often meted out in the form of summary executions of prisoners. Near the end of 1847, a military courier was ambushed on the outskirts of Mexico City. The rider survived the attack and, supported by a squad of dragoons, returned to the scene of the incident to apprehend his assailant. The dragoons seized a Mexican found hiding in a hedge and quickly established his guilt to their satisfaction, whereupon one of them shot the man first in the chest with his musket and then in the head with his pistol. "I am quite satisfied that I did my duty properly," the soldier later testified when asked to justify the killing, "and probably saved the lives of some of Uncle Sam's soldiers."[48]

Nor were all such acts random incidents committed by private soldiers in the heat of the moment. Colonel Ethan Allen Hitchcock, appointed by General Winfield Scott to the post of military governor of Mexico City, recorded rather laconically in his diary that "many" prisoners were "put to death" in retaliation for Americans killed by guerrilla sniping in the occupied city. The reprisals, Hitchcock noted succinctly, "cleared the streets," and after only ten days the city was "quiet."[49] He failed to add whether these prisoners were afforded the opportunity of a trial.

The war with Mexico, although short and in many respects unlike America's previous conflicts, nevertheless added to the nation's experience in addressing prisoner-of-war problems. Once more the benefits of securing the swift repatriation of American prisoners was demonstrated, as was the policy of granting immediate paroles to enemy captives when circumstances precluded adequately guarding or provisioning them. The practice of meting out severe punishments to prisoners deemed traitors was confirmed, and for the first time, American forces made good on threats to execute captives in order to influence enemy behavior.

In summary, the Revolution, the War of 1812, and the Mexican War each revealed the difficulties attendant in managing prisoners. America had entered these conflicts completely unprepared to deal with such challenges, and the cost of that absence of planning had been high. One might reasonably expect that Union and Confederate planners would have drawn on the lessons afforded by these earlier conflicts to anticipate similar problems and ensure that their governments were prepared to resolve them before they arose, but such would not be the case. Both sides would enter the Civil War woefully unprepared to address the challenges that managing thousands of prisoners would bring, and ultimately the dreadful cost of that lack of preparation would be borne by the captives themselves.

CHAPTER 2

"The Crisis Is Fast Approaching"

The Initial Prisoners

THE FIRST AMERICANS who become prisoners during the Civil War were captured long before the armies of the North and South ever met in battle. Indeed, they were taken before the Confederate States of America had even been established. Following a protracted debate, South Carolinians voted on 20 December 1860 to secede from the Union—a decision that placed Major Robert Anderson, commander of the Federal forts of Charleston Harbor, in a very difficult position. Anderson desperately hoped to avoid the "effusion of blood" that was sure to result from an armed confrontation with the hotheads of the South Carolina militia, and with this objective in mind, he decided to transfer his garrison from their quarters in Fort Moultrie, a shore installation vulnerable to ground attack, to the more secure location of Fort Sumter, out in the harbor. To avoid interference from watchful militia commanders, Anderson accomplished the move in secret during the late evening hours of 26 December. As the men departed, he ordered the guns of Moultrie spiked, and to ensure no foreign flag would be hoisted on a Union staff, he directed that the fort's flagpole be cut down.[1]

The leaders of South Carolina were incensed when they learned of Anderson's move. On the following day Governor Francis W. Pickens ordered Castle Pinckney, another of the island forts in Charleston Harbor, seized before its equipment could be destroyed by the garrison. At that time, the facility was occupied by only a caretaker and a repair party of thirty-five soldiers. At four o'clock on the afternoon of 27 December, a contingent of about 150 state militiamen under the command of Colonel James J. Pettigrew rowed out to the island, scaled the fort's wall with ladders, and demanded the surrender of the garrison in the name of the government of South Carolina. Lieutenant R. K. Meade, the Federal officer commanding the work detail, protested the assault, but as he was powerless to resist, he surrendered to Pettigrew and the Carolinians. With this act, Meade and his subordinates gained the dubious distinction of becoming the first prisoners of the American Civil War.[2] Their captivity, while galling to the Union soldiers and workers, was mercifully short; after only a few hours Governor Pickens ordered that they be released and allowed to join their countrymen in Fort Sumter. This was, after all, the twilight period between secession and the initiation of hostilities, and Pickens, while full of bluster and determined to demonstrate the resolve of the people of South Carolina, had no more desire than Anderson to see events in Charleston Harbor escalate into a shooting war.[3]

Only two months later, civil authorities in Texas faced the same hard choices presented to Governor Pickens. When Texas seceded from the Union on 1 February 1861, just over 2,700 officers and enlisted men—almost 20 percent of the entire regular army of the United States—were assigned to the score of forts and other installations that constituted the Military Department of Texas. Brevet Major General David E. Twiggs, one of the nation's four general officers and second in seniority only to Commanding General of the Army Winfield Scott, had assumed command of the department in the closing months of 1860. Twiggs was a veteran soldier with almost half a century of service. He had seen action in both the War of 1812 and the Mexican War, but—as he was soon to discover—nothing in his long years of experience had prepared him for the political intrigue and turmoil he would face at his new post in Texas.[4]

Even as Twiggs was becoming familiar with his new responsibilities, Texans were debating the question of secession. Despite the objections of Governor Sam Houston, sentiment for disunion was running strong. On 13 December 1860 Twiggs anxiously wrote General Scott, advising him of the potentially explosive situation in Texas and requesting guidance on what action to take should the state secede. Scott's aide answered that the commanding general was "laboring under an attack of sickness" and could not respond personally, but that he wished Twiggs to do whatever he deemed necessary to "protect the property of the United States without waging war or acting offensively."[5]

As Scott's instructions were rather short on details as to how these seemingly contradictory instructions were to be accomplished, Twiggs sought additional guidance from Lieutenant Colonel Lorenzo Thomas, the assistant adjutant general of the army. In a succession of letters penned in the opening week of January 1861, Twiggs assured Thomas that "Texas will certainly go out of the Union the latter part of this month." Again he pleaded for "instructions as to what disposition will be made of the troops now in this department. Arrangements should be made at once," he warned. "There is no time to lose. . . . The crisis is fast approaching."[6] In spite of such desperate entreaties, Twiggs never received definitive instructions from his superiors in Washington, and, just as he predicted, the crisis was not long in coming. On 28 January 1861 two delegates from each county and district in Texas convened to debate the question of secession, and only four days later they voted to take the state out of the Union.[7]

With secession, Twiggs and his command were converted into armed agents of a foreign power on the soil of Texas. On 5 February, the state's Committee of Public Safety appointed three commissioners to "visit Major-General Twiggs, commanding the Eighth Division, stationed at San Antonio, and confer with him, and in the name and by the authority of the people of Texas, in convention assembled, to demand, receive, and receipt for all military, medical, commissary, and ordnance stores, arms, munitions of war, and public moneys, &c., under his control, within the limits of the State of Texas."[8]

Echoing the sentiments of Governor Pickens in South Carolina, the committee's members expressed the hope that the transfer of property could be accomplished peacefully, but they prepared for the worst. On 3 February they appointed former Texas Ranger and Mexican War veteran Benjamin McCulloch to the rank of colonel in the army of the Republic of Texas and ordered him to "hold [himself] in readiness to raise men and munitions of war whenever called on by the commissioners of San Antonio, and to be governed as directed by the secret instructions given said commissioners."[9] The committee also admonished the commissioners to "do everything in [their] power to avoid any collision with the Federal troops and to effect the peaceable accomplishment of [their] mission." But if the Federals refused to turn over their equipment and leave the state, the commissioners were empowered to direct McCulloch to "call out and take the command of such force of the volunteer and minute men" as might be necessary to compel Twiggs to comply.[10]

In the early afternoon of 8 February the commissioners met with Twiggs at his headquarters in San Antonio. The general was a native of Georgia, and while the delegation found him to be "strongly in favor of Southern rights," they also noted that he displayed no enthusiasm for surrendering the men or the property entrusted to him unless authorized to do so by his superiors in Washington. Negotiations continued in this inconclusive vein until 16 February, when, as Twiggs succinctly stated later, the talks were "abruptly terminated by the entrance into this city . . . of an armed body of State troops, numbering over 1,000 men, under Col. Ben McCulloch."[11]

Unbeknownst to Twiggs, the commissioners had concluded early on that the Federal garrison would not surrender without a show of force, and they had sent for the old Ranger and his "minute men." The Texans swiftly took possession of the Federal headquarters located in the Alamo, whereupon McCulloch demanded that the Union general "deliver up all military posts and public property held by or under your control." Twiggs quickly judged that resistance to McCulloch and his band would be futile. Upon receiving assurances that his troops would be allowed to "march out of the city, taking with them their arms, clothing, camp and garrison equipage, and all the necessaries for a march out of Texas," he promptly surrendered all the men, equipment, stores, and facilities under his command.[12]

The windfall in installations, weapons, and other military gear that accrued to the State of Texas as a result of Twiggs's surrender was enormous. Forty-four pieces of field artillery, 2,300 small arms, two Federal magazines full of ammunition, 500 wagons, 950 horses, 500 sets of harnesses, and vast stores of fodder, rations, clothing, and tools were collected at San Antonio. The total value of these items, exclusive of the buildings and real estate, was estimated at a whopping $1,229,500, and much of it was employed to outfit a Confederate brigade that General H. H. Sibley would lead in operations in the territories of Arizona and New Mexico.[13] Thrilled with the fruits of their labors and greatly relieved that their stunning victory had been as bloodless as it had been complete, the commissioners could afford to be magnanimous, and in a public circular they urged Texans to assist Twiggs and his men in their departure from the state. "They are our friends," they reminded their fellow citizens. "They have heretofore afforded to our people all the protection in their power, and we owe them every consideration."[14]

This effusion of good will proved short-lived. Shortly after his surrender, Twiggs was informed that the route specified for his "march out of Texas" would be severely circumscribed by state officials. He had planned to move his men overland through the state to the nearest post still under U.S. control, but the commissioners feared that the appearance of Federal soldiers in the territories of New Mexico, Arizona, or Kansas might incite Unionist support and leave Texas with a "nest of hornets to deal with in the future."[15] Twiggs was therefore informed that his troopers would be allowed to quit the state only "by the way of the coast." The general protested, but, as he informed his superiors, he complied out of fear that unless he "yielded that point there would be an immediate collision." In his official report of the surrender, Twiggs contended that the superior numbers of McCulloch, coupled with his orders to avoid violence, precluded resistance; as a result, he had "reluctantly agreed" to the commissioners' demands.[16] Fiery old Sam Houston, now ousted from the governor's office in favor of a prosecession replacement, was outraged by Twiggs's capitulation. As he wrote in a departing salvo aimed at the state legislature, "It is the first time in the annals of our country that a General of the United States Army has conspired with a revolutionary committee to overthrow and supplant Executive authority, which it was his duty to sustain and defend."[17]

Officials in Washington agreed with Houston's assessment, and Twiggs's contention that he swiftly capitulated only to avoid a bloody confrontation failed to ring true. The general's defense had also been weakened by stunningly poor timing, for in a letter of 15 January he had confided to Scott that "as soon as I know Georgia has separated from the Union I must, of course, follow her."[18] Suspicion grew that Twiggs's surprising readiness to accede to the demands of McCulloch and the commissioners might have had other roots, and on 1 March he was removed from command of the Department of Texas. Twiggs left for New Orleans, but angry northerners soon filled newspaper columns with charges that the general had gotten off too lightly. One typical letter demanded that "the villainy of Twiggs" and his "military family" be thoroughly investigated though a full court-martial. President James Buchanan ordered an inquiry into Twiggs's conduct, and following a short investigation, he directed that Twiggs be dismissed from the army for "treachery to the flag of his country." The general seemed to corroborate this harsh judgment when on 22 May 1861 he accepted a commission as a major general in the Confederate States Army.[19]

Following Twiggs's departure, Scott directed Colonel Carlos A. Waite, the commander of the Union garrison at Camp Verde, Texas, at the time of the Federal surrender, to assume command of all Federal forces in the state. In accordance with the terms agreed to by Twiggs, the colonel ordered the soldiers from all the garrisons in Texas to move to an assembly point at Green Lake, twenty miles from the coastal town of Indianola, to await the arrival of ships that would transport them to a port still under Union control.[20] Initially, the Texans allowed Waite's plan to proceed unhindered. Soon, however, the growing concentration of Federal troops, none of whom had yet been officially declared prisoners of war and all of whom were still fully armed and equipped, became a matter of great concern, and the state appealed to the newly constituted government of the Confederate States of America for assistance.

Confederate secretary of war Leroy Pope Walker shared the Texans' apprehensions that Waite's troops might pose a threat, and on 11 April 1861 he ordered Colonel Earl Van Dorn to "repair to Texas with the least practicable delay and there assume command." This intervention in Texas also signaled a decisive change in policy concerning the status of the Union soldiers in the state, for the Confederate government decided to set aside the terms negotiated by Twiggs and the Texas commissioners. Van Dorn was informed that "the whole of the U.S. force, both officers and men, must be regarded as prisoners of war," and he was ordered to "intercept and prevent the movement" of these troops from the state. Additionally, the Confederate commander was directed to recruit from among the Federal forces "such of the men as may be disposed to join the C. S. Army," while ensuring that those who declined such service were securely incarcerated. Drawing on American experience in previous wars, the Rebel government informed Van Dorn that "the commissioned officers may be released on parole," along with soldiers and noncommissioned officers who swore never to take up arms against the Confederacy. The remainder of the enlisted men were to be retained under guard within the confines of Bexar County.[21]

From 23 April until 13 May, Van Dorn's troopers energetically intercepted groups of Union soldiers en route to the concentration point at Green Lake and placed them under guard. Confederate ships blocked the channel leading from Indianola to the Gulf of Mexico, and the one Federal steamer already in position—the *Star of the West* of Fort Sumter fame—was boarded and seized. Waite and the officers under his command furiously protested the actions of the Confederate government, but there was little they could do but accept Van Dorn's offer of parole and ship out for friendly ports.[22]

For many of the officers, the trip to freedom would be a long one indeed. Lieutenants Zenas R. Bliss and J. J. Van Horn, for example, were shipped initially to Richmond, where they were assured they would be paroled pending exchange for Confederate officers of like rank. Negotiations broke down, however, and Bliss and Van Horn were confined in the southern capital until an agreement was brokered. Finally, on 6 April 1862 a flag-of-truce boat transported the two officers within the Union lines at Fort Monroe, Virginia.[23]

As for securing Confederate recruits from the captives in Texas, Van Dorn experienced only limited success. His most notable conquest in this area was Major E. Kirby Smith, an officer of exceptional ability who would eventually rise to the grade of lieutenant general and command the Department of the Trans-Mississippi during the war.[24]

Upon assuming command in Texas, Van Dorn immediately implemented the Confederate secretary of war's orders terminating the practice of paroling Union enlisted men who refused to change allegiance. This action left about three hundred prisoners in southern hands, and they were marched off to Fort Van Dorn, a hastily created prisoner-of-war camp on Salado Creek, seven miles east of San Antonio. Earl Van Dorn thus became the first Confederate general to face the daunting challenge of managing large numbers of enemy captives. At first, the task seemed easy enough; with the capitulation of the last of the Federal garrisons, Van Dorn assumed the most difficult portion of his service in the Lone Star State was over. "I have taken all the U.S. Troops in Texas prisoners of war," he crowed in a letter to his wife, "and now lean back in my chair and smoke my pipe."[25]

But his contentment proved no more permanent than the smoke of his pipe, for the arrival of additional scores of Yankee captives quickly exceeded the capacity of the makeshift camp on Salado Creek. Van Dorn first sought to solve the overcrowding by granting the prisoners passes to visit San Antonio and other nearby towns, but this liberal policy quickly aroused the ire of local residents. Articles and letters complaining that the presence of these "damnable prisoners" constituted a "great nuisance" began to appear in local newspapers; a number of these missives called darkly upon camp officials to "treat those prisoners as they deserve."[26] In response to this public outcry, Van Dorn restricted the captives to the confines of the camp. The facility proved incapable of sustaining the population, however, and in September 1861 the prisoners were divided into six groups and relocated to recently vacated Federal installations across the state.

Most of the men were incarcerated near Camp Verde, sixty-five miles north of San Antonio. There, on open ground, the captives were forced to construct their own shelters. Rations were skimpy, conditions were harsh, and prisoners were routinely subjected to taunts and other forms of abuse by ill-disciplined guards and local civilians. In December, the men were moved back to the San Antonio area, where they constructed and occupied a succession of camps. Finally, in January 1863 they were transported to Baton Rouge, Louisiana, where they were exchanged after almost twenty-two months of captivity.[27]

Even as Waite and his men were being rounded up in Texas, a similar series of events that would result in the incarceration of the first Confederate prisoners of war was being played out in Missouri, far to the north. On 13 March 1861 Captain Nathaniel Lyon, a dedicated, politically connected Unionist and veteran of the guerrilla war in Kansas, was appointed to the command of the U.S. troops at the Federal arsenal in St. Louis. This section of Missouri was a hotbed of secessionist sentiment, and Lyon was directed by Secretary of War Simon Cameron to "arm the loyal citizens" of the city in anticipation of an attack on the arsenal by the pro-Confederate state militia under the command of Brigadier General Daniel M. Frost.[28]

On the evening of 8 May, Lyon received word that a steamer bearing arms and equipment destined for militia use was being secretly off-loaded at the St. Louis docks, preparatory to an attempt by Frost to seize the arsenal. Lyon determined that a preemptive strike was in order, and on 10 May at 3:15 P.M. the intrepid captain led a "large body" of his newly inducted troops to Camp Jackson, the local militia training site. Upon arrival, he surrounded the facility and demanded the unconditional surrender of Frost and his men. After vociferously protesting the dubious legality of the action, Frost complied. As Lyon reported to Washington, "some 50 officers and 639 men" were marched off to confinement in the arsenal.[29] Lyon's bold action made him an instant hero in the North, and he was immediately advanced from the grade of captain to that of brevet brigadier general. Like the Federal officers in Texas, however, the Missouri militiamen would not long suffer the pains of captivity. On the very next day, Lyon released the whole lot (excepting one defiant captain) "on their parole of honor not to fight against the United States during this war."[30]

By the time Frost and his soldiers were paroled, Fort Sumter had been fired upon and the shooting war had begun. Still, this first battle of the Civil War produced no long-term prisoners. The terms under which Major Robert Anderson surrendered the fort were actually quite generous. As one of Anderson's subordinates recalled, the Federal garrison was allowed to fire a fifty-gun salute as the national colors were lowered. Then, with "banners flying and with drums beating Yankee Doodle," the garrison was allowed to depart aboard the Union transports that had remained anchored outside the harbor.[31]

These early prisoner-of-war experiences in South Carolina, Texas, and Missouri all shared common characteristics. First, there were no casualties sustained by either side as a result of enemy fire. The single death at Fort Sumter was Union private David Hough, who was killed in the explosion of a cannon during the firing of the ceremonial salute after the battle, and the lone casualty in Texas occurred when a Federal lieutenant, unkindly characterized as "notoriously nearsighted," fell from one of the evacuation ships and drowned.[32] In all the actions, most of the prisoners were offered swift release through parole, and no challenges were raised as to the legal status of the captives. All of the men, whether soldiers of the regular army of the United States or citizen soldiers of the Missouri militia, were recognized as bona fide prisoners of war, and all were treated as such. The months from the seizure of Castle Pinckney to the standoff in Missouri had been a time of much posturing and little fighting, a time of bloodless confrontations in which the solution to the question of what was to be done with captured soldiers had been the same: they were to be immediately paroled.

After Fort Sumter, the answers would never again be so simple. With the explosion of the first shot above the battlements in Charleston Harbor, Americans both North and South were forced to face the stark reality that all hope for a peaceful resolution of the secession crisis was gone. As the summer of 1861 approached, armed clashes between Union and Confederate forces became more numerous and increasingly bloody, and all questions relative to the conduct of the war assumed a new urgency and importance. No problem the two governments faced during this period would prove more vexing or complex than those posed by prisoners of war, and the first such challenge was not long in coming.

Around mid-morning on 5 June 1861, the masthead lookout aboard the USS *Minnesota* sighted a sail on the horizon and moved to investigate, in accordance with her mission as a member of the Atlantic Blockading Squadron. The sail proved to be that of the U.S. brig *Perry*, but it was not alone. In tow was the *Savannah*, a 50-ton schooner out of Charleston with a crew of twenty. The schooner had been seized while operating as a commerce raider in the service of the Confederacy, but in his report of the circumstances attending her capture, the captain of the *Minnesota* made plain that he did not consider the *Savannah* a legitimate ship of war. She was instead a "piratical schooner," a renegade vessel stalking the sea lanes in an immoral search for unsuspecting prey. And the commission under which she sailed was signed by none other than Jefferson Davis, president of the Confederate States of America.[33]

That commission was a "letter of marque and general reprisal." On 17 April 1861 Davis had offered to provide such letters to the masters of private vessels if they would agree to attack Union shipping, and on the following day that news was widely reported in northern newspapers. On 6 May the Confederate Congress officially sanctioned the president's action, lauding the use of privateers as an excellent means of employing "the whole land and naval force of the Confederate States . . . against the vessels, goods and effects of the Government of the United States."[34]

Privateering under letters of marque and reprisal had long been an accepted practice in war, and especially so in the United States. In the first year of the American Revolution, the Continental Congress had prescribed a commission for "commanders of private ships of war . . . to attack, seize, and take the ships and other vessels belonging to the inhabitants of Great Britain," and no less than 1,679 privateers mounting almost 600 guns and crews numbering over 55,000 sailors had ravaged British shipping under this authorization. The practice was revived during the War of 1812, when 500 privateers flying the Stars and Stripes seized or sank 1,300 British ships.[35] Given this precedent, the Union government's assertion that the sailors of the *Savannah* were no more than pirates was dubious indeed, but in truth the reasoning behind this charge had nothing to do with the legality of letters of marque. Rather, it signaled the reappearance of the contentious question of the legal status of combatants taken under arms.

In a decision reminiscent of that taken by Britain during the Revolution, the administration of President Abraham Lincoln had ruled that Confederate combatants were to be regarded as traitors engaged in armed insurrection rather than bona fide soldiers in the service of an opposing sovereign power. The president doggedly maintained that no state had the right to secede, and he directed his administration carefully to avoid any action that might be construed as legitimizing secession or providing a de facto recognition of the Confederacy as an independent nation. To proceed otherwise, Lincoln reasoned, would transform the war from one to preserve the Union to one of simple conquest, and this was a point he steadfastly refused to concede. The crewmen of the *Savannah* were therefore branded as rebel pirates rather than as sailors of a belligerent nation. Their treatment demonstrated that the Lincoln administration wished to make this distinction indisputably plain to the people of the North.

On 15 June the sailors were disembarked at the Battery in New York Harbor. Then, as a vast crowd looked on, they were clapped in irons and, guarded by civilian policemen rather than soldiers, paraded through the streets of the city. Their journey ended at the Tombs, a city prison notorious for the dreadful condition of its cells and for the fact that only "lunatics" and the most despicable criminals were confined within its walls.[36]

Two days after the Confederate president's declaration authorizing letters of marque and reprisal, Lincoln had responded with a counterproclamation warning that crews taken while operating under such letters would be "held amenable to the laws of the United States for the prevention and punishment of piracy." The punishment for piracy prescribed by those laws was death, and the Federal government now moved to ensure that it was implemented.[37] The men of the *Savannah* were brought before the Second Circuit Court of New York, where they were charged with "piratically, feloniously and violently" attacking ships sailing under the flag of the United States.[38]

News of the *Savannah*'s capture soon reached Richmond. On 19 June, Jefferson Davis directed officials at Charleston to contact the commander of the Union blockading fleet and propose a prisoner exchange that would free the privateersmen. But when the proposal of exchange was presented to the Federal commander, he replied only that the men in question were not on board any of the vessels under his command.[39] This obviously evasive response heightened Confederate concerns, and their worst fears were confirmed when newspapers from the North arrived reporting that the sailors had been incarcerated in the Tombs and were under indictment for piracy. Jefferson Davis was never a man to back away from a challenge, and he reacted swiftly and decisively to this news.

On 6 July, Davis dispatched to Lincoln the first correspondence between the two presidents concerning prisoners of war. The letter contained the initial statement of Confederate intentions about the treatment of prisoners, and it contained an ominous warning of swift retaliation should southern captives be mistreated. "It is the desire of this Government," Davis wrote,

> so to conduct the war now existing as to mitigate its horrors as far as may be possible; and, with this intent, its treatment of the prisoners captured by its forces has been marked by the greatest humanity and leniency consistent with public obligations; some have been permitted to return home on parole, others to remain at large under similar conditions within this Confederacy, and all have been furnished with rations for their subsistence, such as are allowed to our own troops. It is only since the news has been received of the treatment of prisoners of war taken on the *Savannah* that I have been compelled to withdraw these indulgences, and to hold the prisoners taken by us in strict confinement.

Nor did Davis's threats of retaliation end there. Speaking directly of the Union threat to hang the sailors interned in the Tombs, he warned Lincoln that

> a just regard to humanity and to the honor of this Government now requires me to state explicitly that, painful as will be the necessity, this Government will deal out to the prisoners held by it the same treatment and the same fate as shall be experienced by those captured on the *Savannah,* and if driven to the terrible necessity of retaliation by your execution of any of the officers or the crew of the *Savannah,* that retaliation shall be extended so far as shall be requisite to secure the abandonment of a practice unknown to the warfare of civilized man, and so barbarous as to disgrace the nation which shall be guilty of inaugurating it.[40]

Davis had, in fact, already set the machinery of retaliation in motion. On the day before he wrote Lincoln, the Confederate president had ordered the commandant of the Richmond prisons to select and place in close confinement a lieutenant colonel and two captains who had been free in the city on parole.[41] On these men would fall the blows of southern retribution promised by Davis, and on 30 August the Confederate Congress demonstrated its support of the president's decision by authorizing the chief executive to "inflict such retaliation, in such measure and kind as may seem to him just and proper."[42]

Still, all hope for a bloodless resolution of the crisis was not lost. In the closing paragraph of his letter to Lincoln, Davis offered the Union president a means of aborting the cycle of reprisals and counterreprisals initiated by the treatment of the southern sailors. "With this in view," he wrote, "and because it may not have reached you, I now renew the proposition made to the commander of the blockading squadron to exchange for the prisoners taken on the *Savannah,* an equal number of those now held by us, according to rank."[43]

In Lincoln's eyes, however, agreement to such an exchange would have constituted an official acknowledgment of the existence of the Confederate States of America as a sovereign power, which ran counter both to the president's core beliefs and his most basic interpretation of the war. Lincoln had first articulated his view on 15 April 1861, in his initial proclamation following the surrender of Fort Sumter, when he had called upon the states to furnish 75,000 volunteers. The men were required not for the purpose of defeating an opposing nation, he explained, but for service against factions in the seven seceded states who were bent on obstructing the rule of law. These "combinations," as he called them, were "too powerful to be suppressed by the ordinary course of judicial proceedings"[44] Lincoln reemphasized this interpretation in his address to a special session of Congress on 4 July. The conflict must not be construed as a war between the United States and the government of the Confederate States of America, he told the assemble legislators; that would be to accede to the southern contention that secession was constitutional and the union of states only temporary. "What is now combated," Lincoln insisted, "is the position that secession is consistent with the Constitution." Throughout the next four years he sustained what historian David Donald has aptly characterized as the "legal fiction" that the war was an "insurrection" led by influential individuals in the South who had rebelled against the laws of the United States. In this construction Confederate soldiers were no more than traitors, and privateersmen—even those operating under letters of marque—were simply pirates.[45]

By the fall of 1861 northern jails held the crews of numerous privateers, and Lincoln's determination to try them in civil courts initially garnered enthusiastic support. The editors of the *New York Times* spoke for many in the North when they insisted the trials go forward and the sailors be hung if convicted. "Let [the sentence] therefore be inflicted," the *Times* thundered, adding that any action less forceful would be tantamount to abandoning the shipping of the country to "numberless vessels of the same description now haunting the seas." Threats of Rebel retaliation, the editorial insisted, should not be allowed to diminish northern resolve, for "to pause because the enemy threatens sanguinary reprisals, would be the merest weakness."[46] All through the summer such calls for stern action rang out across the North, and prospects for the crewmen of the privateers seemed dark indeed. The Federal marshal in charge of the incarcerated crew of the *Savannah* was so certain they would be convicted that he ordered death cells prepared to receive them upon their return to the Tombs following trial.[47]

When the crews of the privateers actually came to trial that fall, however, most of the outcomes were far different. A New York jury failed even to reach a verdict in the trial of the crew of the *Savannah,* while in Philadelphia, the proceedings against the crew of the privateer *Petrel* were abruptly terminated when the presiding judge angrily dismissed the case rather than "trying charges against a few unfortunate men here out of half a million that are in arms against the government."[48] Such was not the case in a second Philadelphia trial, where the jury convicted the crew of the brigantine *Jeff Davis* of piracy and, after only a short deliberation, sentenced all of them to be hanged. Upon learning of the judgment passed on the crew of his namesake, Davis vowed to make good his threat to retaliate in kind. He again ordered a like number of Union prisoners culled from the captives in Richmond, and he warned Lincoln that if the men of the *Jeff Davis* were executed, the prisoners in Richmond would suffer the same fate.

The seriousness with which the Confederate president's words were taken became clear when J. H. Ashton, the district attorney for the city of Philadelphia, appealed to U.S. Attorney General Edward Bates for guidance in scheduling the execution of the privateersmen. Ashton must have been puzzled by Bates's reply, for instead of offering a proposed date for the hangings, the attorney general wrote that the men were not to be executed. With Davis's threats in mind, Bates circumspectly informed Ashton that "there are indeed some political reasons, very operative on my mind, although prudently not proper for publication just now, which make it desirable to hold these cases up to await certain important events now and in the near future." What had happened, as one Lincoln biographer concedes, was that the president of the United States had been "outplayed" by his counterpart in Richmond. Faced with the certainty that Davis would execute one Union officer for each Confederate sailor who went to the gallows, Lincoln had refused to enter into a "competition in hanging." The "temporary" postponement directed by Bates became indefinite, and none of the southern sailors were ever executed. Instead, they were retained in confinement until the summer of 1862, when they were released and allowed to return home.[49]

Although the clash of wills sparked by the capture and disposition of the privateersmen lasted only a few months, it revealed a number of important insights into the manner in which the two belligerent governments would confront the challenges attendant in establishing and operating prisoner-of-war systems. First, it demonstrated that both Lincoln and Davis clearly understood that prisoner-of-war issues carried implications of sovereignty and national legitimacy that reached far beyond the immediate problems of the prisoners themselves. Second, it provided the first indication of the official policy the United States would follow concerning the legal status of Confederate prisoners. Mirroring the course of action adopted by the British in the American Revolution, Lincoln insisted throughout the war that soldiers and sailors of the "so-called Confederate States of America" were no more than rebels in the service of an insurgency. But, also like the British, he quickly abandoned the practice of treating Confederate prisoners like convicted felons or prosecuting them in civil courts on charges of treason.[50] Finally, the actions of both governments in this early clash of wills demonstrated the alacrity with which each would resort to acts of retaliation against prisoners in order to secure national objectives or influence enemy behavior. Each of these factors would play a vital role in shaping both Union and Confederate prisoner-of-war systems. And even as the fate of the privateersmen was being debated in the North, a desperate battle near a small creek in northern Virginia signaled that the time for the construction of those systems was at hand.

CHAPTER 3

"They Had Not Been Expected in Such Numbers"

The Confederate Prisoner-of-War System, July–December 1861

"YOU ARE GREEN, it is true," Lincoln conceded to the capable but inexperienced Brigadier General Irvin McDowell, "but they are green also. You are all green alike." What McDowell thought of this less-than-rousing assessment from his commander in chief, history does not record; but this prod to action was the nearest thing to a presidential vote of confidence he received before he led his army, then the premier fighting force of the Union, out of Washington on 16 July 1861. Five days later that army crashed into a Confederate force led by the mercurial and obstinate Major General Pierre Gustave Toutant (P. G. T.) Beauregard near the northeastern Virginia hamlet of Manassas. This first major clash of the opposing forces in the Civil War was as confused as it was vicious, and the uneven and sometimes unexplainable manner in which soldiers on both sides conducted themselves more than confirmed the pithy assessment Lincoln had offered McDowell.[1]

Thirty-five thousand Yankees grappled with almost 32,000 Rebels in the broiling heat of that Sunday, and for much of the battle the outcome was in doubt. Late in the afternoon, however, the Confederates gained the upper hand, and by sunset McDowell's army had been ingloriously routed and was in full flight back to Washington. For the southerners, victory proved almost as costly and disorienting as defeat had been for their enemies; although Beauregard held the field, his forces were too frazzled to do any more than just that. The battle was by far the largest up that point in the war, and it was also the bloodiest. Union casualties totaled 481 men killed and 1,011 wounded, while Confederates counted 387 dead and 1,582 wounded. And when Union commanders finally regained control of their demoralized soldiers, they found that over 2,000 of them were missing. Most of this number had been captured, and by 22 July the initial group of these unfortunates had begun their journey south to confinement as prisoners of war.[2]

For the soldiers captured at Manassas, the journey into captivity proceeded in a sequence that would be repeated in much the same form thousands of times during the war, and the experience was as bewildering as it was terrifying. When captured, the Yankees were disarmed and marched under guard to a collection point in an open field about seven miles south of the battlefield. Here the soldiers, some of whom were wounded, spent their first night of captivity. Just after sunset a heavy thunderstorm blew in, and the rain pelted down in sheets throughout the night. Although a few soldiers managed to find shelter in a nearby empty barn, most of the men were forced to endure the storm bereft of shelter or blankets. Around mid-morning of the following day the prisoners were marched through the rain and mud to the railroad station at Manassas Junction, where they were packed into cars of the Virginia Central Railroad. By the time the trains lurched out of the station, most of the captives had guessed their destination—Richmond.

Confederate planners had never intended for Richmond to become a final destination for Federal prisoners. Because of the city's central location in the eastern theater of the Confederacy and its extensive road and railroad network, it was initially viewed only as a large receiving station. Captives shipped there would be classified, segregated, and then transported out of the city to locations throughout the South, where they would be interned in prisons located in secure areas far from the front lines. Such was the plan, but—as would often be the case in much of the Confederate planning concerning prisoners of war—it was quickly overcome by events.[3]

Word that the prisoner trains were likely bound for the Confederate capital was passed from car to car; as this piece of information spread, it was coupled to another, more sinister rumor that upon arrival in the city the captives would be set upon by vicious and uncontrollable mobs bent on avenging the Rebel losses suffered at Manassas. Assurances from the commander of the guard accompanying the prisoners that he would permit no harm to come to any Yankees did little to assuage the captives' fears. As it turned out, they need not have worried. The trains did not arrive in the capital until late in the evening of 23 July, whereupon the men were off-loaded and moved through dark and empty streets to the corner of Main and 24th Streets. There they filed into their new residence, a large, empty brick warehouse that until recently had housed the tobacco factory of Ligon and Company.[4]

The citizens of Richmond, caught up in the frenzy of excitement and martial ardor that swept the South following the victory of First Manassas, were initially quite proud that Yankee prisoners were confined in their city. Here, within the bleak confines of the Ligon warehouse, could be seen living, tangible proof of the veracity of the oft-voiced claims of the superiority of southern arms, and each announcement that additional shipments of prisoners from Manassas were arriving set the city abuzz. Curiosity-seekers gathered on the platforms of depots or lined the streets to gawk at the sullen "bluebellies" who shuffled past under guard, and the capital's citizens often greeted the city's newest residents with shouts of mock congratulation at being the first to fulfill the Union's "on to Richmond" strategy.[5]

Yet beneath all this bravado lay a sense of uneasiness. While southerners were pleased that the captives were securely confined in their city, no one in the Confederate capital knew quite what should be done with them. "They had not been expected in such numbers," recalled one citizen honestly, "and due preparation had not been made for their reception. There was not a Confederate official in the land who had any experience in taking care of prisoners of war."[6] Truer words had never been spoken. It was not until the Federals taken at Manassas were actually filing into the filthy, gloomy confines of the Ligon warehouse that it began to dawn on southern leaders that they had made no preparations for actually billeting, feeding, or otherwise caring for the hundreds of prisoners of war that the trains were disgorging into the city.

This is not to say that no thought had been accorded the subject of enemy prisoners. The issue had been a topic of some concern to both military and civilian leaders in Richmond. Out of these discussions had come the initial laws intended to regulate the incarceration and treatment of Yankee captives, and in these early provisions one may find the origins of the policies and practices that would shape the development of the Confederate prisoner-of-war system.

In 1861 the Confederate States Army adopted regulations governing the treatment of prisoners that were, like many of the other operational instructions of the southern land and naval forces, virtual copies of those then in the manuals of the U.S. army and navy. These regulations stipulated that captives were to be "disarmed and sent to the rear . . . as soon as possible." Other than horses, which were to be confiscated, the private property of prisoners was to be "duly respected," and each captive was to be treated with "the regard due to his rank." Prisoners were to be provided a daily subsistence of "one ration each without regard to rank," and wounded captives were to be treated with "the same care as the wounded of the Army."[7]

In the days following Fort Sumter, questions concerning the management of enemy prisoners were also raised on the floor of the Confederate Congress. On 21 May 1861 Congress approved an act regulating the treatment and disposition of "all prisoners of war taken, whether on land or at sea . . . during the pending hostilities with the United States." These prisoners, section one of the act stipulated, were to be "transferred by their captors . . . to the . . . Secretary of War," who, "with the approval of the President," would "issue such instructions to the Quartermaster General and his subordinates as shall provide for the safe custody and sustenance of prisoners of war." The act concluded by requiring that prisoners were to be furnished rations that were "the same in quantity and quality as those furnished to enlisted men in the army of the Confederacy." This seemingly innocuous phrase would become the subject of endless charges and debate, for throughout the war the Davis government would be compelled to answer allegations that the Rebels were deliberately starving Union prisoners.[8]

Laws and regulations, no matter how comprehensive and well intentioned, are but empty words if not supported by action, and this sad fact was amply demonstrated that summer in Richmond. Those to whom the absence of Confederate preparation most rapidly became apparent were, of course, the Federal prisoners themselves. The Ligon warehouse was a cavernous, three-story building measuring thirty feet wide and seventy feet long; its selection as the first of the city's prisons for Federal captives had been driven primarily by expediency. Because municipal officials had designated the structure as an emergency holding pen for rebellious Negroes in the event of a slave insurrection, iron bars had already been fitted over the windows of its first two floors. This feature, along with the size and sturdiness of the building, rendered the warehouse as near a prison as any structure in Richmond, and for that reason it was chosen.[9]

Upon their arrival at Ligon's, all of the prisoners were forced into the upper two floors of the building. The rooms were soon so tightly packed that the men had difficulty finding even enough space to lie down. The Federal officers expected that they would be provided accommodations separate from those of the enlisted men, according to custom, and some were so naive as to have believed the assurances of Confederate guards that they would immediately be granted paroles and allowed to roam the city at will. It soon became apparent that such would not be the case. All of the prisoners—officers included—spent their first night in Richmond sleeping in whatever space they could find on the rough plank floor of the warehouse.[10]

Moreover, this was no ordinary assemblage of Union officers; among their number were two well-known political personalities from New York State. The first was Colonel Michael Corcoran, a militia officer and politician who wielded considerable clout among the Irish of New York City. At Manassas, Corcoran had been slightly wounded and then captured while in command of the famous

69th New York. The second political celebrity captured during the battle was Congressman Alfred Ely, a serving member of the U.S. House of Representatives. Ely was one of the many civilians who had journeyed by buggy out from Washington that fine Sunday morning to see the Rebels get whipped, and he was one of the few who had not been able to dash back to the capital when the Rebs had refused to perform according to that script.[11]

So it was that Ely, Corcoran, and their fellow prisoners came to spend their first night of captivity on the grime-encrusted floor of Ligon's. The following morning, the prisoners were awakened to a breakfast of dry bread, boiled beef, and coffee. As they were ingesting this first taste of prison fare, they received a surprise visit from an officer who would become one of the most important architects of the Confederate system of prisons, Brigadier General John Henry Winder.[12]

Winder was descended from a prominent Maryland family that had furnished officers in each of the nation's wars. His grandfather had served with distinction during the Revolution; his father, William H. Winder, was a career officer in the regular army. Promoted to brigadier general shortly after the War of 1812 began, the elder Winder distinguished himself as an aggressive and resourceful leader. Captured in the battle of Stony Creek in 1813, he soon found himself one of the American hostages held under sentence of death as a result of Crown threats to try Irish-American soldiers on charges of treason. Happily for future generations of Winders, the general was not executed. It was largely because of his skill in facilitating negotiations between the belligerents, in fact, that the cycle of retaliation and counterretaliation was broken and the American hostages freed. Upon his exchange he was ordered to assume command of the forces charged with the defense of Washington. These orders set in motion a series of events that would end in the complete destruction of the general's personal military reputation and the disgrace of the entire Winder family.[13]

Upon reporting to his new command, William Winder quickly ascertained that he was woefully short of reliable troops and supplies. Repeated requests to the secretary of war for reinforcements and additional provisions yielded little of either, and Winder—overworked, indecisive, and increasingly despondent—made poor use of the limited combat power that was available to him. He repeatedly withdrew as the British advanced through Maryland, and by the time he finally decided to make a stand outside Washington, it was too late. The British easily routed his hodgepodge force at Bladensburg, and Americans who were not killed or captured were soon in headlong flight. The "Bladensburg races," as the rout was aptly labeled, left the road to Washington totally undefended, and on 24 August 1814 the British entered the capital and set it afire.[14]

Military and congressional courts of inquiry convened after the war officially exonerated Winder, but the general's military career was at an end; he would be forever known as the "most unfortunate general" of the war. He resigned his commission to practice law, and in time he came to terms with his fate. Not so his eldest son. John Henry, then fourteen years old, was in his first year as a cadet at West Point at the time of the Bladensburg debacle. He was exceedingly proud of his father's military exploits and achievements, and although he bore the Bladensburg slights and innuendoes of his classmates in silence, he vowed that his own record of military service would be so exemplary that it would erase the "stain of Bladensburg." In the opening days of the Civil War, fate provided him with a golden opportunity to do just that.[15]

January 1861 found Winder, then a major in the Third U.S. Artillery Regiment, in command of a small garrison in Florida charged with the security of Pensacola Bay. Due to a serious illness resulting from a combination of malaria and general physical exhaustion, he had been absent from his command for almost a year. On 10 January, Florida seceded from the Union and demanded that all Federal garrisons in the state be immediately surrendered. The lieutenant commanding the Pensacola installations in Winder's absence flatly refused to do so. Under pressure from encroaching Florida and Alabama troops, he moved the Federal garrison from the mainland to Fort Pickens on Santa Rosa Island.[16]

Winder's duty was now clear. As a commissioned officer in the U.S. army, he was required to rejoin his soldiers in Fort Pickens and defend the post to the best of his ability. Such had been the decision of his old friend and fellow southerner, Major Robert Anderson, at Fort Sumter; but Winder, uncertain whether his native state of Maryland would remain in the Union, procrastinated. Then, while visiting his brother in Baltimore, Winder witnessed firsthand the bloody riot that erupted on April 13 when citizens attacked U.S. troops en route to Washington. Convinced that both Maryland and his adopted state of North Carolina would soon secede, Winder finally acted. In a letter dated 20 April he tendered his resignation to the assistant adjutant general of the army. The "unfortunate state of the country," he wrote, required that he "sever the ties" that had bound him to the army through almost forty years of service. Had he returned to his post at Fort Pickens and been steadfast in its defense, Winder's name might have been joined to that of Anderson as a hero of the Union, and the "stain of Bladensburg" might finally have been expunged. But he chose instead to follow the South into secession, and on 30 April, at the age of 61, he set out for North Carolina to offer his services to the Confederacy.[17]

Winder's efforts to secure a military appointment through his home state came to naught; although the governor promised him an advisory post in the grade of general officer, another appointee was selected to fill the position. Ever sensitive to real or perceived slights, Winder fired off a blistering letter in which he accused the governor of damaging his reputation. When offered a colonel's commission and the command of a regiment of North Carolina infantry, he refused on the grounds that it was an "inferior command." Sensing that there would be no offer from North Carolina commensurate with his previous rank and experience, Winder traveled to Richmond, where he joined the hundreds of other southerners seeking military or civilian appointments. He spoke personally with Jefferson Davis and with General Samuel Cooper, a close friend from the prewar army who had recently been named adjutant general of the Confederate army. Winder's lobbying efforts paid off on 22 June, when he was offered a brigadier general's commission and an appointment as inspector general of the military camps that were springing up throughout the Richmond area. Deeming both the position and the rank appropriate, he accepted them.[18]

Prior to the Civil War, Richmond had been a rather tranquil city of 38,000, but its selection on 27 April 1861 as the capital of the new Confederacy transformed it. Throughout May and June, thousands of soldiers and civilian volunteers from all over the South streamed into the city, and by July its population had doubled. Although the majority of these new arrivals sought only an opportunity to enlist and train with the new regiments that were forming, a sizable number went looking for less wholesome and patriotic diversions. They found them. Drunkenness, knifings, shootings, prostitution, gambling, and thievery of all sorts became common in the camps around the city, and as the early illusions of swift glory and heroic service gave way to the harsh realities of endless drill and numbing fatigue details, many of the farmboys-turned-soldiers simply deserted their units for the high life in town. Crime rates in all categories of offenses skyrocketed, and when the capital's minuscule police force proved incapable of dealing with the crisis, Mayor Joseph Mayo appealed to Winder for assistance. Winder moved swiftly to rectify the problem through measures that were both harsh and effective.[19]

In an action that anticipated the manner in which he would deal with the coming crush of Federal prisoners, Winder transferred all the Confederate soldiers and sailors then held in the civilian jails of the city into a single large building, where they were kept until they were tried and released to their units for disposition. To accomplish the tough and dangerous job of ridding Richmond's streets of drunken soldiers and deserters, Winder recruited a group of equally tough civilian "detectives." This force, dubbed the "Plug Uglies" by locals, moved with equal aggressiveness when their mission was expanded to include rounding up alleged Union sympathizers. Richmond's citizens initially applauded these efforts, but as the strictures of martial law tightened around the capital, Winder and his Plug Uglies became increasingly unpopular. By the end of the year, the general had acquired the rather unflattering sobriquet of "military dictator of Richmond."[20] But his reputation did not keep the citizens of Richmond from turning to him when a new crisis gripped the city, and they were quick to support Secretary of War Leroy P. Walker's decision to add the responsibility of coping with the problems presented by the Manassas prisoners to Winder's growing list of duties.[21]

In their analyses of southern prisons, most historians have agreed that one of the main reasons for the deplorable conditions in those facilities was that the Confederacy never developed a comprehensive, centralized system through which it could administer its vast network of prisoner-of-war camps. In his classic 1930 work, for example, historian William B. Hesseltine argues that the prison system developed in the South was "less worthy of the name than that of the North" and owed its existence to "a series of accidents." Confederate prisons, he contends, "came into existence without definite plans, to meet the exigencies of the moment."[22]

No one who has studied the creation and growth of the Confederate prison system would contest the assertion that it was initially shaped by expediency. The same was true of the northern system in the first months of the war. Both belligerents failed to draw on the lessons of the nation's previous conflicts, which amply illustrated the necessity of having a clearly defined set of prisoner-of-war policies and procedures in place when the fighting began. The first southern prisons did indeed come into existence "without definite plans," for leaders in Richmond had formulated no policies or procedures for managing the thousands of prisoners shipped south following Manassas. Yet once this deficiency was realized, the Davis administration moved aggressively to create a system through which it could direct the establishment of a network of camps and exercise national control over those facilities. That system would become increasingly centralized and more complex as the war progressed.

Evidence of this new centralization of control became clear even as Winder moved to accomplish his duties. On his first visit to Ligon's warehouse, the general was alarmed by its overcrowding and quickly ascertained that additional space would be required to house incoming prisoners. He assured his "celebrity prisoners" that he would find separate accommodations for Union officers, and on the day following the arrival of this initial group of prisoners in Richmond, Winder commandeered Howard's factory and ordered all Federal officers transferred there. Still, prisoners from Manassas and other engagements continued to flow into Richmond, and Winder was continuously pressed to find more space. By October 1861 the number of Yankee captives topped 2,685, and there was still no end in sight. The only structures suitable for confining large numbers of men were the city's factories and warehouses, such as Ligon's and Howard's, which the general moved to convert into prisons. Buildings housing Atkinson's, Barret's, Palmer's, Grant's, Mayo's, Scott's, Ross's, Smith's, and Taylor's tobacco factories were appropriated, as were the Crew and Pemberton and Gwathmey tobacco warehouses. As each new facility was occupied, it was hoped that no more would be required, but the crush of hundreds of new prisoners arriving from battles such as Ball's Bluff and Bethel always combined to make additional acquisitions imperative.[23] Winder was soon confiscating suitable structures and filling them with prisoners without even paying their owners. Such was the case with the warehouse of W. H. Gwathmey. When the indignant proprietor complained to the secretary of war that Winder had seized his warehouse "as a prison for the use of the Government" without offering compensation, the secretary summarily dismissed the outraged merchant with terse instructions that he "present his account" to the government of the Confederate States.[24]

Winder's prodigious efforts notwithstanding, Confederate leaders fully understood that even with the acquisition of additional buildings, Richmond would never be able to house all of the prisoners that were being taken in the eastern theater of the war. Accordingly, as summer faded into fall the Davis administration intensified its efforts to locate suitable prison sites outside the capital. One of the most attractive locations proposed was North Carolina, and inquiries as to the possibility of establishing a major prison there had been initiated soon after the state seceded. North Carolina governor Henry T. Clark appointed a commission to determine if a suitable site could be found, and on 25 October he notified Secretary of War Judah P. Benjamin, who had replaced the ailing Walker, that the owners of the abandoned Rowan cotton factory in Salisbury were willing to sell the facility for $15,000, payable in Confederate bonds. The buildings of the factory were capable of housing between four and five hundred prisoners, the governor reckoned, and he hastened to add that with the addition of a fence to enclose its seven acres of grounds, "accommodation could be made for as many more."[25]

Back in Richmond, this offer was welcome news indeed to Benjamin and his hard-pressed staff, and on 27 October the secretary authorized his representative in North Carolina to purchase the Rowan factory at the full $15,000 asking price.

Benjamin's eagerness to complete the transaction was evident in his instructions to his agent. "Inform me by telegraph the instant you complete the purchase," he wired, "and report what further enclosures, buildings, &c., can be advantageously erected, with the view if possible of making the depot sufficient for the reception of some 2,000 prisoners."[26] The transaction was completed on 2 November, and Benjamin wasted no time in taking full advantage of the new facility. "How many prisoners could be sent immediately with safety?" he inquired of the governor only two days later. Even before he received an answer, he ordered his subordinates to hasten preparations to transfer the first group of prisoners out of Richmond.[27]

But on 27 November, Benjamin received disturbing news from a North Carolina businessman who had recently visited the Salisbury site. "It is much out of repair," the merchant informed him, "and will not be fit for the safe-keeping of prisoners for a long time."[28] Benjamin could have postponed the proposed occupation date for the new facility, but after consultations with Winder he judged that the prisoner situation in Richmond was too grave to permit any delay. He ordered that Confederate soldiers awaiting trial by courts-martial in jails near Salisbury be employed in renovating the Rowan site, and he proceeded with plans to transfer prisoners out of Richmond to North Carolina immediately. The first shipment—120 soldiers captured at Manassas—arrived at Salisbury on 12 December, and another 176 joined them on the 26th.

In spite of Benjamin's efforts, the first arrivals found that warnings of the factory's poor condition were unfortunately quite accurate. Repairs had barely progressed, the single well was completely inadequate for a population of hundreds of men, and—most distressing of all to the Confederate guards who had accompanied the prisoners—no provisions had been made to constitute a guard force to keep watch over the detraining Yankees. To answer this need, desperate Confederate officials promptly pressed into service a company of students from nearby Trinity College. Under the unlikely command of a minister who also served as the institution's president, these students watched over their charges until a proper guard could be mounted some weeks later.[29]

Work on enclosing the compound at Salisbury continued after the arrival of the first captives. When completed, a board fence eight feet high surrounded the sixteen-acre site. Along the outside of this wall, guards patrolled along an attached parapet about four feet off the ground. The parapet allowed them an unobstructed view of the interior of the compound, in which stood the principal factory building (a ninety by fifty–foot brick structure), an engine house, six four-room tenements, a superintendent's house, and three small sheds. At full capacity, Benjamin and his staff planned to confine two thousand men at Salisbury, thereby alleviating some measure of the overcrowding in Richmond.[30]

But the secretary knew that ultimately this would not be enough. Even as Salisbury was being occupied, he continued his search for additional locations where the government might establish prisons. Tuscaloosa, Alabama, seemed at first to offer hope of relief, and on 25 October Benjamin asked Alabama governor A. B. Moore whether the state might be able to assist in housing prisoners. "I am told," Benjamin wrote, "you have at Tuscaloosa not only legislative buildings, but an insane asylum and a military institute, all unoccupied. We are greatly embarrassed by our prisoners as all our accommodations here are required for our sick and wounded. It would be a great public service if you can find a place for some, if not all, of our prisoners. We have now over 2,000 here."[31]

Moore responded that he would accept the transfer of a limited number of prisoners, and on 21 November Colonel A. C. Myers, the Confederate quartermaster general, dispatched an officer to Tuscaloosa, where, in accordance with the provisions enacted by the Confederate Congress assigning the responsibility for prisoners to the quartermaster corps, he was to assume command of the city's captives.[32] The relief afforded by Tuscaloosa was short-lived, however, for less than one month later all available space in the city except the insane asylum (which continued to house patients) had been consumed. On 19 December the newly elected governor of the state, John G. Shorter, notified Benjamin of the situation in a rather brusque note. "Better send no more prisoners to Tuscaloosa," he advised. "Accommodations exhausted." To preclude any notion the secretary might have held concerning confiscation of the asylum, Shorter added that the "lunatic asylum will not be leased," for its conversion to a prison would surely "disorganize the institution and arouse the indignation of a loyal and Christian people." For Benjamin, such reports were exceptionally bad news, and he responded to the governor in an equally brief and sharp message. "I shall send no more prisoners to Tuscaloosa," he declared, testily closing the two-line missive, "Never thought of seizing asylum."[33]

Other initiatives aimed at relieving the overcrowding in Richmond were more successful. Groups of prisoners numbering between 150 and 200 were shipped to Atlanta and New Orleans, where they were interned in existing jails. The governor of South Carolina volunteered to confine 150 men in the Columbia jail and another 200 "of the better class" at the city's fairgrounds.[34] A contingent of 154 prisoners, characterized by the editor of the *Charleston Mercury* as "among those who had evidenced the most insolent and insubordinate dispositions" while interred at Ligon's, were confined in the jail of that city and in Castle Pinckney.[35]

A final group of about the same size was transported to Macon, Georgia, where they were incarcerated in the dank holding pens of a slave market.[36]

Thus by the end of 1861, Confederate leaders had firmly established the foundation of the system by which they would administer the dozens of camps established over the course of the war. Army regulations and legislation enacted by the Confederate Congress specified the treatment to be accorded captives, and these provisions adhered to President Jefferson Davis's admonition that prisoners be treated with "kindness and courtesy."[37] Although the thousands of prisoners taken following Manassas had caught the government completely unprepared, following its initial shock the Davis administration had moved aggressively to acquire confinement facilities in Richmond and to establish installations in other states.

While there had been some successes, the first six months of the Confederate prison system also exposed the frightfully serious and complex problems that would plague it throughout the war. The first of these was the shortages of food, medicines, and basic supplies in all categories. Rations were a problem in Richmond from the moment the first prisoners arrived. The regulations of 1861 governing the treatment of captives directed that they receive the same daily rations as Confederate soldiers in the field:

3/4 pounds of pork or bacon or 1 1/4 pounds of fresh or salted beef
18 ounces of bread or flour or 12 ounces of hard bread or 1 1/4 pounds of cornmeal.

In addition to the items provided for each individual, the following were to be supplied every hundred rations:

8 quarts of peas or beans or 10 pounds of rice
6 pounds of coffee
12 pounds of sugar
4 quarts of vinegar
2 quarts of salt.[38]

Unsurprisingly, the bill of fare never satisfied this requirement in either quality or quantity. In Richmond, Congressman Alfred Ely and the officers with whom he was confined ate as well as any prisoners in the Confederacy. They were fed three times daily, but, as one of the captives later recalled, the ration provided usually consisted of "boiled beef steak and bread," a monotonous and nutritionally deficient offering that could be supplemented only if one possessed the funds to purchase such items as coffee, potatoes, corn, and eggs from the local merchants who were authorized to peddle their wares in the prison. For the enlisted men, the daily ration was far more meager. In August, a wounded prisoner wrote from his hospital bed to ask a friend to "send along . . . a piece of cornbread . . . for we don't see any of that article in these parts." Another captive related that the men on his floor were fed a morning ration consisting of bread, boiled beef, and water, and an evening ration of bread and a soup concocted from the beef "taken from the slops of the day previous." Supplemental items like those available to Ely and the officers could be purchased only irregularly, and on 12 September the rations of coffee and sugar that had been dispensed daily since July were terminated.[39]

Provision of supplies in other categories fell far short of requirements as well. Prisoners were provided no clothing to replace worn-out uniforms. "I am almost entirely naked," one soldier in a Richmond prison informed friends back home. "The shirt I have on, I have worn for nearly three weeks. It was very much torn when I put it on, and now it is all in ribbons." Bedding for the rough plank floors of the warehouses consisted solely of "ticks," small cotton bags that soldiers stuffed with straw, and most of the men had no blankets.[40]

Medical supplies were also wanting. By the fall, stores of lint and plaster had been drawn down to almost zero, and Confederate medical personnel were quick to attribute the shortage to the Yankees themselves. "Tell your master, Lincoln, to raise the blockade, and then we'll have enough to treat you," one prison surgeon demanded of an ailing Federal. "We haven't enough for our own patients, and they must be served first."[41]

A second problem in the southern prison system that became evident during this formative period was the administrative and supervisory inadequacies of the Confederate military and civilian leaders charged with directing daily operations in the individual camps. Shortages of rations and other supplies were exacerbated by poorly conceived and executed distribution plans, so that available stocks of food, medicines, and blankets often were not distributed in a timely and consistent manner. The monumental problems the Confederacy would face in prioritizing shipments over its limited railroad network surfaced at this time, as did the shortage of trained and experienced clerks and supervisors who would be required to ensure that adequate stocks of food and supplies for prisoners were properly requisitioned and distributed.[42]

Nor did those charged with directing the southern system of prisons seem able to provide an adequate force to guard their captives. At Salisbury prison, the company of college students hurriedly pressed into service as guards were completely untrained and poorly equipped. Securing an adequate guard force would continue to be a problem at Salisbury, and in Richmond the situation was no better.[43] Major J. T. W. Harriston, assigned to command in the network of Richmond prisons in the fall of 1861, recalled that "the guard was relieved every morning at nine o'clock, a new regiment being furnished every day at that hour. The regiment was always composed of new recruits, who were sent thither mainly to learn the duties of a soldier." These new recruits were generally "awkward and inefficient."[44] Throughout the war, the majority of soldiers detailed as guards at southern prisons would either be inexperienced and inept recruits (much like those provided Harriston) or men deemed too old or infirm for service in line units. Such men were often exceptionally harsh in the performance of their duties, and at best proved decidedly uninterested in bettering the conditions of the captives they guarded.

Serious deficiencies in the standards that Confederate leaders would employ in choosing, preparing, and maintaining their prisons also appeared in this early period. Conditions within Confederate camps did not become bad as a result of diminishing resources or any other combination of factors over the course of the war. While conditions in southern facilities would worsen as the war progressed, they were atrocious from the start. This was due in large part to the pattern routinely followed in occupying those facilities. Confederate leaders would select a location for a prison and then direct the site to be occupied without ensuring that it had been adequately prepared to receive prisoners. Once the captives arrived, they would be marched into the prison—be it a stockade or some preexisting building—and the gates would swing shut. Improvements to the facilities following the arrival of prisoners would be effected only when compelled by security requirements, as was the case at Salisbury, or when health and sanitation conditions became so bad that the prisoners' lives were threatened. Improvements in this second category, in the few cases where they were undertaken, would almost always prove to be grossly inadequate.

Further, the mission of the Confederate garrisons assigned to the camps was almost always limited to guarding prisoners, dispensing rudimentary medical care, and distributing available rations and supplies. Missing from this list of duties was the requirement to complete the routine inspections and modest construction projects necessary to sustain the health and welfare of the prisoners. Such was the case when the very first Federal captives entered the prisons of Richmond, and such would continue to be the case over the life of the Confederate system.

The effects of this policy of deliberate neglect were predictable. No latrines, for example, were provided for the hundreds of men incarcerated in Ligon's. Fortunately, as a young New Hampshire soldier remembered, "The floor of the room in which some of us were at first confined . . . was not level, and the foul black stream of mud and water from the sink settled on one side of the room to a depth of one to two inches. We succeeded in huddling on the other side of the room, and so most of us kept out of the mud at night." Most of the inmates might have successfully employed this tactic, but not all, for the soldier recalled that "one of our company became insane and spent his time splashing around in the filth until he was taken out of the room and we saw him no more."[45] Conditions in the Smith warehouse prison were similar. Latrine facilities there consisted only of a hole cut in the floor in one corner of the room. The opening extended from the levels where the soldiers were confined all the way down to the basement of the building, and as the basement filled with excrement, a nauseating stench rose to permeate the upper floors.[46]

Yet another problem that appeared at this time and became progressively worse was the increasing hostility with which many southerners came to view the presence of prisoners. Although the arrival of the first Federal prisoners in the heady days immediately following Manassas sparked outbursts of pride and patriotism among the citizens of Richmond, such feelings quickly wore thin when it became apparent that rather than simply serving as a distribution point, the capital would be forced to house thousands of prisoners on a long-term basis. Complaints that the captives were consuming too great a portion of the city's limited fuel and food supplies increased, as did fears of the security threat posed by hundreds of prisoners who might escape or be freed by marauding bands of Union cavalry.[47] In September 1861, the *Richmond Enquirer* calculated that the weekly cost of maintaining the 1,700 prisoners confined in the city was a staggering $11,000, and the paper echoed the sentiments of many citizens when it angrily charged Winder with confining the captives in conditions better than they had known in the Union army. By October, the good-natured taunts and teasing that had greeted the initial prisoners had been replaced by angry threats, hoots, and jeers.[48]

A final deficiency revealed in this early period was the absence of an adequately manned, permanent staff tasked with the responsibility and provided the authority to direct the developing Confederate prison system. Throughout 1861 all orders directing the establishment and administration of camps were issued by the secretary of war. Although this certainly indicated that the development of a comprehensive, nationally directed prisoner-of-war system was an important priority of the Davis administration, it was becoming increasingly evident that as the demands of war increased, the secretary of war simply did not have time to administer the complex and rapidly growing network of Confederate camps.

By December 1861 the hard realities of war had long since overwhelmed the Confederacy's feeble plans for prisoner management, and the squalid pens of Richmond were already horribly overcrowded. Although his authority technically extended no further than Confederate capital, Winder had been forced by necessity to become the de facto director of a developing prisoner-of-war system that encompassed most of the Deep South. As hundreds of additional prisoners streamed into the capital, he furiously cobbled together arrangements to transfer them to camps in other states, but it was obvious that this cumbersome arrangement would prove inadequate in the long run. Recalling the great success with which the nation had employed the office of commissary general of prisoners during the War of 1812, Winder proposed that a single leader provided with full authority be appointed to direct the development and administration of the Confederate prisoner-of-war system. Only such an appointment, he insisted, could bring order out of the chaos of 1861. As the number of reports detailing the dreadful conditions in the camps continued to rise, many within the Confederate government were coming to agree with him.[49]

CHAPTER 4

"A State of Perpetual Twilight"
The Union Prisoner-of-War System, June–December 1861

THE ORIGIN of the Union prisoner-of-war system, like that of the Confederacy, can be traced to summer of 1861, and in many respects the development of the two systems during the first seven months of the war was similar. Both clearly mandated humane treatment. U.S. army regulations, revised in 1861, directed that the private property of captives was to be "duly respected" and that each prisoner was to be treated "with the regard due his rank." Wounded prisoners were to be "treated with the same care as the wounded of the [Union] army," and all captives were to receive "one ration per day." Lastly, as in the southern army, prisoners were to be transported as quickly as possible to the rear, where they would become the responsibility of the quartermaster general.[1]

A second similarity between the two systems can be found in the helter-skelter manner in which their initial camps were established. As was the case in the Confederacy, Union military and civilian leaders were completely unprepared to receive prisoners at the outbreak of the war, and this lack of preparedness resulted in a confused and sometimes desperate scramble to locate suitable places of internment for the first Rebel captives. Due to Lincoln's determination to avoid any action that might be construed as recognition of the Confederacy as a belligerent state, the first southern captives—the privateersmen taken following Fort Sumter—were confined in the Tombs and treated as traitors rather than as bona fide prisoners of war. Given the political statement that Lincoln wished to convey to the country and the nations of Europe, such treatment might be expected. Less well known, however, is the fact that the conditions under which Confederate soldiers were imprisoned in other northern facilities during this early period were not much better.

Like Richmond in the South, New York City stood astride the most modern and extensive transportation net in the North. Because there were no plans for confining prisoners elsewhere, this fact alone made the city an attractive location for depositing captives. Accordingly, when General George B. McClellan telegraphed the War Department on 13 July 1861 requesting "immediate instructions . . . as to the disposition" of the Confederates captured by his command in western Virginia, he was directed to send the captives to Fort Lafayette in New York Harbor.[2]

That installation, which stood on a small rocky outcrop in the Narrows between Staten Island and Long Island, was one of the series of forts constructed following the War of 1812. Originally intended to defend the approaches to the city, it was showing its age by 1861, and there was little to recommend it as a place to confine enemy prisoners other than the fact that it lay offshore and in close proximity to New York City. Still, a suitable place had to be located for confining the hundreds of prisoners being taken by McClellan and other Union generals, so the army ordered that cells be created in the fort by bricking up the entrances to the rooms housing the structure's two main batteries and four smaller casements. The enclosures thus created were damp, foul-smelling spaces, cluttered with gun carriages, rope, and other impedimenta of coastal defense. Because they were lighted only by small slit embrasures, the lower reaches of the rooms remained shrouded in what one inmate described as "a state of perpetual twilight." Beds for all the men would not fit in the cramped spaces, and many were forced to sleep on the cold stone floors with only thin bags of straw for mattresses.[3]

Because of these grim conditions, Fort Lafayette became widely known as the "American Bastille"—a moniker rendered all the more suitable by the fact that its first inmates were political prisoners jailed as a result of Lincoln's suspension of the writ of habeas corpus.[4] The fort's maximum capacity had originally been estimated at fifty inmates, and had confinements in the facility been limited to prisoners of state only, the available space might have been adequate. Unfortunately, Union unpreparedness to billet prisoners mirrored that of the Confederacy, and the result was desperate overcrowding. Arriving prisoners of war were simply stuffed into cells already holding dozens of political internees, and the fort's inmate population was quickly pushed to three times its projected capacity. Prisoner rations were of low quality and poorly prepared, the water—drawn from a contaminated cistern—was foul, and prisoners were forced to spend most of their time restricted to their cells because the overcrowding precluded exercise periods.[5]

As Fort Lafayette filled beyond capacity, officials in the War Department began to cast about for other installations that might be quickly converted to prison use. That search led them to Governor's Island, another of New York

Harbor's defense facilities. The island, situated off the southern end of Manhattan, was home to two installations, Castle Williams on its southern tip and Fort Columbus on its northern end.

Castle Williams, a circular fortification with walls forty feet high and eight feet thick, had been competed in 1811; in the late summer of 1861, it was designated as a prison for Confederate enlisted men.[6] Even after converted for prison use, its rooms were more spacious than those of Fort Lafayette, but with the arrival of hundreds of Confederate soldiers captured following the fall of Hatteras Island, it too was swiftly filled far beyond capacity. Soon every space was crammed to bursting, despite attempts to meet the crisis by transferring some inmates to a small installation on nearby Bedloe's Island and erecting dozens of tents to house the unceasing flood of new arrivals.[7] With the overcrowding, conditions in Castle Williams plummeted. "Our men are now suffering very greatly from disease," Sergeant Andrew Norman, a spokesman for the captives of the Seventh North Carolina, wrote to Union secretary of war Simon Cameron on 29 September. "To-day 115 of the 630 are confined by disease which threatens to prostrate us all." He pleaded with the secretary to grant the Carolinians parole. The ranks of the prisoners were being depleted due to "the want of room and the presence of contagious diseases among us," he informed Cameron, warning of the likely consequences of further confinement under such conditions. "Four of our men have died within the past five days," he explained, "and many others are dangerously ill."[8] Union physicians charged with monitoring conditions within the fortress prison agreed with Norman's assessment. Following a health and welfare inspection conducted at the end of September, Surgeon William J. Sloan notified his superiors that

> the condition of the Fort Hatteras prisoners in the castle at this post is such as to require the immediate attention of the Government. They are crowded into an ill-ventilated building which has always been an unhealthy one when occupied by large bodies of men. There are no conveniences for cooking except in the open air, no means of heating the lower tier of gun rooms and no privies within the area. As the winter approaches I cannot see how these 630 men can be taken care of under the above circumstances. These men are without clothing and are not disposed to use the means prescribed by me for the prevention of disease unless compelled to do so. Everything necessary in a sanitary point of view has been urged upon them but is only carried out by the persistent efforts of the officer in charge of the castle. Under all these circumstances with the effect of change of climate and the depression result-

ing from their situation disease must be the result. There are now upwards of eighty cases of measles amongst them, a number of cases of typhoid fever, pneumonia, intermittent fever, &c. I have taken the worst cases into my hospital and am preparing it with beds to its full capacity for other cases. Every building upon the island being crowded with troops, with a large number in tents, I know not how the condition of these prisoners can be improved except by a change of location to some other place for all or a portion of them, the present condition of things resulting principally from deficiency of quarters and not from causes within our control.[9]

The island's other facility, Fort Columbus, was a brick structure dating from the end of the eighteenth century. Here Confederate officers were imprisoned in converted buildings that had formerly housed Union officers posted to the fort, and although the overcrowding was not as dire as that found in Castle Williams, conditions were not much better. Colonel Gustavus Loomis, the commander of all facilities on the island, concurred with Sloan's assessment that conditions in the two prisons were debilitating. He also agreed with the surgeon's warning that with the onset of the frigid New York winter the number of deaths would spiral out of control, and he notified his superiors in Washington that there were only two courses of action that would avoid this catastrophe. Either they authorized him to construct suitable barracks for all the prisoners, or they allowed the prisoners to "be removed before cold weather comes."[10] Wishing to avoid the trouble and expense of constructing new housing for hundreds of prisoners, the War Department selected the second option. The question was, where could the prisoners be moved?

One option was to transfer the captives to other prisons that were already in use on the East Coast. Baltimore's Fort McHenry, for example, had housed Confederate prisoners since July 1861. One segment of its captive population was unique, the direct result of the consuming wrath of the commanding general of the army, Winfield Scott. In response to McClellan's request for instructions as to the disposition of the prisoners taken during his campaign in western Virginia, Scott magnanimously told the general to "discharge" all enlisted and noncommissioned officer prisoners who were willing to swear allegiance to the Union. Specifically exempted from this provision, however, were Confederate officers who had formerly served under the Stars and Stripes. "You will except from this privilege," Scott wrote to McClellan on 14 July, "all officers among your prisoners who have recently been officers of the U.S. Army or Navy and who you may have reason to believe left either with the intent of bearing arms against the United States. The captured officers of this description you will send to Fort McHenry."[11]

By the fall of 1861 the fort was manifesting many of the deficiencies that plagued the facilities on Governor's Island. Construction had been completed in 1812, and the buildings within its massive, star-shaped walls were in poor repair. And like the prisons on Governor's island, Fort McHenry was already overcrowded, in part because it could claim the dubious distinction of being one of the few facilities to hold considerable numbers of three categories of prisoners. Along with southern prisoners of war, its cells contained civilian prisoners of state and Union soldiers convicted of crimes punishable by imprisonment. This combination pushed the number of internees well beyond capacity.[12]

Such was also the case in prisons that had been established in the nation's capital. Prisoners captured in northern Virginia during the summer of 1861 were sent to the District of Columbia, where they were originally confined in the Washington County Jail, a structure built in 1830 and designed to house a maximum of one hundred inmates. This capacity was more than adequate when the jail held only civilian offenders, but the arrival of Civil War captives quickly pushed the prisoner population to more than double that number. Cells constructed to hold two prisoners were crammed with ten, and sanitary facilities were overtaxed. Conditions in the jail became so deplorable that Lincoln's own secretary of the interior was moved to liken the facility to "the Black Hole of Calcutta."[13]

In an effort to relieve the overcrowding, the city's provost marshal commandeered the Old Capitol building and converted it to prison use. Iron bars were affixed to its windows, and the yard surrounding the structure was enclosed with a board fence. It was to this facility that Confederates captured at Manassas were marched through vengeful crowds shouting, "Kill them! Kill them!" and it is likely they would have done so had the marine escort not pushed the mob back at bayonet point. The prisoners survived, but by October 1861, only two months after it was opened, the Old Capitol prison was filled beyond capacity.[14]

Still, something had to be done to relieve the terrible overcrowding on Governor's Island. Deaths from measles, pneumonia, and a host of other illnesses were reaching epidemic proportions, and winter was fast approaching. With all existing prisons in the East already filled to bursting, General Scott decided to expand the Union system of prisons yet again. On 26 October the War Department issued orders directing that "prisoners of war confined at the several posts in New York Harbor be sent by sea under charge of a vigilant officer and strong guard to Fort Warren, Boston Harbor."[15]

While this emptying of the prisons in New York Harbor undoubtedly occasioned great joy among the Confederate inmates, it unfortunately came as a complete surprise to Colonel Justin E. Dimick, the officer designated to receive the men being shipped to Boston. Dimick was commanding Fort Monroe in Virginia when, on 19 October, he received orders from the headquarters of the army assigning him to Fort Warren. The orders also directed Dimick to "take charge of the political prisoners and prisoners of war who may be sent there for safe-keeping" and provided specific guidelines to follow in accomplishing this mission. While prisoners were to be "securely held," they were also to be "allowed every privilege consistent with this end, including opportunity to take air and exercise and be treated with all kindness." Prisoners were to be permitted to supplement their standard rations and equipment through purchases from local merchants. They were to be allowed to receive food, clothing, and "small sums" of money from home; subject to the inspections of government censors, they could post letters to friends and relatives. Dimick was advised that General Scott desired that the facility be prepared for use as soon as possible, for "the order . . . transferring the prisoners from New York Harbor cannot be given until you are established at Fort Warren." The directive closed with assurances that "the Quartermaster's and Subsistence Departments have given orders for putting the quarters at Fort Warren in comfortable condition," and that the quartermaster officer in Boston had been instructed to secure rations for the shipment of prisoners that would soon be en route to the fort.[16] All this specificity and detail notwithstanding, there was one grievous flaw in Dimick's orders. The colonel was advised to expect only one hundred prisoners in the shipment from New York, and the quartermaster in Boston was instructed to obtain rations for that number for thirty days only.[17]

On the afternoon of 31 October, Dimick received word that the *State of Maine*, a vessel chartered by the War Department to transport the prisoners from New York to Boston, was entering the harbor. The colonel was waiting on the dock to meet his new charges, and it was there that he learned that instead of the 100 prisoners he expected, the holds of the *State of Maine* were stuffed with 155 political prisoners and just over 600 prisoners of war. Dimick was in no way prepared to accommodate this number for even one evening, and he informed the distraught captives that they would have to remain on the ship overnight. When the Federal officer in charge of the Confederate prisoners explained that the crowded conditions on the ship would surely lead to an outbreak of disease should the men be required to spend another evening on board, Dimick relented and allowed four companies of North Carolina infantrymen to come ashore and be billeted in the fort. The remainder of the men were compelled to spend yet another uncomfortable and unhealthy night afloat.[18]

Of all the prisons occupied by Confederate soldiers during the war, only Fort Warren would secure the reputation as a place where conditions were adequate and captives were treated humanely. That reputation was due primarily to the standards and philosophy of command instilled by Colonel Dimick in the initial weeks of the camp's operation. Given the huge number of men transferred into the installation at one time, it is not surprising that accommodations were at first inadequate. Prisoners were forced to subsist on short rations; as one North Carolina officer reported, missed meals were not uncommon. The rooms in which the captives were billeted were small and hopelessly overcrowded, and due to the shortage of furniture, many men were forced to sleep on crude pallets constructed of scraps of lumber and cloth.[19]

Dimick worked tirelessly to ameliorate these hardships, and he was largely successful. To relieve the overcrowding, he granted Confederate officers limited freedom to walk about the island. Sympathetic citizens in Boston were permitted to contribute food, clothing, and bedding for the prisoners' welfare, and the captives' health needs were met by competent and attentive medical personnel. Conditions for enlisted prisoners were less comfortable, but soldiers who had endured the grim cells of Fort Lafayette or Castle Williams had no doubt that they were better off in Fort Warren. As one North Carolina soldier fresh from the cramped confines of Castle Williams later wrote, "We were not so crowded . . . were better fed, and our quarters were greatly improved."[20] Dimick and his staff dealt firmly yet fairly with their charges, and in their personal correspondence the captives were lavish in their praise for the commandant. One prisoner recalled that Dimick "did all in his power to render our condition more tolerable," while another observed that "we experienced none of the rudeness and insolence we had daily to encounter at Fort Lafayette."[21]

The Union's scramble for prison facilities was not restricted to the eastern theater of the war. Battles were also being fought in the Department of the West, and commanders in that theater soon found that their government had made no provisions for confining prisoners taken in those engagements. During the last half of 1861, Missouri remained the most hotly contested state in the western theater. For years, irregular armed bands of northern and southern sympathizers had clawed at each other in a vicious guerrilla war, and the arrival of regular troops from the Union and Confederate armies ensured that both the scale and intensity of the fighting would increase. Federal authorities headquartered in St. Louis knew that with fighting would come prisoners of war, and in September

1861 they began to cast about for a suitable facility in which to confine them. Ironically, the location they chose was Lynch's Slave Pen, late the property of Bernard M. Lynch, a slave trader who, as one resident of the city remembered, fled south when the political tide in the city began to run against him and "the traffic in human beings suddenly ceased."[22] The pen was a two-story brick structure deemed capable of holding around 100 prisoners; because it was located on Myrtle Street, it soon became known as the Myrtle Street Prison. The facility had been open less than a week when the first contingent of 27 prisoners, a mix of local southern sympathizers and regular Confederate troops, was escorted through its doors. Through the fall that number grew to 150, but when word arrived that 2,000 more prisoners would soon be shipped to St. Louis from the battlefields of southwest Missouri, George E. Leighton, the city's provost marshal, knew that a much larger facility would be required.

As he had done in the selection of Lynch's Slave Pen, Leighton looked for a structure that was not only suitable for the incarceration of prisoners, but one that had once been the property of a secessionist who had been forced to flee the city. The McDowell Medical College met both of those characteristics. Dr. Joseph N. McDowell had come to St. Louis from Tennessee, and in 1840 he founded the college that bore his name. Enrollment at the institution climbed steadily during the decade, and in 1847 McDowell erected a large, octagonal stone building at the corner of Eighth and Gratiot Streets to house it. The doctor did not limit his interests to the operating table and lecture hall, however. He became active in local politics, where he was one of the city's leading advocates of slavery and secession. In anticipation of the war he was sure would come, he began to stockpile small arms and even cannon in the rooms of the college. On 30 May 1861, shortly after Lyon's preemptive strike against Frost's militia, detachments of the pro-Union "Home Guards" stormed the building hoping to seize the weapons, but McDowell was one step ahead of them. The arms had been shipped to Tennessee, and the wily physician was not far behind them. Authorities confiscated the college, and for three months it saw service as a temporary barracks, but in December 1861 Provost Marshal Leighton ordered it converted into a military prison. Bunks and stoves were moved into the classrooms and lecture halls, a kitchen and mess hall were constructed in the dissecting room, and the name of the finished structure was changed to the Gratiot Street Prison.[23]

Direction of the prison fell under the control of Major General Henry W. Halleck, commander of the Department of the West. Although local estimates placed the number of prisoners that could be confined in the structure at two thousand, the general was convinced that this figure was far too optimistic. On

25 December he presented the War Department with an alternative to using the Gratiot Street facility as a traditional prison. "I have between 2,000 and 3,000 prisoners of war," Halleck wrote to Adjutant General Lorenzo Thomas, and "no proper building here for keeping them. If [the] Governor of Illinois consents to use of State Prison at Alton, now nearly unoccupied, will the General-in-Chief authorize me to fit it up and use it as a military prison?"[24] Halleck's plan, in short, was to employ the Gratiot Street Prison as a transfer point where Confederate prisoners of war, civilian prisoners of state, and Federal soldiers awaiting trial would be assembled and then shipped to the larger facility at Alton. Prisoners would be retained at Gratiot Street Prison only if the capacity of Alton was exhausted. The proposal was approved, and on 26 January 1862 Halleck ordered Alton to prepare to receive its fist shipment of captives from St. Louis.[25]

To direct operations at the Gratiot Street installation, Halleck selected Colonel John W. Tuttle, the regimental commander of the Second Iowa Volunteers, and to ensure the prisoners were accorded humane treatment, the general furnished the new commander with a set of very specific instructions. Prisoners were to be provided the full daily ration specified. To facilitate the policing and sanitation of their barracks, they were to be "divide[d] . . . into squads, say twenty or more, each under a chief selected from among themselves by election or of your appointment as you may deem expedient." Prisoners were to be supplied an area where they might "take exercise when the weather permits," they were to be permitted "to wash themselves," and they were to be allowed packages of food and clothing from friends and relations. "In regard to the sick," Tuttle was instructed, "every proper facility will be afforded to the surgeon in charge in the matter of sending for necessary supplies, &c." Rations provided to patients in the prison hospital were to be "the same . . . as is given to U.S. sick in hospitals," and prisoners deemed seriously ill by camp surgeons were to be "sent to the nearest general hospital designated by the medical director."[26]

Halleck thus had every intention of ensuring that soldiers who became prisoners of war in his department were treated humanely, but—as would be the case in nearly all prisons both North and South during this formative period—events on the battlefield soon rendered such intentions moot. On 18 December 1861 Union troops under the command of General John Pope surprised a poorly led force of Confederate regulars and militia near Milford, Missouri, and when the smoke cleared, the Yankees found they had bagged just over 1,300 prisoners. Pope shipped the whole lot to St. Louis by train, and when the Rebels arrived on 22 December they were moved through raucous, jeering crowds to the Gratiot Street Prison. Here the southern captives were forced to undergo an experience eerily akin to that being endured by their northern counterparts in the tobacco warehouses of Richmond. The trains brought in three times more prisoners than the building could accommodate, and, as Halleck had feared, the capacity of the prison was quickly exceeded. The overwhelming number of prisoners jammed onto each floor rendered the sanitary standards prescribed by Halleck impossible, and the supply of available rations soon ran short. The plan for an expeditious transfer of prisoners to Alton stalled, and untrained and overtaxed guards became increasingly more ruthless. By New Year's Day 1862, after only three weeks of operation, a deadly epidemic of measles was raging through the prison. Gratiot Street thus joined the lengthening list of Union pens in which southern captives were sickening and dying at an alarming rate, and Halleck was forced once more to search for locations where he could establish additional prisons.[27]

One option that was not available to the general involved transferring prisoners from Gratiot Street to Camp Chase, the other major western prison established in the summer of 1861. Located in Columbus, Ohio, the camp had originally been intended as a Union recruit training depot, but when Ohio regiments engaged in the western Virginia campaign of General George B. McClellan captured large numbers of prisoners, the governor of Ohio, William Dennison, volunteered a portion of the camp to confine them. Three frame wooden buildings were erected in the southeastern corner of the camp, and this facility, officially designated "Prison No. 1" by camp authorities, was enclosed by a plank fence twelve feet high.[28]

Although judged capable of confining 450 prisoners, the buildings stood on only a half-acre of ground, a fact that ensured overcrowding would be a problem from the start. Military prisoners were soon outnumbered by civilian prisoners of state shipped in from Virginia and Kentucky, and after only one month of operation, Governor Dennison was pleading with Secretary of War Cameron for assistance in managing the crush. No help was forthcoming, however; and with the onset of the frosts of October, the situation became desperate. The Confederates had no blankets, their clothes were in tatters, and overcrowding precluded adequate winterizing of the frame barracks. Conditions became so bad that Dennison wrote Cameron again, urging that the suffering prisoners be discharged as soon as possible. "Some arrangement," Dennison insisted, "should be made by which these applications can be speedily disposed of as such prisoners are accumulating very rapidly."[29] Dennison surely now questioned his decision to become involved with enemy prisoners of war at all, and he would probably have been happy to be rid of the steadily worsening problems of Prison No. 1. The reply from the War Department did nothing to relieve his consternation, for on

16 November he learned that "improvements and a permanent extension" to the site, to be designated "Prison No. 2," had been approved. Camp Chase, although hurriedly established, poorly constructed, and badly administered, would continue to hold Confederate captives, and it would become one of the most hellish northern prisons of the war.[30]

Yet another similarity in the manner in which the Union and the Confederacy attempted to cope with the hoards of prisoners in 1861 resulted from the fact that both governments failed to authorize the appointment of a commissary general of prisoners to direct prisoner-of-war operations. As a result, in the North the responsibility for establishing and maintaining prisons and directing the transfer of prisoners from one facility to another in the eastern theater fell directly to the War Department. Secretary of War Cameron, General Scott, and other senior officers were overwhelmed by the minutiae of billeting, feeding, securing, and transporting thousands of captives. The situation was even worse in the distant Department of the West. Because prisoner issues became the responsibility of the field commander in that theater, General Halleck and his staff officers were forced to expend precious time and resources directing prisoner operations rather than focusing on defeating the Confederate forces arrayed against them. Like their counterparts in the South, these Union military and civilian leaders quickly realized that as the war grew in scope and intensity, the responsibilities of their offices would soon severely hamper their ability to deal effectively with prisoner-of-war problems.

The final similarity in the early development of the Union and Confederate prisoner-of-war systems grew directly from this failure to appoint a commissary general of prisoners. In both the North and the South, the most insistent pleas for the establishment of this position came from the two officers most intimately involved in resolving prisoner-of-war issues. In the South, General John Henry Winder did not suggest the creation of such an office until late in 1861, but his Union counterpart had called for such an appointment almost four months earlier. That officer was Brigadier General Montgomery C. Meigs, the quartermaster general of the army.[31]

Meigs was a career soldier who quickly identified the deficiencies in Union planning for prisoners of war. Others might have been lulled by the promise of a short and glorious war, but Meigs was certain that the conflict would be both desperate and protracted. He was also sure that it would present the nation with challenges for which there had been little preparation, one of the most important of which would be the inadequacy of planning for prisoners of war. By regulation, that responsibility fell to him as quartermaster general, but he knew that the tasks associated with managing captives would be too great for him to accomplish along with his other duties, and he moved with characteristic energy to propose an alternative. On 12 July, less than a month after he had been promoted to the rank of brigadier general and appointed quartermaster general, Meigs wrote Secretary of War Cameron, warning him that "in the conflict now commenced it is to be expected that the United States will have to take care of large numbers of prisoners of war" and "respectfully" advising the secretary of the "propriety of making some arrangements in time." He reminded Cameron that army regulations specified that prisoners of war were entitled to "proper accommodations, to courteous and respectful treatment, to one ration a day, and to consideration according to rank," and that "heretofore when the Government has had prisoners to care for a commissary of prisoners has been appointed." This officer, Meigs explained, would be tasked with keeping the muster list of prisoners, arranging exchanges, and negotiating with the representatives of the enemy to ensure captives held in their prisons were treated humanely. Because the position was one of "high power and importance," Meigs cautioned that the officer appointed should be "an accomplished gentleman" who possessed a level of "knowledge of military law and custom" equal to the "delicate questions" he would have to face. Meigs reminded Cameron of the exemplary service John Mason had rendered as commissary general of prisoners in the War of 1812, and in the closing lines of his letter he again "respectfully" recommended that "some person be designated as commissary of prisoners . . . charged with the care of the prisoners now in our hands and preparations for those likely to fall into our possession."[32]

In both the North and the South, then, the two officers designated to assume the management of enemy captives as an additional duty called for the formal appointment of an officer tasked with the specific responsibility for directing the emerging prisoner-of-war systems. The two governments responded very differently to this request. Winder's entreaties failed to change the minds of Confederate leaders, who were determined to retain the policy of employing Richmond as collection point from which prisoners would be dispatched to the growing number of prisons throughout the South. As provost marshal of Richmond, the task of caring for the prisoners in the capital and supervising their transfer to outlying camps continued to fall by default to Winder, but he was not formally appointed as commissary general of prisoners and the authorization of a staff to oversee this complex operation was withheld.[33]

Initially it appeared as though Meigs's appeal would also be denied, for the entire summer passed with no reply from Cameron. Yet prisoner-of-war issues were growing ever more immediate, and on 29 August Meigs again wrote the secretary, "respectfully" repeating his request that a commissary general of prisoners be appointed. "All this," Meigs wrote of the increasingly numerous and complex problems that were consuming a growing portion of his time, "requires the care and supervision of a special officer."[34] Still there was no response. By October, however, the prisoner-of-war situation had become so serious that Meigs's request could no longer be ignored, and Cameron directed him to recommend an officer for appointment as commissary general of prisoners. On 3 October, Meigs acknowledged receipt of Cameron's instructions and notified the secretary that he already made his selection—Lieutenant Colonel William Hoffman.[35]

Hoffman was "an officer of rank and experience," Meigs assured Cameron, and in this assessment the general did not exaggerate. The son of a career officer, Hoffman had spent his childhood on a succession of army posts, and in 1825 he received an appointment to West Point. There he was a diligent if not brilliant student, graduating in the top 20 percent of his class four years later. For the next thirty years he served in a variety of challenging assignments around the country, always performing his duties in a manner that earned him a reputation as an exacting taskmaster and a stern disciplinarian. He also became known as an officer whose considerable personal pride and sense of honor were easily wounded, and the readiness with which he bristled at real or perceived slights earned him the nickname "Old Huffy."[36]

In October 1860, Hoffman was appointed lieutenant colonel in the 8th Infantry, one of the regiments policing the frontier in the Department of Texas. He knew that Texas was on the verge of secession, and because he was reluctant to expose his family to such a politically volatile situation, he asked that his date of departure for San Antonio be delayed. His request was denied, and on 11 February he assumed command of the departmental headquarters barracks at the Alamo. Only five days later, Ben McCulloch and his minutemen stormed into the town. When Hoffman learned that McCulloch planned to demand the surrender of the garrison, he brought his men to full readiness and urged his commander, General David Twiggs, to resist any attempt to disarm the Federal troops. But the secession-minded Twiggs wished to avoid bloodshed at all costs and refused to allow the distribution of ammunition to the regiment. The garrison was easily overcome, and Hoffman and his soldiers were informed they would be allowed to depart San Antonio for the coast, where they would board Union transports for New York.[37]

On 23 April 1861, the situation for the Union troopers changed yet again, for officers of the newly constituted Confederate States Army arrived with orders to detain Hoffman and his fellow officers as prisoners of war. The captives were given two choices. They could either remain in Texas under close confinement, or they could return to the North after signing a parole in which they promised not to take up arms against the Confederacy until exchanged. For professional soldiers, the choice was an agonizing one; but after agreeing that they could be of more service to their country if they returned to the North, the officers selected the latter alternative.[38] On 24 April, Hoffman signed the following parole:

> I do hereby declare upon my honor and pledge myself as a gentleman and a soldier that I will not take up arms or serve in the field against the Government of the Confederate States of America under my present or any other commission that I may hold during the existence of the present war between the Union States and the Government of the Confederate States of America; that I will not correspond with the authorities of the United States, either military or civil, giving information against the interest of the Confederate States of America, until regularly exchanged.[39]

Hoffman interpreted these terms quite strictly. Upon his arrival in Washington, the War Department had some difficulty in finding duties he felt he could perform without violating his parole. He declined an assignment as a recruiting officer, for example, but consented to serve as a member of courts-martial panels at West Point and as a disbursing officer in Pittsburgh. Hoffman was an ambitious man, and he chafed under such dead-end, administrative assignments. Anxious to obtain a transfer to what he termed "a more active sphere of duty," he asked to be posted to Oregon, where he might assume command of the Department of the Pacific. But on 30 September, he received orders of a very different kind. He was directed to report immediately to the War Department, where he was informed that he had been selected to become the commissary general of prisoners.[40]

To say that Hoffman was displeased with the War Department's decision would be something of an understatement. As soon as he heard the news, he enlisted the support of two powerful backers—Generals George B. McClellan and John E. Wool—to engineer his return to full service. Wool asked that a special exchange of prisoners be arranged under which Hoffman and a Confederate officer would be "mutually released from their paroles."[41] The southern officer to be exchanged was selected, and all seemed in order when Hoffman received devastating news. The Confederate had indeed been exchanged, but for another Union officer. Although assured that the switch had been necessary because the Confederate was of lesser rank, Hoffman took the whole affair very personally.

Bypassing the established military chain of command, the enraged colonel fired off a letter directly to the secretary of war. He complained to the secretary of the "extreme mortification" he felt when informed that the prisoner for whom he was to be exchanged had been traded instead for an Union officer "recently promoted to the rank of major and still more recently as announced in the newspapers as placed on the retired list." Words could not express the "profound humiliation" he felt at this "palpable slight." To drive home his point, Old Huffy closed the letter with assurances that he "fully appreciate[d] the indignity" that had been done him.[42] Hoffman's protest was in vain, however. Having identified the man he deemed perfectly suited for the post of commissary general of prisoners, Meigs was not about to give him up. On 23 October the War Department published orders detailing Hoffman "for duty as the Commissary General of Prisoners" and directing him to report to Meigs for instructions.[43]

Hoffman's initial instructions from Meigs revealed a second major difference in the ways in which the North and the South had determined to shape the development of their prisoner-of-war systems. On 7 October, Meigs directed Hoffman to

> proceed to the group of islands known as the Put-in-Bay, and Kelley's Island, off Sandusky in Lake Erie, and . . . examine them with reference to the lease of the ground upon some of them for a depot for prisoners of war. You will report which of the islands affords on the whole the greatest advantages for the location of such a depot, the price at which a suitable tract of land can be leased during the war and such other matters as may be of importance. Should other localities in that vicinity appear to you to be better fitted for the purpose you are authorized to visit them also. You will complete this duty as soon as practicable, and returning to this city report in writing the result of your examination, making a report also upon the steps necessary to establish a depot and prepare it for the reception and safe detention of prisoners.[44]

Whereas southern leaders had opted for a system under which prisoners would be confined in existing facilities throughout the South, such as the cotton factory in Salisbury or unoccupied government buildings in Tuscaloosa, Meigs had decided that Confederate captives would be consolidated in a single depot specifically designed and constructed for that purpose.

Whatever misgivings Hoffman might have had concerning his appointment as commissary general of prisoners, he immediately put them aside and set off for Lake Erie as directed. Upon arriving, he conducted an inspection of the islands as specified, and on 22 October he submitted a detailed report that illustrated the high degree of diligence and thoroughness that had characterized his entire career. The three small Put-in-Bay islands, he informed Meigs, were too thickly inhabited and too close to Canada to permit the establishment of a large prison. While the larger Kelly's Island did offer two possible locations, Hoffman judged one too exposed to the weather and the other too near "large vineyards and a wine and brandy establishment" that would surely constitute "too great a temptation to the guard to be overcome by any sense of right or fear of punishment."[45]

Hoffman's report was not all bad news, for he had also reconnoitered Johnson's Island, located about three miles out in the bay opposite the city of Sandusky. He told Meigs that the island was "decidedly the best location" he had seen, and he recommended it be selected as the site of the prison depot.[46] Lumber was cheap in Sandusky, Hoffman noted. He recommended the construction of frame barracks 105 feet long and 24 feet wide, to house 180 enlisted prisoners apiece, estimating that each structure could be erected at a cost of $800. For officer prisoners, he advised the construction of barracks 112 feet long and 29 feet wide, divided into twelve rooms, which would each have a capacity of 48 officers. He estimated that each of these barracks could be built for $1,100. Other necessary construction included quarters for a guard force of 100 to 150 men, a "substantial plank fence" to enclose the barracks area on three sides, elevated platforms for patrolling sentinels, blockhouses, a hospital, storehouses, and kitchens. The barracks would also require stoves for warmth and cooking. Hoffman ended his report with an itemized listing of expenses that placed the total cost of building a depot capable of confining 1,280 prisoners at $26,266, and he estimated that construction could be completed by 1 January 1862.[47]

Shortly after submitting the report, Hoffman learned that winterization of the barracks would raise the cost of construction to $30,000, but in spite of this increase Meigs remained pleased with the work done by his new appointee. He forwarded Hoffman's report to the secretary of war with the recommendation that "Johnson's Island, Sandusky Bay, be rented and buildings for the accommodation of 1,000 prisoners be erected immediately."[48] The secretary approved the recommendation without amendment, and on 26 October 1861 Meigs telegraphed Hoffman to "proceed at once to establish a depot for prisoners of war on Johnson's Island, in Sandusky Bay, according to the plans which you have submitted." Meigs expressed full confidence in Hoffman's "discretion and knowledge," but this expression of confidence did not prevent him from reminding his subordinate that the work on Johnson's Island was to be accomplished with "the strictest economy consistent with security and proper welfare of the prisoners."[49]

This last line, seemingly so innocuous at the time, was in truth an early indication of the overriding importance that economy would assume in the formulation of the policies that would shape daily operations in the Union system of prisons. The origins of this imperative for thrift lay in the culture of the army in which career officers like Hoffman and Meigs had served. In the years following the Mexican War, funding for the army was so low that virtually every aspect of military life was severely constrained by lack of funds. Commanders were held strictly accountable for all equipment issued and every penny spent, and expenditures deemed extravagant were rigorously investigated for evidence of fraud. Army pay was so meager that the families of officers bereft of personal fortunes were forced to live in a perpetual state of genteel poverty. Even the most rudimentary training was impossible, and construction appropriations were so spare that the War Department sanctioned the building of only those barracks that were deemed absolutely necessary and constructed of materials "of the cheapest kind."[50]

Anxious to improve the quality of frontier life despite constrained appropriations, commanders developed innovative methods of supplementing troop rations. Soldiers on many posts in the Great Plains spent their days growing crops rather than drilling, and alternative means of funding were developed to acquire items not provided by the government. One of the most common was the post fund, a scheme in which soldiers' rations that were deemed to be excess, or beyond the daily level of subsistence actually required, were resold to the commissary from which they were drawn. Money accrued through these sales was then placed into the fund and spent to procure items that would make life in the forts more healthful or enjoyable.

Operating under such constrained financial conditions had been a daily challenge for professional soldiers like Meigs and Hoffman. In response, Meigs had developed a reputation for frugality that was known throughout the army, and when he assumed responsibility for prisoners of war he certainly did not become any freer with the government's purse. In August 1861, for example, he was asked if replacement clothing might be furnished Confederate prisoners whose original uniforms had been reduced to rags. "Prisoners are entitled to no other allowances than one ration per day," Meigs testily reminded the petitioner. "If they need clothing, they should be placed where they can earn it by their labor."[51]

During his thirty years of service Hoffman had also been required aggressively to develop and implement plans to overcome deficiencies in government funding. While constructing Fort Atkinson on the Santa Fe Trail, he proudly had submitted to the secretary of war a program in which his soldiers grew crops for themselves and the post's livestock; as the commander at Newport Barracks, Kentucky, he had maintained a successful post fund that financed such improvements as a "ten pin alley," an ice house, and vegetables to supplement the diet of his men.[52] Such schemes had conditioned both Meigs and Hoffman to a preoccupation—almost an obsession—with economy, and that preoccupation would exert a dark and terrible influence on the Union prisoner-of-war system throughout the war.

On 15 November 1861 the agreement leasing Johnson's Island to the Federal government was signed, and Hoffman directed the Sandusky firm of Gregg and West to commence construction of the depot.[53] To prevent the arousal of local public opinion against locating a military prison so near the city, he cautioned the contractors to keep the details of the project quiet, and as workmen began erecting the barracks and palisade, Hoffman busied himself with the task of selecting the man who would command the facility.[54] Given that the individual chosen to fill this demanding position would require a comprehensive knowledge of army regulations and procedures, Hoffman might have been expected to select a career officer with experience in such matters. He did not. Instead he tapped William S. Pierson, a civilian who had never been in uniform prior to the war. In notifying the War Department of his choice, Hoffman described Pierson as an "experienced man of business" who maintained the "strictest integrity" in his daily life. Pierson was also a former mayor of Sandusky, and while his integrity and business experience were certainly laudable, it was probably this political connection that led to his selection. To compensate for the new commander's complete lack of experience in military affairs, Hoffman advised Pierson to seek the counsel of an officer possessing "experience in the usage of military posts." In orders that reflected his own leadership style, Hoffman urged the freshly minted lieutenant colonel to issue orders "without any preliminary discussion" and never to "permit his views to be questioned."[55]

Hoffman next turned his attention to securing a guard force for the prison. These men, like Pierson, were all recruited locally, and although officially mustered in as the 128th Regiment, Ohio Volunteer Infantry, they chose to adopt the more distinctive designation of the Hoffman Battalion. Hoffman directed the commander of the guard to ensure that his men were drilled to a "perfect state of discipline" before they arrived at the depot; to further hone their skills he ordered that they practice mounting a small guard each day until the first shipment of prisoners arrived. Work on the prison proceeded rapidly, and in only six weeks the facility was almost completed. Pierson and an initial contingent of twenty-five guards arrived at the site on 28 December, and all indications were that the first prisoner-of-war depot constructed by the United States since the War of 1812 would be ready to receive its first inmates as scheduled.[56]

What Meigs and Hoffman could not know was that even before the final planks for the palisade of the new prison were pounded into place, the sheer scope of the Civil War had rendered their plans completely inadequate. To men accustomed to duty on primitive frontier posts typically garrisoned by less than two hundred soldiers and operated on shoestring budgets, the construction of an installation capable of confining 1,280 captives and built at a cost of $30,000 seemed a mammoth undertaking that would surely solve the Union's prisoner-of-war problems. And as planned and constructed by Meigs and Hoffman, Johnson's Island was to be much more than just another prison. It was to be a prisoner-of-war depot, a single location to which all the captives taken by Union forces could be sent and maintained under Hoffman's direct control.

But even before the facility was finished, the number of prisoners held in the North far exceeded its capacity. Only three days before Pierson and his guards moved to the island, General Henry Halleck had dashed off a desperate telegram alerting the War Department that in St. Louis he held "between 2,000 and 3,000 prisoners of war" with "no proper building . . . for keeping them."[57] This number alone would have completely overwhelmed the depot on Johnson's Island, but the problems of the North did not end there. Fort Lafayette and Fort Warren were filled to bursting, and the unceasing influx of prisoners in the eastern theater had necessitated the reopening of the wretched camps on Governor's Island.[58]

After eight months of operation, the men directing the development of the Union prisoner-of-war system thus found themselves stymied by the same problems that bedeviled the prison system of the Confederacy. The costs of transporting and maintaining thousands of enemy captives were spiraling out of control, and the staggering administrative and logistical burden of providing guards, rations, supplies, and other necessary equipment threatened to collapse the nascent system entirely. The greatest problem both systems faced was that of locating and securing facilities sufficient to confine the growing number of captives. In both sections, camps filled beyond capacity as soon as they were established, necessitating a continuous search for additional sites that would, when opened, also be deluged with prisoners. Throughout this unending cycle, conditions in the camps of both governments continued to deteriorate.

As 1861 drew to a close, a growing number of leaders and ordinary citizens in both the North and the South were becoming convinced that there would never be enough camps to quarter the number of prisoners being taken. The only sure means of ending the suffering of soldiers held captive, they believed, lay in securing their swift repatriation through a general exchange of prisoners. And in Washington as well as in Richmond, pressure was building for the adoption of just such a course of action.

CHAPTER 5

"Our Government Must Change Its Policy"

The Move to the Exchange Cartel of 1862

IN JANUARY 1862, Mrs. Sylvester R. Knight, the wife of a Union soldier held prisoner in Richmond, wrote Abraham Lincoln to plead for his assistance in obtaining her husband's release. In reply, Lincoln assured her that although he sympathized deeply with her plight, as well as that of the "many others in like condition," he was certain that she did not "appreciate the difficulty" of what she was asking. The president did not exaggerate. Obtaining the release of an individual soldier at this point in the war was possible only through a complex and convoluted process that offered no guarantee of freedom for the captive. What Lincoln elected not to tell Mrs. Knight in his letter, however, was that the central source of the "difficulties" was the policy that he himself had chosen and directed his subordinates follow in all negotiations concerning the exchange of prisoners.[1]

As 1862 opened, no systematic process existed for repatriating prisoners. Exchanges of captives, when they occurred at all, were generally limited affairs, conducted in accordance with terms concluded by opposing armies in the field and encompassing only the captives under the direct control of local commanders. By the end of that July, exchanges between the Union and Confederate governments would be national in scope, repatriating thousands of prisoners daily in all theaters of the war according to the provisions of a single cartel. While historians have provided numerous accounts of exchanges under this cartel, the story of how the two governments came to agree to it has been largely overlooked.[2] Such an examination reveals that neither the North nor the South moved easily to an acceptance of a general exchange of prisoners. Calls for the establishment of such an arrangement were alternately supported or rejected by the belligerents depending on the vicissitudes of the war; and in spite of the fact that a cartel promised the repatriation of thousands of suffering prisoners, both governments repeatedly delayed its implementation through acts that were both duplicitous and self-serving. The story of how Union and Confederate leaders finally consented to a general exchange is one of soaring hopes born of humanitarian necessity and of how those aspirations were time and time again dashed on the hard rocks of political and military expediency. It is also a story of immense importance in the history of the Union and Confederate prison systems.

In early 1862, Federal policy governing prisoner-of-war exchanges was still driven by the concern that formal exchange negotiations with southern leaders would be perceived as a recognition of the Confederate States as a sovereign nation. From the opening of the war Lincoln had assured his countrymen that they were engaged in a just and noble crusade to preserve "free government upon the earth," through measures that were "without guile . . . with pure purpose" and anchored in a firm "trust in God." Recognition of the Confederacy as a bona fide state with full belligerent rights would support the southern claim that far from being a holy endeavor, the war was no more than an illegal and immoral invasion of a neighboring state, undertaken for simple conquest. This Lincoln was determined to avoid at all costs, even if it meant that Mrs. Knight's husband and thousands of Union soldiers like him remained confined in southern prisons.[3]

This is not to say that Lincoln's concerns were groundless. From the moment the first southern captives were taken, the administration of President Jefferson Davis pushed aggressively for a general exchange of prisoners, and it did so for good reasons. The dearth of confinement facilities, which became evident after the battle of First Manassas, worsened as bloody engagements in the fall and winter of 1861 produced hundreds more captives. In addition, Davis and his lieutenants fully appreciated the fact that the Union possessed nearly three and a half times more white men of military age than the South. This disparity forced southern leaders to press aggressively for liberal exchange agreements that would permit the speedy return of captured Rebels to the ranks.[4] But, just as Lincoln always maintained, southern support for a general exchange of prisoners was also a component of a strategy targeted at securing the recognition of the Confederacy as a sovereign state. "By the exchange of prisoners," Davis admitted after the war, the Union conceded that "actual war existed," acknowledged the "belligerent rights" of the Confederacy, and "explod[ed] their theory of insurrectionary combinations."[5]

The first test of Lincoln's policy of denying southern proposals for a formal government-to-government exchange was the capture of Confederate privateers in the summer of 1861, and initially the president's decision to refuse Confederate entreaties garnered widespread support.[6] The Supreme Court and Congress concurred with Lincoln's characterization of the war as a rebellion led by lawless elements in the South, and Union newspapers sustained this view. "The case against them," the *New York Times* maintained in its report of the capture of the Savannah's crew, "is complete in all its particulars. They were without any charter or characteristic to distinguish them from pirates." Echoing the sentiments of most northerners, the paper urged that Lincoln stay the course in the prosecution of the southern sailors.[7] But this initial public support proved fleeting, and soon the case of the privateers was generating the first challenge to the president's policy.

Problems for Lincoln began in November, when Davis learned that Walter W. Smith, the captain of the Confederate brigantine *Jeff Davis,* had been convicted of piracy and sentenced to hang. Upon hearing this news, the Confederate president moved swiftly to make good on his threat to retaliate in kind. On 9 November 1861 Secretary of War Judah P. Benjamin, acting on instructions from Davis, ordered General John Henry Winder "to choose, by lot, from among the prisoners of war, one who is to be confined in a cell appropriated for convicted felons, and who is to be treated in all respects as if such convict, and to be held for execution in the same manner as may be adopted by the enemy for the execution of the prisoner of war Smith, recently condemned to death in Philadelphia."[8] In accordance with these instructions, Winder proceeded to the officer's prison in Howard's factory, where he asked the imprisoned congressman Alfred Ely to draw from a tin case one of six ballots upon which he had written the names of the most senior Union officers then confined by the South. Ely at first declined this request, but after being assured by the Federal officers that they would bear him no ill will, he consented. In a stroke of unbelievable good fortune for the southern cause, the name on the slip of paper he chose was that of Colonel Michael Corcoran, the most famous and most flamboyant officer held in the entire Confederacy.[9]

Corcoran had immigrated to the United States from Ireland in 1849. He settled in New York, where he amassed both wealth and local notoriety as the proprietor of the exclusive Hibernia Hotel. He became a political and civic leader in the Irish immigrant community, was appointed commander of the Irish 69th New York Regiment, and achieved a status very nearly approaching immortality among the Sons of Erin when he refused to parade his command in ceremonies honoring the visiting Prince of Wales. Although court-martialed for his disobedience, Corcoran was spared the inconvenience of a trial by the onset of the war. His contribution to the Union war effort both began and ended at Manassas, but following his capture he made sure his supporters back home remained appraised of his fate through letters in which he detailed his "gallant conduct" while confined in the Bastille of the South.[10] From the moment of his capture, Corcoran—always a master at promoting his own fortunes—had added to his notoriety by "allowing" northern newspapers to publish letters he posted from prison. Missives to constituents, political leaders, and even "personal" correspondence to Mrs. Corcoran from her "affectionate husband" appeared in major city papers for all to read.[11] Following his selection as the hostage for the condemned privateer captain, Corcoran redoubled his writing efforts, posting letters to a dizzying array of newspapers, congressmen, and Irish admirers in New York. In these messages the self-serving colonel was at his best. "The fear of dying is nothing," he heroically proclaimed in one well-publicized letter, "but to be brought down to the level of a skulking, cowardly pirate is a degradation that my soul revolts at. Languishing in the dungeons of your country's enemy . . . is a most awful fate."[12]

Corcoran's prewar activities in New York had won him many influential friends, who now began relentlessly to pressure the government for action to repatriate their hero. Judge C. P. Daly, a power in Tammany Hall politics, wrote directly to Secretary of War Edwin Stanton demanding to know what the government had done "toward the release of Colonel Corcoran"; he was so impatient for an answer that he told the secretary that he would await a reply at the telegraph office. The harried Stanton did respond immediately, assuring the judge that "the Government has taken the measures they deem proper to effect the release of Colonel Corcoran . . . and will disclose what they have done when proper to be disclosed." The secretary, no doubt weary of answering dozens of similar petitions penned by Corcoran advocates, closed the telegram by admonishing Daly that "it is hoped that the rash indiscretion of persons pretending to be Colonel Corcoran's friends may not induce the rebels to prolong his imprisonment or refuse his exchange."[13] Nor was Secretary of State William Seward able to escape the ire of Corcoran's supporters. Informed by a prominent Massachusetts politician that large crowds of Irishmen had rallied at Faneuil Hall in Boston and Tammany Hall in New York to demand that the government secure the colonel's release, Seward could only reply weakly that "measures for those objects have for some time past and still are in progress."[14]

Pressure on the Lincoln administration to change its policy also came from other sectors. Descriptions of the terrible conditions in the prisons of Richmond began to filter north shortly after the Manassas prisoners were taken; along with Davis's promise to retaliate in kind should southern prisoners held by the Union be harmed, they led even the most steadfastly proadministration newspapers to question the government's stance. In an editorial of 1 August 1861, the *New York*

Times—the same newspaper that only two months earlier had angrily declared that the captured privateersmen should be hung—conceded that "the current of events may render it necessary to act with caution . . . and not take a position which may augment greatly the horrors . . . of this civil war." The mere fact that the North held thousands of prisoners supplied proof enough of the Confederacy's status as a belligerent power, the editors reasoned, and the indisputable reality that battles were raging everywhere surely provided evidence sufficient to convince "even [Lincoln] . . . that we are at war with somebody." To exchange prisoners, the *Times* argued, would not be tantamount to recognizing the Confederacy as a sovereign state. In a follow-up article four days later, the paper's editors echoed the sentiment of many in the North when they allowed that "we know of no other mode in which these prisoners may be returned to us except by exchange."[15]

Calls for a change in the administration's policy also came directly from the Union prisoners themselves. On 24 July, after only one day of confinement in Ligon's, the prisoners taken at Manassas prevailed upon Congressman Ely to prepare a petition to Lincoln. In the document, Ely later recalled, the soldiers confirmed that they were "prisoners of war, in close confinement in Richmond, Virginia, and requested that immediate steps be taken by our government—by exchange or otherwise—to effect their release." The petition, signed by forty officers and six hundred enlisted men, elicited no public response from Lincoln, but it was published in newspapers across the North.[16]

Pleas from individual prisoners also received wide play in northern papers. In a letter to the *Washington Star,* for example, Lieutenant Isaac W. Hart wrote of the "pale, sickly, half-clad and heart-broken soldiers" who shared his confinement, and he called on Lincoln to "institute a system of exchange at once, which, as viewed from this standpoint, every principle of justice and humanity seems to demand."[17] Implicit in this request (and others like it) was the very real possibility that the government's refusal to authorize a general exchange would result in reduced enlistments at home and diminished morale among soldiers in the field. Yet Hart's letter—like the petition from the inmates at Ligon's—generated no response from the administration. As Ely noted in his diary, "This question does not attract the attention of our Government with the solicitude that belongs to its importance." He was confident that this would soon change. "Public sentiment," he felt, "will very soon urge upon Mr. Lincoln the necessity of an exchange."[18]

That sentiment was indeed growing, and those seeking a change in northern policy were becoming increasingly insistent. The wife of a Pennsylvania soldier confined in Richmond wrote Confederate secretary of war Simon Cameron, begging that he and the president do everything in their power to ensure that "justice is done to the poor prisoners everywhere through the land." By this point in the war, however, most petitioners were neither as eloquent nor as patient in their demands. In a typical letter, one father of a Union soldier reminded Cameron that while "a good deal is being said in the county in relation to the course pursued by the Government at Washington in the matter of the exchange of prisoners with the Rebels or Confederates or whatever they may be called," precious little was actually being done to secure the release of the prisoners. "Public opinion," the angry father continued, "demands some other course and will expect some method—some plan adopted by which an exchange can be made."[19]

Calls for a change in policy also came from the three Union military commanders who had been the most successful in the battles of 1861. General George McClellan had favored immediate exchanges from the beginning of the war, while Henry Halleck and his subordinate, Ulysses S. Grant, had at first steadfastly refused to support them, agreeing with the administration that they might imply a de facto recognition of the Confederacy. But by November 1861, Grant was burdened with so many prisoners that he was driven by military necessity to endorse a policy through which he could swiftly dispose of them.[20] Halleck was an even more important convert, for he was considered a preeminent authority on international law. Like Lincoln, Halleck was wary of Confederate attempts to parlay exchanges into a means of securing official recognition from the European powers; but as the number of prisoners held by both sides continued to mount, the general was forced to put those fears aside. He had witnessed firsthand the horrors produced by overcrowding in the prisons of St. Louis, and with those dreadful scenes in mind he notified his superiors that "after full consideration of the subject I am of the opinion that prisoners ought to be exchanged." The act of exchanging prisoners, he judged, constituted no more than "a mere military convention" that would have little bearing on the legal status of the persons being exchanged. "A prisoner exchanged under the laws of war," Halleck wrote, "is not thereby exempted from trial and punishment as a traitor. Treason is a state or civil offense punishable by the civil courts; the exchange of prisoners of war is only a part of the ordinary *commercial belli*."[21]

By the end of 1861, even members of Lincoln's own cabinet were pressing the president to authorize exchanges. In early December a delegation of judges and attorneys representing the New York legal community attended a Cabinet meeting to speak on behalf of the exchange of all prisoners, and especially of Colonel Corcoran. In his diary, Secretary of the Treasury Salmon P. Chase wrote that when the men had departed, "some conversation took place on the subject," and that he and Postmaster General Montgomery Blair had advised the president that the time for a change in policy had come. Chase argued that the United States had already "acknowledged the Rebels as belligerents by the institution of the blockade, but not as National belligerents," and he suggested that as long as negotiations were conducted through military channels, the government could propose the exchange of Corcoran for the privateer captain William Smith. "Nothing was decided," Chase recalled, "but the matter is still reserved for further consideration."[22]

Lastly, the U.S. Congress added its weight to the growing pressure on the Lincoln administration. As the number of northern prisoners grew and knowledge of the deplorable conditions in southern prisons became more widespread, constituent demands for swift action to obtain the release Federal captives rapidly mounted. Legislators were deluged not only by letters from family members seeking the return of sons, brothers, and husbands, but also by missives from the prisoners themselves. Typical of the latter category was a letter to a Michigan congressman from a prisoner who wrote "in behalf of 72 Sons of Michigan" held in the prisons of Virginia, the Carolinas, Alabama, and Louisiana, who were "sustained only by the hope that it will not much longer continue thus and that a speedy exchange will restore them to their families and friends." The author, himself a prisoner in Richmond, assured his representative that while the men "did not wish to embarrass the action of our Government in the least," they could "not understand how a full exchange will do more injury than acts already done." As he explained, "We enlisted to serve our country and if necessary die for it, but we would prefer a different death than the one awaiting us here. It makes my face burn to . . . think that over four months have passed and nothing done for our relief." If the Federal government persisted in its current policy, the prisoner closed, the plight of the prisoners should be taken directly to the people, for he was certain that "an appeal to the people of our State would be promptly met."[23] He was correct. Less than one week after his letter was received, the legislature of Michigan opened hearings which would produce joint resolutions declaring that it had become "expedient that arrangements should be made for the exchange of prisoners" and instructing the state's congressmen in Washington to "use their power to bring about such arrangements."[24]

Assailed by such demands from all sides, the U.S. Congress acted. In a joint resolution of 11 December, legislators observed that while there had been no official government endorsement of exchanges, prisoners had been "indirectly" exchanged by Union commanders in the field since the time of the surrender of the Texas garrisons. Such exchanges had increased "the enlistment and vigor of the Army" while serving "the highest interests of humanity." All this, the solons noted, had been accomplished without necessitating "a recognition of the rebels as a government." The House and Senate therefore now "requested" that the president expand these "indirect exchanges" into "systematic measures for the exchange of Prisoners."[25]

The indirect exchanges cited in the resolution had largely occurred as a result of negotiations between opposing commanders in the field, and they were of three types. The first was a straightforward exchange of prisoners, rank for rank, as practiced in the War of 1812. Confederate general Gideon Pillow exchanged captives with Union general Lew Wallace in Missouri under such an agreement in August 1861, and Halleck had authorized a more extensive exchange of the same type between General John C. Fremont and General Sterling Price in the same theater in October.[26]

The second type of agreement negotiated by officers in the field was the special exchange, in which specific captives were traded. In a letter of 7 December 1861, for example, U.S. navy flag officer Lawrence M. Goldsborough notified Major General Benjamin Huger, the Confederate district commander at Norfolk, Virginia, that he was prepared to exchange "a number of individuals, late officers of the U.S. Navy and Marine Corps avowing secession principles," for U.S. navy officers confined in the South.[27]

The third type of indirect exchange involved paroling specific prisoners in order that they might return home and personally arrange their exchange for soldiers held by the enemy. The parolees were granted a specific period of time to complete the exchange. If successful, both groups of prisoners were released from the terms of their paroles and could remain free. If the paroled soldiers were not able to arrange an exchange in the allotted time, the terms of their parole required them to return to prison when their specified period of freedom expired. Paroles of this sort might be granted to individual soldiers, as was the case when Confederate lieutenant William Biggs was granted a thirty-day parole from Fort Warren in order that he might proceed south and arrange his exchange for Lieutenant William E. Merrill, a Union officer imprisoned in Richmond. Whole groups of prisoners might also be paroled under these provisions, as happened on 13 December 1861, when 249 Confederate prisoners captured in the fall of Hatteras Island were allowed to depart Fort Warren for their home state in search of Federal prisoners for whom they might be exchanged.[28]

This kind of exchange, like most in the eastern theater of the war during 1861, was arranged by the offices of Major General John E. Wool, the Federal commander at Fortress Monroe, Virginia, and Major General Benjamin Huger. In each transaction, Wool was careful to reiterate that the exchange was no more than an agreement between field commanders and in no way implied recognition of the Confederacy as an independent nation. Huger, for his part, missed no opportunity to remind Federal authorities that such exchanges were accepted by the Confederacy only out of "a sense of humanity," and that in refusing to authorize a general exchange of prisoners, the Union was guilty of perpetrating "a system unknown in the rules and usages of warfare."[29]

The exchanges managed by Wool and Huger typically involved less than a hundred prisoners. Yankees to be exchanged would be transported from Richmond to Norfolk by train, where they would be placed aboard Federal flag-of-truce ships and taken to Fort Monroe. Rebels would be sent by steamship from prisons in the North to Fort Monroe and then reembarked on smaller vessels that would take them across the James River to Norfolk.

While these sorts of exchanges did free a small number of prisoners, they also created confusion about the legal status of those released. As no formal government-to-government agreement set the terms of their release, there were no standardized provisions regulating the conditions of their parole or formal exchange, as had been the practice during the War of 1812. Instead the prisoners were exchanged under a number of locally negotiated and often convoluted arrangements that rendered their legal status uncertain at best. Union soldiers were often released only after they had taken an oath not to bear arms against the Confederacy, and southerners obtained their freedom only if they had taken an oath of allegiance to the United States or at least swore "not to take up arms . . . or serve in any military capacity whatever . . . until regularly discharged according to the usages of war from this obligation." What those "usages of war" might be, no one could say.[30]

Although both sides emphasized the humanitarian nature of these exchanges, the criterion used to select the prisoners to be freed suggests that both the Union and the Confederacy also wished to limit the advantages such altruism provided their foes. On 8 November, the Federal War Department instructed Colonel Dimick that selections for release from Fort Warren were "to be made from the most feeble and infirm" prisoners. Similarly, in Richmond, one of Winder's subordinates reported with obvious pride that the prisoners he had recommended for exchange were "those least likely to be efficient for harm to the Confederacy in the event, not probable, that they again enter the service of the United States."[31]

As much as the Lincoln administration feared that loosening the restrictions regulating exchanges might lead to the recognition of the Confederacy, by the end of 1861 demands that the government modify its policy had grown too numerous and insistent to ignore. In a move designed to limit policy changes as much as possible while responding to Congress's "request" that "systematic measures" for exchange be instituted, the administration opted officially to endorse the already ongoing practice of indirect exchange.[32] This shift in policy was evident in a 2 January 1862 memorandum, in which Secretary of State William H. Seward directed General McClellan to allow 500 captives to go south and seek exchanges for themselves as soon as the 250 Hatteras prisoners previously released under such conditions had secured their freedom. On 7 January the War Department authorized General Ambrose Burnside, then preparing for an expedition against Roanoke Island, North Carolina, to exchange any prisoners taken for Federal soldiers who might be captured.

Evidence of the administration's eagerness to implement the new policy was also apparent in the western theater of the war. On the same day that Burnside received his instructions, the War Department ordered General Halleck to secure the exchange of five officers and 240 enlisted men who were still held in Texas. Halleck was nonetheless admonished that his efforts should "not commit the Government of the United States." When the punctilious general posed the very reasonable question of exactly how he was to effect the exchange of prisoners without "committing the government," he was instructed that "the intention is not to commit our Government by formally acknowledging the existence of a government in the so-called Confederate States."[33] Confusion and contradictions notwithstanding, the instructions to Burnside and Halleck were significant, for they constituted the first official acknowledgment by Washington that exchanges in the field were being negotiated.[34]

Lincoln hoped that this measured and closely controlled shift in administration policy would be sufficient to mollify the concerns of Congress and anxious citizens, and at first it appeared as if it might do so. The *National Intelligencer* echoed the conviction of many in the North in an editorial confidently declaring that "all questions [concerning exchanges] may be regarded as solved by the arrangements into which our government has entered."[35] But even as Lincoln and his lieutenants were working feverishly to implement this new direction in exchanges, a combination of events and circumstances was building that would render their efforts totally inadequate.

The first of these arose from the continuing saga of Michael Corcoran. Demands for the colonel's release continued to build, until finally Seward had no choice but to direct McClellan to have Wool inquire of Huger whether Corcoran might be exchanged for William Smith, the master of the *Jeff Davis*, who had been sentenced to hang. Impatient for an answer, Seward then telegraphed Mc-Clellan a second time, advising him of the "great anxiety of the friends of Colonel Corcoran" and asking whether any answer had been received from Huger.[36]

Huger had indeed received Wool's inquiry, but sensing the desperation of the Federals, he perceived the time was right to press for a more sweeping change in Union policy. "The proposition," he wrote of Seward's offer to Confederate secretary of war Judah Benjamin, "is a complete giving away of the principle heretofore asserted by them. It appears to me they should go a step further and make [the exchange] general."[37] Benjamin agreed and decided to up the ante even further. "I decline taking into consideration any proposition for exchange of our privateers taken in our service on the high seas until there is an absolute unconditional abandonment of the pretext that they are pirates, and until they are released from the position of felons and placed in the same condition as other prisoners of war," the secretary wired Huger. He continued, "And I decline receiving any proposals in relation to the hostages whom we are forced unwillingly to treat as felons as long as our fellow-citizens are so treated by the enemy."[38]

Huger passed this to Wool and, eager to rid himself of the burden of serving as the southern point of contact in such negotiations, he added the suggestion that the two governments appoint agents to manage exchanges in the future. Wool, equally weary of the responsibility, concurred. On 24 January he forwarded Huger's suggestion to the War Department with the recommendation that it was certainly "worthy of consideration." To that point, Lincoln had steadfastly rejected all proposals calling for direct contact with civilian representatives of the Confederacy and had allowed only military commanders in the field to conduct exchange negotiations, but the combination of Benjamin's refusal to exchange Corcoran and rising northern sentiment in favor of general exchanges clearly signaled that this strategy was no longer tenable. The timing of Wool's recommendation was therefore fortuitous, providing Lincoln with the opportunity for yet another incremental policy shift that would limit contact with the Rebel government while assuring an increasingly anxious populace that everything possible was being done to relieve the suffering of northern prisoners.[39]

Only one day after receiving Wool's telegram, Union secretary of war Edwin M. Stanton issued an order appointing the Reverend Bishop Edward R. Ames of the Methodist Episcopal Church and Congressman Hamilton Fish of New York as commissioners and directing them "to visit the prisoners belonging to the Army of the United States now in captivity at Richmond, in Virginia, and elsewhere, and under such regulations as may be prescribed by the authorities having custody of such prisoners relieve their necessities and provide for their comfort at the expense of the United States." Additionally, the commissioners were authorized to provide Confederate authorities "the assurance that on like condition prisoners held by the United States may receive visitation and relief." On 30 January the secretary notified Quartermaster General Montgomery Meigs of the appointment of the commissioners and ordered him to "take such measures as may be necessary to establish a depot of clothing . . . combs, brushes, soap, and such other articles as may be deemed necessary to the personal cleanliness and health of the said prisoners . . . at Fortress Monroe" and to "deliver the same" to Ames and Fish as they required. On the same day, Stanton directed the surgeon general of the army to "supply the senior medical officer at Fortress Monroe with a sufficient quantity of medicines of all kinds necessary for supplying the wants of the Union prisoners in the South." To cover any extra expenses Ames and Fish might incur, Stanton deposited $20,000 into a New York City bank account from which either of the two could draw.[40]

With these instructions the Lincoln government was not only proposing the initiation of direct civilian contact between representatives of the two governments, but also offering to relieve the Confederacy of the expense of caring for Union prisoners. Still, Lincoln still could not bring himself to sanction a general exchange of prisoners. Completely frustrated with Union alternatives that consumed enormous amounts of effort for little gain, the Davis government determined that the time for a showdown had come. On 26 January, Benjamin issued an ultimatum: either the North agreed to a general exchange or he would immediately terminate all exchanges. The secretary of war directed General Joseph E. Johnson, the senior field commander in the Confederate army, to notify General McClellan, recently promoted to commander of all the armies of the United States, that the Confederacy would no longer be a party to "a system so partial in its operation, so cumbersome in detail and so difficult of execution." Johnson was to inform McClellan that the South, as always, stood ready to "enter into arrangements for a general exchange of prisoners on fair terms and on some definite basis to be agreed on," but that absent such an agreement, the Confederacy would be "forced to decline making any further exchanges on the anomalous system which now exists and which experience has satisfied us must prove impracticable."[41]

When Ames and Fish arrived at Fort Monroe on 4 February, Huger delayed receiving them pending the arrival of definitive instructions from Richmond. While awaiting permission to continue their journey, the two commissioners informed Huger that Seward had ordered the privateer crewmen moved from their cells in the Tombs to Fort Lafayette. Henceforth, they assured Huger, the men would be treated as prisoners of war rather than felons. While this news was certainly welcomed in the South, it did nothing to aid Ames and Fish in their mission. Following a cabinet meeting in which Davis and his advisors discussed possible responses, Benjamin prepared for Huger's signature a letter welcoming the Yankee commissioners but informing them that they would not be allowed to proceed to Richmond as they had planned. Instead, they would be met at Fort Monroe by two Confederate commissioners empowered to discuss terms for the "restoration of all the prisoners to their homes on fair terms of equal exchange." Ames and Fish had no authority to enter such negotiations; upon seeking additional guidance from Stanton, the two envoys were ordered back to Washington.[42]

Faced with the collapse of the Ames–Fish mission and renewed pubic anger at yet another failure to secure the release of northern prisoners, Lincoln and his advisors were forced to reevaluate their policy of refusing to authorize a general exchange. By this time they understood that incremental adjustments would no longer suffice. Stanton directed Wool to contact Huger and reiterate that only he was empowered to arrange exchanges. While this was simply a restatement of existing Union policy, but the secretary also authorized Wool to confer with "any other person appearing" to "arrange for the restoration of all the prisoners to their homes on fair terms of exchange."[43]

News of Stanton's approval of negotiations to effect a full exchange of prisoners was met with great acclaim throughout the North, and many attributed the change in policy to the Ames–Fish mission. On 15 February, the *New York Times* reported that the mission had been "crowned with unexpected and most splendid success," and the *Times*'s editors confidently predicted that because of the commissioners' efforts, "it will not be many days before all those brave fellows, for whom families and friends have been pining hopelessly will be at home." Ames and Fish also believed that repatriation was at long last a certainty, and they were quick to congratulate the government for securing the release of prisoners without compromising its "National existence."[44]

Hopes for a speedy repatriation were soon dashed, however. Huger, finally granted his wish to be relieved as the Confederate point of contact in exchange matters, was replaced by Brigadier General Howell Cobb, and on 23 February Cobb and Wool met on a flag-of-truce boat near Craney Island, Virginia, to finalize a cartel of exchange. At first the talks went smoothly and swiftly. Both men agreed that the terms of exchange should be based on the cartel employed during the War of 1812; even tricky procedural questions—such as exchanges when one side held an excess of prisoners—were resolved. Excess prisoners would be delivered to the country of origin on parole until both sides amassed a sufficient number of captives to permit exchanges according to the terms of the cartel.[45]

Final agreement on a cartel seemed almost certain; but then Cobb proposed the inclusion of an article that would have required that all prisoners taken by either side be "released . . . within ten days of capture . . . and delivered on the frontier of their own country free of expense to the prisoners and at the expense of the capturing party." Wool, believing that he did not possess the authority to agree to such a proposition, telegraphed Stanton for additional guidance. The secretary sustained Wool's objection, noting that he found Cobb's proposal to be "obnoxious in its terms and import and wholly inadmissible." He accordingly directed Wool to "make no arrangement at present except for actual exchanges."[46]

Stanton never explained his abrupt refusal to accept Cobb's proposition, but there are two possible explanations for his action. First, he might have thought that accepting Cobb's contention that the Confederacy possessed a "frontier" was uncomfortably close to acknowledging that it was a sovereign state with identifiable borders, a notion that the Lincoln administration continued to deny unequivocally. The secretary's refusal might also have been based on changes in the existing balance of prisoners. Up until February 1862, the South held more prisoners than the North, but campaigns by Ulysses Grant and Ambrose Burnside had netted almost 18,000 Rebel prisoners, and agreeing to transport this huge number of captives for release at the frontier would have been both expensive for the Union and tactically advantageous to the South.[47]

Wool informed Cobb on 27 February that the cartel was unacceptable as proposed. He suggested that the two schedule further meetings, adding the caveat that in accordance with Stanton's instructions, all future negotiations would be "exclusively limited to the exchange of prisoners as presented to Major-General Huger the 13th February, 1862."[48] Cobb, fully aware that Wool had earlier insisted that he alone was "clothed with full powers for the purpose of arranging for the exchange of prisoners," judged Stanton's abrupt entry into the negotiations to be no more than Yankee duplicity. "As I expected," he telegraphed Benjamin, "they have backed down from their own proposition." Unwilling to continue the special exchanges, Benjamin directed Huger to decline all such arrangements in the future. On being told of Benjamin's orders, Stanton fired off an angry message of his own, informing Wool that as the War Department had "exhausted all the means in a fruitless effort to establish a just and liberal system of exchange with the enemy," no further instructions concerning exchanges would be forthcoming. Like most citizens in the North, members of Congress had believed that an agreement on a general exchange of prisoners was imminent. Upon learning of

Stanton's decision, the shocked lawmakers demanded that he explain why the talks had been suspended. This was precisely the sort of congressional intrusion the Lincoln administration always sought to avoid, but the crafty Stanton proved equal to the challenge. In response to a letter of inquiry from the Speaker of the House, the secretary placed the blame for the "protracted delay in the exchange of Colonel Corcoran" squarely on the South. "There is no other cause known to this Department," Stanton insisted disingenuously, "than the disregard by the rebel forces of an arrangement for the mutual exchange of prisoners negotiated between Maj. Gen. John E. Wool and the rebel general Howell Cobb."[49]

So things stood in March 1862, and so they might have continued indefinitely, but even as the two governments were hardening their resolve to suspend exchanges, battles then raging from the shores of the Atlantic to the banks of the Mississippi were making such a position impossible to sustain. On 8 February, Burnside bagged 2,500 Confederate prisoners when Roanoke Island fell to his amphibious assault; this number, while considerable, was dwarfed only eight days later when Grant's victory at Fort Donelson netted an additional 15,000 Rebel captives. Although Burnside had received War Department permission to negotiate battlefield exchanges with his Confederate opponents, no such authorization had been afforded to Grant. Halleck, Grant's superior, was therefore again faced with the onerous task of identifying locations where prisoners might be secured.[50] As existing prisons at St. Louis and Alton were already overflowing, Halleck appealed to the governors of Indiana and Illinois for help. Happily for the general, both rallied to his call. "We can take 3,000 prisoners if necessary," Governor Oliver P. Morton of Indiana telegraphed Halleck, while Illinois governor Richard Yates assured him that "if quarters for prisoners are wanted we have barracks [at Springfield] that will accommodate 3,000 to 4,000 and at Chicago for 8,000 or 9,000."[51]

Meanwhile, officials back in Washington were scrambling to develop a plan for dispersing the Fort Donelson prisoners among the available camps. McClellan's first concern was that Halleck quickly "get them over the Ohio River to . . . points where they can be securely kept." Captured Confederate generals, field officers, and "all the rebel officers taken who have been heretofore in our Army" were to be shipped to Fort Warren, where they would be closely confined, and McClellan assured Halleck that instructions for disposing of the thousands of remaining prisoners would follow shortly.[52]

Those instructions could come none too soon for Grant, for the sudden influx of 15,000 destitute and utterly disoriented prisoners into his camp had produced nothing short of absolute chaos. Feeding the Rebels swiftly depleted available stocks of rations, and because the captives had no overcoats, blankets, or tents, they suffered horribly in the freezing rain and snow that swept the grounds where they were penned. So great was the confusion that when Grant ordered his officers to secure the assistance of ranking Confederate general Simon B. Buckner in collecting the prisoners and "supplying their wants," Buckner could not be located, although Grant's staff was reasonably certain he was somewhere in the camp.[53]

Two days later, orders finally arrived directing that 3,000 of the prisoners be sent to Springfield, 3,000 to Indianapolis, and 5,000 to Chicago. Five hundred sick and wounded men were to be dispatched to hospitals in Cincinnati. The remainder were to be scattered among small facilities in Terre Haute, Richmond, Lafayette, and Fort Wayne, Indiana.[54]

This distribution of prisoners boosted the number of permanent Union prisons by three: Camp Butler in Springfield; Camp Morton in Indianapolis; and Camp Douglas in Chicago. Although the need for these new camps was indisputable, they further exacerbated the administrative problems plaguing the Union prisoner-of-war system. The resolution of these challenges should have fallen to William Hoffman, as commissary general of prisoners, but although he had held the post for almost five months, neither the colonel's appointment nor the scope of his responsibility and authority were common knowledge in the army. In truth, Hoffman had not been kept informed of events by Meigs, and so he was completely isolated from the most pressing prisoner-of-war problems. His ignorance of the crisis triggered by the fall of Fort Donelson was so complete that even as Halleck was struggling to dispose of thousands of captives, Hoffman was proudly reporting to Meigs that the newly constructed depot on Johnson's Island was "ready to receive a limited number of prisoners, say 500 or 600."[55]

Hoffman's isolation was about to end, however. On 24 February he received orders from Meigs to "visit Chicago, Indianapolis and other places to which the prisoners taken in Tennessee have been sent" and "report what is absolutely necessary to prevent their suffering." Meigs stipulated that all requests for supplies should be made with a view to strict economy. He reminded Hoffman that only supplies and equipment essential to "prevent real suffering" should be requisitioned, and even those items were to be provided at the lowest possible cost to the government. "Much clothing not good enough for [Union] troops," Meigs offered as one means of fiscal conservation, "has by fraud of inspectors and dealers been forced into our depots. This will be used."[56] Hoffman required no such prompting; if anything, his obsession for thrift was even more consuming than that of Meigs. Armed with his superior's directive and eager to assert his authority, Hoffman immediately set off to inspect the new facilities hastily created by Halleck. He soon discovered that conditions within those prisons had already sunk to the level of the installations that had been operational since the early days of the war.

The first prison Hoffman visited was Camp Morton, a five-acre cantonment area established on the Indiana State Fairgrounds. While the camp's garrison was quartered in a set of rather ornate Victorian structures near the entrance of the grounds, the five buildings that had been selected to confine prisoners were drafty exhibition halls, stables, and barns with dirt floors. Four of these dilapidated structures were designated as prisoners' barracks, and the fifth was slated to serve as the camp's hospital. They were enclosed by a board fence with an elevated platform that served as a walkway for the guards.[57]

Although the prospect of confining a large body of prisoners so near the city concerned many of Indianapolis's citizens, the local newspaper called on its readers to display a kindly spirit toward the Rebels when they arrived and to refrain from hurling insults at men powerless to counter them. The first train bearing prisoners from Fort Donelson arrived on 22 February, and most citizens heeded the paper's request for civility. Detraining prisoners chatted amiably with bystanders before being marched through generally good-natured crowds to the cantonment area. As the Rebels soon discovered, these would be last pleasant moments they would experience for some time.[58]

Although the capacity of Camp Morton had originally been estimated at 2,000 prisoners, more than 3,000 were delivered in the initial shipments. Guards dutifully shoehorned them into the stables and sheds that had been designated as barracks, even as trains from the south brought still more captives. By April, the number of men confined at the facility had climbed to over 4,200, and harried officers at the camp were notified that more were on the way.[59]

Because there had been little effort to convert the fairgrounds into a site actually suitable for a prison, conditions at the camp would have been poor even if the number of prisoners had been capped at the projected capacity of two thousand. With more than twice that number confined on the five-acre plot, conditions at Camp Morton rapidly became terrible.[60] Prisoners housed in the stables and barns slept on a thin covering of straw in the stalls or wherever they could find sufficient space to lie down. The buildings had been cheaply constructed for summer use only, and all of the plank walls sported wide cracks through which the howling wind blew rain, sleet, and snow. In the hospital, these gaps were so large that patients were forced to tack their only blanket to the walls to shield them from the elements.[61] Latrines consisted simply of open pits dug in the center of the camp. When they filled to overflowing, they were haphazardly covered with a few inches of dirt and new pits were dug in another part of the camp. This process was repeated until much of the cantonment area was transformed into one large, poorly covered latrine. Effluent from these sinks pooled on the ground and seeped into the wells that supplied drinking water, and as a result the capabilities of the primitive camp hospital were soon overwhelmed by dozens of desperately ill patients.

Guards were also a problem at Camp Morton. Colonel Richard D. Owen, the camp commander, had been furnished only one regiment to guard four thousand men, and in an effort to solicit the prisoners' cooperation and forestall escape attempts, he instituted a number of very liberal practices. Tobacco and stationery were dispensed to the prisoners free of charge, and limited numbers of captives were allowed to go into Indianapolis under guard to purchase food and supplies not available through regular supply channels. Enterprising Rebels turned these liberties to other purposes; soon, local newspapers were reporting that paroled southerners had become regular fixtures in the city's taverns. In response, Owen suspended the privilege and tightened security.[62]

Hoffman arrived for his inspection of Camp Morton on 5 March 1862, and what he saw disturbed him. The "very dark and close," conditions in the prisoner barracks, he noted, would inevitably lead to "much sickness unless improvements are made." Accordingly, he ordered the installation of windows to provide additional air and light. To relieve overcrowding, he authorized the construction of seven additional barracks, and to upgrade medical care he obtained Meigs's permission to expend $2,500 for an addition to the Indianapolis hospital.[63]

In directing these improvements, Hoffman firmly adhered to the mania for thrift he and Meigs shared. To defray the cost of improvements at Camp Morton, the colonel thus directed the establishment of a prison fund, notifying the prison's quartermaster that the camp commissary was to "withhold any part of the ration which may be in excess of what is really necessary and semi-monthly pay to Colonel Owen the value of the ration so retained, thus making a fund to be distributed by the colonel for the benefit of the prisoners." Such a fund, Hoffman believed, could be used to purchase "many articles which now have to be furnished by the Government . . . such as brooms, buckets, and table furniture," as well as "all articles that may in any way be of benefit to the sick."[64]

The next stop on Hoffman's inspection tour was Camp Douglas, originally a recruit training depot. Located on the south side of Chicago, the prison was created by setting aside twenty acres near the center of the camp. Sixty-four wooden barracks stood within the designated area, each of which was deemed capable of accommodating 95 prisoners, bringing the estimated capacity of the prison to just over 6,000 men. On 21 February 1862 the first shipment of 3,200 prisoners arrived. Although camp officials had been alerted the group was en route, little had been done to prepare for them, and the price of this lack of preparation would be high indeed. Federal soldiers were still quartered in the barracks designated to house the captives, and for two days Chicagoans were treated to the unique spectacle of soldiers in blue and gray living side by side. By the time camp officials untangled the mess and moved the Yankees out, a second contingent of almost 1,300 prisoners had arrived, and this group was followed shortly by 2,000 more.[65]

Confusion reigned in other areas as well. The prisoners had been shipped north so rapidly that no clear division of responsibility between the Federal government and the state of Illinois had been established. Both now claimed authority to direct operations at the prison. When presented with this delicate political question, the Union quartermaster at the camp turned to Quartermaster General Meigs for clarification. "I am ordered by the State authorities to supply clothing, camp and garrison equipage to all the prisoners arriving," the befuddled officer wrote. "Shall I do it?" To the irascible Meigs, the lines of authority had never been in doubt. "The prisoners are the prisoners of the United States," he fired back. "The supplies to be issued are the property of the United States. You are an officer of the United States. The State of Illinois has no more right to give you orders than the State of Massachusetts. State authorities are entitled to respectful attention and consideration but they have no right to give orders to an officer of the United States." Despite such blunt pronouncements, disputes over the separation of Federal and state powers would continue to complicate operations at the camp.[66]

Command of Camp Douglas fell to Colonel Joseph H. Tucker, an Illinois militia officer whom Governor Yates had chosen to oversee the construction of the prison in 1861. Before the war, Tucker had been an influential member of the Chicago Board of Trade, but his successes in business did little to prepare him for the staggering responsibilities he now faced. He soon discovered that the guard force allotted to the camp was completely inadequate and that the prisoners' escorts departed immediately after delivering their charges. Even more alarming was the physical condition of the arriving prisoners. Unaware that Hoffman had been appointed to resolve such problems, Tucker appealed directly to Halleck for assistance. "The prisoners," he informed the general, "are being made comfortable in barracks, but they arrive in much confusion—parts of regiments and companies together—and many are thinly clothed and sick and no surgeons with them." On learning of this, Halleck was furious. "Confederate surgeons separated from their regiments will be sent on immediately," he replied. "Their separation was made by the stupidity of subordinates and contrary to my orders."[67]

Nor was the absence of guards and medical personnel the only problem the frazzled Halleck was forced to remedy. Because it had been occupied in such haste, no stockade had been constructed to enclose the prisoner barracks at Camp Douglas, and Confederate officers routinely took advantage of this lack of restraint and the high level of confusion in the camp to stroll into Chicago, where they wined and dined at the city's finest restaurants. Furious citizens insisted the mayor put a stop to this outrage, and the state's adjutant general, A. C. Fuller, demanded an explanation of Halleck. "Will you advise me what character of discipline shall be enforced upon prisoners in our camps so I may instruct commandants at camps?" Fuller inquired. "The military and civil authorities at Chicago are doing everything to make the prisoners comfortable, but the mayor telegraphs me this evening that there is much indignation that the rebel officers have been feasted at the principal hotels. Shall I order a strong enclosure around the barracks?" By this point Halleck must have been wondering what else could go wrong at Camp Douglas, and his answer betrayed his growing frustration. "All prisoners of war must be [well] treated and made comfortable," he informed Fuller. "They must not be permitted to go to the city but be confined within the limits of the camp. It was contrary to my orders to send officers either to Springfield or Chicago."[68]

Hoffman's stay at Camp Douglas was short, but after only a cursory inspection he felt he had seen enough to pronounce prisoners in the facility "well provided for in every way." Tucker had been replaced by Colonel James A. Mulligan on 26 February, and Hoffman concluded his visit with praise, advice, and instructions for the new commander. On 7 March, Hoffman informed Mulligan that he was "pleased" with conditions in the camp. The barracks were more than adequate, and the hospitals were "well organized." But there were several areas where the commissary general wished Mulligan to modify operating procedures at the prison, and chief among these was the liberal policy of visitation that had been instituted at the insistence of Governor Yates. "The presence of so many visitors to the prisoners," Hoffman admonished Mulligan, "is attended with much inconvenience and detriment to the service, and I therefore request that hereafter none may be admitted." Families or friends should not be permitted to have direct contact with the prisoners, but should these visitors wish to provide prisoners with "contributions," including "small amounts" of money, the donations would be "gladly received and distributed as requested" by camp staff.[69]

As always, Hoffman insisted on thrift in all aspects of operations. While he assured Mulligan that "all articles absolutely necessary for the health and comfort of the prisoners" would be provided, he urged the commander to "consult economy in this as much as possible." And just as he had done at Camp Morton, Hoffman urged Mulligan to establish a prison fund at Camp Douglas. "The regular ration is larger than is necessary for men living quietly in camp," he explained, "and by judiciously withholding some part of it to be sold to the commissary a fund may be created with which many articles needful to the prisoners may be purchased and thus save expense to the Government."[70]

At the time of Hoffman's inspection, Camp Douglas held about 5,500 prisoners, a number well within its capacity. Rations were adequate both in quantity and quality, and medical care, while not exemplary, was sufficient. In early April, however, the battles of Shiloh and Island No. 10 produced thousands more prisoners, and although Colonel Mulligan begged that no additional captives be sent to Chicago, both Halleck and Governor Yates countered that the colonel was being too conservative in his estimation of the facility's capacity and that the prison could sustain many more Rebels. Accordingly, new shipments soon began arriving at Chicago's depots, and by 15 April the prisoner population at Camp Douglas had ballooned to almost 9,000 men.[71]

Predictably, the newcomers' impact on conditions within the camp was both swift and devastating. Available barracks space was quickly exhausted, and in desperation Mulligan began billeting prisoners in the post's dilapidated stables. These "temporary barracks," as they were designated, were rickety structures that offered little protection from either the cold or the rain, and the prisoners housed in them suffered miserably. An outbreak of smallpox combined with a deadly array of respiratory diseases to push deaths in the camp to 230 by the end of April, and with the spring thaw came a host of sanitary problems that increased the rate of sickness and death exponentially. Brackish water mixed with the effluent of overflowing latrines stood ankle deep in many portions of the camp. Garbage, rotting bones, and other food waste from the kitchens was simply dumped in huge piles on the prison grounds, and the stench that arose from the crowded, unventilated barracks was nauseating.[72]

Command of the camp changed hands three times between April and June, perpetuating the administrative chaos that had prevailed in the prison since its creation and ensuring that even the most basic standards of sanitation would not be maintained. By spring, conditions had become so desperate that an inspector from the U.S. Sanitary Commission advised Hoffman that "the absolute abandonment of the spot seems the only judicious course." The barracks at Camp

Douglas, he found, were so filthy and vermin-infested that "nothing but fire can cleanse them."[73]

Since his cursory visit to Camp Douglas in March, Hoffman's only concern had been that the facility be operated economically. On 17 May, he unknowingly added to the misery of the prisoners by ordering the camp's bakery closed because of high fuel costs. When he found that his instructions directing the establishment of a prison fund had been ignored, he bypassed the camp commander and ordered the post quartermaster to implement such a program immediately. The distressing report of the Sanitary Commission inspector caught him by surprise, and in a letter to Meigs he asked for permission to fund construction of a waterworks and other projects that would improve the level of sanitation in the camp. Now, however, it was the parsimonious Meigs's turn to emphasize economy, and in a terse reply he left no doubt that he considered such expenditures for prisoners to be superfluous. "The United States has other uses for its money," he chastised Hoffman. Conditions in Camp Douglas continued to deteriorate.[74]

If the news from Camp Douglas was bad, however, the situation at Camp Butler—the last of the three major camps Halleck had established to receive prisoners from Fort Donelson—was much worse. This camp, located five miles from Springfield, Illinois, had received its first prisoners on 22 February, and conditions there were ghastly from the first. Like many other Federal prisons, Camp Butler had first seen service as a recruit training depot. When Governor Yates volunteered to convert a portion of the facility to a prison, twenty-one of the camp's wood-frame barracks, each with a capacity of one hundred prisoners, were designated for that purpose. As no fence had been constructed to enclose these structures, security at the prison was poor; but the greatest problem at Camp Butler was the health of the prisoners confined there.[75]

Although Springfield's brutally cold winter certainly contributed to the high rates of sickness at the prison, the main source of the problem lay with the poor performance of the camp's staff. The installation was commanded by Colonel Pitcairn Morrison, a doddering, white-haired officer of forty-one years of military service whom a local newspaper had very charitably characterized as a "kindly old gentleman." Morrison exercised little control over operations at the facility, and the standards of discipline and sanitation he set were abysmal. On 9 March, Hoffman submitted the report of his inspection of Camp Butler to Halleck, wasting no verbiage in his assessment. Sanitary conditions in the camp were "not at all satisfactory." Sickness was so prevalent among the captives that the staff had been compelled to convert three barracks initially intended to billet prisoners into hospitals, and still there was not adequate space for those requiring medical attention. "Some of these have been sick some days without any medical attendance and all of them were without that attention which sick men should have," he told Halleck, continuing, "The hospitals are in a very offensive condition and are too limited to accommodate all the sick. Something should be done immediately to relieve the sick from their sad condition."[76]

Hoffman notified Colonel Morrison that conditions in every other part of the camp were equally unacceptable, and he tendered a number of very basic remedies that would save the prisoners from "real suffering." Barracks should be ventilated and bedding routinely aired. Policing of the camp should be improved, and the supply of potable water for the captives should be increased. To aid in the care of the sick, Hoffman ordered the construction of an addition to the prison hospital, and he contracted the services of a Springfield physician to assist the camp surgeon. Deficiencies in clothing, blankets, and the tools deemed "absolutely necessary" to facilitate camp police, he assured Morrison, would be furnished by the quartermaster. But to this authorization, Hoffman also appended instructions on how such items could be obtained at the least possible cost. Again he urged the creation of a prison fund. "The daily ration provided prisoners," he instructed Morrison, "is larger than is necessary, and by withholding a part to be sold to the commissary a fund may be created with which necessary articles may be bought for them and expense saved to the Government." And while he authorized the issue of shoes "as far as may be necessary to keep [the prisoners] from suffering," he admonished the quartermaster that "there are many sick who can do without them."[77]

In the end, very little was done to relieve the suffering at Camp Butler, and although Hoffman's report clearly documented that Morrison and his staff were utterly incapable of providing for the basic necessities of the prisoners already in their charge, Halleck continued to ship additional prisoners to the prison. As there was no room for these later arrivals in the camp's overcrowded barracks, they were quartered in tents, and the number of deaths from exposure continued to climb. The plight of the captives was so obvious and so pitiful that it soon attracted the attention of the Springfield press. "The sickness among the prisoners has almost assumed the features of an epidemic," reported one local newspaper. "We learn that on the afternoon of Friday [7 March 1862] no less than nine deaths occurred, and in the previous days the daily average of mortality was three or four."[78] By the end of March, 148 prisoners had succumbed to pneumonia and had been buried in the facility's newly designated Confederate cemetery.[79]

Nor was the high death rate the only problem at Camp Butler. As the camp had no fence, prisoners quickly discovered that escape was relatively easy. Morrison and his staff seemed powerless either to prevent such departures or to recapture the offenders. Guards routinely accepted bribes to facilitate such escapes, and accountability in the camp was so slipshod that authorities often could not even establish the actual date prisoners had gone missing. In May 1862 the construction of a twelve-foot-high fence enclosing the barracks was finally begun, and in the following month the aged and incompetent Morrison was belatedly relieved of command in favor of a younger, more energetic officer. But while these actions went far to improve security at the installation, they did nothing to relieve the misery and suffering of the prisoners.[80]

Even as the new camps were being established, conditions in the Union prisons founded earlier in the war continued to decline. By this time Hoffman was fully aware that he had drastically underestimated the requirements for prisoner barracks at Johnson's Island, and he notified Meigs of plans to initiate a fourfold enlargement of the facility. "The ground," he wrote, "is laid off for ten more buildings . . . which will accommodate easily 3,000 men." Much more ominously, for the first time in the war Hoffman suggested that the Union adopt a policy of deliberate filling its camps beyond capacity. "By crowding, the ten buildings will quarter near 4,000 men, making with the buildings now up room for about 5,000 men," he informed Meigs. From this point forward, deliberate overcrowding would become an accepted part of Union prisoner-of-war planning, and the effect on the prisoners would be devastating.[81]

Even with planned overcrowding, a capacity of five thousand men fell far short of satisfying Meigs's initial objective of employing Johnson's Island as a depot where all captured Confederates could be confined. By March 1862 the Union held many times that number. Thus, even before he received approval for the first round of expansion at the facility, Hoffman was frantically searching for more room to confine prisoners on the island. Then, quite surprisingly, Secretary of War Edwin Stanton abruptly put an end to the need for such plans. Since the beginning of the war, prison commanders had complained that overcrowding in their camps often necessitated the billeting of officers and enlisted prisoners in the same barracks. Such mixing, the commanders maintained, provided Rebel officers with an opportunity to incite enlisted men to resistance and escape. To resolve the problem, Stanton decided to change the mission of the Johnson's Island depot. On 13 April he ordered Hoffman to "cause the officers, prisoners of war . . . to be removed without delay to the Sandusky depot, which will hereafter be held as a prison for officers alone."[82]

Although many of the prisoners who arrived on Johnson's Island in the early spring and summer of 1862 might have agreed with one Johnny Reb who found the camp "a salubrious, pleasant place," such sentiments vanished in the howling winds of the region's fabled winter storms. Warm days and balmy nights soon gave way to sleet, snow, and biting cold. As was the case in most Union prisons, the barracks at Johnson's Island had been hastily constructed of green, unseasoned lumber; as the planks dried, huge gaps appeared in the exterior walls and floors. Hoffman, economy-minded as ever, had declined to authorize the construction of either interior walls or ceilings, and as the gales off Lake Erie cut through the walls of the barracks, the prisoners suffered mightily.[83]

In spite of these harsh conditions, most of the Confederate officers initially welcomed the opportunity to leave their old prisons behind. This was certainly the case for the officers from Camp Chase, where overcrowding and an inept and inexperienced garrison combined with political squabbles to render life particularly trying for inmates. Throughout 1861, most of the captives confined at Camp Chase were political prisoners held in two small blocks of barracks that were prosaically designated Prison No. 1 and Prison No. 2. On 19 February 1862, the character of the installation was forever changed when Halleck ordered all of the Confederate officers captured in the fall of Fort Donelson to proceed to Camp Chase on their word of honor, adding that he would hang any officer who violated this parole.[84]

The first contingent of 104 parolees arrived at Camp Chase on 24 February; over the next week they were joined by 800 additional officer and enlisted prisoners. By 1 March the inmate population stood at just over 1,200, a number that far exceeded the camp's capacity. To accommodate these new arrivals, Prison No. 3, an addition containing more barracks space than Prison Nos. 1 and 2 combined, was erected; but even as this facility was being occupied, special trains bearing Rebel prisoners taken at Island No. 10 and Shiloh were arriving at Columbus's stations. Prison No. 3 was quickly filled to bursting, even though the staff resorted to such drastic measures as sleeping prisoners three to a bunk.[85]

In January 1862 David Tod succeeded William Dennison as governor of Ohio, and while Tod made no attempt to influence operations at Johnson's Island, he wasted no time in declaring that all activities at Camp Chase fell under his control. Tod, who was fond of signing all his official correspondence "Governor and Commander in Chief," named Granville Moody as camp commander. Moody was a local minister, and although appointed to the grade of colonel in the Ohio militia, he had almost no military experience. Not surprisingly, this amalgam of supposed qualifications produced an administration at Camp Chase that might most kindly be described as erratic.[86] Moody was given to hosting prisoner prayer meetings, and he was fond of personally conducting tours of the camp for local dignitaries. Security under his administration was so slipshod that it was not unusual for the citizens of Columbus to see Confederate officers in full uniform and sidearms walking the streets of their city, often attended by their slaves, who had accompanied them into captivity. Rebels frequented local bars and hotels where, as the *Cincinnati Commercial* indignantly reported, they brazenly registered as members of the "C.S. Army" and toasted Ohio's secessionist element.[87]

In Moody's defense, the spectacle of armed Confederates strolling through the streets of the state capital could be attributed in large measure to the confusing and contradictory orders issued by Halleck and Hoffman. Halleck had allowed paroled Confederate officers to retain their sidearms, and Hoffman had advised Governor Tod that "paroles to visit the city may be granted."[88] Regardless of the source of the transgressions, however, it was Stanton who came under fire from outraged citizens, who demanded he immediately remedy the situation in Columbus. On 30 March he responded by directing Halleck to remove Moody. Upon hearing of the order, "Governor and Commander in Chief" Tod attempted to intervene on behalf of the hapless reverend, but when the legislature of Ohio forwarded to the U.S. Congress a joint resolution condemning the laxity at the prison, the governor gave way. Tod also promised to ensure that the freedoms heretofore allowed to prisoners would be restricted, but Stanton was taking no chances. On 13 April, the secretary ordered all of the officers confined at Camp Chase shipped at once to Johnson's Island.[89]

In spite of these transfers, Camp Chase remained badly overcrowded, and during the spring of 1862 conditions rapidly deteriorated. Hearing of this decline, Hoffman dispatched Captain H. M. Lazelle to inspect the prison, and the captain swiftly discovered that there was little good news to report. The prison buildings were filthy, and basic sanitation was so wanting that a "nauseating and disgusting stench" permeated the entire area. The interior walls of the barracks were begrimed with untold layers of soot and grease, and the grounds between the buildings were filled with heaps of the "vilest accumulations of filth." Latrine facilities for the thousands of prisoners consisted of no more than "open excavations with a single rail placed over them lengthwise," and following each rain the runoff of effluent from these sinks collected in vast, fetid pools near the prison hospital. Nor was sanitation the only problem. The prisoners were "in rags," and rations at the camp were "very inferior." The beef, which Lazelle found to be composed of necks and shanks, was "only tolerable," the bread was "sour and dark and heavy," and the rice "floury and wormy." This combination of unsanitary conditions and unhealthful rations was wreaking havoc on the health of the prisoners. At the time of Lazelle's inspection, the prison hospital was filled to three times its capacity, and the post surgeon was so overworked that many of the sick went untreated.[90]

Lazelle informed Hoffman that the prisoners were "gladly willing to do anything that will improve their condition," but that their pleas for help had fallen on deaf ears. "Suffice it to say," he wrote, "that while it is a matter of constant representation and of the loudest complaint from all the prisoners, all the soldiers and all the doctors, the commanding officer and Governor, not a single step has been taken to remedy this terrible abomination." Although he left specific instructions directing improvements at the camp, Lazelle closed his report with the gloomy prediction that it was highly unlikely that they would ever be implemented.[91]

His pessimism was well founded. At Stanton's insistence, Governor Tod had removed Moody and appointed Colonel Charles W. Allison to command of Camp Chase, but this change in leadership did little to remedy the problems at the prison. Tod, it seems, was possessed of the rather bizarre notion that the most important qualification for a camp commander was that he be a good lawyer, and while Allison was indeed an attorney of local renown, his primary qualification appears to have been the fact that he was also the brother-in-law of Ohio's lieutenant governor. But, as Lazelle bluntly reported to Hoffman, Allison was "not in any degree a soldier." To the contrary, he was "completely ignorant of his duties" and "surrounded by the same class of people." Making a bad situation even worse, the enlisted men assigned as prison guards were as inexperienced as their commander. Lazelle found that Allison and his officers had neither the knowledge nor the desire to instruct their subordinates in the proper performance of their duties. This freed the guards to devise their own procedures for maintaining control over their charges, and they routinely meted out severe punishments for even the most minor breaches of prison regulations.[92]

Sadly, the terrible conditions at Camp Chase were also common to the Federal prisons in the East. In the wake of operations such as McClellan's Peninsula campaign, thousands more Rebel prisoners were sent north for confinement, and because all of the prisons established in 1861 were already filled beyond capacity, officials were once more forced to seek locations where these new captives might be interned. The most infamous eastern prison established in response to this new demand was Fort Delaware, a brooding granite structure situated on Pea Patch Island in the Delaware River. The facility had housed a small number of military and political prisoners since 1861, but Meigs determined that it would now be converted into a major prison in the Union system. On 22 April 1862 he telegraphed the deputy quartermaster general in Philadelphia to "prepare shanties for 2,000 prisoners of war . . . outside the fort but under its guns." This brief message initiated operations at the camp that would become one of the most dreaded and deadly of all northern prisons.[93] The clapboard shanties that Meigs ordered constructed at the post were not fit for habitation, the rations supplied the captives were unappetizing and unwholesome even by prison standards, and the medical care provided the sick was spotty at best.[94]

Hoffman inspected Fort Delaware two months after Meigs ordered it to be opened, and in a report to Stanton he judged the island to be "a very suitable place for the confinement of prisoners of war." The report listed no problems among the 1,000 prisoners confined there at the time of his visit. Hoffman was so pleased with the site, in fact, that he recommended the commander of the facility be directed to "have immediately erected sheds for 3,000 more prisoners," adding that if necessary, "even a greater number may be conveniently guarded there."[95]

Meigs accepted without challenge Hoffman's glowing assessment of conditions at Fort Delaware, but an urgent request submitted by the camp commander only two weeks after Hoffman's inspection provides a very different assessment. At the time Hoffman visited the prison, the prisoners' uniforms were in tatters. Many were almost naked. Hoffman did not—or perhaps chose not—to see this very obvious problem. Captain A. A. Gibson, the commander of the prison, had made repeated requests for additional supplies to feed, house, and clothe the captives, all of which had yielded no response from the War Department, and soon the situation was urgent. "The necessity for clothing," Gibson very tactfully advised his superiors, "begins to be pressing," and he again petitioned Hoffman for an immediate shipment of pants, shirts, shoes, and blankets.[96]

Hoffman's attention was elsewhere, however. Even with planned overcrowding and the hurried expansion of existing facilities like Fort Delaware, the demand to locate additional space to confine Rebel prisoners was relentless. In accordance with Stanton's directive of 13 April, he ordered the Confederate officers interred at Fort Columbus and Fort Delaware transferred to Johnson's Island in mid-June, but this offered little respite. In a letter to Stanton he proposed that "sheds for the accommodation of five thousand" additional prisoners be erected on Governor's Island, and he suggested the construction of more bunks in Castle Williams dramatically to increase the capacity of that installation as well.[97]

The continued presence of problems such as overcrowding, shortages of supplies, and inadequacies in rations and medical care in Federal prisons begs the question of why more was not done to ameliorate the suffering of the captives. The answer to this troubling question may be found in the fact that the Union planning and execution of its prisoner-of-war system was terribly deficient in three critical areas. First, the paucity of Union preparation to receive large numbers of prisoners at the onset of the war cannot be overstated. Because of this lack of planning, military and civilian leaders were placed in a desperate situation as they struggled to house, feed, clothe, and care for each successive wave of prisoners shipped north. These shortfalls were exacerbated by Meigs's and Hoffman's insistence that prisoners be confined at the least possible cost to the government. In accordance with this drive for economy, Hoffman continuously emphasized that captives were to be provided only those supplies that were "necessary to save them from real suffering," and he refused all requests for expenditures that he deemed in excess of this minimum level of subsistence.[98] In their efforts to determine and maintain this fine line of sufficiency, Hoffman and the camp commanders often erred; and when they did, prisoners were not provided the basic necessities essential for their health and welfare.

The third and most important cause of the terrible conditions in northern prisons, however, was that in the summer of 1862—after a full year of war—the Union still lacked a clearly defined and functioning system to manage prisoners of war. This deficiency made the identification of shortcomings difficult and rendered impossible any concerted action to remedy them. Twelve months had passed since Meigs first recommended the appointment of a commissary general "charged with the care of prisoners," and although Hoffman had been named to that post, his authority to serve as the single point of contact in resolving prisoner issues was still not recognized.[99] This became abundantly clear to Hoffman shortly after his appointment. On 7 December 1861 he made the first of several attempts to confirm his position and assert his authority. He advised the adjutant general of the army that "the office and duties of commissary-general of prisoners are not familiar to the service," and to "avoid embarrassment" he requested "that those who are in charge of prisoners of war, civil or military, may be notified that I have been appointed to that office and that any directions I may give in relation to prisoners may be complied with."[100]

When this request failed to elicit a response from the War Department, Hoffman was incensed, and he turned to his immediate superior, Quartermaster General Meigs, for assistance. On 26 February 1862, Old Huffy complained that

my position as commissary-general of prisoners has never been announced to the Army, and in order that my authority might not be recognized merely through courtesy on the 7th of December last I requested that the Adjutant-General would notify those in charge of prisoners of war of my appointment and the extent of my authority. I am not aware that any such notice has been given, and to avoid embarrassing conflict of authority I desire to call your attention to the subject in the hope that what is proper in the case, will be done.[101]

Help from Meigs was not soon forthcoming, as demonstrated by the fact that although Halleck, Stanton, and even the governors of Ohio, Illinois, and Indiana all played a major role in the decisions regarding the disposition of the thousands of prisoners taken at Fort Donelson, Island No. 10, Shiloh, and a host of other battles, the one officer specifically designated as the commissary general of prisoners was never even consulted. Upon learning that this mammoth project was underway, Hoffman launched a belated attempt to assert his authority, but to no avail. Completely frustrated, he again pleaded with Meigs for assistance. In a testy message of 19 March, Hoffman protested that his position as commissary general was being ignored and that officers and even local politicians were routinely overstepping their authority. "I beg leave respectfully," Hoffman wrote,

to inquire what officers are properly in authority over prisoners of war. Up to this time generals whose troops have captured prisoners have exercised control over them whenever they thought proper to do so. General Halleck has given orders in relation to the prisoners taken at Fort Donelson, even when they were beyond the limits of his department. My office is not known to the generals, and any information I have about the movements of prisoners I pick up from the newspapers or other chance sources. This system must lead to delays, confusion and expense, and I would respectfully suggest that all places where prisoners are or may be confined should be under the charge of one person, who should keep the commanders in the field advised of the capacity of these places and who should have entire control of all prisoners received at them.[102]

Meigs passed the message on to the adjutant general of the army, reminding him Hoffman's previous requests for a delineation of duties and responsibilities had been ignored and urging that the army publish a formal announcement of Hoffman's appointment and scope of authority.[103]

This time Meigs's intercession achieved the desired result. On 2 April the Office of the Adjutant General published General Orders No. 32, amending the revised regulations for the army that had been adopted in 1861. But while the revision did announce the creation of the post of commissary general of prisoners, it also clearly indicated that the War Department had not kept abreast of the latest developments in the prisoner-of-war situation. It still spoke of the creation of a "general depot . . . under the command of the commissary-general of prisoners," implying that this installation might serve as the repository for all prisoners of war. Nor did the orders furnish Hoffman with the unequivocal statement of authority he sought. Rather than placing the disposition of captives directly under his control, it provided that generals commanding departments or field armies "at their discretion" could terminate their responsibility for enemy prisoners by sending them to the general depot. The implication was that should those commanders wish, they could retain control of prisoners and designate locations other than the depot for their confinement. Nor did the vagueness of the orders end there. Although the commissary general of prisoners was granted the authority to "visit places at which prisoners may be held," he was not empowered to assume direct control of the captives. The orders provided only that he might "recommend to the general whose guards are responsible for [the prisoners] whatever modification in their treatment may seem to him proper or necessary and report the same to the War Department."[104]

Given the ambiguous division of responsibility evident in General Orders No. 32, it is not surprising that much of the army remained ignorant or uncertain of the scope of authority vested in Hoffman's office. Help finally came in mid-June, when the War Department endeavored to clarify the lines of responsibility and authority through the publication of General Orders No. 67, which, at last, assigned control of prisoners of war sent by generals in the field to any camp "entirely" to the commissary general of prisoners. Specifically, the orders tasked Hoffman with the responsibility of establishing "regulations for issuing clothing to prisoners," and he alone was empowered to "direct the manner in which all funds arising from the saving of rations at prison hospitals or otherwise shall be accounted for and disbursed." He was further directed to provide "such articles as may be absolutely necessary for the welfare of the prisoners," and he was granted the authority to select the locations for prisons and to direct the construction of new facilities as required. He was required to visit all camps each month. In the case of "extreme illness" among prisoners, he was accorded the power to grant paroles "on the recommendation of the medical officer attending the prison." Finally, the orders specified that "all matters in relation to prisoners" were to be directed through the office of the commissary general, and that in the performance of his duties Hoffman was to be "subject only to the orders of the War Department."[105]

But even the sweeping provisions of General Orders No. 67 did not immediately resolve Hoffman's difficulties in dealing with general officers in the field. A full month after the orders were issued, he was notified by a subordinate at Camp Chase that the officer in charge of the prisoners "desired to be informed if you had the entire charge of the prisoners" and whether or not the authority of the commissary general of prisoners superseded that of his immediate chain of command.[106]

Throughout the war Old Huffy would frequently complain that military and civilian authorities had bypassed him to correspond directly with Stanton or officers in the War Department, and on occasion his orders were simply ignored. In June 1862, he angrily warned superiors by letter and telegraph that his exclusion from the deliberations concerning the dispositions of the thousands of prisoners taken in the battles around Corinth, Mississippi, would likely lead to "some embarrassment" and unnecessary expense for the War Department.[107]

Still, General Orders No. 67 supplied Hoffman with the clear and comprehensive statement of responsibility and authority he had sought, and armed with its provisions he could now set about establishing his control over the Union prisoner-of-war system. No such clear delineation would be provided General John Henry Winder, however. Although the challenges he faced by were every bit as daunting as those plaguing Hoffman, Winder would be forced to address them without even the pretense of national authority.

Conditions in southern prisons throughout the first half of 1862 were mixed. Prisoners confined at Salisbury, for example, found that while rations were bland, the portions provided were adequate. Nor was overcrowding initially a problem. On 7 January 1862 prison commandant Braxton Craven reported that only 295 captives were confined at the facility, and although subsequent shipments of prisoners from Richmond swelled this number to 1,425 by early April, Salisbury's six acres proved spacious enough to contain the prisoners and still leave room for the popular new game of baseball. One prisoner found Salisbury to be more like a college campus than a prison during this period; in a letter home, another described a drowsy existence in which "our time is spent in playing ball, chess, walking, smoking, snoozing, philosophizing, speculating, criticizing and—like McCawber—waiting for something to turn up."[108]

In Richmond, the situation was quite different. Life for Yankee captives confined in the capital had never been good, and as the prisoner population in the city ballooned during the winter of 1861–1862, conditions plummeted in the prisons Winder had established during the first months of the war. Rations were insufficient and issued irregularly, the uniforms of the prisoners were reduced to rags, and the medical facilities designated to attend to the increasing number of sick and wounded proved completely inadequate. In the spring of 1862 the transfer of prisoners to other camps and the limited and special exchanges negotiated by Wool and Huger provided a small measure of relief, and the chronic shortage of clothing was temporarily eased by the distribution of two thousand sets of uniforms sent south by the Union.[109] This brief respite ended with the termination of cartel negotiations between Wool and Cobb. Exchanges slowed to a trickle and overcrowding swiftly returned. The situation was further exacerbated because during the period of reduced prisoner population, the surgeon general had secured permission to convert four of Winder's prisons into hospitals for Confederate wounded.[110]

Winder was again forced to scramble for space to confine prisoners, and he lit upon the cavernous structure housing the ship chandlery of L. Libby and Son. Exercising the same degree of tact employed in earlier such confiscations, Winder summarily notified Libby that his warehouse had been appropriated by the Confederate government and that he had forty-eight hours to vacate the premises. On 7 March the first captives from crowded facilities across Richmond were transferred to Libby. Their arrival initiated the transformation of this nondescript warehouse into the most infamous of Richmond's Civil War prisons.[111]

To its first inmates, Libby doubtless appeared little different from the warehouse prisons they had previously occupied. Prisoners were housed on the top two floors of the facility. These floors were divided into three rooms, each of which was 103 feet long and 42 feet wide. There was no furniture, and as one captive recalled, the light admitted by the small windows at each end was so dim that there was a forty-foot space in the center of each room where newsprint could not be read. Ventilation was poor, and although the building had running water, it was drawn directly from the muddy and polluted James River.[112]

To command the prison Winder chose Lieutenant Thomas P. Turner, a twenty-one-year-old Virginian with no military experience. His second in command was Richard ("Dick") R. Turner, no relation, also an inexperienced lieutenant in his early twenties. While the occupants of Libby found the aloof Thomas to be something of a martinet, they soon learned that Dick was possessed of a ferocious temper and a proclivity to violence that would earn him the abiding hatred of all prisoners with whom he came in contact.[113]

Libby's very first occupants found the facility to be less crowded than other Richmond prisons, but after only three days of operation additional transfers pushed the population to seven hundred inmates, and that luxury vanished. More than one hundred men were confined in each of the structure's dark and forbidding rooms, and that number continued to climb as prisoners captured during McClellan's Peninsula campaign began to arrive in the capital. As the two armies grappled within sight of the capital, Richmond was inundated by over five thousand Confederate wounded as well, and for three days an unending train of ambulance wagons creaked through the streets of the capital. As hospital matron Sallie Putnam recorded in her diary, "Death had a carnival in our city." Every available room and building was pressed into service to care for the casualties; as Putnam recalled, "We lived in one immense hospital, and breathed the vapors of the charnel house."[114] Close behind the Confederate wounded came hundreds of Union captives.

With space in Libby exhausted and no hope of quickly finding another empty warehouse to convert to prison use, Winder looked for locations outside the capital to confine these newest arrivals. He selected the fairgrounds at Lynchburg, Virginia. But even as the first prisoners were arriving at that site, Winder's subordinates notified him in no uncertain terms that the facility was completely unacceptable. On 18 June, Colonel George C. Gibbs, the commander of the post, apprised Winder that the conditions under which Lynchburg's 2,260 prisoners were confined were appalling. "The premises occupied as a prison are entirely unsuited to the purpose," Gibbs wrote. "The sleeping quarters of the prisoners, are vacant (open) stalls. There is no hospital . . . no prison surgeon . . . and the prisoners were without food for the twenty-four hours ending at noon to-day." Confederate quartermaster general Abraham C. Myers concurred with this dismal assessment. He notified Secretary of War George Randolph that reports from his subordinates at Lynchburg indicated that "it is almost impossible to obtain supplies to feed the prisoners in this place," adding his assessment that only the "speedy exchange of prisoners of war or their disposal otherwise" could avert a catastrophe.[115]

With cartel negotiations between the two governments stalled, Winder knew that a speedy exchange was not likely, and again he initiated a search for other means to dispose of the swelling prisoner population in Richmond. Once more he scoured the city in search of suitable warehouses he might confiscate and convert to prison use, but most had already been pressed into service as hospitals to care for Confederate wounded from the Peninsula campaign. Although he was able to add one additional warehouse, a millhouse, and a tobacco factory to his growing list of impromptu prisons, Winder knew that these acquisitions would be insufficient to house the hundreds of prisoners arriving daily. He had to identify new options. Although no more suitable buildings were available to confine captives, he discovered one piece of real estate in the city that seemed ideally suited to just such a purpose. That spot was Belle Isle, an eighty-acre island in the James River just southwest of Libby Prison.

At first glance, there was much to recommend Belle Isle. The island, as its name implied, was a beautiful place. Its trees, abundant wildlife, and grassy slopes had long made it a favorite recreation spot for local residents. The site had no barracks, but with the coming of spring, the prisoners could be comfortably billeted in tents. The river would furnish abundant fresh water and would also provide the Yankees the opportunity to bathe frequently and wash their clothes. "Their condition," the editors of the *Richmond Enquirer* wrote, would certainly be "more enviable than that of the several thousand of other comrades now in city prisons." Finally, Belle Isle also satisfied the security requirements sought by Winder and his staff. The one bridge that joined the island to the mainland could be easily guarded, and the swiftness of the river's current would discourage escape attempts.[116]

Although life in the open air might well be preferred by prisoners over the monotonous and unhealthful existence that had been their lot in the crowded warehouses, Winder's decision to establish a confinement facility on Belle Isle was not without grave risks. Should the Confederate government fail to supply adequate numbers of tents to shelter the prisoners from the oppressive heat and torrential rains of summer, life on the island would be miserable. And if the use of the site stretched into the region's brutal winter, the failure to erect heated barracks to house the captives would surely result in disaster. All this Winder understood, but he was forced by necessity to operate in the short term, and in mid-June he ordered the transfer of enlisted prisoners from the warehouses to Belle Isle to begin.

Capacity of the island was placed at 3,000 prisoners, and a maze of large Sibley tents soon sprouted to house them. In only two weeks, however, the estimated capacity was exceeded. As the battles outside Richmond pushed the number confined to over 5,000, the quartermaster department ominously reported that the supply of tents had been exhausted and food for the captives was running low. Still, the unending lines of soldiers in blue continued to shuffle across the bridge over the James. Once on the island, they were left to fend for themselves. Bereft of shelter of any sort, they suffered mightily in Richmond's blistering summer heat and torrential downpours. Their only recourse was to seek relief in holes burrowed into Belle Isle's once-verdant slopes and to add their voices to those of the thousands of prisoners in blue and gray praying for salvation through exchange.[117]

Exchange negotiations had never completely ceased, although talk of a cartel had been muted following the angry charges of duplicity traded by Benjamin and Stanton in March; but it was not long before the twin spurs of public outrage and undeniable economic necessity put the negotiations back on track. The greatest pressure in the North arose from continuing demands for the release of Colonel Michael Corcoran. In a resolution of 24 March, the U.S. House of Representatives again pressed Stanton to disclose "the cause, if any for the protracted delay in the exchange of Colonel Corcoran," and the secretary, bowing to the immense political pressure generated by Corcoran's admirers and powerful political associates, reauthorized Wool to seek the colonel's release through negotiations with Huger. Although Confederate secretary of war Benjamin had publicly proclaimed only a month earlier that requests for special exchanges would not be entertained, the twin specters of desperate overcrowding and the burgeoning cost of maintaining thousands of prisoners compelled the Davis administration to agree to a resumption of negotiations.[118]

So Wool and Huger met once more, and by 9 May they had drafted an agreement under which Corcoran and the other Union prisoners held hostage would be exchanged for the Confederate privateersmen. Stanton, at last accepting the inevitable, approved the plan and ordered the southern sailors shipped to Fort Monroe to await the arrival of the hostages. All seemed in readiness. But the long-delayed exchange was fated to be derailed yet again, for now it was a Confederate official who took a turn at duplicity. In the middle of negotiations, Secretary of War Benjamin had been replaced by George W. Randolph, and when Huger asked Randolph to forward the hostages from Richmond to City Point, the new secretary answered rather evasively that the Yankees were not confined in the capital, but in Salisbury. Puzzled by this response and fearful that any delay might imperil the agreement, Huger replied that he considered himself "pledged to deliver the hostages upon the arrival of the privateersmen," and he requested the "authority to order them from Salisbury."[119] The wily Randolph replied that "there are no longer any hostages in our hands, the persons so treated having been considered as other prisoners of war since the privateersmen received the same consideration from the enemy. An equivalent for the privateersmen will be furnished from the persons who were hostages according to the cartel agreed on. Until you know the number and rank of the officers among the privateersmen I do not see how that equivalent can be determined."[120]

Huger now sensed that something was amiss, and his suspicions proved correct. Despite Randolph's assertions to the contrary, the secretary never intended to exchange the Union hostages. Instead, he hoped to trick the Yankees into releasing the privateersmen and, once certain that they were securely under Confederate control, declare them "exchanged" for northern soldiers that had earlier been passed through the lines. If his gambit had been successful, the secretary would have scored the double coup of securing the release of the southern sailors while continuing to hold the immensely valuable Corcoran as a pawn to be played at a later date to force the Union to accede to a general exchange.[121]

Unlike Randolph, Huger was an honorable man, and he was incensed when he learned that he was being used as an unwilling dupe in the secretary's intrigues. On 28 May he angrily dispatched a message to Randolph, reminding him that under the terms negotiated with Wool "all the persons formerly held as hostages" were to be exchanged for "all the privateersmen," and that while the secretary's scheme might "fulfill the letter" of the agreement, it certainly did not fulfill the spirit. Randolph's semantic hairsplitting was as detestable as that attempted by the Yankees in March, the outraged Huger continued, and he would have no part in it. As he stated flatly, "I must comply with the terms, or I shall be guilty of similar conduct to that pursued by General Wool, to which I cannot consent. I repeat my request that I have authority granted me to send for and deliver over on parole all officers once held as hostages provided General Wool delivers to me all the privateersmen." Along with being innately dishonest, George Randolph was an exceedingly proud man, and he did not take a rebuke from a subordinate lightly. Charging that Wool had outwitted Huger in the exchange negotiations, he relieved Huger of all authority for exchanges and pushed on with his crude attempt to bamboozle the Yankees.[122]

On 2 June, just as Wool and Huger had agreed, a Federal colonel arrived opposite the Confederate lines at Petersburg, Virginia, with the eighty-five privateersmen to be exchanged; but instead of receiving Union hostages, he was presented a telegram from Randolph claiming that Huger's promise to Wool had been "misunderstood" and that further negotiations would be necessary before the Union prisoners could be released. Correctly interpreting Randolph's vague note to mean that the hostages would not be presented for exchange, the colonel promptly returned his prisoners to the Union lines. When Stanton learned of Randolph's attempt at trickery, he immediately ordered that the hapless southern sailors be returned to their cells in Fort Lafayette.[123]

Randolph's machinations had extinguished hopes for the speedy conclusion of a general exchange, and now both governments had ample reason to distrust any proposition offered by the other. By this time, commanders in the field had become impatient with such political sparring. Finding themselves increasingly burdened with enemy prisoners and concerned about the fate of their own men held captive, McClellan and Lee decided to circumvent the squabbling between Washington and Richmond and proceed with exchanges on their own authority. The two generals resumed army-to-army exchanges, and on 8 June, without notifying Stanton, McClellan proposed that these arrangements be further formalized. "I fully agree that a general exchange or cartel would be preferable," McClellan wrote to Lee, "and should it be agreeable to you would be very glad to designate a general or staff officer to meet one to be selected by you for the purpose of endeavoring to arrange the details." By the time Stanton heard of McClellan's overture he could do little but add his grudging consent, but he appended a warning that the general should be "on guard" against Confederate perfidy. And he emphasized Lincoln's insistence that exchanges must be limited to prisoners actually under the direct control of the two armies.[124]

After obtaining permission from Randolph to act on McClellan's proposition, Lee appointed General Howell Cobb to meet with McClellan's representative, Colonel Thomas M. Key. On 15 June the two men met between the lines, where almost at once Cobb sought to expand the scope of the discussions from local exchanges to a general exchange of all prisoners. When Key informed Stanton of Cobb's proposal, the secretary severely reprimanded the colonel for exceeding his powers. Stanton then fired off a second brusque telegram reminding McClellan that Lincoln had personally forbidden negotiations encompassing general exchanges and directing the general to ensure that talks remained restricted to exchanges between the two armies.[125]

Yet time was running out for both Lincoln and his policy, for northerners were becoming increasingly impatient with the failure to conclude a general exchange. In books, pamphlets, and public addresses, prisoners who had been released through the limited exchanges recounted the trials of their captivity to a public eager for such news; lurid drawings and sensational articles detailing the terrible conditions in southern prisons became a staple in the newspapers of northern cities. Typical of these journalistic offerings was a *New York Times* editorial that called upon its readers to "think of the crowded and filthy tobacco warehouses, the brutal keepers, the sanguinary guards, the rotten food, the untended wounds, the unmedicated disease, the miserable marches through the blazing South, and the reincarceration in other jails, more remote than the first, which a voice from home does hardly ever reach."[126]

Even more troubling for Lincoln, increasing numbers of newspaper editors were moving beyond simply reporting conditions for prisoners of war to place the blame for their suffering squarely on the president and his administration. In the same editorial, for example, the *Times* lamented that "we are more than grieved to learn that on the apathy of our own Government is chargeable the failure to have a system adopted for the exchange of prisoners. We have hoped that the supposed 'political necessities' under which it was justified had yielded to the claims and instincts of humanity. We are sorry to find that it is not so."[127] The ultimate cost of Lincoln's recalcitrance, the paper predicted, would extend far beyond prolonging the misery of the prisoners. "Should we fail to have quick responses to calls for new armies," the *Times* warned, "the Government may begin to find that its apathy to the sorrows and sufferings of those who have already periled life and lost liberty in battling for it, is producing an aversion to military service. We cannot be reconciled to this. Our Government must change its policy."[128]

Congress was also feeling the renewed wrath of outraged constituents. Letters demanding the institution of a general exchange poured into congressional offices, and legislators responded by increasing the pressure on the administration. On 23 June, for the third time in only three months, Congress served Stanton with a joint resolution directing him to "communicate to the Senate any information he my have in regard to the exchange of prisoners or of negotiations therefore."[129]

In the South, meanwhile, the need for a general exchange was growing desperate. The administrative and economic burden of maintaining thousands of Union prisoners was crushing, and conditions in the prisons of the Confederacy were becoming more horrific with each passing day. The staggering burden of disposing of prisoners was also beginning to hinder southern military operations in the field. On 3 July, Lee, in a typical understatement, wrote Randolph that "it would be a great relief to us if we could arrange a general exchange." To spur the secretary to action, the general suggested that Cobb be immediately authorized to negotiate such an agreement with Wool. Then, without waiting for the secretary's response, Lee notified McClellan that "notwithstanding such care as we have been able to give the wounded of your army who have fallen into our hands, in addition to that of your own medical officers, I learn with regret that they are dying rapidly," and he proposed to release immediately and unconditionally 2,500 Federal wounded. McClellan commended the "humane spirit evinced by General Lee" to Stanton, and in the name of "our soldiers who are suffering in captivity" he added his voice to the multitudes demanding a general exchange. In a separate note sent directly to the president, McClellan offered a more practical reason for his support for an exchange. "I am very anxious," he explained to Lincoln, "to have my old regiments filled up rather than have new ones formed."[130]

McClellan was very astute to correspond directly with Lincoln in this matter, for in the last analysis the question of whether or not the North would agree to a general exchange rested with the president alone. For the most part, Lincoln had remained silent on the subject of prisoners. Other than his insistence that no action that might lead to recognition of the Confederacy be undertaken, the president had deliberately distanced himself from the controversies over the establishment of prisons and the treatment of captives. He would take great care to remain aloof from prisoner issues throughout the war.

But Lincoln's stance should not be taken as evidence that he was not aware of the suffering of prisoners or that he never took a hand in determining their fate. Gruesome accounts of the ordeals of Union captives were a staple in the newspapers Lincoln read. These descriptions were supplemented by published journals of former captives. The most popular of these accounts was the Richmond journal of Representative Alfred Ely, which the congressman closed with a plea that northerners remember the plight of those who remained "within the wretched confines of a Confederate prison." In addition to these published accounts, Lincoln received firsthand information about the sufferings of prisoners from personal meetings with repatriated captives. On 18 August 1862, for example, the president hosted a dinner for recently released prisoners. Although Lincoln attempted to shift the conversation at these gatherings away from the horrors of the camps, the prisoners' tales of misery were inescapable. Finally, evidence that the president was thoroughly aware of the suffering of Union captives is confirmed by the fact that a report on prisons, prisoners of war, and exchanges constituted a lengthy and important section of the president's annual report to Congress.[131]

Nor could Lincoln have remained unaware of the conditions under which southern prisoners were held in Union camps. As all students of Lincoln's presidency have noted, the president was a frequent visitor to the War Department telegraph office, where he closely monitored correspondence from units and commanders in the field; this would have included the hundreds of messages and telegrams concerning the state of Confederate prisoners in Federal prisons that flowed in and out of the department during 1862.[132] Many northern newspapers also carried full accounts of the abysmal conditions in Union camps. Among this group could be found the paper from the president's hometown of Springfield, Illinois, which regularly reported on the terrible conditions at Camp Butler.[133]

In spite of such evidence, Lincoln's involvement in the policies and directives that determined the conditions in Union prisons has been largely ignored by historians. Scholars who have addressed this subject have all maintained that when the president did become personally involved in such issues, he consistently exerted a moderating influence.[134] Frequently such was the case, for Lincoln often received pleas for relief directly from southern prisoners or their families begging for presidential intervention. On 9 April 1862, he responded to one such telegram by directing Halleck to mitigate the "rigor of confinement" for a prisoner threatened by the smallpox epidemic raging at Alton; in August of that same year he ordered the commander of Camp Chase to allow a prisoner confined there to telegraph his wife.[135]

But it is also true that the president's intercession often derived from decidedly less charitable motives. He repeatedly intervened to order the release of Rebel prisoners known either to him or his friends, and on numerous occasions—such as when he ordered a special exchange be arranged to return a Union colonel deemed essential to the retention of the Republican congressional majority in a key northern state—his actions were politically motivated.[136] Nor was the president's intervention into prisoner affairs always aimed at freeing captives. He often directed that applications for release be denied even when, as was the case in the soldier at Alton, to do so meant almost certain death. And when Tennessee governor Andrew Johnson proposed that "seventy vile secessionists" be imprisoned and offered in exchange for "seventy east Tennesseans" held in Rebel prisons, the president's support was enthusiastic. "I certainly do not disapprove of the proposition," he wired Johnson, and the plan went forward.[137]

Far from being ignorant, uninformed, or uninvolved, Abraham Lincoln was acutely aware of all prisoner-of-war issues throughout the Civil War; but any intervention or attempt on his part to ameliorate the lot of prisoners, either Union or Confederate, stemmed from his personal or political objectives rather than from appeals for mercy or his inherent good nature. So when the political pressure for exchange became intolerable in July 1862, the president intervened without hesitation. Had the situation permitted, Lincoln would have continued his policy of refusing a general exchange, no matter how terrible the plight of Union prisoners, for he believed that such a policy best served the greater cause of preserving the Union. But with Congress, the northern press, the public, and even his own military leaders all clamoring for the acceptance of a general exchange, the president was at last forced to concede that his policy of refusing to support such an agreement had become politically untenable. Therefore, on 12 July, Stanton, at the president's direction, authorized General John A. Dix, the commander of the Department of Virginia, to "negotiate a general exchange of prisoners with the enemy." The secretary directed Dix to employ the British–American cartel of 1813 as a guide in formulating the agreement, and in a warning that surely originated with Lincoln, he admonished the general to observe "proper caution against any recognition of the rebel Government."[138]

Due to the illness of Cobb, Randolph appointed General Daniel H. Hill as the Confederate commissioner to the talks, and on 18 July, Hill and Dix met at Haxall's Landing on the James River to compose a cartel for general exchange. In only one day the men completed their task, and a draft of the document was submitted to Stanton and Randolph. Both secretaries approved the compact as drafted, and on 22 July the agreement was signed and ratified by Dix and Hill. Ironically, the provisions of the cartel in its final form were essentially the same as those proposed by Wool and Cobb almost five months earlier.

The Dix–Hill cartel was composed of nine articles. Articles one through three provided a detailed schedule of rank equivalents to be followed in calculating the value of persons to be exchanged. A flag officer or major general was to be exchanged for "officers of equal rank" or "forty privates or common seamen," while army captains and navy lieutenants were to be traded for officers of like ranks or six privates or common seamen. Article four mandated the discharge on parole of all prisoners within ten days of capture and specified that they be transported to "points mutually agreed upon at the expense of the capturing party." Once paroled, prisoners would be officially exchanged in accordance with the schedule. "Surplus prisoners" not officially exchanged due to a shortage of captives on one side or the other would continue in a parolee status and would "not be permitted to take up arms . . . or discharge any duty usually performed by soldiers, until exchanged under the provisions of this cartel." Article five required each government to submit lists of "officers and men relieved from parole" so that a like number could be returned to full military duty by the other side, and article six declared that the provisions of the cartel were to be "of binding obligation during the continuance of the war," no matter which party held a surplus of prisoners.[139]

Articles seven through nine of the agreement were listed as "supplementary articles." Article seven provided that the transfer of prisoners was to take place at Aiken's Landing on the James River for captives confined in the eastern theater of the war and at Vicksburg, Mississippi, for those held in the western theater. These points could be changed should the "vicissitudes of war" require, but the article stipulated that exchanges were to proceed regardless of the difficulties either belligerent might encounter. Under the provisions of article eight each government was to appoint an "agent of exchange" whose duty it would be to "communicate . . . by correspondence and otherwise, to prepare the lists of prisoners, to attend to the delivery of the prisoners at the places agreed on and to carry out promptly, effectually and in good faith all the details and provisions of the said articles of agreement."[140]

The final article of the cartel was perhaps the most interesting. While the cartel of 1813 contained a provision allowing either of the signatories to declare that agreement "null and no longer binding" with only six months' notice, the agreement penned by Hill and Dix included no such escape clause. "Misunderstandings," article nine stipulated, were to "be made the subject of friendly explanations" and were not to be allowed in any way to "defeat" or "postpone" the purpose of the agreement or to "interrupt the release of prisoners on parole."[141]

News that the cartel had been ratified was met with great joy in both the North and the South. The *New York Times* assured its readers that "the good to be effected by an exchange . . . far exceeds any advantage that could be gained by retaining the rebel prisoners." One of the first effects of the institution of the cartel, the *Times*'s editors confidently predicted, would be "an immense stimulus to volunteering," which would add "one hundred thousand recruits" to the rolls of the army. To many in the South, the agreement represented not only a humanitarian victory but a diplomatic one as well. "It seems that the Federal Government has at last condescended to recognize the Confederacy," the *Richmond Dispatch* crowed when the negotiations between Dix and Hill began in earnest, and the paper applauded the "very proper" general exchange that resulted.[142]

To the soldiers confined in Union and Confederate camps, word of the agreement constituted nothing less than a new lease on life. Civilians both North and the South prayed that this cartel, unlike the temporary arrangements of the past, would be permanent, and the provisions of article nine of the cartel ensured that such would be the case. Or so it seemed.

CHAPTER 6

The Period of Exchange under the Cartel

July 1862–December 1863

ON THE HOT summer morning of 3 August 1862, two ships docked at Aiken's Landing, a muddy spit of land on the James River near Fort Monroe, Virginia. Although one of the ships was Union and the other Confederate, on this day each flew a flag of truce, since their purpose in meeting was other than combat. The cargo of these vessels was unique, for they bore the first detachments of prisoners designated for exchange under the provisions of the Dix–Hill cartel. Aboard the Union ship were southern captives who had been imprisoned at Forts Warren and Delaware; the Confederate vessel held Yankee prisoners drawn from camps across the South. Shortly after docking, officers from each of the ships disembarked, traded rosters of the prisoners, and, in accordance with the table of equivalents stipulated in the cartel, began to work out the details whereby each of the men would be exchanged. Among the Federal prisoners declared exchanged as a result of this initial meeting was Colonel William Hoffman, the Union commissary general of prisoners who had been released on parole following his capture in Texas. Also freed at long last was Colonel Michael Corcoran, who promptly became the darling of New York society and began work on the florid memoir in which he claimed for himself the title of the "Hero of Bull Run."[1]

With minor modifications, the exchange procedure followed that day would be played out dozens of times during the coming months. As soon as the cartel was ratified, the officials who directed the prisoner-of-war systems in both the North and the South shifted their focus from simply maintaining captives to arranging for their swift exchange. The benefits offered by the cartel were enormous. Most obviously, thousands of soldiers were freed from the prisons where they faced privations, disease, and very often death. Exchange under the cartel also offered significant advantages to the Union and Confederate governments. It answered the demands of northerners and southerners who had been clamoring for the swift repatriation of their loved ones, and it supplied a means for returning veteran soldiers to the ranks. Additionally, it relieved the enormous drain of resources the two governments were expending to confine enemy captives. Officers charged with managing prisoners and the enlisted soldiers tasked with guarding them could now be reassigned to duties at the front, while the immense quantities of money, transportation assets, billeting space, and supplies and equipment of every sort that had been required to maintain prisoners could now be allocated for other purposes.

Given the cartel's many advantages, one might have thought that Union and Confederate leaders would have worked tirelessly to keep it in place. Such was not the case, however. After only six months of operation the cartel began to break down; in less than a year it had ceased to function altogether. An examination of the short life of the agreement reveals that both governments had a hand in its demise.

The mechanics of the cartel were simple. As soon as it was signed, Colonel Robert Ould was selected as the Confederate agent of exchange, in accordance with the agreement's eighth article. A prominent attorney and dedicated advocate of southern rights in his native District of Columbia, Ould had resigned his appointment as U.S. district attorney and had moved to Richmond upon the inauguration of Lincoln in 1861. There he joined the Confederate government, rising to the post of assistant secretary of war before he was named to head the Bureau of Exchange and serve as the cartel's southern agent.[2] Union secretary of war Edwin Stanton deferred naming a Union agent of exchange until Commissary General of Prisoners William Hoffman received complete rolls of the Confederates held prisoner. As soon as these were in hand, the secretary instructed General Lorenzo Thomas, the adjutant general of the army, to add this responsibility to his existing list of duties.[3]

Initially the Confederate secretary of war appointed Major N. B. Watts to serve as the southern agent at Vicksburg, the exchange point in the western theater of the war. Predictably, the system of maintaining two independent agents directing operations hundreds of miles apart soon led to complications, and it was discarded in favor of maintaining Ould as the sole Confederate agent of exchange, with headquarters in Richmond. In the southern system, Vicksburg became simply a point where prisoners in the western theater were collected. From there Watts, operating under instructions from Ould, provided his superior with the names, ranks, and numbers of prisoners he received, as well as the number of paroles and exchanges granted. No Union agent was appointed for the western theater, but under instructions from General Thomas, Hoffman ordered two of his subordinates, Captains Henry M. Lazelle and Henry W. Freedley, to superintend the delivery of the southern captives to Vicksburg. On 9 August, Thomas arrived at the site personally to direct exchanges.[4]

Although the terms of the cartel included no specific duties for Hoffman, Thomas assigned him the responsibility of assembling the Rebel prisoners and ensuring they were transported to the applicable point of exchange. Hoffman determined that the 12,000 prisoners held at Camp Chase, Johnson's Island, Camp Douglas, Camp Butler, and Alton Penitentiary would be shipped to Vicksburg for exchange, and—as was the case in all the duties he was assigned—his supervision of this transfer was exceedingly thorough. He ordered the commanders of the five prisons to dispatch the prisoners by rail in groups of one thousand men to Cairo, Illinois, where he made arrangements for the captives to be transported down the Mississippi to Vicksburg by steamboat. Prisoners whom surgeons determined were too ill to travel were to remain in the prisons under the care of army medical personnel. During visits to each of the prisons, Hoffman personally issued detailed instructions on how the commanders of the guard detachments should secure their charges while en route. He directed that the routes to Cairo were to include the fewest changes of railroad cars possible and that the trains were to carry sufficient rations to provide for the prisoners during the entire trip. In Cairo, the ration supply was to be replenished for the trip downriver, but at no time were the commanders to allow liquor or other contraband to reach the prisoners. Upon arrival at Vicksburg, guard commanders were to sign the prisoners over to Captain Lazelle, who would then meet with the Confederate representative and arrange for the actual exchange.[5]

As always, the commissary general took great pains to ensure that all movements of prisoners were accomplished at the least expense possible to the government. Expenses of this sort had fallen under Hoffman's budget knife even before the cartel became effective. "I hear that you give transportation to released prisoners," he had curtly telegraphed one commander in March 1862. "It is not authorized."[6]

In spite of Hoffman's prodigious efforts to ensure that the transfer of prisoners went off without a hitch, he was bedeviled with problems at nearly every turn. Medical care for the captives transported from Camp Chase was inadequate, and one group of Johnson's Island prisoners was delayed for almost two weeks at Cairo because Union transportation officials would not allow them to proceed south until the convoy of vessels was completely filled.[7]

The most serious and persistent problem Hoffman faced, however, was shoddy record keeping. Prison commanders would often dispatch shipments with prisoner rolls that failed to list such vital information as the ranks of the captives, the date, time, and place of their capture, or the unit to which they had been assigned. Hoffman's frustration was further heightened because long before the first exchanges occurred, he had alerted his commanders that they would be required to account precisely for their prisoners. "A general exchange of prisoners of war is expected to take place immediately," he had warned on 31 July 1862, "and for this purpose you will prepare a roll of all prisoners of war in your charge." This advance notice went for naught, and the accounting in the initial rosters was atrocious.[8] Exchanges were delayed until the errors and omissions were corrected, and Hoffman repeatedly blasted Union commanders for the "embarrassment" caused by the "careless manner" in which they prepared their rolls. One roll contained a whopping 178 errors, and as Old Huffy acerbically assured his subordinates, "this [was] not a singular case."[9]

In an effort to remedy this problem, Hoffman ordered the preparation of a standardized form that would supply all the information required about the prisoners to be exchanged. Each page of the form was headed by the statement that "we the undersigned, Prisoners of War, give our parole of honor that we will not take up arms again . . . until exchanged under the provisions of the Cartel entered into July 22, 1862"—a clever addition ensuring that even as the prisoners signed the document, they were pledging to abide by the terms of parole stated in the cartel. But even with such aids, slipshod accounting of prisoners continued to plague Union administrators throughout the war.[10]

General John Henry Winder, like Hoffman, was assigned no specific duties under the terms of the cartel. Implementation of the agreement nonetheless increased the scope of his responsibilities dramatically, for while Ould arranged the paroles and exchanges of Confederate soldiers in the eastern theater of the war, it fell to Winder to carry them out. Typically, Ould would notify Winder of the dates of upcoming exchanges and the anticipated number of prisoners to be passed through the lines. Winder would then supply Ould with rolls containing the name, rank, unit, and physical description of each soldier to be exchanged. Through correspondence with the commanders of prisons in Virginia, Georgia, Alabama, and both Carolinas, the general would arrange to have those prisoners shipped to Richmond, where they would be consolidated before being sent on to Ould at the point of exchange. This procedure added to Winder's responsibilities in another way as well, for while implementation of the cartel rapidly reduced the number of Yankees held in prisons outside Richmond, the city's use as the point of concentration for prisoners awaiting exchange ensured that the population of captives under Winder's direct control remained high.[11]

These difficulties notwithstanding, the rate at which exchanges proceeded under the cartel was astounding. In late July 1862, Hoffman had reported to Stanton that the camps of the North held 20,500 prisoners of war. Existing Union prisons were so overcrowded that he had been forced to direct his subordinates to conduct "careful examinations" of the recruit training depots at Albany, Utica, Rochester, Buffalo, and Elmira, New York, to "ascertain their capacity" for quartering prisoners.[12] After only one month of exchanges at City Point and Vicksburg, the number of prisoners held in the North had diminished to 13,241, obviating the requirement for additional prisons.[13] By the end of September, exchanges had reduced the number of Confederate captives to 5,012; at the close of 1862 the commissary general of prisoners reported to the secretary of war that only 1,286 Confederate prisoners remained in Union hands. Hoffman consolidated most of them in Alton, Camp Chase, and Johnson's Island. With the exceptions of Forts Delaware, Pickens, and Lafayette, each of which held civilian prisoners of state, Hoffman was able to close all the remaining camps in the North.[14]

In the South, the story was much the same. Although the number of Yankees held at Belle Isle, Libby, and the other Richmond prisons remained high, exchanges under the cartel rapidly drew down the number of prisoners in other installations of the Confederate prisoner-of-war system. Local newspapers reported that the last inmates held at Salisbury Prison departed at the end of August; by the fall of 1862 Winder had also completely emptied the prisons at Macon, Lynchburg, Charleston, Mobile, Atlanta, and Tuscaloosa. Ould's representatives at the Vicksburg point of exchange had processed and released 16,000 prisoners by 21 August, almost all of the captives held in the Confederacy's prisons in the western theater.[15]

Not all prisoners chose to be exchanged. Soldiers on both sides opted to take oaths of allegiance to the governments that had captured them, a decision that usually ensured they would be released from prison but would not be repatriated. Winder found units where Yankees who sought to remain in the South and serve in the Confederate States Army could enlist; for those who sought only to remain neutral, he found places of employment.[16]

In the North, Stanton directed Thomas to retain all "persons who decline to be exchanged," and shortly after the cartel was ratified Hoffman confirmed that captives who took the oath of allegiance would not be repatriated to the Confederacy. To facilitate accountability, Hoffman devised yet another of his standardized forms, on which the name, rank, regiment, place of capture, and physical description of each of these prisoners was recorded. Upon signing an oath swearing that they would "support, protect, and defend the Constitution and Government of the United States against all enemies, whether foreign or domestic," the men were released.[17]

War Department General Orders No. 107 of 15 August 1862 directed that oaths of allegiance "must in all cases be a voluntary act," and Hoffman's form expressly stipulated that such oaths must be given "freely and voluntarily." Still, coercion often played a part in the southern soldiers' decisions, and border-state soldiers with strong secessionist sentiments became the particular targets of threats. Those who opted not to take the oath when given the chance knew that their refusal would likely lead to continued imprisonment. Confederate officers from Kentucky, for example, were advised that if they did not "voluntarily" agree to take the oath they would not be considered for exchange.[18]

The most blatant case of the manipulation of exchange roles for political gain occurred as the result of collusion between President Abraham Lincoln and Andrew Johnson, the military governor of Tennessee. As soon as it became likely that exchanges under the cartel would soon begin, Johnson wrote the president to ask that he be permitted personally to approve all releases of prisoners from Tennessee. Lincoln, always ready to become intimately involved in prisoner issues when the political stakes were high, asked the governor to clarify his request. "Do you really wish to have control of the question of releasing rebel prisoners so far as they may be Tennesseeans?" he wrote to Johnson. The governor responded unequivocally that he did. "I have to state," he explained, "that I do believe we can prescribe such terms of release & so dispose of the question as to exert a powerful influence throughout the state in our favor." The fact that selecting out prisoners in this manner constituted a clear violation of the Union's own General Orders No. 107—as well as the terms of the cartel—was obviously not as important to Lincoln as the political gains possible under Johnson's scheme, for the president readily granted the governor's request, allowing Johnson to send an agent into prisons where Tennesseeans were confined to explain the "benefits" of renouncing the Confederacy. Throughout the period of the cartel Johnson, with Lincoln's assistance, maintained a firm control over releases in order to enhance Unionist power in his state.[19]

As exchanges reduced the number of prisoners held in northern and southern prisons, both Hoffman and Winder acted to improve operations at individual camps and increase their authority over their respective prisoner-of-war systems. In July 1862 Hoffman consolidated his many recommendations to prison commanders into a single circular that detailed the regulations to be observed in the administration of camps. During the respite provided by the cartel he moved to ensure that it was distributed and implemented at "all stations where prisoners of war are held."[20] This circular represented Hoffman's most determined effort to date to establish his personal control over the Union prisoner-of-war system, and its provisions touched on virtually every aspect of prison and prisoner management. The commanding officer at each camp was to be held strictly accountable for the "discipline and good order of his command and for the security of the prisoners," and he was further charged to "take such measures as will best secure these results." Comprehensive reports detailing the number and status of prisoners were to be compiled daily and forwarded to the office of the commissary general monthly. Any changes in the reports required a complete explanation, and the authority to parole or release prisoners was reserved to the War Department and the commissary general of prisoners.[21]

According to the circular, prisoners were to be divided into companies upon entering the camps, and they were to "give up all arms and weapons of every description and all moneys which they have in their possession." Prisoners could not "hold or receive money"; all their funds were to be "taken charge of by the commanding officer who will give receipts for it to those to whom it belongs." Commanders were to establish individual accounts from which inmates could draw to purchase approved items from camp sutlers. Packages sent to the prisoners from friends or relatives, "if proper," were to be "carefully distributed as the donors may request." Unauthorized visits to the camps "out of mere curiosity" were "in no case to be permitted"; persons having valid reasons to enter the camps were to "remain only long enough to transact their business." Seriously ill prisoners might receive "short visits" from "their nearest relatives, parents, wives, brothers or sisters," but "under no other circumstances" would visitors be permitted to see prisoners without Hoffman's personal approval. Prisoners were to be allowed to write letters of "one page of common letter paper" only. Should the letters be anything other than "strictly of a private nature," they were to be destroyed.[22]

The circular also contained provisions for the care of the sick. Each prison hospital was to be "placed under the immediate charge of the senior surgeon who will be held responsible to the commanding officer for its good order and the condition of the sick." Funds allocated for the operation of these facilities were to be "kept separate from the fund of the hospital for the [U.S.] troops and . . . disbursed for the sole benefit of the sick prisoners on the requisition of the surgeon approved by the commanding officer."[23]

Naturally, Hoffman also included detailed instructions on how the camps were to be maintained at the least possible cost to the government. Requests for clothing to be issued to prisoners were to be initiated by camp quartermasters, but prison commanders were told to subject each of these requisitions to a "careful inquiry" to determine its "necessity." Valid requests were then to be submitted to Hoffman for final approval. To restrict the issue of clothing, the commissary general directed that "from the 30th of April to the 1st of October neither drawers nor socks will be allowed except to the sick." Every prison was to establish a "general fund for the benefit of the prisoners" by "withholding from their rations all that can be spared without inconvenience to them and selling this surplus under existing regulations to the commissary." Detailed accounts were to be maintained by the army commissary officers who received the "surplus" rations, and prison commanders were required to furnish Hoffman a report on the status of the funds at the close of every month. The general fund was to be used to purchase "all such articles as may be necessary for the health and comfort of the prisoners and which would otherwise have to be purchased by the Government." Confirming his penchant for minutiae in matters of economy, Hoffman went on to list the sorts of items that could be purchased with money from the fund. Approved items included "table furniture and cooking utensils, articles for policing purposes, bedticks and straw, the means of improving or enlarging the barrack accommodations, extra pay to clerks who have charge of the camp post-office, and who keep the accounts of moneys deposited with the commanding officer, &c., &c." A similar fund was to be established in each prison hospital to defray the cost of "articles for policing, shirts and drawers for the sick, the expense of washing, and all articles that may be indispensably necessary to promote the sanitary condition of the hospital." A final source of income to reduce the cost of prison operations was to come from the sutlers who peddled their wares in selected camps. For this "privilege," the merchants were to be "taxed a small amount by the commanding officer according to the amount of trade," and the money accrued by this means was to be deposited in the general fund.[24]

While the provisions of Hoffman's circular were extensive, his efforts to standardize and gain control of daily operations in the Union camps did not end with its publication. Most prison commanders were inexperienced officers who had been recently recruited from civilian life, and from bitter experience Hoffman had learned that changes in prison operations and administration would come about only if he exercised strict supervision. He thus notified camp commanders that he would personally inspect each camp monthly and that he would dispatch officers from his office when required to supervise the implementation of his directives. The instructions he issued to a supervisor sent to a troubled camp in the summer of 1862 were typical. The officer was to remain at the camp "until all instructions which you may have received are completely put in force and carried out minutely in daily practice under your immediate supervision by the commanding officer at that place, and that they be so fully understood by him, that further instructions to him from this office regarding the regulations of matters appertaining to the prisoners as detailed to you will be unnecessary; as it is not sufficient in these cases simply to give orders, but to see them carefully executed."[25]

In the South, Winder also took advantage of the period of the cartel to consolidate operations and increase his control over the portion of the Confederate prisoner-of-war system that he administered. He first turned his attention to operations in the prisons of Richmond. Anticipating that the prisoner population would balloon with the arrival of captives en route to the point of exchange, he ordered Captain Norris Montgomery, the commander on Belle Isle, to increase his guard force and extend the four-foot-high embankment around the facility so that it might provide temporary accommodations for up to two thousand additional men. Like Hoffman, Winder also sought to bring unauthorized visits to prisons under control. To do so, he directed Montgomery to limit contact with the prisoners to only those persons approved by the provost marshal general's office.[26]

In an effort to better facilitate operations under the cartel, Winder instituted long-overdue changes among the commanders and staff officers in his department. Aware that he could no longer personally direct operations in Richmond's many prisons, Winder appointed Henry Wirz to command of all Richmond prisons. Wirz was a recently promoted captain who had previously directed operations at the Tuscaloosa, Alabama, camp, where he had been very popular among the Yankee prisoners. Upon his assignment to Richmond, however, he began to establish the reputation for cruelty and capriciousness that would eventually cost him his life. Winder also made changes in the leadership of the capital's prisons. Montgomery had been assured in August that he would continue in command at Belle Isle, but when he failed to implement the provost marshal general's new regulations restricting visits to the site, Winder relieved him and assigned Captain Thomas P. Turner, formerly the commander of Libby, in his place.[27]

Winder increased the size of his personal staff as well. His son, William Sidney Winder, had served as his adjutant since October 1861, and in the summer of 1862 Winder added his second cousin, Richard Bayley Winder, to his staff. Richard Winder, a thirty-five-year-old native of Accomac County, Virginia, had been a wealthy planter before the war. In 1861 he joined a Virginia regiment, where he established a reputation for competence and rose to the rank of captain.

Upon learning that his regiment was to be disbanded, he sought out the elder Winder and offered his services. They were eagerly accepted, and on 13 August 1862 Richard was named assistant quartermaster general.[28]

For Winder, as well as for the captives confined in Richmond, exchange under the cartel had come none too soon. In mid-July the capital's prisons were crowded with 7,847 Federal prisoners, and Winder was finding it increasingly difficult to find sufficient rations for them. Even supplies of flour for bread were almost exhausted. By 16 July the situation had become so critical that Winder warned General Robert E. Lee that the lack of adequate rations would likely provoke a prisoner uprising that his guard force would be unable to quell. To this Lee could only reply that Winder should "make arrangements to supply the prisoners with their rations" and that he could "see no reason for their being in want of bread."[29] Such banal responses did nothing to alleviate the desperate challenges Winder faced, and only the initiation of large-scale exchanges under the cartel averted a catastrophe in Richmond's prisons that summer. As soon as the agreement went into effect, Winder made every effort to empty the facilities under his control as swiftly as possible. Each day the citizens of Richmond were treated to the spectacle of long lines of Yankees shuffling under guard through the streets of the capital on their way to City Point. When processing difficulties in outlying prisons threatened to retard the exodus, Winder dispatched Wirz on a whirl-wind tour of those facilities to undo the snarls and accelerate the shipment of prisoners to Richmond, where they would be quickly passed on for exchange.[30]

Although Winder made impressive gains in improving the efficiency of prison operations during the early months of exchanges under the cartel, he continued to be hampered by the muddled system of command and control in the Confed-erate prisoner-of-war system. As provost marshal general and commander of the Department of Henrico, his control over prisons in the Richmond complex was absolute, but he had no clear authority to direct operations in prisons outside the capital, although he often was required to do so. As a result, his orders directed to officials in outlying camps were frequently challenged by military department commanders who viewed him as an interloper and by governors anxious to retain operational control of the prisons in their states. Winder thus could never be sure that his instructions to camps located in Georgia, Alabama, and the Carolinas would be executed, and his requests for even the most fundamental information from these facilities were frequently ignored. When directed by the secretary of war to provide the number of prisoners held by the Confederacy, for example, he could supply accurate information only for the camps in Richmond and Lynch-burg. The numbers of captives held in Alabama and at Salisbury, he confessed, were only "approximations," for "changes have been made by the officers in command in Alabama and North Carolina which have not yet been reported." As for the number of prisoners held in the western theater of the war, Winder had no clue; as he reported, "The prisoners captured in the West and Southwest have never been reported here and I know nothing of them."[31]

Like Hoffman, Winder was soon frustrated by a system that was quick to enlarge his responsibilities while denying him the requisite authority to carry them out. Also like his northern counterpart, he appealed to his superiors for help, and his requests frequently met with success. When he complained to Secretary of War George Randolph that his efforts to direct operations at Salisbury were being countermanded by Brigadier General James G. Martin, the commander of the District of North Carolina, Randolph immediately fired off a terse note to Martin reaffirming that "the prisoners and prison-guard [at Salisbury] are under the sole control of Brig. Gen. John H. Winder and this arrangement should not be interfered with except in case of emergency."[32]

Although effective in solving problems on a case-by-case basis, direct intervention of this sort failed to address the basic weakness in the Confederate prisoner-of-war system. Simply put, the system was crippled by deficiencies in command and control, and those problems would continue until the authorities in Richmond placed all prisoner-of-war operations under the direction of a single officer. Although the Davis administration expected Winder to fulfill the same role as his northern counterpart Hoffman, responsibility for prisoners in the Confederacy remained diffused. As a result, the development of an efficient and effective prisoner-of-war system in the South began to fall behind that being established in the North.[33]

Although exchanges under the cartel proceeded apace once the agreement was ratified, the process was fraught with difficulties from the start. Only one day after the cartel was signed the first of these problems surfaced when Union general John Pope, newly appointed to command the Army of Virginia, issued his infamous General Orders No. 11. On 21 June, Secretary of War Stanton had granted military commanders operating in the seceded states the authority to seize any personal or private property belonging to citizens deemed to be in sympathy with the Confederate cause. Pope's order expanded Stanton's declaration. It permitted the expulsion of disloyal male citizens residing within Union lines and provided that they could be executed as spies if they ever returned. Davis blasted Pope's order as nothing less than a "policy of pillage, outrage upon unarmed, peaceable people, arson and ruthless insult to the defenseless," as well as a breach of the cartel.[34]

Even as Davis was determining how best to deal with General Orders No. 11, a second problem arose. Pope's declaration had obviously touched a nerve among southerners; the *Richmond Dispatch* branded him a "scoundrel." Only five days after the hated order was issued, Virginia governor John Letcher wrote Secretary of War Randolph, challenging the provisions of the cartel. Letcher requested that Virginians who fell into Confederate hands while serving as officers in the units raised by Unionist Francis H. Pierpont be surrendered to state officials so that they could be tried on charges of treason and inciting servile insurrection. He further asked that the cartel be amended to mandate the transfer of all such cases to state control in the future.[35]

Unwilling to relinquish national control of the Confederate prisoner-of-war system, Davis denied Letcher's request, and on 25 July the captured soldiers from Pierpont's units were exchanged, along with Yankees taken in other states of the Confederacy. Still, the Confederate president believed that he had to register a firm denunciation of Pope's policy, and this he did in a letter to Lee on 31 July. "Scarcely had the cartel been signed," Davis wrote, "when the military authorities of the United States commenced a practice changing the character of the war from such as becomes civilized nations into a campaign of indiscriminate robbery and murder." Davis announced that in response to Pope's order, the Confederate War Department had issued General Orders No. 54, "recognizing General Pope and his commissioned officers to be in the position which they have chosen for themselves—that of robbers and murderers and not that of public enemies entitled if captured to be considered as prisoners of war." Davis instructed Lee to "communicate to the Commander-in-Chief of the Armies of the United States the contents of this letter and a copy of the ... general orders, to the end that he may be notified of our intention not to consider army officers hereafter captured from General Pope's army as prisoners of war."[36]

Davis further added the threat of wider retributions should General Orders No. 11 not be rescinded. As he advised Lee, "For the present, we renounce our right of retaliation on the innocent ... but if after notice [has been given] to the Government at Washington of our confining repressive measures to the punishment only of commissioned officers who are willing participants in these crimes these savage practices are continued, we shall reluctantly be forced to the last resort of accepting the war on the terms chosen by our foes until the outraged voice of a common humanity forces a respect for the recognized rules of war." Exchanges under the cartel would nonetheless proceed, Davis wrote, for although Pope's order "would justify our refusal to execute the generous cartel ... a sacred regard to plighted faith ... prevents our resort to this extremity." Implicit in this declaration that exchanges would continue was the clear warning that they could just as easily be terminated.[37]

The ink on Davis's letter to Lee had scarcely dried when a third incident arose that threatened the existence of the cartel. On instructions from Randolph, Lee had written General George McClellan on 6 July to demand an explanation of the execution of William Mumford, a citizen of New Orleans who had been hanged on the orders of Union general Benjamin F. Butler for hauling down the U.S. flag that flew over the government mint in that city. Also in Lee's letter was a demand for information concerning the Federal execution of Colonel John L. Owen, an officer in the Missouri State Guard who, according to Confederate accounts, had been charged with bridge burning and executed without trial. McClellan, professing ignorance of these acts, had sent the letter on to Stanton, but the secretary had declined to reply. On 1 August, Davis therefore ordered Lee again to demand a reply from McClellan about Mumford and Owen, and also to ask whether the actions of Generals David Hunter and John W. Phelps, two Federal officers accused of inciting slaves to murder their masters, and Colonel Graham N. Fitch, charged by Confederates with the murder of two civilians, were sanctioned by the Lincoln administration. Davis knew that Lee's first request for information had gone unanswered, so he directed Lee to inform McClellan that if no reply was received within fifteen days, the Confederate government would "assume that the alleged facts are true and are sanctioned by the Government of the United States," and that Davis would order retaliation as deemed appropriate.[38]

On 9 August, Henry Halleck, now general in chief of the U.S. army, did respond to Lee's inquiry; but Halleck's missive was anything but the answers Davis sought. Halleck wrote that he found Lee's letters to be "couched in language exceedingly insulting to the Government of the United States," declined to receive them, and returned them to Lee without supplying the explanations demanded. Upon hearing of Halleck's action, Governor Letcher renewed his bid to increase his state's degree of control over northern prisoners by requesting that officers in Pope's command who were captured in Virginia be remanded to that state's courts for trial. Other Confederate solons called for more draconian responses to what they perceived as Yankee depredations. Tennessee senator Gustavus Henry asserted that the South should "neither ask nor receive quarter from this day henceforward," and Senator James Phelan of Mississippi agreed, declaring that he had always "been in favor of fighting this contest under the Black Flag."[39]

Davis remained steadfast in his determination to retain national direction of the Confederate prisoner-of-war system, but in an address on 18 August, he advised the Confederate Congress that the time for retaliation had come. Hunter and Phelps, he told the congressmen, were "engaged unchecked by their Government in exciting servile insurrection," and Butler was possessed of "instincts so brutal as to invite the violence of his soldiery against the women of a captured city." Protests from the Confederate government had "failed to evoke from the authorities of the United States one mark of disapprobation," and this Federal refusal to discipline its commanders in the field left the South with only one course of action. "Deeply as we may regret the character of the contest into which we are about to be forced," Davis asserted, "stern and exemplary punishment can and must be meted out to the murderers and felons who disgracing the profession of arms seek to make of public war the occasion for the commission of the most monstrous crimes."[40]

The Confederate Congress agreed. On 20 August the War Department issued General Orders No. 59, which directed that if captured, Fitch was to be confined as a felon rather than a prisoner of war. Officers under his command who fell into Confederate hands were to be "set apart by lot" and executed in numbers equal to the number of "peaceable citizens" Fitch was alleged to have ordered to be executed. One day later, this edict was followed by the publication of General Orders No. 60, which stipulated that Hunter and Phelps were to be "no longer treated as public enemies of the Confederate States, but as outlaws." If either of the generals or any of their officers "employed in drilling, organizing, or instructing slaves with a view to their armed service in this war" were captured, they were to be treated not as prisoners of war, but to be "held in close confinement for execution as a felon, at such time and place as the President shall order."[41]

Although edicts such as General Orders Nos. 59 and 60 were certainly a threat to the long-term survival of the cartel, they did not call its basic provisions into dispute. After only a few weeks of exchanges, however, Union and Confederate leaders were presented with a question not specifically addressed in the cartel. What classes of prisoners qualified for exchange, and what classes remained outside the provisions of the cartel and could therefore be retained indefinitely in confinement? One class of captives that sparked this debate was the former members of the Missouri State Guard. On 27 July 1862 M. Jefferson Thompson, a brigadier general in the Missouri State Guard, wrote Secretary Randolph to complain that Union prisons at Alton, Chicago, and St. Louis held "a number of persons" who had once been assigned to the Missouri Guard but had been discharged following the expiration of their term of enlistment. These men, Thompson protested, were "nevertheless taken by the enemy in Missouri because it was known that they were Southrons and would probably re-enlist in the C. S. Army." The Federals were now refusing to classify them as prisoners of war and thus subject to exchange. Also held in these prisons were officers who had been captured while recruiting soldiers for southern service, even though they themselves had not yet been mustered into the Confederate States Army. These "gentlemen" were being held not as Missouri guardsmen but as regular Confederate officers, Thompson insisted. He warned that unless the War Department moved quickly to amend their status, "the enemy will require regular officers in exchange."[42]

Questions of classification also arose in the North. On 29 July, Stanton wrote Adjutant General Thomas to "direct [his] attention specially" to securing the release of a number of civilian "telegraph operators" and "hospital assistants and private persons who were in attendance upon the sick" when captured. These noncombatants should "not be held as prisoners," Stanton declared. Equally important to the hard-nosed secretary, they should not figure in exchange calculations. An additional class of prisoners Stanton directed Thomas to exclude from exchange was those Confederate prisoners "who decline to be exchanged." As long as there were "enough of the others to be exchanged for all our troops held as prisoners," the secretary allowed, southerners who wished to remain in the North should be allowed to do so.[43]

The number of categories of southern prisoners to be exempted from exchange was further increased when Union secretary of the navy Gideon Welles called Stanton's attention to the fact that northern prisons held "many pilots and seamen who were captured on board vessels seized for violating the blockade." It was "through the experience and skill of these men that vessels succeed in running into and out of the blockaded ports," Welles maintained, and it was therefore "of great importance that they should not be released and again engage in their profession." To prevent this, he urged that none of them be released without the express approval of the Navy Department.[44] The final group of Rebels to be denied exchange was a collection of Johnson's Island prisoners who had been accused of being "bushwackers and guerrillas" rather than regular soldiers. As exchanges emptied the depot during the summer of 1862, these men retained in confinement.[45]

Ould became increasingly alarmed by the growing number of categories of southern prisoners being excluded from exchange, and on 5 October he wrote Lieutenant Colonel William H. Ludlow, the acting agent for exchange (in reality, the Union's primary agent), to demand a meeting to resolve in person "difficulties" that he contended were too numerous to resolve by correspondence. Among the problems enumerated by Ould were the confinement of the Missourians and the crews of blockade runners, the designation of Confederate "partisan rangers" as guerrillas not liable for exchange, and Ben Butler's illegal practice of continuing to confine prisoners in New Orleans after they had been lawfully exchanged.[46] Ludlow passed Ould's letter to Thomas, and in a surprising act of conciliation the Federal general suggested to Stanton that he be allowed to reply positively to most of the southern agent's protests. Specifically, Thomas proposed that although the arrest of Missourians should stand because the state had never seceded, the guardsmen and partisan rangers should henceforth be treated as prisoners of war and that Butler should be ordered to release the prisoners held in New Orleans. Stanton refused to allow Thomas to send this response, but Ould was notified through other channels that the corrective actions it proposed would be implemented.[47]

Even as Thomas was composing his reply to Ould , the Lincoln government was attempting to resolve the greatest challenge it faced during the entire period of the cartel. This challenge, ironically, arose not from problems associated with confining enemy captives, but from the difficulties attendant in managing the thousands of Union troops paroled under the cartel. Unless otherwise instructed, Confederate officers routinely paroled all Union prisoners immediately upon the conclusion of a battle. While this course of action quickly freed Union captives and relieved the Confederacy of the burden of confining thousands of enemy soldiers, it presented northern leaders with the thorny problem of maintaining the parolees until they were officially exchanged and could return to full military duties. During the first year of the war the Union had solved this problem by furloughing parolees until they were exchanged or granting discharges to soldiers who wished to terminate their military service. When it became obvious that the cartel would be adopted, however, Federal planners correctly surmised that the trickle of parolees returning to the North would soon become a flood and that discharging so many men would constitute an unacceptable drain on Federal manpower. Accordingly, Union planners scrambled to devise a method of retaining the men on active duty until exchange permitted their return to the ranks. On 28 June the War Department published General Orders No. 72, which contained new instructions for the disposition of Federal parolees. Although completely unforeseen at the time, the method of parolee management specified in this document would have an enormous impact in shaping the future of the Union prisoner-of-war system.

General Orders No. 72 rescinded the provisions of the existing regulations that had authorized furloughs for all paroled prisoners and discharges for those who no longer wished to serve in the military. Under the new orders, soldiers on parole were no longer to be granted furloughs. Soldiers currently on parole or who might be paroled in the future were directed to "immediately repair" to "Camps of Instruction" established at various locations throughout the North. Men belonging to regiments raised in "New England and the Middle States" were to report to a newly established facility near Annapolis, Maryland, which bore the appropriate if unimaginative name of Camp Parole. Soldiers belonging to regiments from Virginia, Tennessee, Kentucky, Ohio, Indiana, and Michigan were to repair to Camp Chase at Columbus, Ohio, while men from regiments raised in Illinois, Wisconsin, Minnesota, Iowa, and Missouri were to report to Benton Barracks, a former recruit training depot near St. Louis. Upon their arrival in the camps, the soldiers would be assigned duties "compatible with their parole as may be assigned to them by the officers in command." Camp commanders were to organize the men into companies and battalions, taking care to keep "those of the same regiment and of the same State as much together as possible." Anticipating that some of the affected soldiers might be somewhat less than eager to abide by these new instructions, General Orders No. 72 also included enforcement and punitive provisos. Mustering and recruiting officers at stations across the North were admonished to "use their utmost exertions" to ensure that the order was "faithfully carried out," and governors were "respectfully solicited to lend their efforts to the same end." Any officer or enlisted parolee who failed to comply as directed "within the space of time necessary for them to do so" would be "accounted deserters and dealt with accordingly."[48]

Most parolees did comply. By the thousands they dutifully terminated their furloughs and reported to the camps of instruction as directed. But they quickly found that outside of publishing General Orders No. 72, their government had done little to prepare for the implementation of this new system of parolee management. The experience of parolees from Iowa who reported to Benton Barracks was typical. Considerable numbers of soldiers from the Eighth and Twelfth Iowa Regiments had been cut off and captured in the battle of Shiloh; following a short period of imprisonment at camps in Tuscaloosa and Macon, they were paroled. On returning to friendly lines, they were assured that they would receive all their back pay and be discharged from the service, but these proved to be empty promises. In fact, the men received no back pay, and on 9 July 1862 they were informed that instead of being granted furloughs and discharges, they had been ordered to report to Benton Barracks.

Upon their arrival in St. Louis, the Iowans discovered that the barracks' staff had made virtually no preparations to receive them. There was no equipment for cooking rations; nor were there eating utensils, and the men were forced to make do with the single tin cup and plate they had been issued in the Rebel prison in Tuscaloosa. The level of subsistence, as one soldier recalled, was "not much over half-rations, and these of the poorest quality, having sour bread and rotten meat." Another Iowan remembered that while those who had experienced the horrors of southern prisons sincerely considered the acceptance of parole to be an honorable alternative to dying "in filth" without "a morsel of bread to fill our stomachs," the camp staff considered them cowards. And as none of the regiments' officers had accompanied them to Benton Barracks, the men had no one to speak in their behalf. "We have been treated little better since our release," a third soldier wrote in summary, "than we were while in the South."[49]

The parolees' most common complaint was that they were being assigned duties that violated the terms of their parole. Each of them had signed an oath pledging on their "most sacred honor" that "during the existing war between the Confederate States and the United States of America" they would not "bear arms or aid or abet the enemy of said Confederate States or their friends directly or indirectly in any form whatever until exchanged or released." Soon after their arrival at Benton Barracks, however, they were ordered to relieve a Missouri regiment that was then guarding the camp.[50] This the Iowans refused to do. As one of their number wrote in a letter of appeal to Iowa governor Samuel J. Kirkwood, "Necessity compels us to state to you that we have orders . . . to be fully armed and equipped so that we can relieve the Twenty-third Missouri, now on duty . . . and there is not a man who has signed [a parole] but would prefer to return to their southern prisons before perjury." The Iowans were jailed in wholesale numbers for refusing to stand guard, but they remained resolute. "Already forty of us are in the guard-house," Kirkwood was informed by another of his constituents, "and the rest are ready to go at a moment's notice. No telling of the consequences."[51]

In an attempt to influence those consequences, parolees of the Twelfth Iowa appealed to N. B. Baker, Iowa's adjutant general, "to see into this affair and see what shall be done." In response, Baker dispatched a curt inquiry directly to Stanton.[52] "Will not Iowa soldiers of the Eighth, Twelfth, Fourteenth and Sixteenth Iowa sent home on parole be furloughed until exchanged?" he angrily demanded. "Who has a right to detail them for further service? Was not the detail for relief of the Twenty-third Missouri a violation of their parole?"[53] Stanton passed Baker's letter to Halleck with a request that the general draw upon his considerable knowledge of international law and tender a ruling on whether requiring parolees to stand guard constituted a violation of their paroles. Halleck, always adept at crafting legal opinions that supported existing government policies, did so. In brevity and directness, his answer of 19 July rivaled Baker's inquiry to Stanton. "Paroled prisoners are obliged to do guard, police and fatigue duty for the proper order of their own corps," he wrote. "Those who refuse are mutineers."[54]

Halleck's blunt answer quieted protests for a time, but Baker was not to be put off. Writing to Stanton two days after Halleck's ruling, he restated his objection to Iowa parolees being forced to do "anything which might by implication or indirection make them violate that parole," and he repeated his request that Stanton "not allow punishment to brave and gallant men who have done their duty."[55] The secretary of war at last acquiesced, and on 26 July he ordered the practice of assigning parolees as guards at Benton Barracks be terminated.[56]

The general orders defining the scope of Hoffman's authority as commissary general of prisoners had required that "all matters in relation to prisoners will pass through him," and Old Huffy, interpreted this mandate to include not only Confederate captives but the Union parolees who were now reporting to the camps of instruction.[57] Accordingly, Hoffman became as involved in the operation of the camps of instruction as he was in the direction of camps that held enemy prisoners. He quickly learned that discharging this additional responsibility would be no less challenging.

While conditions at Benton Barracks were every bit as bad as parolees claimed, Hoffman found that the situation at Camp Parole in Annapolis was even worse. Because the camp had been hastily established, there were insufficient barracks to house parolees. When the barracks were filled, soldiers were billeted in tents, and when the supply of tents was exhausted, the men threw up hovels of whatever materials they could scrounge. Private S. C. Sears wrote home that he and two comrades were able to find shelter in a "shanty of wood," and he counted himself lucky. This haphazard scramble for housing sufficed during the summer months, but with the onset of the cold and damp Chesapeake winter, the men began to suffer terribly. Their misery was compounded because camp authorities had also failed to issue adequate clothing. When protests to Federal officials yielded no improvement in camp conditions, Wisconsin parolees appealed directly to Governor Edward Salomon for relief. Salomon in turn demanded an explanation from the War Department. In a letter to Stanton on 20 October, the governor charged that men from his state confined at Camp Parole had been "two weeks without tents or shelter, on small rations, without cooking utensils and unprovided with clothing," and that "the sick in particular [were] being ill-provided for." Stanton ordered Hoffman personally to investigate the "alleged ill-treatment of paroled soldiers from Wisconsin," and Hoffman's ensuing report to the War Department indicated not only that the complaints of the parolees were fully justified, but that the conditions under which they were being held would not soon improve.[58] He conceded that there had been "a good deal of exposure and suffering among the paroled troops at Camp Parole," but this had been "unavoidable" due to "large numbers [of prisoners] being sent there before adequate provision had been made for them." As to the adequacy of government efforts to alleviate the suffering, Hoffman could offer only the weak assurance that "all the troops now there are as well provided for as they can be in tents, and with few exceptions they are suitably clothed."[59]

In truth, Hoffman had found conditions at Camp Parole much worse than the War Department dared tell Governor Salomon. The care of the sick was entirely inadequate; Hoffman was so dismayed by what he saw that he sent a lengthy list of deficiencies to the medical director of the military department in which the camp was located. The camp's hospital contained an insufficient number of stoves to provide adequate warmth, and "save putting the sick on cots in tents," he could ascertain "little that was done to alleviate the many privations which sick men in the camp are exposed to." The camp surgeon failed to "appreciate the importance of not only prescribing for the sick, but also as far as in his power of providing for the many wants which must be met to diminish their sufferings and insure a speedy recovery," and records charting the treatment of ill soldiers were incomplete and poorly maintained.[60]

Nor were deficiencies in housing and medical care the only problems Hoffman discovered at Camp Parole. Discipline in the camp had never been exemplary, but by November 1862 crime was so widespread that one disgusted parolee appealed directly to Stanton to take steps to end the lawlessness. "Drunkenness, fighting, burglary, robbery, gambling, &c., are witnessed by us daily, and even murder is not of unfrequent occurrence," the petitioner recounted. Violence had become so prevalent that "a person is not safe to step out to meeting or anywhere else after dark." He begged the secretary to act swiftly to put down the "reign of rowdyism" that threatened law-abiding soldiers.[61]

On being notified of this rampant lawlessness by Stanton, Hoffman telegraphed Lieutenant Colonel George Sangster, the commander of Camp Parole, demanding an explanation of why discipline had been allowed to slip so far. Old Huffy's message also contained specific punitive actions to restore discipline to the camp. "Require [the parolees] to be drilled twice a day," Hoffman ordered, "and see that all officers attend the drills." Soldiers would pay a high price for past offenses, he insisted. He also directed Sangster to "permit no exchanged officer or soldier to leave the camp unless by orders through me or from higher authority."[62]

Union parolees sent to Camp Chase found conditions there every bit as grim as those experienced by their comrades at Benton Barracks and Camp Parole. Because Confederate prisoners awaiting exchange were still being confined in the camp's barracks, arriving parolees were housed in tents, and this deplorable situation took a decided turn for the worse when the camp's supply of tents was exhausted. The camp commander was instructed by the War Department to "cause temporary sheds to be erected," but until these makeshift barracks could be built, parolees without tents had no choice but to sleep in the open.[63]

Nor was the lack of housing the only problem at Camp Chase. Many of the soldiers had not been paid in over a year, and although they had been promised that they would receive both the back pay and allowances due them upon their arrival at the camp, neither was forthcoming. By September the men had become, in the words of one of the garrison's officers, "clamorous and mutinous for pay." Following a visit to the facility, Ohio governor David Tod heartily concurred in this ominous assessment. "It will be impossible to bring them to any kind of order or discipline until they are paid," the governor wired Stanton.[64] But when camp officials requested immediate disbursement of the money owed the parolees, they were informed that the government of the United States had no currency to issue. "It has been impossible for the Treasury to furnish funds to meet the heavy payments recently required," Assistant Paymaster General C. H. Fry replied; the regional paymaster in Columbus, Ohio, was "out of funds."[65] As a result, there would be no pay for the men interned at Camp Chase.

Morale among the parolees at the camp sank lower still when they learned that they had been selected to test a War Department scheme concocted to remedy a serious problem that had arisen since the ratification of the cartel. Shortly after the agreement had gone into effect, Union officers discovered that considerable numbers of soldiers, believing that falling into enemy hands would lead to a speedy parole and discharge from the service, were intentionally straggling from their units or otherwise placing themselves in circumstances that ensured they would be captured. As General Don Carlos Buell complained in August, the system of paroles established by the cartel had "run into intolerable abuse" from soldiers seeking capture and a trip home.[66]

With the cessation of discharges and furloughs for paroled soldiers, parole camp commanders soon were confirming the fact that many of the men in their camps had allowed themselves to be captured to escape the dangers and rigors of service. "I find by inquiry that there are not 500 men here that know what army corps they belong to," the commander of Camp Parole wrote to Hoffman. "If the men of my camp were a sample of our Army we would have nothing but a mob of stragglers and cowards. I am convinced more and more every day that three-fourths of paroled men are stragglers and cowards."[67]

Others in positions of authority in the North shared these sentiments. Following the wholesale surrender and immediate parole of over four thousand Yankees in the battles of Richmond and Mumfordsville, Kentucky, Governor Tod was moved to share his convictions with Stanton. On 9 September 1862, he telegraphed the secretary, "The freedom in giving paroles by our troops in Kentucky is very prejudicial to the service and should be stopped. Had our forces at Richmond, Ky., refused to give their parole it would have taken all of Kirby Smith's army to guard them." Stanton had obviously given much thought to this problem before receiving the governor's letter, for he immediately responded that he agreed with Tod's assessment. "The evil you mention," he replied, "is one of the most dangerous that has appeared in our army and it is difficult to see what remedy can be applied. There is reason to fear that many voluntarily surrender for the sake of getting home." To curb the practice, Stanton added in closing, he had "sent 1,500 to Camp Chase," under orders that they be "kept in close quarters and drilled diligently every day, with no leave of absence."[68]

Although Tod concurred with Stanton's decision to make an example of shirkers, the addition of this vexatious lot to the hundreds of surly parolees already confined in his state was not at all what he had in mind. Preserving order over such a mixed mob at Camp Chase would pose a "great difficulty," he advised Stanton. Instead, Tod proposed a punishment that would, not incidentally, ensure that the troublesome parolees were sent far from Ohio. Sioux Indians were again wreaking havoc on the Minnesota frontier, and "if the Indian troubles . . . are serious and the paroled Union prisoners are not soon to be exchanged," Tod asked, "would it not be well to send them to Minnesota?" Stanton was taken with the idea on the spot. In the final telegram between the two that busy day, he wired Tod that "your suggestion as to the paroled prisoners being sent to the Indian borders is excellent and will be immediately acted upon."[69]

"Immediately" turned out to be not fast enough. Before Stanton could complete the arrangements for sending any of the soldiers west to fight the Sioux, the situation at Camp Chase became very bad indeed. On 16 September Tod frantically telegraphed the War Department that the number of parolees confined in the camp had swollen to over four thousand men, all of whom the governor assessed as being in "a very demoralized state for want of organization." He urged Stanton quickly to send an officer who could take charge and move the soldiers out of the camp and on to Minnesota, and on the following day Stanton responded by assigning this difficult mission to Major General Lew Wallace.[70]

Wallace was a veteran of the Mexican War, and as a regimental and division commander he had acquitted himself well in combat at Fort Donelson and Shiloh. None of his past experience, however, could have prepared him for the absolute bedlam he found at Camp Chase. On his first day of duty at the camp he wired Stanton to suspend all further shipments of prisoners, for he had quickly ascertained that it was "impossible to do anything with those now in Camp Chase." The parolees, he wrote, "generally refuse to be organized or do any duty whatever, and every detachment that arrives only swells a mob already dangerous." Not surprisingly, Wallace discovered that "the Eastern troops are particularly disinclined to the Indian service," and he pleaded with the secretary to allow him "time to do something with those now on hand before the task thickens."[71]

Meanwhile, Lincoln had judged that the stakes were high enough to require his involvement in prisoner affairs, and he enthusiastically supported sending the parolees to Minnesota. On 20 September he directed Stanton to send the parolees west "with all possible dispatch." The internees at Camp Parole alone, Lincoln wired the secretary, required "four good unparoled regiments to guard," and his solution to this unacceptable drain on Federal manpower was simple. "Arm them and send them away just as fast as the Railroads will carry them," he directed, because "each regiment arriving on the frontier will relieve a new regiment to come forward."[72]

Lincoln's wishes notwithstanding, Wallace continued to beg that no more parolees be sent to Camp Chase. In a follow-up telegram to Adjutant General Thomas on 28 September, he provided a detailed description of just how volatile the situation at the installation had become. "There had never been such a thing as enforcement of order amongst them," he wrote of the parolees at Camp Chase, and

> with but few exceptions officers abandoned the men and left them to shift for themselves. The consequences can be easily imagined. The soldiers become lousy, ragged, despairing and totally demoralized. In addition to that it seems each man became possessed with an idea that because he was paroled he was until exchanged exempt from duty of any kind, even from the most ordinary camp duty. A large number in fact hold paroles which they have sworn to, obligating them not to go into camp or take arms for any purpose in behalf of the United States, and not merely as against the Confederate States but as against any power or authority. When I announced my purpose in camp that I was to organize them for service against the Northwestern Indians a

very few received it with favor. Nearly the whole body protested. Especially was this the case with the Eastern troops. Every objector intrenched himself behind his parole. If I had had a reliable regiment at hand to enforce my orders a guard would have been instantly thrown around the camp and every protestant arrested. My authority should have been recognized at all hazards. But no such regiment was present. Force was out of question. I endeavored to reason with the men, but when my back was turned they jeered and groaned at me. I promised them their pay and a complete uniform without charge. They would believe nothing I said. The motive of all this was easily understood, viz., a disinclination to longer service.[73]

Many of the parolees who had been sent to the camp had already deserted, Wallace noted, and he was able to coerce a portion of the remaining men into companies only by threatening to withhold their back pay and new clothing to replace their tattered and filthy uniforms. Those who cooperated he moved to another part of the camp in order to separate them from the "mutinous soldiery" who were refusing all orders, but he candidly added that even parolees who had consented to be reorganized would be of little future use to the Union, for the great majority of them had promptly deserted as soon as they were paid. The few who remained, Wallace argued, should be given a dishonorable discharge and sent home.[74]

Stanton hardly had time to digest the contents of Wallace's alarming assessment when a more serious challenge to the Union policy for managing paroled soldiers arose from another quarter—the governors of the states in which the parolees had been recruited, who had never been fond of General Orders No. 72. From the time the directive had gone into effect, letters from parolees complaining of the shabby treatment they were receiving had poured into statehouses across the North. Governor Kirkwood of Iowa had responded to such protests almost immediately, writing Lincoln to request that all parolees from Iowa be removed from Benton Barracks and retained instead at the recruit depot in Davenport. As soon as Stanton's intention to dispatch parolees to Minnesota became known, the governor's request was quickly echoed by the chief executives of other states.[75] On 2 October, Governor James F. Robinson of Kentucky called Stanton's attention to reports of "the greatest disorder" at Camp Chase; to save the Kentuckians confined there from "demoralization," he asked that they be relocated to camps in Louisville. Robinson's letter was followed only two days later by a telegram from Governor Israel Washburn of Maine requesting that parolees from his state be released from Camp Chase and allowed to return home until exchanged. On 14 October, Governor A. G. Curtain of Pennsylvania forwarded to Stanton a petition in which soldiers from his state chronicled the "unjust treatment" they were enduring at Camp Parole. Conditions at the camp were so bad, Curtain fumed, that "many of [the parolees] would prefer to be returned to Richmond," and he "earnestly" asked that "the people of this State now at Annapolis be brought within our borders." One week later Governor Oliver P. Morton of Indiana requested that the secretary transfer all Hoosiers to Camp Morton near Indianapolis. Wisconsin's governor, Edward Salomon, had been largely silent since his angry note recounting conditions at Camp Parole back in October, but upon learning that other governors were trying to have their parolees transferred to installations nearer home, he again took up his pen to demand that Stanton afford "the same privilege" to soldiers from his state.[76]

The Union's plan for handling paroled soldiers had clearly been a disaster, but Stanton stubbornly refused all requests to transfer parolees to camps in their home states. To accede to such demands, he contended, would "operate as an inducement to shameful surrender"; to safeguard the strength of the Union army, parolees must remain interned in camps of instruction until exchanged.[77] Nor did Stanton heed the governors' protests against sending the recalcitrants against the Sioux, and the parolees surely would have been dispatched to the Minnesota frontier had not General Pope succeeded in quashing the uprising before the plan could be implemented. But by the time Stanton was notified of Pope's victory, he had already set in motion the events that would precipitate the greatest of all the calamities associated with Union parolee management.

On 15 September 1862 the Union suffered one of its most humiliating defeats of the Civil War when the entire garrison at Harper's Ferry, Virginia, surrendered after only token resistance during the early stages of the Lee's Antietam campaign. On that single day Stonewall Jackson's corps bagged 12,520 Yankees. The fast-moving Confederates paroled their prisoners on the spot, but as soon as the parolees reentered Union lines, ten thousand of them were unceremoniously rounded up and sent off to Annapolis for disposition. The fact that these enlisted soldiers had played no part in their officers' decision to surrender the post mattered not at all to Stanton; having determined that they belonged in the category of soldiers meriting punishment for capitulating too easily, he sent General Thomas to Camp Parole to organize them and pack them off to Minnesota to battle the Sioux.[78]

When Thomas arrived at Camp Parole, he found it teeming with just over twelve thousand parolees. After disbanding one regiment whose period of enlistment had expired, he combined the remaining eight thousand Harper's Ferry parolees with four thousand who were already in the camp and initiated the process for packing them all off to Saint Paul. Under normal circumstances Thomas would have sent the men to Camp Chase, where they would have been organized into regiments, issued arms and equipment, and then shipped on to Minnesota. In this case, however, the general made the fateful decision that Columbus was "out of the direct route," and he telegraphed Stanton that he was sending the men to Camp Douglas at Chicago instead. In a masterful understatement, Thomas added that assignment to Indian fighting duties in Minnesota had come as a "bitterly distasteful" surprise to the parolees, for their Confederate captors had assured them that they would be immediately discharged when they returned to the North. One regiment from Ohio, he noted, had pointedly informed him that while they would be pleased to accept the government's offer of transportation as far as their home state, they would be "departing" the train as soon as they entered Ohio and returning to their homes. Thomas had no doubt that the men were quite serious, and he warned Stanton to expect much straggling and many desertions before the group reached Chicago.[79]

The men traveled west under the command of General Daniel Tyler, a no-nonsense sixty-four-year-old veteran who relished the opportunity to whip the disgruntled parolees into shape. The Harper's Ferry soldiers, Tyler informed Thomas, were "perfectly disorganized," for all of their field grade officers had been recalled to Washington, leaving only junior officers to accompany them to Minnesota. Nor did the accommodations the government provided for the trip west—freight cars without either water or toilets—do anything to improve the parolees' attitudes. When they finally arrived at Camp Douglas on 28 September, the men found that the barracks were completely occupied by eight thousand recruits training at the post; as a result, they were billeted in a block of stables adjacent to the camp. "The floors of the apartments," wrote one lieutenant who managed to retain his sense of humor, "were laid in mud, and the roofing perforated so as not to exclude the refreshing rain."[80]

By this juncture the parolees were absolutely spoiling for a fight with their keepers, and on 30 September the first of many clashes flared when a Vermont regiment refused to obey Tyler's orders to perform guard duty. Tyler was not a man who took insubordination lightly, and he promptly called in a loyal regiment from outside the camp to enforce his orders at the point of a bayonet. The Vermonters relented, and an uneasy quiet settled over the installation until 5 October, when, in an extraordinary example of either poor timing or deliberate mischief-making, the editors of the *Chicago Tribune* chose to devote a portion of that day's paper to the publication of the terms of the Dix–Hill cartel. This was the first time most of the parolees had actually been able to examine the document in full, and after reading it they decided that its terms obviously exempted them from guard duty and drill, let alone from being dispatched on campaigns against rampaging Indians. Tyler privately agreed with this interpretation; he confided to Thomas that "under the last clause of article 6 the parole forbids performance of 'field, garrison, police, guard or constabulary duties.' If we comply with this paragraph, it appears to me it leaves little else for us to do with the men but feed and clothe them and let them do as they please." But cartel or no, Tyler was determined to bring the men to heel, and when they again refused guard duty, he responded by canceling furloughs and increasing the parolees' daily regimen of drill, camp policing, and inspections.[81]

This was much akin to putting a match to dynamite, and Camp Douglas exploded. For a full three weeks the installation was consumed by a full-blown insurrection, during which parolees—often led by their officers—burned barracks and fences, demolished the hated guardhouse, and stoned garrison troops who attempted to bring them under control. Damage to the camp and adjoining structures was estimated at over $15,500, and the level of violence and destruction was so great that Chicagoans feared, as one resident recorded, "that a volcano existed at the camp which might at any time break forth and overwhelm the city." The riot was not quelled until 23 October, when Tyler brought in regular army troops with orders to shoot to kill any soldiers who refused to comply with camp regulations. When the rioters refused to desist, the regulars opened fire, killing two parolees.[82] Tyler's lethal response quickly restored order, and for the next month he ruled the facility with an iron hand. Still, officials in Washington feared a recurrence of the mayhem, and as soon as it became obvious that the men would not be needed in Minnesota, the War Department moved with all speed to remove them from Camp Douglas. By the end of November, almost all of the parolees had either been discharged or exchanged and dispatched to rejoin regiments at the front.[83]

Meanwhile, debate continued to swirl around the question of exactly what duties the parolees who remained in camps of instruction could be assigned. Ultimately, it fell to Hoffman to resolve this problem, and his solution was nothing if not ingenious. Hoffman reasoned that while it was true that the cartel seemed to preclude military service of all types, it was not the individual soldier but his government who had given the parole. It therefore followed that the government, rather than the individual, should set the limits on the assignments a parolee could lawfully accept. Hoffman acknowledged that parolees from volunteer regiments would never accept this line of reasoning, but he had a solution to this problem as well. Conceding that such men were "almost beyond the reach of rules and articles of war," he recommended that the "most economical course" for dealing with them was to muster them out of service until they were exchanged. Discharge would terminate their status as parolees, but the government would then be free to recall them into the army, where they could lawfully assume full military duties just as if they were new recruits. Although clearly a violation of the spirit if not the letter of the cartel, Hoffman's solution was speedily adopted by the War Department.[84]

As the North was attempting to resolve the problem of how to manage its parolees, the South was awaiting a response to Robert Ould's questions concerning the continuing confinement of the Missouri home guards, the crews of blockade runners, Confederate partisan rangers, and the prisoners held by Butler in New Orleans. On 10 November, Jefferson Davis's patience ran out. The president directed Judah P. Benjamin, then secretary of state, to have Secretary of War George Randolph demand the immediate exchange of the partisan rangers and other Confederate prisoners who had been paroled but were still being held in New Orleans. Randolph ordered Ould to "present these facts to the enemy's agent," along with yet another demand for an explanation of Butler's execution of Mumford. To ensure this query would not also be ignored, Randolph further directed Ould to warn William Ludlow that unless a satisfactory answer was received in fifteen days, "all commissioned officers in our hands will be retained."[85]

Ould passed Davis's ultimatum to Ludlow, and on 3 December the Union agent replied that "orders had been issued . . . to send all the prisoners in the West belonging to irregular organizations to Vicksburg for exchange," and that the same orders would apply to the prisoners held by Butler.[86] Once again, however, no explanation of Mumford's execution was offered. So when the fifteen days allotted for a satisfactory reply had expired, Davis acted. On Christmas Eve 1862, the Confederate president issued a proclamation that would ultimately prove to be yet another nail in the coffin of the cartel. It opened with a detailed recounting of the South's four unsuccessful attempts to secure information about Mumford's execution, declaring, "The silence of the government of the United States . . . affords evidence only too conclusive that the said government sanctions the conduct of said Butler, and is determined that he shall remain unpunished for his crimes." Davis then pronounced Butler "a felon, deserving of capital punishment," and he ordered that the officer in command of any detachment fortunate enough to capture the Union general was to "cause him to be immediately executed by hanging." In addition to this death sentence for the Beast, Davis decreed that all officers serving under Butler's command were, if captured, to be "reserved for execution" and that "no commissioned officer of the United States taken captive shall be released on parole before exchange until the said Butler shall have met with due punishment for his crimes."[87] Davis's proclamation clearly constituted a direct violation of the terms of the cartel signed by the Confederate government only five months earlier, but southern support for the decree was overwhelming. Echoing public sentiment, the *Richmond Dispatch* found that the president's proclamation against Butler "comes up to the full measure of the public expectations," and its editors asserted that "the black flag is the only answer to the unheard of crimes of these enemies of the human race."[88]

The stunning news that the same Confederate government that had repeatedly insisted that the war be conducted according to the "usages of civilization" was now ordering the summary executions and the indefinite retention of Union officers clearly placed the future of the cartel in jeopardy. Most damaging to the exchange agreement was the proclamation's final paragraph. "All negro slaves captured in arms," Davis decreed, were to be "at once delivered over to the executive authorities of the respective states where they belong, to be dealt with according to the laws of said states."[89]

On first reading, this provision for the disposition of "slaves captured in arms" seems to be an incongruous attachment to a proclamation detailing the retaliation to be visited upon offending Union officers, but in truth it addressed a question that had been troubling white southerners since the Union first made known its intention to employ blacks as combat soldiers. On 17 September 1862 the Confederate House of Representatives had requested that Davis provide information on "what disposition is made of negroes captured by the Army and whether any general orders have been issued to facilitate their restoration to their owners." Secretary of War Randolph had answered that his department had "not been informed of the capture of any slaves," and while the secretary's reply temporarily assuaged the legislators' concerns, the announcement of Lincoln's preliminary emancipation proclamation on 21 September 1862 prompted the resurgence of fears that armed ex-slaves in blue might soon be loosed against the Confederacy.[90] Thousands of ex-slaves were already seeing combat in regiments of the U.S. Colored Troops, and Confederate leaders determined that at the first opportunity they would take action to dissuade additional slaves from running away and volunteering for such service.

That opportunity came on 14 November 1862, when Brigadier General Hugh W. Mercer, commander of the Department of South Carolina, reported that "six negroes in Federal uniforms with arms (muskets) in their hands" had been "encountered" during operations on Saint Catherine's Island. Two of the black soldiers were killed in the encounter. Among the four taken prisoner was "a boy named Manuel" who had been turned over to Charleston "negro brokers" for sale. Believing that "these negroes must be made an example of," Mercer had reclaimed the boy. As he maintained to his superior, General P. G. T. Beauregard, soldiers like Manuel were in fact no more than "slaves taken with arms in hand against their masters and wearing the abolition uniform." Upon such captives, Mercer insisted, "some swift and terrible punishment should be inflicted that their fellows may be deterred from following their example." Beauregard appealed to the War Department for "guidance in such cases," and James A. Seddon, Randolph's successor as secretary of war, forwarded the report to Davis with a recommendation that "the negro be executed as an example."[91]

After conferring with Davis, Seddon informed Beauregard that the president agreed that "summary execution must be inflicted on those [ex-slaves] taken," but by the time Davis issued his proclamation of 24 December, he had elected not to follow his secretary of war's recommendation.[92] Although unwilling to issue a national directive ordering such executions, Davis agreed that something had to be done to stem the flow of ex-slaves into Colored Volunteer regiments, especially because this phenomenon was sure to become more widespread if Lincoln made good on his threat to issue a preliminary emancipation proclamation in November. This was why he appended to his proclamation against Butler the provision remanding all ex-slaves captured in arms to their states of origin to be disposed of as those states saw fit.

With his proclamation, Davis was implementing a strategy that had served the South well in the past—the threat of retaliation. Threats of retaliation against northern prisoners had won the release of the privateer crews and had wrested agreement to the exchange cartel from a reluctant Lincoln. Such threats, southern leaders were convinced, had also forced the Yankee government to rescind the hated general orders of Pope and Hunter; they had even led to Pope's banishment to the wilds of Minnesota. Time and again, Confederate threats had been effective in shaping northern policies, and Davis and his lieutenants were confident they would do so once again.[93]

What neither the president nor his subordinates yet comprehended, however, was that two key circumstances governing the relationship between the Union and the Confederacy had changed, and that because of these factors, southern threats of retaliation would never again be as effective as they had been earlier in the war. By the beginning of 1863, the balance of excess prisoners held had shifted in favor of the Union—a fact that would progressively strengthen the North's hand in all negotiations with the South. Second, and more important, was the fact that the Union had experienced bitter and divisive trials in the management of its own parolees. Newspaper accounts of the deplorable conditions under which these men were being held in the camps of instruction had created a public relations nightmare for Lincoln and had gained for his administration the enmity of the governors, legislatures, and ordinary citizens of many of the most politically important and powerful states in the Union.

At the same time, the military and civilian officials most closely associated with managing parolees had become increasingly convinced that most of the men in the camps had somehow allowed themselves to be captured in the expectation that they would be discharged or furloughed when paroled. When discharges and furloughs were not forthcoming, parolees had complained to their governors and representatives, refused assignment to basic military tasks, deserted in droves, mutinied, rioted, destroyed thousands of dollars of government property, and fought pitched battles against all who had sought to restore order. In the opinion of Lincoln, Stanton, and a host of other ranking Federal officials, these problems had arisen as a direct consequence of the cartel, and the sooner that agreement was terminated, the better. As a result, southern threats to abrogate portions of the cartel carried little power of persuasion. This fact was clearly evident in Stanton's response to Davis's proclamation. On 28 December the secretary directed Ludlow to terminate immediately all exchanges of Confederate officers.[94]

Davis's hopes that threats of retaliation might induce Lincoln to suspend issuance of the Emancipation Proclamation also came to naught, and on 1 January 1863 the proclamation went into effect as planned. Addressing the Confederate Congress on 12 January, the Confederate president maintained that the proclamation constituted nothing less than a call to slaves to rise in "a general assassination of their masters"; as such, he avowed, it should be branded "the most execrable measure recorded in the history of guilty man." But in response to the proclamation, Davis could do little but turn once again to threats of reprisals. Exchanges of enlisted soldiers would continue under the terms of the cartel, he announced, but Federal officers were to be subjected to even harsher punishment than that prescribed by his proclamation of 24 December. As he told the congressmen, "I shall, unless in your wisdom you deem some other course more expedient, deliver to the several State authorities all commissioned officers of the United States that may hereafter be captured by our forces in any of the States embraced in the proclamation that they may be dealt with in accordance with the laws of those States providing for the punishment of criminals engaged in exciting servile insurrection."[95]

Neither William Ludlow nor Robert Ould had any part in the actions precipitating this latest round of retaliation and counterretaliation, but as the Union and Confederate agents of exchange, it now fell to them to keep the cartel operational in spite of the pronouncements of their governments. Two days after Davis's congressional address, Ludlow wrote Ould to inquire whether the Confederate government actually intended to implement Davis's proposal. He also asked whether the South truly planned to retain all Union officers, and he proposed that he and Ould meet to discuss these issues. In reply, Ould suggested a compromise through which a limited exchange of officers might be continued. Writing to Ludlow on 17 January, he confirmed that although Davis's proclamation of 24 December would indeed be strictly observed, nothing in the president's message precluded the continuation of the direct, officer-to-officer exchanges that the two governments had employed in the past. "If you have any Confederate officer in your possession and will deliver him," Ould offered, "an officer of like grade will be delivered to you and they will be mutually declared to be exchanged." Paroles of enlisted men, Ould assured Ludlow, would continue unabated under the terms of the cartel.[96]

As it turned out, Ludlow need not have worried about Davis's threat to deliver captured Union officers over to the states for trial as criminals. Alabama senator William L. Yancey challenged the legality of the measure shortly after the president's address; later, at Yancey's insistence, the question was referred to the Senate Judiciary Committee for a ruling. Following a heated debate, the committee ruled that as no state laws were in effect against the Union, retaliation against soldiers of the United States could be implemented only by the national government of the Confederate States.[97] Davis's threat remained a dead letter.

Although Ludlow and Ould had worked well together during the first six months of exchanges under the cartel, relations between the two were becoming increasingly strained. The fact that the North now held almost ten thousand more prisoners than the South allowed Ludlow to become progressively more rigid in dictating the conditions under which exchanges would occur. When Ulysses Grant complained that by continuing to use Vicksburg as the western point of exchange, the Union was reinforcing a garrison that he was attempting to reduce, Ludlow notified Ould that prisoners taken in the fighting at Arkansas Post would be confined in Alton Penitentiary until they could be transported to the eastern point of exchange instead. Ould vigorously opposed this unilateral departure from the terms of the cartel, but in the end there was little he could do but lodge protests.[98]

Ludlow's primary objective in the spring of 1863 was to craft an agreement that would secure the release of Union officers who had been retained in the South under Davis's proclamation of 24 December. The conditions under which these captives were being held, he learned early in March, were rapidly deteriorating, and he was determined to get as many of them as possible out of Richmond before new rounds of retaliation made their release even more difficult. Like Davis's proclamation, Stanton's order of 28 December 1862 had terminated any general exchanges of officers, but with the plight of the captives in Richmond in mind, Ludlow set about convincing the secretary to allow special exchanges along the lines proposed by Ould on 17 January. "It is very necessary to get our officers out of prison," he admonished his superiors on 25 March. "If not authorized to deliver all Confederate officers, cannot authority be given to deliver an equal number or equivalent to ours and get the latter out of prison?"[99]

Stanton, in fact, had for some time been receiving reports of worsening conditions in the Richmond prisons, and Ludlow's appeal presented the secretary with a difficult choice. On the one hand, he was loath to authorize any course of action that might prolong the life of the cartel (and with it, the problems attendant in operating the parolee camps). At the same time, he was equally anxious to avoid a recurrence of the 1862 storm of protest generated by the Lincoln administration's refusal to agree to general exchanges. Ludlow's proposal that the government sanction a return to the precartel policy of special exchanges seemed to offer an acceptable solution to this dilemma. On 27 March the Union agent was thus notified that Stanton had authorized "exchanges of officers, man for man, without reference to the cartel."[100]

Fully understanding that this latest opportunity to free Union officers might also quickly pass, Ludlow wasted no time setting in motion the mechanism for exchange. On the same day that he received Stanton's authorization to proceed with special exchanges, he telegraphed Hoffman to "send me immediately all Confederate officers you have at Washington, Baltimore and Fort Delaware, and order all at the West to be sent to you that I may use them for exchange. Our officers are suffering greatly."[101]

On 3 April Ludlow notified Ould that while only special exchanges of officers would be authorized until "the offensive order of Mr. Jefferson Davis" was revoked, the Union had begun concentrating southern officers at Fort Monroe and stood ready to pass them through the lines as soon as Confederate officials agreed to "exchange . . . U.S. officers equivalent in number or rank."[102] Ould agreed, and officer exchanges under the restrictions enumerated by Ludlow resumed. Still, the Confederate commissioner was not about to allow Ludlow's assertion that the South was to blame for the demise of the cartel to pass unchallenged, and in a letter of 11 April Ould vented his frustration and anger. "You have charged us" he wrote furiously to Ludlow,

> with breaking the cartel. With what sort of justice can that allegation be supported when you delivered only a few days ago over ninety officers most of whom had been forced to languish and suffer in prison for months before we were compelled by that and other reasons to issue the retaliatory order of which you complain? Those ninety odd are not one-half of those whom you unjustly hold in prison. Is it your idea that we are to be bound by every strictness of the cartel while you are at liberty to violate it for months and that too not only in a few instances but in hundreds? If captivity, privation and misery are to be the fate of officers on both sides hereafter let God judge between us. I have struggled in this matter as if it had been a matter of life and death to me. I am heartsick at the termination but I have no self-reproaches.[103]

Even as Ould and Ludlow were trading accusations, the chances that general exchanges under the cartel would be resumed were being further weakened by the decisions of their governments. In the North, Stanton remained preoccupied with the problem of Union soldiers surrendering in droves in order to avoid the rigors and hazards of soldiering, and the War Department tightened the conditions under which a parole given by a Federal soldier would be considered valid. On 29 February these efforts had resulted in the publication of General Orders No. 49, which was specifically designed to counter the Confederate practice of simply declaring masses of captives "paroled" following each battle. The order specified that the U.S. government would no longer recognize such "battlefield paroles" in the future. Henceforth, duplicate sets of parole certificates would be required for all captives, and only commissioned officers would be empowered to give paroles for themselves and their subordinates. Any officer who agreed to a battlefield parole for himself and his men would be considered a deserter, and any officer or enlisted man who tendered his parole under terms other than those authorized in General Orders No. 49 would be "bound to return" to the enemy and "surrender . . . as a prisoner of war."[104]

In the South, meanwhile, Confederate legislators continued to wrestle with the question of how black soldiers and their white officers should be treated. On 1 May they produced a joint resolution requiring that captured black soldiers be "delivered to the authorities of the state or states in which they shall be captured, to be dealt with according to the present or future laws of such state or states." National courts alone would decide the fate of white officers who commanded black soldiers. "Every white person," the resolution declared, "being a commissioned officer, or acting as such, who, during the present war, shall command negroes or mulattoes in arms against the Confederate States . . . shall be deemed as inciting servile insurrection, and shall, if captured, be put to death, or be otherwise punished, at the discretion of the court."[105]

The resolution also granted Davis increased latitude to "cause full and ample retaliation" for any alleged Union "violation of the laws or usages of war," and opportunities for the president to test this expanded power were not long in coming.[106] Only three days after the resolution's passage, Confederate captains William F. Corbin and T. G. McGraw were tried by northern military courts on the charge of recruiting behind the lines in Kentucky. The men were found guilty and executed. When the Confederate government learned that Lincoln had personally approved the sentences, Ould notified Ludlow that "the Confederate Government has ordered that two captains now in our custody shall be selected for execution in retaliation for this gross barbarity," and that the order would be "speedily executed."[107] Ludlow promptly recommended to Hoffman that all Confederate officers, including those who had already been exchanged and were awaiting shipment south, be retained until further notice; he then warned Ould that "for each officer so executed one of your officers in our hands will be immediately put to death and if this number be not sufficient it will be increased."[108]

Davis's second opportunity to apply his expanded powers of retaliation came when Union raiders under the command of Colonel Abel D. Streight were captured in northern Georgia. Although Streight's command was composed exclusively of Indiana troops, Alabama governor John G. Shorter insisted that among the raiders were two companies of Alabama unionists and that one objective of the raid was to incite slaves to rise against their masters. Shorter maintained that under the provisions of the congressional resolution of 1 May, Streight and his officers should be tried by national courts or remanded to the state of Alabama for punishment. Davis agreed, ordering the Federal officers held for trial in national courts. Even after it was confirmed that neither Alabamians nor blacks rode with Streight, the colonel and his officers were ordered confined in Libby and excluded from consideration for exchange.[109]

Chances for the resumption of full exchanges were further diminished by the publication of regulations more tightly constricting the circumstances under which Union soldiers could tender their paroles. On 24 April 1863 the War Department issued General Order No. 100, a wide-ranging summary of the laws of war authored by Francis Lieber, a renowned professor and authority on international law at Columbia University. Section seven of the document, which specically addressed the circumstances and procedures under which paroles might be given and received, reiterated the provisions stated earlier in General Orders No. 49. Only commissioned officers were allowed to give paroles for themselves and their men, all parolees were to be individually documented, and paroles granted through the Confederate practice of summarily releasing large numbers of prisoners on the battlefield were considered invalid.[110] On 20 May, Hoffman dispatched a copy of General Order No. 100 and General Orders No. 49 to Ludlow with instructions to regard "all paroles exacted or accepted by the enemy from our troops in violation of this stipulation . . . null and void." Troops who gave their paroles illegally, Hoffman continued, would "be ordered to duty as if no parole had been given."[111] Ludlow forwarded copies of both regulations to Ould, and when the Confederate agent inquired as to the effective date of the orders, Hoffman instructed Ludlow to reply that the restrictions embodied in General Orders No. 49 should be considered operative from the date of its publication.[112]

By this point, exchange negotiations were "plunging into an awful vortex," as Ould wrote Ludlow; given the increasingly acrimonious environment, it was clear that the cartel could not long survive.[113] Hoffman thus suggested to Stanton that "it would seem to be advisable to prepare barracks at Fort Delaware to accommodate in all 10,000 prisoners of war," and the secretary concurred.[114] By 25 May, exchanges of officers had been terminated completely. The Confederate strategy of threatening retaliation was derailed when Brigadier General W. H. Lee, the son of Robert E. Lee, was wounded and captured during the battle of Brandy Station. The younger Lee was held in close confinement at Fort Monroe under threat of execution should the two Union officers held hostage in Libby be hanged. "His retention," Ludlow noted succinctly, "settles all questions about hanging our officers."[115]

At this juncture, virtually every advantage in prisoner-of-war deliberations lay with the North. In a dramatic attempt to regain some measure of control over the exchange process, Jefferson Davis accepted Confederate vice president Alexander H. Stephens's "patriotic offer" to do what he could to prompt a resumption of exchanges. Davis dispatched Stephens on a desperate mission to meet personally with Lincoln for the purpose of "endeavor[ing] to establish the cartel for the exchange of prisoners on such a basis as to avoid the constant difficulties and complaints which arise."[116] Stephens proceeded to Hampton Roads on 4 July, but there his journey north ended. Lincoln refused to meet with him, and northern victories at Gettysburg and Vicksburg—both of which occurred while Stephens awaited permission to proceed—placed Lincoln in an even stronger position to deny any demand or entreaty that Davis might make.

On 3 July 1863 the Union War Department issued its final adjustment to parole procedures with the publication of General Orders No. 207. The order emphasized that in accordance with article seven of the original cartel, "all captures must be reduced to actual possession and all prisoners of war must be delivered at the places designated, there to be exchanged, or paroled until exchange can be effected." The only exception allowed was when commanders of two opposing armies agreed to "exchange prisoners or to release them on parole at other points mutually agreed upon by said commanders." Ould was duly notified that all releases deemed not in conformity with this order would be considered "null and of no effect."[117]

But even as the order was being distributed, northern designs were dealt a setback when Ulysses Grant summarily paroled nearly thirty thousand prisoners taken at Vicksburg and George Meade released almost twelve thousand following the battle of Gettysburg. This number was boosted further still on 9 July, when seven thousand Rebels were paroled upon the fall of Port Hudson. General Henry Halleck was stunned by these releases. As he relayed to Grant in a telegram of 8 July, "paroling the garrison at Vicksburg without actual delivery to a proper agent, as required by the seventh article of the cartel, may be construed into an absolute release." Once freed, Halleck fumed, the men might "be immediately placed in the ranks of the enemy," for "such has been the case elsewhere." These admonitions were quickly transformed into War Department policy. The North would make no further large releases.[118]

In the late summer of 1863, Stanton moved to terminate exchanges completely through a blatant violation of the terms of both General Orders No. 207 and the cartel. Indeed, less than two weeks after the publication of General Orders No. 207, Stanton demonstrated that he had no qualms about ignoring the Union's own regulations if he perceived an advantage in doing so. The "mutually agreed upon" point of exchange in the east was City Point, but on 13 July Stanton directed General Ethan Allen Hitchcock, recently appointed as commissioner of exchange, to inform Ludlow that no more prisoners of war would be forwarded to that location "till further orders." As justification for his decision, Stanton cited the danger that the Confederates would immediately press the parolees into service defending Richmond.[119]

Ludlow was stunned by the decision, and he found the secretary's justification pitifully inadequate. Protesting that he had "no reason to believe that any such prisoners are put into the field without having been properly exchanged," he warned of the likelihood that "unless deliveries [of southern prisoners] continue, no more of our men will be delivered." Desperately he pleaded for clarification. In reply, Hoffman provided the true reason for Stanton's decision. "I am informed," Old Huffy wrote, "that there will be no more deliveries of prisoners of war until there is better understanding in relation to the cartel and a more rigid adherence to its stipulations on the part of the rebel authorities." In the meantime, a new camp was being established to confine excess prisoners until "the matter of exchanges" was "satisfactorily arranged."[120]

From this point, all hope of resuming exchanges under the cartel rapidly faded. On the same day that Stanton's order suspending deliveries of prisoners to City Point was issued, Ould unilaterally declared twelve Confederate general officers and three colonels captured at Vicksburg exchanged, informing Ludlow after the fact that equivalents could be chosen from Union officers paroled in May after the battle of Chancellorsville. Ludlow rejected Ould's action as a gross violation of the cartel, and he assured the Confederate agent that the North would agree to no such special exchanges until Colonel Streight and his officers were released.

Although Ludlow did not know it at the time, this would be his final communication as the northern agent of exchange. On 25 July he was removed in favor of Brigadier General Sullivan A. Meredith. Ould charged that Stanton had ordered the change because Ludlow had dared to challenge the secretary's order suspending exchanges at City Point, and all available evidence indicates that Ould was probably correct. Relations between Ould and Meredith were acrimonious from the start. In their first meeting Ould proposed that exchanges be resumed under the provisions of General Orders 49, 100, and 207; as a demonstration of good faith, he stated that the South stood ready to exchange Colonel Streight and all other Union officers except those captured while in command of black troops, which would be retained in accordance with the joint resolution passed by the Confederate Congress. Ould was also eager to resume exchanges of enlisted soldiers. Yet he insisted on exceptions, adamantly asserting that southerners would "die in the last ditch" before giving up the right to send captured slaves back into slavery. Meredith, citing the South's refusal to exchange black soldiers and the officers who commanded them, promptly declined the proposition.[121]

Ould's next move came as a result of Confederate attempts to resolve a problem that had so terribly vexed leaders in the North—the disposition of large numbers of parolees. Up to this point, the maintenance of parolees had posed no significant problem in the South, but upon Grant's release of thousands of captives following the fall of Vicksburg, Confederate leaders were forced to establish a camp at Demopolis, Alabama, for parolees awaiting exchange. At Demopolis, it was not long before all the difficulties that had plagued operations in the northern camps of instruction quickly surfaced. "Paroled prisoners," the camp's commander complained to Secretary of War Seddon, "are determined to believe that they cannot be held to service until exchanged. The men are coming in, but will not stay." By 15 August desertions and mutinous behavior at Demopolis had reached such an alarming level that Jefferson Davis felt compelled personally to reassert the Confederacy's right to hold the men until they were exchanged. Still, the soldiers continued to defy authority and desert in droves; by 19 August so many had deserted that the War Department had no choice but to declare the Vicksburg parolees "furloughed" until exchanged.[122]

Although this expediency went far to ameliorate the immediate problems at Demopolis, it did nothing to speed the process of returning parolees to combat duty. Confederate leaders knew that if the Union persisted in its determination to refuse exchanges, the men might never rejoin their regiments, and this the manpower-poor South could not allow. On 16 September, the Confederate War Department therefore published General Orders No. 123, declaring most of the Vicksburg parolees and all southern prisoners who had been delivered at City Point at any time prior to 25 July 1863 exchanged.[123]

Northern authorities learned of the declaration only when it was published in the *Richmond Enquirer*. A furious Halleck immediately branded the exchanges illegal under the terms of the original cartel; after perusing the article, Hoffman informed Stanton that General Orders No. 123 would return no less than 1,208 officers and 22,879 enlisted men to the Confederate ranks. When converted to private soldier equivalents (forty privates for each major general, six for each captain, and so on), this number ballooned to 29,433 men. Using the same formula, Hoffman calculated that the number of Federal troops then on parole awaiting exchange totaled only 19,109, leaving a Union balance of 10,024 men. Following Hoffman's recommendation, Hitchcock instructed Meredith to declare immediately exchanged all officers and enlisted men who had been paroled up to 1 September 1863; because this number would still not equal the total number of Vicksburg parolees declared exchanged by the South, Meredith was further ordered to demand that Ould release sufficient prisoners confined in Richmond to make good the difference. But "on no account," or "by any accident," Hitchcock emphasized, was Meredith to enter into any agreement that would result in the release of southern prisoners who had been retained in the North following Stanton's suspension of exchanges.[124]

As the dispute over the Vicksburg parolees wore on, conditions plummeted for the Union captives in Richmond. Reports of their suffering soon filled the columns of newspapers in the North, and, as had been the case in the days prior to the cartel, editors charged that northern boys were dying in southern pens while the Lincoln administration bickered over technicalities. In an editorial on 10 November, for example, the *New York Times* insisted that "the Government ought at once to take measures to bring about a general exchange," for "whatever the merits of the controversy between Mr. Ould and Gen. Meredith may be, it will hardly be maintained that it is better to let ten or twelve thousand of our soldiers be starved to death than to give way."[125]

Public clamor for a resumption of exchanges rose to a crescendo, and in response Meredith proposed a plan to Hitchcock that he thought would quiet the restive populace. Meredith suggested that he be allowed to present to Ould a letter in which the North would once more propose, for "motives of humanity," an exchange of officers, "man for man, according to grade." Should Ould find this offer unacceptable, the letter would contain an alternative proposal calling on each of the belligerents to assume responsibility for maintaining its respective soldiers currently in enemy prisons. Meredith conceded that there was "but little hope" that Ould would accept either proposal, but he maintained that if the southern agent refused the offer as expected, the letter could be of immense propaganda value if released for publication in the major newspapers in the North. "If it is presented to him and then published," Meredith offered in summary, "it will have the effect of allaying any public feeling against the Government as to the suspension of exchanges."[126]

Hitchcock forwarded Meredith's suggestion to Stanton with a note that he believed the proposal that each government feed and clothe its own prisoners to be "impracticable." Hitchcock also judged the initiation of a special exchange of officers to be unwise, for to undertake such a course of action would be impossible without "impliedly acquiescing in the formal determination of the rebel authorities . . . to make a distinction between officers of the Federal Army taken prisoners while serving with white troops and those serving with colored regiments."[127] Stanton concurred with Hitchcock's assessment.

But by the middle of November, even Halleck was forced to concede that the conditions under which northern prisoners were being held were "even more barbarous than that which Christian captives formerly suffered from the pirates of Tripoli, Tunis, and Algiers."[128] Public demands that the government take some action in behalf of the captives could no longer be ignored, and Stanton reluctantly authorized the implementation of Meredith's proposal. Twenty-four thousand army rations were sent through the lines for the prisoners in Libby; but by this point in the war, relations between the North and the South had become so bitter that even this simple gesture of humanity foundered.[129] Ould denied requests that northern agents be allowed to observe the distribution of the rations, and false reports that Confederate guards were consuming the food soon began to circulate in the North. Meredith, who in official correspondence had recently accused Ould of being afflicted with "the habit of special pleading and of perverting the truth," confronted the southern agent with the reports, whereupon Ould retorted that southern attempts to aid Union prisoners had occasioned nothing but "vilification and abuse," and proclaimed that no more deliveries would be allowed.[130]

Although Hitchcock might have found some of Meredith's proposals wanting, he obviously saw much merit in the Union agent's suggestion that the government enlist the northern press to sway public opinion; with Stanton's approval, the commissioner submitted a letter of his own for publication in the *New York Times*. "The public," Hitchcock's letter of 28 November began, "appears to be in need of information on the subject of exchanges of prisoners of war." He was determined to provide that information and much more. Hitchcock began with a detailed history tracing the demise of the cartel and went on to assure his countrymen that the blame for the termination of that agreement rested solely with the Rebels. As an example, he offered Ould's unilateral declaration of exchange of the Vicksburg parolees. "The Government of the United States would not haggle about a few men, more or less," he insisted, but Ould's insistence that the Union "deliver to him all of the prisoners in our possession, amounting now to about 40,000 men, and receive in return about 13,000 men" was entirely unacceptable. Such an arrangement would have provided the South with a favorable balance of "about 27,000 men" whom Ould, "judging by what he has actually recently done," would have illegally declared exchanged and returned to the field, where they would once more have been free to "fight against national troops standing under an unstained national flag."[131]

Such violations were serious, Hitchcock insisted, but the primary reason that the Union was refusing to resume general exchanges lay in the southern treatment of captured black soldiers and their officers. Davis and the Confederate Congress were guilty of the "wildest threats of vengeance" against black soldiers and their white officers, Hitchcock maintained. Although he conceded that "what has actually been done up to the present time in the South in obedience to this spirit of vengeance ... may be impossible to determine in detail," he asserted that the very absence of such information surely indicated that the Confederacy had embarked upon a policy that would result in "the destruction of this class of troops whenever and wherever they unhappily fall into their power." White officers of black regiments were being summarily executed when captured, Hitchcock alleged, while black soldiers taken prisoner were either murdered, sold into slavery, or imprisoned without hope of exchange. He concluded on a firm note: "The Government of the United States in authorizing the employment of colored troops for the suppression of the rebellion bound itself . . . to use its utmost power to throw over that class of troops the protection of the laws of war, and stands engaged before the world to make no compromise whatever which shall jeopardize the claim of this class of troops when captured to be treated with that humanity which is due to all other troops in like circumstances according to the laws of civilized warfare."[132]

Meanwhile, events were taking a very bizarre turn in Stanton's search for a strategy that would quiet northern discontent without granting an advantage to the Confederacy. Following his stormy sojourn in New Orleans, General Benjamin Butler had been transferred to command at Fort Monroe. On 17 November, the Beast—the Union officer most hated in the South and the only Federal soldier still under Davis's death sentence—wrote Stanton to propose that he was just the man to get exchanges back on track. Butler was certain that if given a chance, he could convince Ould to resume man-for-man exchanges, but Stanton rebuffed him on the grounds that the Rebels would never agree to include black soldiers and their officers in the exchanges. Stanton then attempted to dismiss Butler by informing him that although his suggestions were certainly welcome, they should be forwarded not to the secretary of war, but to General Hitchcock, the commissioner of exchange.[133]

Butler was nothing if not persistent, however. He countered that relations between Meredith and Ould had become "sufficiently acrimonious to have lost sight of the point of dispute." Productive negotiations between the two, he charged, were now impossible. "No one will go further in exerting every power of the Government in protecting the colored troops and their officers than myself," Butler assured Stanton. In his opinion, the treatment of black soldiers was not blocking exchanges. Rather, Meredith and Ould had become so fixated on the question of numbers that Union soldiers were being "starved to death upon the proposition of inequality in the computation and value of paroles." He continued, "If you will examine the correspondence, it will be seen that the whole question turns upon that point; not a suggestion is made that color, caste, or condition has anything to do with the dispute." The time had come for someone other than Meredith to treat with Ould, Butler insisted. Through his own sources he had obtained reliable information that "the rebel authorities will exchange every officer and soldier they now hold in custody, whether colored or not, upon receiving an equivalent number and rank from us." The strategy of the North should be to exchange as many soldiers from white regiments as possible, for at the completion of such exchanges Federal prisons would still hold an excess of ten thousand Confederates upon whom the Union could "work both retaliation and reprisal to the fullest extent to wring from the rebels justice to the colored soldier."[134]

Stanton was certainly not eager to resume exchanges, and he probably saw Butler's proposals as unwelcome interference, but he was also keenly aware that the number of northern citizens who held the Federal government responsible for the suspension of exchanges was growing.[135] In an editorial of 2 December, for example, the *National Intelligencer* had asserted that the prevailing opinion in the North was that the entire issue of the treatment of black soldiers was simply an excuse invented by the Lincoln administration to terminate exchanges.[136] And in fact, such was the case. The plight of black soldiers had figured not at all in Stanton's decision to halt exchanges at City Point back in July; only after the public began to clamor for a resumption of exchanges did the administration adduce the treatment of black captives as the reason behind their suspension. By the time the *Intelligencer* editorial was published, sentiment against the Federal position was so overwhelming that Hitchcock took up his pen in a second attempt to convince an unbelieving populace that the "Negro question" did indeed stand at the center of the administration's policy of refusing exchanges. The commissioner's "postscript," as the *New York Times* titled it, consumed two full columns of verbiage, but contained little to bolster the administration's position.[137]

Indeed, the northern public now identified Hitchcock as one of the primary obstacles to a general exchange. By 3 December public sentiment was running so strong against the general that he was moved to assure Stanton that he was "perfectly willing either to withdraw altogether or to be set aside temporarily" if that might "promise relief to the sufferers in Richmond prisons."[138] Stanton refused the offer, but Federal efforts to find some course that might assuage public demand for the resumption of exchanges without granting too great an advantage to the Confederacy increased in tempo. On 7 December, Halleck tried his hand at opening exchange negotiations directly with Lee, but the southern general refused to participate in discussions he considered outside the parameters of the cartel.[139]

From Fort Monroe, the tireless Butler continued to insist that he alone could succeed where all others had failed. When he learned that smallpox was raging among the prisoners in Richmond, he deduced that the time had come for opening a fresh line of communication with the Rebels. On his own initiative, he sent to the southern capital enough smallpox vaccine to inoculate six thousand men. The Confederates permitted the distribution of this initial shipment, but when

Butler attempted to expand this tenuous contact by offering to send more, there was no reply from Richmond.[140]

Still, Stanton was forced to concede that Butler's overtures had been the most successful of all that had been attempted, and on 17 December the secretary appointed him "special agent for exchange of prisoners at City Point." Meredith was "relieved from further duty as commissioner of exchange" and ordered to Fort Monroe for service as Butler's subordinate. The new special agent was directed to authorize only those exchanges that would return "man for man" and "officer for officer." In all deliberations, he was to ensure that "colored troops and their officers" were "put upon an equality . . . with other troops," and he was cautioned to take no action that "compromised . . . the honor or dignity of the Government."[141]

As 1863 drew to a close, it was obvious that exchanges under the Dix–Hill cartel were at an end, and both governments sought to assure themselves and their constituents that they were blameless in its demise. On 5 December, Stanton submitted to Lincoln his annual report on military operations, which was substantially the same as Hitchcock's account in the *New York Times*. It was long on assertions that the Rebels had violated the cartel through illegal declarations of exchange and their refusal to treat black prisoners equitably, but there was no mention of the fact that Stanton himself had ordered the actual termination of exchanges in July. The sole reason for the termination of general exchanges, Stanton claimed, was Rebel deceit and vengefulness. He piously asserted that even after being treated so shabbily, the Union remained "ready at a moment" to exchange "man for man, officer for officer" the forty thousand prisoners it held.[142] Such was the northern explanation of why the cartel had failed.

In a message to a joint session of the Confederate Congress on 7 December, President Jefferson Davis presented the southern version of the cartel's demise. "I regret to inform you that the enemy have returned to the barbarous policy with which they inaugurated the war, and that the exchange of prisoners has been for some time suspended," the president announced. Northern policymakers had been "consistently perfidious," he insisted; their willingness to abide by the terms of the cartel had been based solely on whether or not they held an excess of prisoners. There was much truth in the president's assessment of northern motives, but—like Stanton's version of events—Davis's explanation was as remarkable for what it did not say as for what it did. He made no mention, for example, of the debilitating effect of the Confederacy's decisions concerning the treatment of black soldiers and their officers. Nor did he discuss the impact of Ould's unilateral and illegal declaration of exchange for the Vicksburg prisoners.[143]

The real losers in the failure of the cartel were the prisoners themselves. From the time general exchanges were terminated in July 1863 to the final demise of the cartel at the end of that year, the two governments continued to rationalize and justify their own actions while heaping accusations upon the enemy. Each steadfastly asserted that the other was at fault. Still, two facts were inescapable: once more the camps were filling beyond capacity, and once more the conditions within them were swiftly degenerating. The failure to resume general exchanges led to a crisis in the prison systems of the North and South during the last seven months of 1863, and that crisis, in turn, precipitated the horrors that would be visited upon the men in those systems in the following year.

Commissary General of Prisoners William Hoffman (right) and his staff outside his office in Washington, D.C., in 1865. *Courtesy of the Library of Congress.*

Brigadier General John H. Winder as he appeared in 1862 when he assumed de facto control of the developing Confederate prisoner-of-war system. *Southern Historical Collection, University of North Carolina.*

Southeast view of the interior of the stockade at Camp Sumter, Andersonville, Georgia. The trough-like structure in the foreground is the open latrine (sinks) constructed along the bank of the creek that was the camp's primary source of drinking water. Prisoner shelters (shebangs) and caves can be seen beyond the creek. *Collection of The New-York Historical Society. Digital ID # aa 02062.*

Burying Union dead in the prisoner cemetery outside the stockade of Camp Sumter on 17 August 1864. By this point in the prison's history, individual graves and coffins had long since given way to mass burials in trenches. *Collection of The New-York Historical Society. Digital ID # aa 02063.*

The Union steamer *New York*. Used throughout the war to transport exchanged prisoners, the steamer is seen here tied up at the exchange point at Aiken's Landing. *Courtesy of the Library of Congress.*

"Swallowing the eagle" at Point Lookout, Maryland. Confederate prisoners, each with his hand on a Bible, stand at attention beneath a draped American flag as the Union officer on the dais at right administers the oath of allegiance to the United States. *Collection of The New-York Historical Society. Digital ID # ae 00007.*

This front and side view of Libby Prison was taken by Alexander Gardner shortly after the fall of Richmond. The bottom half of the structure was whitewashed so that escaping prisoners would be highlighted against the walls should they attempt a night escape. *Courtesy of the Library of Congress.*

Washington May 20th 1864

Abraham Lincoln
        President United States
            Sir

            Enclosed please
find the photographs of four re
turned prisoners, whose likenesses
were taken by order of the com
mittee on the conduct of the War
    Some of these will form a
part of the likenesses to be pub
lished in the forthcoming report
on the condition of returned prison
ers
        Very respectfully
            Yours &c   B. F. Wade

42904

Letter accompanying the photographs of exchanged prisoners sent to President Lincoln by Benjamin F. Wade, chairman of the Joint Committee on the Conduct of the War. The photographs were taken as part of the committee's investigation of the terrible condition of prisoners returned from southern camps to Annapolis, Maryland, in May 1864. The captions for each of the photographs are the originals assigned by the committee. *Abraham Lincoln Papers, Library of Congress.*

Private Isaiah G. Bowker, Co. B: 9th Maine Vols. Admitted per Steamer *New York* from Richmond, Va., March 9th 1864. Died May 16th 1864 from effects of treatment received while in the hands of the enemy.

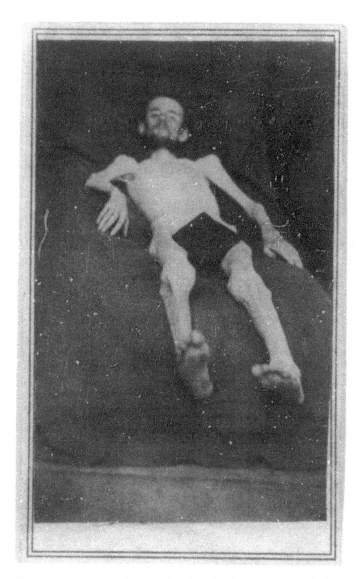

Private L. H. Parham, Co. B, 3d W. Tenn. Cav. Admitted per steamer *New York* from Richmond, Va., May 2, 1864. Died May 10, 1864, from effects of treatment while in the hands of the enemy.

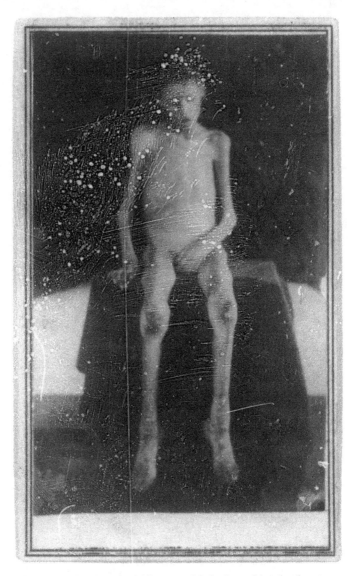

The caption identifying this soldier is too faded to be read, but the photo is one of the four "likenesses" Wade sent to Lincoln on 20 May 1864.

CHAPTER 7

Prelude to Catastrophe
Union and Confederate Prisons, July–December 1863

MOST HISTORIANS WOULD agree that conditions in Civil War prisons reached their nadir in 1864, and descriptions of the terrible conditions and horrible suffering in the camps during that year are available in dozens of camp histories and prisoner narratives. Yet these accounts share a common shortcoming. They present the events of that dreadful year in isolation and fail to acknowledge the fact that their origins are to be found in the last seven months of 1863. It was then that the men who directed the Union and Confederate prisoner-of-war systems very deliberately developed and implemented the policies and directives that led to the hellish camps of 1864. As a direct result of those policies, the quantity and quality of prisoner rations, shelter, essential supplies, and medical care would be slashed to the bone, while the rates of starvation, sickness, and death would skyrocket to the highest levels of the entire war.[1]

The immediate effect of the termination of general exchanges in the summer of 1863 was that the prisons of the North and South once more filled far beyond capacity. Exchanges under the cartel had allowed the two belligerents to empty and close most of their prisons; in the expectation that exchanges at some level would shortly resume, both were reluctant to expend the considerable resources required to reopen old facilities or construct new ones. By the time each accepted the fact that there would be no resumption of exchanges, the few remaining prisoner-of-war camps were desperately overcrowded, and captives were sickening and dying at an alarming rate. As a result, both governments were forced into a frantic scramble to identify locations for new prisons and to reopen old camps. Officials responded to this demand for additional space by confining captives in existing structures that were obviously unfit for use as prisons and by ordering the hasty construction of inadequate facilities at locations that would prove fearfully unhealthful.

Finally—and most importantly—it was during the last seven months of 1863 that the men who directed the prisoner-of-war systems became increasingly hardened to the pitiful plight of the men in the camps. Military and civilian leaders, with full knowledge of the consequences of their actions, began to implement policies that dramatically increased the incidence of sickness and death among the captives under their control. They also came to embrace the notion that massive retaliation against helpless prisoners was a just and warranted response to charges that their own men were being systematically mistreated in enemy camps. By the end of 1863, these new attitudes—combined with the staggering demands of managing unprecedented numbers of prisoners—would ensure that the Union and Confederate prisoner-of-war systems during 1864 would be the darkest of the war.

Exchanges under the cartel had allowed Union commissary general of prisoners William Hoffman to reduce the number of prisoners incarcerated in the North to only a fraction of the total that had been confined before the agreement went into effect. In January 1863, Union prisons held only 1,286 captives; but as disputes and successive rounds of retaliation progressively reduced the number of men being exchanged, the prisoner population began to climb rapidly. By the end of the year, camps in the North held almost 35,000 Rebel captives. Predictably, conditions in Union prisons plummeted. In the penitentiary at Alton, Illinois, for example, smallpox had first been diagnosed among the prisoners in late 1862, but because exchanges reduced the number of inmates to a manageable level, Major Thomas Hendrickson, the facility's commander, was able to launch an aggressive inoculation and quarantine program that effectively suppressed the disease. When exchanges under the cartel began to slow, Alton again became overcrowded, and the disease flared once more. By midsummer, Hendrickson was warning that "the smallpox still prevails to a considerable extent in this prison, and will, I fear, continue to do so as long as it can have fresh subjects to operate upon." Confessing that he knew of no other acceptable course of action, the harried commander requested that "no more prisoners be sent here for a few weeks" so that the "loathsome disease" could burn itself out.[2]

The crush of prisoners then coming north was so great that Hoffman could not grant Hendrickson even the short respite that he sought. Still, something had to be done to quell the disease. Union surgeon general Joseph R. Smith suggested that the prison could remain open if the infected captives were moved to a separate quarantine facility, whereupon Hoffman telegraphed Hendrickson to locate and acquire such a site immediately. But this proved a rather difficult undertaking. As Hendrickson informed Hoffman, the civilians who lived adjacent to the prison were "strongly opposed" to having scores of smallpox-infected Rebels thrust among them. Hendrickson continued his search for a quarantine site, but even as he did so, Hoffman continued to ship trainloads of prisoners to Alton. By the middle of July, Hendrickson alerted Hoffman that "we have now in this prison about 1,500 prisoners, a number far too great for comfortable accommodation during the warm weather." Medical inspectors had placed the maximum capacity of the facility at "not greater than 1,000," he asserted; moreover, fed by the overcrowding, smallpox at Alton had reached epidemic proportions. It was not until the end of the summer that Hendrickson was able to find a suitable location for quarantining infected prisoners, and even then he had to billet the desperately ill men in tents while he sought approval for the construction of a building where they might receive medical treatment.[3]

Although there was no smallpox at Gratiot Street Prison, the lack of sanitation in this St. Louis facility rendered conditions there almost as unhealthy as at Alton. A medical department officer inspecting the prison in late July 1863 reported that the ceilings and floors were "dilapidated" and that ventilation was poor. The prison was generally filthy, and attempts by the prisoners to clean the walls and floors had been severely constrained due to overcrowding and the fact that "when scrubbing is done the water leaks through from one story to another." The prisoners' diet did not contain "a sufficient variety of vegetable food," and "the leakage from the officers' privy through a badly built wall into a . . . recreating room" was "productive of inconvenience," to say nothing of a host of grisly diseases. Although virtually every structure in the prison was in dire need of cleaning and repair, the inspector discovered that the prison fund—instituted at Hoffman's direction and supposedly maintained to remedy such deficiencies—had "gone on steadily accumulating and now amounts to something near $4,000." He "respectfully" recommended that it be immediately expended to raise conditions in the facility to an acceptable standard.[4]

In June 1863 Camp Douglas stood almost empty. All but a few of the inmates had departed, but the camp was in terrible shape. Its walls were sagging and in need of repair, its water system and latrines were completely inadequate, and its barracks—ravaged through overuse and the destruction inflicted during the parolee riot—had been reduced to a motley collection of burned-out shells and ramshackle huts barely fit for human occupation. U.S. Sanitary Commission inspectors had recommended simply terminating the post's use as a camp for prisoners of war, but as the number of prisoners swelled beyond the capacity of existing facilities, Hoffman was forced to designate Camp Douglas as a major confinement center.[5]

On 13 August, Captain J. S. Putnam, a parolee who had chosen to remain at Camp Douglas to serve as its caretaker commander, eagerly telegraphed Hoffman that the camp was "in good condition to accommodate 8,000 prisoners."[6] When Captain J. A. Potter, the post's experienced and capable quartermaster, heard of Putnam's naive assessment, he lost no time in apprising the commissary general of the camp's true capacity. "I have just learned that you have been told that Camp Douglas would accommodate 8,000," he wired Hoffman on 15 August. "This is an error. Six thousand, including guard, is the utmost limit, and then they will be crowded." And in a clear indication of what he thought of Putnam's leadership capabilities, Potter closed his message by bluntly requesting that Hoffman "please have a commandant sent; a good officer."[7]

A new commander was appointed to oversee the reactivation of Camp Douglas as a prisoner-of-war facility, but the commissary general of prisoners had no part in his selection. Colonel Charles V. De Land, a farmer and sometime journalist before the war, had risen to command of the First Michigan Sharpshooters. When his regiment was assigned to guard duty at Camp Douglas, he was appointed to command of the prison by the commander of the military district in which it lay.[8] This continuing lack of control over such important decisions frustrated Hoffman no end. In July, he had petitioned Secretary of War Edwin Stanton for promotion to brigadier general, maintaining that the advancement in rank would bolster his authority and aid in his dealings with senior field officers, but General Henry Halleck had advised the secretary that Hoffman's duties were not sufficient to merit promotion. The request was refused.[9]

Denied advancement, Hoffman once more appealed to the secretary of war to streamline the chain of command in the Union prisoner-of-war system and to expand his own authority as commissary general of prisoners. "I beg leave respectfully to suggest," he wrote Stanton on 19 September,

> that it would facilitate the management of the affairs of prisoners of war and lead to a more direct responsibility if the commanders of stations where prisoners are held could be placed under the immediate control of the Commissary General of Prisoners. By the interposition of an intermediate commander the responsibility is weakened and correspondence passing through him is necessarily much delayed, and through frequent change of commanders it is impossible to establish a uniform and permanent system of administration. I would therefore respectfully suggest that an order of the following tenor be issued, viz.: Hereafter at all stations where rebel prisoners of war are held they will be under the exclusive control of the commanding officer, who

will be strictly responsible for them to the Commissary-General of Prisoners, and, except from the War Department or the General-in-Chief, he will receive orders relative to prisoners only from or through the Commissary-General of Prisoners.[10]

Stanton took the recommendation under advisement, but Hoffman's problems with senior officers would continue.

De Land assumed command of Camp Douglas on 18 August, and the situation he inherited was desperate from the start. His regiment had been part of the Union force that had cut off and captured General John Hunt Morgan's brigade of Confederate raiders back in July, and on his first day of command he learned that Morgan's men were to be his prisoners. The raiders began to arrive in Chicago in mid-August; in one month they pushed the prisoner population to over four thousand, a number the ramshackle prison was in no way prepared to adequately accommodate. "I tell you frankly," De Land informed Hoffman, "this camp has heretofore been a mere rookery; its barracks, fences, guardhouses, all a mere shell of refuse pine boards."[11]

Hoffman knew that De Land's grim assessment was no exaggeration, and on 23 September he alerted the War Department that the buildings burned by the parolees should be replaced "with as little delay as possible." The recommendation was passed to Stanton, who refused to authorize the construction upon learning the cost of the project. In a message laced with both invective and sarcasm, Stanton directed the adjutant general to inform Hoffman that "the Secretary of War is not disposed at this time . . . to erect fine establishments for prisoners in our hands." Hoffman was authorized to provide only what was "indispensable . . . to prevent suffering," and any meager improvements were to be financed through "ordinary means . . . or by the use of the prison fund if necessary to that end, as far as it will go." Once those monies were exhausted, Hoffman was told, "nothing more will be authorized." In justifying his adoption of this hard line, Stanton offered for the first time the rationale that would become the mantra cited to justify such decisions—it was because of "the treatment our prisoners of war are receiving at the hands of the enemy."[12]

With this pronouncement, a new and decidedly darker chapter in the history of prisoner treatment in Union camps opened. Until this point, basic necessities (such as adequate food and shelter) had been deliberately denied Confederate prisoners only as acts of retaliation, which targeted particular individuals or groups of captives and which was implemented in response to specifically designated enemy misdeeds. What Stanton was now mandating was no less than a fundamental shift in Union policy, which sanctioned withholding essential supplies, services, and shelter simply as a matter of course. This new policy was in direct contravention to the provisions of General Order No. 100. Although retaliation against designated prisoners for specific enemy wrongs was allowed, article 56 of the order stipulated that prisoners were not to be subjected to "cruel imprisonment," and article 75 specified that in the absence of acts of retaliation ordered in compliance with regulations, the only justification for altering the "confinement and mode of treating a prisoner" was the "demands of safety."[13]

Stanton's new, harsher policy severely restricted even the most rudimentary improvements at Camp Douglas, and it had the predictable result. By early October, De Land was pleading with Hoffman for "immediate action as regards the construction of the new barracks for prisoners at this camp." There were "more prisoners than we have barracks for," the commander wrote; as a result, he was reduced to "lodging them in outhouses and kitchens." The level of overcrowding had also far outstripped the capabilities of the camp's medical facilities. "I am now using the chapel for hospital purposes," De Land admitted. He went on to request the construction of "an additional hospital building and a hospital laundry" to supplement the existing accommodations, which he characterized as "meager, temporary, and inconvenient."[14]

If De Land had any notions that the War Department might have been ignorant of the rapidly deteriorating conditions at Camp Douglas, they were erased when Union surgeon A. M. Clark inspected the camp on 9 October. Clark, recently appointed as acting medical inspector of prisoners of war, had been dispatched by Hoffman on a tour of the major camps in the Union system, and at Camp Douglas he quickly discovered that northern claims that Confederate prisoners were being confined under humane conditions were pure bunk. The supply of water for the camp was "utterly inadequate," and the latrines designated for the use of almost 5,000 prisoners consisted only of shallow trenches that had been scratched through the center of the camp. Trenches that had been filled to capacity had not been covered, and there was "apparently no management at all" of the sinks still in use. They were "in filthy condition," Clark noted, and the "removal of offal, &c." was "not well attended to."[15]

Clark estimated that the ragged collection of "tents and huts" in the camp had a maximum billeting capacity of only 4,500 prisoners—a total "utterly insufficient" for the number held at the facility—and that all of the "huts" were "greatly in need of repair." Rations were adequate, but "no attention is paid to cooking by authorities." The captives were "miserably clad and suffer much from the cold"; roughly 1,200 men were "without blankets." In addition, the prisoners were "generally filthy," a condition the surgeon ascribed to "deficient facilities for cleanliness."[16]

Clark further asserted that cleanliness in the prisoners' hospital was "not as good as it ought to be," and because the overall hospital capacity was "very deficient," there were "some 150 sick men lying in the barracks who should be in hospital and receiving attention." The prison chapel was "being prepared as a hospital," but this process was being slowed by "the protest of certain good ministers of Chicago, who claim that the prisoners' souls should be looked after at the expense of their bodies." Ventilation in the hospital had "been utterly lost sight of," there was "not sufficient care taken to prevent disease," and patients suffering from highly contagious diseases—such as typhoid fever, pneumonia, and measles—were "not isolated as they should be." The rates of recovery from such illnesses was "not very ready" but could be greatly improved if the hospital was not overcrowded and better ventilated. Upon inquiring why even basic improvements had not been attempted in the hospital, Clark found that "the excuse given is that there is no hospital fund on hand."[17]

Clark's inspection also uncovered a darker side to operations at Camp Douglas. Faced with desperate overcrowding and an insufficient guard force, De Land had ominously told Hoffman that he had "instituted some extremely severe punishments to restrain the men."[18] In fact, he had deliberately instituted a regime of torture and draconian punishments to cow prisoners into submission. Prisoners who violated camp regulations were hung by their thumbs; another common punishment was sentencing captives to long periods of confinement in the facility's "dungeon," a dank hole that Clark assessed to be "a dungeon indeed," and which could be entered only through a small hatch. Upon inspecting the interior of the small room, Clark discovered that the floor was "laid directly on the ground and is constantly damp." Latrine facilities consisted of a single hole in one corner of the room, "the stench from which" Clark found to be "intolerable." Although the maximum capacity of the dungeon was "three or four prisoners," he found twenty-four men packed into it, in conditions he judged to be "inhuman." Clark readily confessed that he was able to remain in the dungeon "but a few seconds, and was glad to get out, feeling sick and faint."[19]

Upon receiving Clark's report, Hoffman ordered De Land to initiate corrective actions "at once"; but a closer inspection of Hoffman's instructions reveals that the improvements he had in mind were quite limited both in scope and expense. De Land was ordered to correct deficiencies in the maintenance of the barracks and in camp sanitation; he was also directed to provide additional hospital space and furnish clothing for the prisoners. Hoffman included detailed instructions on how to improve cooking and baking at the camp, and he demanded more attention to record keeping.[20]

But in ordering these improvements, Hoffman adhered precisely to Stanton's policy that only items and facilities "indispensable to prevent suffering" were to be provided, and at the least possible expense.[21] Although many of the problems Clark identified could be traced to overcrowding, for example, Hoffman did not authorize the construction of additional barracks. The sole source of financing for all improvements was to be the prison fund. In other words, the cost of raising conditions in the camp to a level at which the captives might survive was to be borne completely by the prisoners themselves. "Nothing more," as Stanton had directed, would "be authorized."[22]

Even more significant was the fact that Hoffman chose to ignore completely Clark's charge that prisoners at Camp Douglas were routinely being subjected to "inhuman" punishments. Hoffman made no mention of De Land's practice of confining large numbers of men in the camp's dungeon, although such punishments were expressly prohibited by General Order No. 100. The prisoners confined in the dungeon at the time of Clark's visit had received that punishment for trying to escape, and although article 77 of General Order No. 100 allowed that "a prisoner of war who escapes may be shot, or otherwise killed in his flight," it clearly stipulated that "neither death nor any other punishment shall be inflicted upon him simply for his attempt to escape, which the law of war does not consider a crime." If the prisoners Clark observed were guilty only of attempting to escape, their confinement in the dungeon constituted a clear and serious violation of General Order No. 100.[23]

Article 75 of the same order further provided that although prisoners were subject to confinement "as may be deemed necessary on account of safety," they were not to be "subjected to other intentional suffering or indignity." Narratives of prison life in Camp Douglas, however, are replete with tales of being sentenced to time in the dungeon for even trivial infractions. One private from a Mississippi regiment was thrown into the hole for drawing water from the wrong well; he later wrote that "one who has not been in such a place cannot have the least conception of it." Although Hoffman knew of De Land's cruelties and was fully aware that such acts were in contravention to Union regulations, he did not object. Neither did Stanton, who had already decreed that the mistreatment of Rebel prisoners was an acceptable quid pro quo for alleged Confederate misconduct toward Union captives.[24]

As a result, the abuse of prisoners at Camp Douglas continued. Escapes at the prison had always been a problem. Prisoners tunneled out of the camp almost at will, and De Land seemed incapable of instituting the sort of discipline in his guard force that would have prevented breakouts. On 3 December, however, he eagerly notified Hoffman that he had implemented a solution that was sure to preclude escapes in the future. "I have ordered all the floors removed from the barracks and cook-houses and the spaces filled with dirt even with the top of the joist," De Land crowed. And in a brutally candid acknowledgment that he was fully aware of the consequences of forcing prisoners to sleep on bare ground in the numbing cold of a Chicago winter, the commandant added that "this will undoubtedly increase the sickness and mortality, but it will save much trouble." This admission elicited no comment—let alone a corrective order—from the commissary general of prisoners.[25]

Although Hoffman did nothing to curb De Land, he knew that he would eventually be compelled to take action to relieve the overcrowding at Camp Douglas. Its maximum capacity had been estimated at just over 5,000 inmates, but, as he informed Stanton in a message of 3 December, its population had risen to "between 6,000 and 7,000 prisoners." Still, Hoffman continued to ship in trainloads of prisoners weekly, even though the overcrowding was exacerbated in November by yet another fire that consumed more precious barrack space. "They are very much crowded," Hoffman admitted, "having now to occupy buildings which were formerly used as cookhouses." But rather than press the secretary for money to improve conditions at the camp, Hoffman proposed to relieve the congestion by transferring "about a thousand" men to a newly constructed prison depot at Rock Island, Illinois.[26]

Rock Island, situated in the Mississippi River between Davenport, Iowa, and Moline, Illinois, had been the site of a Federal ordnance depot since 1840. The island, about three miles long and one mile wide, offered ample space and excellent security, and in the summer of 1863 Hoffman selected it as the site for a prison. The facility, constructed according to plans drawn up by Hoffman himself, was composed of 84 barracks, each of which was 100 feet long by 22 feet wide, with room for 120 prisoners apiece. The entire site was enclosed by a rough board fence 12 feet high.[27] Work on the site began on schedule at the end of August 1863, but from the beginning the quality of construction was shabby because of government insistence that the camp be erected at the least possible cost. Indeed, Quartermaster General Montgomery Meigs specifically admonished the quartermaster responsible for supplying materials that "the barracks for prisoners . . . should be put up in the roughest and cheapest manner—mere shanties, with no fine work about them." The most startling cost-cutting measure at Rock Island came from Hoffman himself: no hospital would be constructed at the prison.

Hoffman had an opportunity to reconsider this decision when he inspected the still-unoccupied camp in early November, but instead he pronounced the site ready for occupation as it stood.[28]

On 3 December, 5,592 prisoners—a combination of transfers from Camp Douglas and recently captured Confederates from Grant's victories at Lookout Mountain and Missionary Ridge—arrived at Rock Island. The facility was blanketed in two feet of snow, and the temperature hovered at a bone-chilling thirty-two degrees below zero. Only three surgeons had been assigned to the prison, and as they frantically worked to treat dozens of cases of frostbite and pneumonia, they made a terrible discovery: ninety-four of the arrivals were infected with smallpox. The surgeons feared that many other men had been exposed to the disease during the long hours in the cramped railroad cars that had transported them to the camp—fears that proved justified when an additional thirty-eight cases were soon diagnosed.[29]

The surgeons realized that only a swift reaction would prevent a full-fledged medical crisis, but they soon discovered that their treatment options were severely restricted. Upon being told that there was no hospital where infected prisoners could be cared for or isolated, Chief Surgeon J. J. Temple converted troop barracks into treatment wards and directed that a "pest house," or isolation site, be erected outside the prison walls. But it took time for these facilities to be fitted out for medical use, and in the meantime infected captives remained billeted with healthy soldiers. Soon smallpox was raging throughout the camp. Temple attempted to stem the contagion by initiating a vigorous program of inoculation, but this proved largely ineffective because the vaccine supplied by the Union medical department was inferior. By the end of December, ninety-four of the infected prisoners had died, and Temple's makeshift wards were crowded with 245 desperately ill patients. The number of new smallpox cases diagnosed increased daily, ensuring that deaths at the new prison would soon be counted in hundreds per month.[30]

Much of the suffering and death at Rock Island could be attributed directly to Hoffman's insistence that the prison be constructed and operated as cheaply as possible. This demand was also a paramount consideration in the construction of Point Lookout, which was the second prison Hoffman opened in 1863, and it would produce the same dreadful results. Point Lookout was situated at the tip of the narrow peninsula formed by the junction of the Potomac River and Chesapeake Bay, a location that should have kept it from ever being selected as a site for a major prison. The forty-acre site was low and subject to regular flooding from the bay, and its sandy soil supported no trees that might provide fuel for heating and cooking or shelter from both the blistering heat of summer and the icy winds that swept up the Chesapeake in winter. Hoffman chose the site simply because it was isolated and easily secured from attack.[31]

Also located on the peninsula was Hammond General Hospital, a mammoth 1,400-bed complex of twenty buildings and one of the largest medical facilities erected during the war. The hospital was of wooden construction, and if wooden barracks had also been provided for the prisoners, conditions at Point Lookout would have been much more bearable. But Meigs, in yet another of his cost-saving initiatives, ordered that only the prison kitchens and storehouses were to be built with wood. Prisoners were to be billeted in "old tents" drawn from surplus stocks and erected "by the prisoners themselves."[32] Army quartermasters scoured supply depots to fill this order, and the assortment of tentage they sent to the camp was astounding. Antiquated French bell tents, Sibley tents, A-tents, pup tents, wall tents, and hospital flys were all shipped to Point Lookout. But while the variety was impressive, all of the tents shared two common characteristics. They were old, and they were in such bad shape that they had been rejected for use by Federal forces in the field.[33]

On 23 July, Halleck named Brigadier General Gilman Marston, a militia officer who before the war had served as a U.S. representative, to command Point Lookout, and on 6 August the new commander informed Hoffman that he was prepared to receive prisoners. The first shipments of captives were transfers from overcrowded facilities in the East, and by the end of September, Point Lookout held almost 1,700 men.[34] Marston at first deemed the use of tents to shelter these prisoners to be acceptable, but he began to have second thoughts as winter approached. On 8 October he asked for permission to erect barracks at the site. Hoffman agreed to forward the request to Stanton, also alerting Marston to the fact that 1,000 prisoners were at that moment en route to Point Lookout and that he would be sending another 2,000 as soon as he could "have tents sent down."[35]

As had been the case at Camp Douglas, Stanton refused to allow the construction of barracks at Point Lookout, but this did not slow the shipments of prisoners. On 17 October, Hoffman wrote Marston, "It will be necessary to have on hand a supply of tents to meet any unexpected arrival of prisoners, and I have, therefore, to request you will make requisition for sufficient tents, with what you have on hand, to accommodate 10,000 prisoners." Money to construct the additional kitchens that would be required to feed this multitude, Marston was told, would have to be drawn from the prison fund.[36]

By the end of October, there were almost 7,000 captives confined at Point Lookout. Conditions at the camp had been marginally acceptable to this point, but serious problems now began to arise. On 26 October, Marston notified Hoffman that "among every lot of prisoners sent from Fort Delaware to this point there have been cases of smallpox." The number of transfers infected with the disease was large enough to "create alarm here among the troops and the citizen employees of the Government," he wrote, requesting Hoffman to ensure that "no more will be sent here."[37] Eleven days later, Marston telegraphed that "many of the prisoners are afflicted with scurvy." The disease had arisen due to the absence of vegetables in the prisoners' diet, and Marston asked that he be allowed to purchase "beets, carrots, turnips, cabbages, and the like" to supplement the daily ration. Hoffman agreed to allow the purchase, provided the expenditure was covered by the prison fund, but he hastened to add that as the amount of vegetables was increased, other items in the daily ration should be decreased in order that "the cost will to some extent be refunded."[38]

On 9 November an additional 1,800 prisoners were shipped to Point Lookout, raising the prisoner population to just over 9,000 men. After five months of overuse, the prisoners' tents offered little protection from the elements. Nor were there sufficient tents to shelter all the prisoners. Although Hoffman had promised to replenish the supply, many of the men were compelled to suffer through the frigid nights with no protection from the elements at all.[39] The effects of this absence of shelter were compounded by the fact that the prisoners at Point Lookout were never furnished with sufficient blankets or clothing. Winter had come to the Chesapeake with a vengeance, and Marston's apprehensions were all coming to pass. Temperatures hovered between zero and freezing in the evenings, and to survive the prisoners huddled together under such blankets as were available. In an effort to provide some relief, Marston procured replacement trousers and jackets from surplus stocks of regulation Federal uniforms, but the district provost marshal refused to allow them to be distributed for fear that they would facilitate prisoner escapes.[40]

Rumors of the terrible conditions at Point Lookout were soon circulating throughout the North, and it was not long before they reached the ears of Frederick Law Olmsted, the general secretary of the U.S. Sanitary Commission. Olmsted believed that the Union was morally bound to operate its prisons as humanely as possible, and he held that it was the duty of the Sanitary Commission to ensure that it did so. Accordingly, he regularly dispatched commission inspectors to northern prisons, and to determine the true state of affairs at Point Lookout he sent one of his best, William F. Swalm.[41]

Swalm's inspection was exceptionally thorough, and on 13 November he submitted his findings in a blistering report. The prison hospital consisted merely of a collection of ragged tents, none of which had either stoves or floors. In these makeshift wards Swalm found "poor emaciated creatures" afflicted with chronic diarrhea sharing beds with prisoners suffering from smallpox, typhoid, or scurvy. The dispensary, which he judged a "poor excuse for one," contained "little or nothing but a few empty bottles." Prisoners were transferred to Hammond General Hospital only when their illnesses were accessed to be life threaten ing. Swalm's inspection of the camp hospital grounds revealed that "they have not, according to looks, been policed for a very long time." Filth was "gradually accumulating," and patients were allowed to "void their excrement in the most convenient place to them, regardless of the comfort of others."[42]

While conditions in the hospital were deplorable, Swalm wrote that "it is in the quarters that we have the most complaint and suffering." There he saw "men of all ages and classes, descriptions and hues, with various colored clothing, all huddled together, forming a motley crew, which to be appreciated must be seen, and what the pen fails to describe the imagination must depict." The prisoners were "ragged and dirty and very thinly clad." Most were "in a pitiable condition, destitute of nearly everything, which, with their filthy condition, makes them really objects of commiseration." Many were without blankets to ward off the cold. Although a number of prisoners had constructed rude fire pits in their tents, they were only rarely provided with fuel. On being shown a typical ration, the Union inspector judged that the men were not receiving "half the amount of meat they are entitled to," and he added that the prison commissary sought to make up the difference by increasing the daily ration of crackers.[43]

Swalm was particularly appalled at the lax discipline in the camp. The sinks were "entirely neglected," a condition which led the men to "live, eat, and sleep in their own filth." He predicted that due to overcrowding and lack of supervision, the camp would "soon become in an impassable condition." In the summary of his report, he bluntly offered his assessment of where the blame for the deplorable state of affairs at Point Lookout should be placed. "It is our fault," he wrote, "when the officer in command fails to place in charge some one . . . capable of giving commands and seeing that they are enforced. I know that [the prisoners] are our enemies, and bitter ones . . . but now they are within our power and are suffering." Should the North discover that Federal prisoners were being held under conditions like those that Rebel captives were enduring at Point Lookout, he asserted, "words would hardly be adequate to express our indignation."[44]

When informed of Swalm's findings, Hoffman's first response was to challenge the Sanitary Commission's authority to conduct such inspections at all.

Marston followed suit, branding Swalm's report as "disingenuous and false."[45] When these protests failed to discredit the report, Hoffman promptly wrapped himself in the flag and attempted to suppress it on patriotic grounds. Writing to the associate secretary of the Sanitary Commission, he maintained that publication of the results of Swalm's inspection "cannot but do much harm to our cause by exciting the friendly sympathies of the people for those who seem to be treated with unnecessary harshness and neglect, and by giving the rebel authorities an apparent excuse for the cruel treatment which they have heaped upon those of our people who have been so unfortunate as to fall into their hands."[46]

Protests of this nature were nothing new to Olmsted. In weathering similar charges in the past, he had developed an argument every bit as Machiavellian as Hoffman himself might have devised. He simply directed his inspectors to reply that "the Commission proceeds upon the ground that every rebel whose life is saved will increase the inducement presented to the rebel authorities to treat carefully all Union men who fall into their hands." Confederates would surely realize that "every Union man whose life is saved by them buys back to them a man of their own, whose life we have saved," Olmsted insisted, arguing that "the more rebel-lives we can have to deal with, the more valuable we make to them the lives of the Union men whom they take prisoners."[47]

Old Huffy continued to fume over the interference of the commission, but not once in all his bluster did he challenge Swalm's findings. On the contrary, he conceded in personal correspondence to Marston that "from the report it appears that there is a great want of clothing among many of the prisoners," and that while it was "the desire of the War Department to provide as little clothing for them as possible, it does not wish them to be left in the very destitute condition which this report represents." As he reminded Marston, there was "an abundance of inferior clothing on hand," and it was better to issue those garments than to risk further inspections and the public outrage that would inevitably follow more negative reports.[48]

Other evidence confirms that Swalm's report was more accurate than either Hoffman or Marston wished to admit. On 23 November, Hoffman notified Marston that Stanton had agreed to allow the prisoners to receive "clothing or other articles . . . from members of their immediate family"—a remarkable concession, indicating that shortages at Point Lookout were every bit as bad as Swalm charged. But the most telling support of Swalm's findings came from General Benjamin Butler, who toured the camp on 24 December. In his report of that visit he noted that the prison fund stood at an astounding $65,000, a sum clearly indicating that the money accrued from reductions in prisoner rations was not being spent as intended on either the upkeep of the facility or the basic needs of the captives.[49]

Hoffman had hoped that the opening of a mammoth prisoner depot at Point Lookout would relieve the overcrowding in camps established earlier in the war. As the number of prisoners coming north continued to climb during the summer of 1863, however, those hopes were dashed. One by one, Hoffman was forced to return to full operation camps that had been almost emptied by exchanges under the cartel. As quickly as they were opened, they filled beyond capacity as well. An examination of operations at Camp Chase, Camp Morton, and Fort Delaware during this period supplies further evidence of how overcrowding and the refusal of Union leaders to provide for the basic needs of the captives combined to produce disastrous results.

At the beginning of July 1863, Camp Chase held only 380 prisoners. By the end of that month, an additional 2,960 prisoners had been shipped to the facility, although Hoffman had earlier confided to Stanton that the camp's "full capacity" was only 1,800 men.[50] By October, the crush of humanity had produced conditions so intolerable that the camp's new commander, Brigadier General John S. Mason, wrote Hoffman to plead for funds to effect improvements "at the earliest practicable period." It was "absolutely necessary" to build an additional hospital. Moreover, Prison No. 3—the largest of the three confinement areas in the camp—had become so "foul from want of sufficient drainage" that it needed to be closed, requiring the construction of a new compound for prisoners somewhere else in the camp. Hoffman had seen firsthand how terrible conditions at Camp Chase could become when the facility was overcrowded, and he forwarded Mason's requests to Stanton with the recommendation that the hospital and new prison construction be approved.[51] As had been the case in similar requests from Camp Douglas and Point Lookout, however, Stanton refused to authorize the construction, leaving Hoffman to suggest to Mason that the "changes proposed" be financed as far as possible with money from the prison fund.[52]

The results were predictable. When Medical Inspector A. M. Clark visited Camp Chase on the last day of October, he found that drainage at the facility was "very bad," a deficiency made all the worse because latrines in the camp were "not drained, not disinfected and not kept properly policed." Putrid effluent mixed with stagnant rainwater and runoff stood in nauseating pools throughout the camp. Echoing Mason's contention, Clark reported that the rates of disease and death among the prisoners could be reduced only if the camp was thoroughly drained or relocated. The one prison hospital was "utterly insufficient in capacity," and Clark repeated Mason's request that "additional hospital accommodation should be provided for at least 150 patients."[53]

As damning as Clark's assessment of conditions at Camp Chase was, the report he submitted on Camp Morton was even worse. In June 1863 the camp commander had recommended closing the facility, but as exchanges of prisoners slowed and finally stopped, trains bearing hundreds of captured Rebels once again began arriving at the depots in Indianapolis. The camp quartermaster, alarmed by this influx and fully aware that the facility was unprepared to supply even the basic necessities for so many men, urgently petitioned Quartermaster General Meigs for authorization to provide additional hospital space, but Meigs refused to approve the request.[54] By fall the camp held 2,362 prisoners. The rapid increase in the number of captives was matched by a shocking rise in the death rate. Over 180 men had died by the time Clark arrived at the camp on 22 October. Upon investigation he discovered that the mortality rate among hospitalized prisoners in September alone was 12.45 percent, and the report he submitted to his superiors left no doubt as to the reasons for this appalling statistic.[55]

Clark found that the general state of the camp was "very bad." The "tents and huts" in which the prisoners were housed were "dilapidated," the two open ditches that served as latrines were "exceedingly faulty" and "very foul," and the facility was crowded far beyond capacity. The condition of the men in the barracks was "exceedingly foul," and the lot of the patients in the hospital Clark characterized simply as "miserable." Laundry and bath facilities were "entirely insufficient," and the supply of blankets and bedding was also "insufficient." Although the hospital fund had been dutifully maintained by reducing the patients' rations, Clark suspected that it was "not expended with sufficient freedom in procuring comforts for the sick." These suspicions were confirmed when his inspection of the two hospital buildings revealed that one was "much overcrowded" and the other was "dilapidated and unfit for use." There were 125 men in the barracks who should have been in the hospital, and there was "no care taken" to prevent the spread of pulmonary diseases, chronic diarrhea, and scurvy, all of which ravaged the prisoners. "As the foregoing report will show," he concluded in disgust, "this camp is a disgrace to the name of a military prison."[56]

If Clark expected that his inflammatory report would rouse the indignation of his superiors and result in a flurry of directives to improve conditions at Camp Morton, he was sorely disappointed. Hoffman's only reaction was to ask the medical department to assign a "competent surgeon" to the post.[57] The arrival of hundreds of additional prisoners taken in the battles around Chattanooga and the onset of brutally cold weather did prompt the commissary general to request that Meigs stockpile fifteen thousand sets of "inferior clothing" and an equal number of blankets to be supplied to the prisoners in western camps if required, but in accordance with Stanton's directive concerning the treatment of prisoners, Hoffman assured Meigs that the clothing would be issued only to those Rebel prisoners "found in a destitute Condition."[58]

In part, Stanton's increasingly harsh policy resulted from reports of the pitiful condition of sick and wounded Federal captives sporadically released from camps in Richmond. Southern leaders deemed such releases humanitarian gestures, but the arrival of these men in the North occasioned no gratitude. One such group arrived at Annapolis, Maryland, on 2 November. The accompanying medical officer, outraged by what he saw, reported that

> every case wore upon it the visage of hunger, the expression of despair, and exhibited the ravages of some preying disease within, or the wreck of a once athletic frame. I only generalize them when I say their external appearance was wretched in the extreme. . . . Their hair was disheveled, their beards long and matted with dirt, their skin blackened and caked with the most loathsome filth, and their bodies and clothing covered with vermin. Their frames were in the most cases all that was left of them. A majority had scarcely vitality sufficient to enable them to stand. . . . Upon those who had no wounds, as well as on the wounded, were large foul ulcers and sores, principally on their shoulders and hips, produced by lying on the hard ground, and those that were wounded had received no attention, their wounds being in a filthy, offensive condition, with dirty rags, such as they could procure, incrusted hard to them. . . . How great must be the mortality, then, of these men. . . . Weak and debilitated, they wished but to die among their friends, a wish which, unfortunately, will be too nearly realized.[59]

On occasion, Stanton invited northern journalists to observe the arrival of these shipments. The reporters were always outraged by what they saw, and the secretary was quick to use their graphic descriptions of the terrible condition of the returnees to justify the savage acts of retaliation he was ordering against southern prisoners.[60]

On 9 November the secretary codified his requirement for retaliatory action in a message to Major General Ethan Allen Hitchcock. "You will please report what measures you have taken to ascertain the treatment of United States prisoners by the rebels at Richmond," he ordered the commissioner for exchange, "and you are directed to take measures for precisely similar treatment toward all prisoners held by the United States, in respect to food, clothing, medical treatment, and other necessities."[61] In his response that same day, Hitchcock asked Stanton to reconsider the order; but his request was not based on humanitarian grounds or a concern that the secretary's directive would almost certainly constitute a violation of the provisions of General Order No. 100 governing the treatment of prisoners. Rather, Hitchcock's objection was prompted exclusively by security concerns. "With respect to that part of your instructions requiring me to subject rebel prisoners in our hands to treatment similar to that which our men receive in rebel prisons," he wrote Stanton, "I would respectfully represent that if the treatment of our people in Richmond prisons is such as rumor represents, it would result in an uprising of the prisoners against their guards at Camps Morton and Chase, and most likely at other places where the means of security are very slender." If the secretary wished the order executed, Hitchcock continued, the prisoners should first "be put under lock and key (as in penitentiaries) or on islands under the control of fortified batteries."[62]

Stanton heeded Hitchcock's advice and for the time being shelved his order for the adoption of a policy of retaliation in kind. But when combined with his earlier edict, which stipulated that only those improvements "indispensable . . . to prevent suffering" would be allowed in prisoner-of-war camps, the secretary's proposal clearly signaled his disapproval of all but the most rudimentary initiatives aimed at mitigating the plight of prisoners. This unambiguous message was understood and implemented by the officers who administered the Union prisoner-of-war system, and it shaped their responses to requests from camp commanders. On 8 November, for example, Colonel Ambrose A. Stevens, the recently appointed commander of Camp Morton, sought permission to issue replacement clothing for the prisoners in his charge. Stevens had good reason for requesting the issue, for the winter of 1863–1864 was one of the coldest on record, and the Confederates, clothed in tatters and shreds of uniforms, were suffering terribly.[63] The commissary general of prisoners was unmoved. Three days after Stanton issued his directive to Hitchcock, Hoffman replied that "for the present, you will issue no clothing of any kind except in cases of utmost necessity."[64]

Any notion that these restrictions might be attributed exclusively to Hoffman's well-documented obsession for economy are quickly dispelled by his additional instructions to Stevens: "So long as a prisoner has clothing upon him, however much torn, you must issue nothing to him, nor must you allow him to receive clothing from any but members of his immediate family, and only when they are in absolute want." Allowing prisoners to receive clothing from family members before they reached the point of "absolute want" would have relieved much suffering at no cost to the government, but it would have been in contravention to Stanton's insistence on harsher treatment for southern prisoners.[65]

In no camp was the effect of this harsher treatment more evident than at Fort Delaware. When the rate of exchanges began to slow in the spring of 1863, Hoffman suggested to Stanton that additional barracks be constructed at the fort to confine temporarily the large numbers of prisoners that might "occasionally" accumulate during exchange interruptions.[66] Stanton approved, and Hoffman issued detailed instructions to ensure that the camp was prepared for occupation as quickly and inexpensively as possible. Unfortunately, things went terribly wrong from the start. The number of prisoners confined at Fort Delaware jumped from 51 at the beginning of June to 3,737 at the end of the month, and by the end of July there were 8,982 men crammed into the prison's eight acres on Pea Patch Island.[67]

The new barracks Hoffman had ordered to house this multitude were actually no more than plank huts; to save money, they had been erected without adequate foundations. As soon as they were occupied, they began to sink into the island's spongy soil. "In some places they have sunk nearly a foot," reported the prison's recently assigned commander, Brigadier General Albin Schoepf, warning that if something was not done quickly to correct the faulty construction, the barracks and the prison hospital would surely "fall over, and the loss of life in all probability will be great." The dark, cramped buildings also lacked sufficient ventilation, and because Hoffman had determined that they should have no ceilings or any other insulation, they were agonizingly cold in the winter.[68]

Inadequate housing was far from the only hardship faced by the prisoners at Fort Delaware. Punishments administered by the guards were both random and brutal. Torture, including thumb hanging, was common. Prisoner George Moffett recalled seeing "six or eight 'thumb hangers' suspended at one time," adding that "in some cases mortification would set in and the thumbs would have to be amputated." Guards were posted nearby with orders to "shoot anyone who interfered" in order to prevent fellow captives from intervening on behalf of their comrades.[69] Rations at the camp were scanty, unwholesome, and poorly prepared, while the drinking water—drawn from muddy canals, a brackish creek, and rainwater runoff—was so foul that it stank. Poor drainage and overflowing latrines meant that the prison grounds were perpetually covered with what one Rebel termed a "bed of mud and filth." The only water available for bathing was backed up in the muddy drainage ditches that crisscrossed the compound; rather than risk sickness from washing in this polluted source, most prisoners remained filthy.[70]

Given such conditions, it is not surprising that Fort Delaware was quickly overrun by a host of grisly diseases. By midsummer, the death rate at the prison was so high that it even came to the attention of northern journalists, prompting editors of national newspapers to question why such a shameful mortality rate was allowed to continue.[71] Their articles prompted the U.S. Sanitary Commission to launch an inspection of the facility in July. The commission's inspector assessed medical care at the prison to be "in a disgraceful condition," and the spiraling mortality at the prison supported this indictment.[72] Of the 9,136 prisoners confined in the facility, 167 men died in August alone. In September, the number of deaths from sickness and disease more than doubled, a fact that inspecting army surgeon John Cuyler attributed to the "wet and marshy ground" and the rampant spread of typhoid, which was facilitated by the prisoners being "crowded together in large numbers in a confined space." Cuyler's superior, the medical director of the Middle Department, concurred in this assessment. "This is a horrid mortality," he wrote to Hoffman on 9 October, going on to contend that "mere humanity should cause us to select a more healthy place for prisoners of war."[73] In a report of inspection one month later, Hoffman's own medical inspector, the indefatigable A. M. Clark, added his voice to those calling for the camp to be closed. The presence of "stagnant mud and partially stagnant water" throughout the camp was "constant . . . rendering the atmosphere in a high degree unhealthy." He concluded that Pea Patch Island was an "utterly unfit location for a prison, much more for a hospital."[74]

Hoffman was not disposed to entertain any calls for a reduction in the capacity of the camp. Indeed, he was proceeding with plans to increase its prisoner population if required. Thus, when Cuyler suggested that one tier of bunks be removed from each of the barracks to relieve congestion and slow the spread of infectious diseases, Hoffman refused on the grounds that "there may be times when the number of prisoners in our hands will make it necessary to fill up the barracks, even at the risk of being overcrowded." Fort Delaware remained open and overcrowded, and in October the first cases of smallpox joined with diarrhea, dysentery, typhoid, and pneumonia to push the number of deaths to 377 in that single month.[75]

The most telling medical evidence of the mistreatment of prisoners at Fort Delaware may be found in the records of the deaths that resulted from scurvy. Rations at the prison, like those in all Federal camps, had been reduced as part of Hoffman's plan to increase prison and hospital funds, and by the end of the year the fund at Fort Delaware held $23,000. Reports from camp medical officers indicated that money was being expended to purchase enough vegetables to combat scurvy among the prisoners, but statistics compiled during an inspection of the camp by army surgeon G. K. Johnson clearly indicated that such was not the case. Johnson found that from 1 November 1863 to 1 February 1864 there were 365 cases of scurvy reported among an average prisoner population of 2,747, and that fifteen of those afflicted with the disease had died. "In this case," Johnson concluded, "the diet, I apprehend, has not been quite sufficient in quantity, nor composed quite largely enough of vegetables." Even more damning was the fact that at Fort Delaware, scurvy was a disease confined almost exclusively to the prisoner population. U.S. army regulations specified that prisoners were to receive the same rations and medical care as Federal soldiers, but Johnson found that during the same three months, only three cases of scurvy—and no deaths from the disease—had been reported among the 1,068 men of the Union garrison at the camp.[76]

In the South, the difficulties stemming from the termination of exchanges under the cartel were exacerbated due to the Confederate War Department's designation of Richmond as the point of concentration for all prisoners either entering or departing the southern prison system. This policy ensured that while most of the major prisons outside the capital were emptied when the cartel was operational, the number of prisoners held in Richmond remained high. It also ensured that when the cartel began to break down, the thousands of prisoners who had been concentrated in the city awaiting the resumption of exchanges were joined by thousands of recently captured Yankees for whom exchange was no longer an option. When these two groups were combined, the capacity to house, feed, and otherwise care for them was rapidly overwhelmed.

Obtaining an adequate supply of food for the large numbers of prisoners confined in Richmond had always been a challenge. In March 1863, General John Winder had been able to provide sufficient bread for the captives only by impressing supplies of flour destined for the city's markets. Although clearly necessary to prevent starvation, Winder's decision was blasted by the Richmond press. Taking bread from the mouths of hungry citizens and giving it to the despised Yankees in their midst, the *Richmond Whig* thundered, was but further evidence of Winder's "insane tyranny." Such measures, the paper charged, would surely result in increased food shortages and fuel the triple-digit inflation that was already ravaging the city.[77]

Unfortunately, this grim prediction proved only too accurate. By April, inflation was pushing the cost of basic food items beyond the purchasing power of most of the capital's residents, and flour was so scarce that it often could not be obtained at any price. "There is a manifest uneasiness in the public mind different from anything I have noticed heretofore," War Bureau chief Robert G. H. Kean recorded in his diary that spring. On the morning of 2 April, the simmering desperation he had sensed among the citizens of Richmond erupted in a full-fledged food riot.[78] Amid shouts of "bread, bread," a mob consisting of women who had initially gathered in peaceful protest and men and boys who happened to be loitering around Richmond's Capital Square began smashing store windows and looting not only food but also clothing, shoes, and luxury items.[79] Some members of the crowd were armed with knives and hatchets; others brandished pistols. Both Mayor Joseph Mayo and Governor John Letcher attempted without success to reason with the crowd, and the riot was halted only when Jefferson Davis appeared, backed by a company of militia with orders to shoot to kill, and threatened that the soldiers would open fire if the mob did not disperse within five minutes.[80]

Believing that news of the riot would be detrimental to the morale of soldiers at the front, Secretary of War James Seddon ordered telegraph operators to relay no news of the "unfortunate disturbance," and he asked the Richmond newspapers to print no reports of the riot. Surprisingly, the press initially acceded to the secretary's request, but the *Richmond Whig* broke the story on 6 April.[81] Like the editors of the *Whig*, many citizens at first blamed speculators and unpatriotic farmers for the paucity of food available in the capital. Others maintained that Union spies were at work in the city, disrupting the distribution of goods and fomenting unrest among the populace. But a growing number of citizens and government leaders were coming to the conclusion that the food shortages could be largely attributed to the thousands of Union prisoners who were consuming vast quantities of the capital's diminishing stocks.[82]

This conviction was trumpeted in the Richmond press. An editorial in the *Whig* noted that inflation had pushed the price of beef to twice its fair market value. "Meantime," it continued, "there are, according to the latest accounts, thirteen thousand Yankees in the city and on Belle Isle. Having nothing else to do, and being naturally greedy, they eat like so many wolves and hyenas." Mirroring many citizens' growing resentment, the editorial concluded, "Certainly the prisoners are to be kindly treated, but if we are forced to choose between them and the wives and children of soldiers in the field, to say nothing of other people, who are threatened with starvation and freezing, there will be but one voice and that will not be in favor of the Yankees."[83]

Winder, in fact, was finding it increasingly difficult to supply even the basic necessities for the prisoners in his charge. The majority of the captives in Richmond were now confined in Libby, Belle Isle, and Castle Thunder, a group of three buildings surrounded by a board fence at the corner of Cary and Eighteenth Streets. In each of these facilities, overcrowding combined with dwindling stocks of food and supplies to produce conditions that were the worst yet seen in the war. As late as September 1863 conditions in Libby had been judged acceptable by visiting Union reporters from the *Christian Observer*—the last positive evaluation for any of Richmond's prisons. Shortly thereafter the number of prisoners in Libby began to rise rapidly, and by mid-October just over one thousand Union officers were confined in the facility. There was barely room for the men to stand, and cleaning the rooms became impossible. A layer of filth several inches thick covered the floors, and infestations of lice, fleas, and other vermin added to the misery of the captives.[84] Rations consisted of about half a pound of boiled beef, cornbread, and soup issued twice daily. This meager fare could be supplemented with private purchases of vegetables, fruit, and other delicacies, but the high cost of such items quickly exhausted the funds of most prisoners.[85]

On Belle Isle, life was immeasurably more difficult. The prison had been returned to full operation in May, and by September 1863 it held almost 5,400 prisoners, all of them enlisted men. As prisoner Joseph C. Helm later recalled, those lucky enough to have any shelter at all were crowded into "a few old tents that would hardly shed rain"; almost half of the captives on the island did not have even that. Those unfortunates, Helm remembered, sought refuge from the elements in holes dug in the ground, or else they "collected in groups of three or four hundred and stood through the night, pressing against each other." And while the rations issued to the officers imprisoned in Libby were certainly spare, they were sumptuous compared to the fare provided the enlisted captives on Belle Isle. The men drew rations only once daily, Helm vividly recalled, and this allowance consisted either of "a piece of bread, made from unbolted corn meal, not to exceed four inches square, and a pint of thin soup made from rice or 'nigger' beans, or a piece of meat . . . weighing three or four ounces; or a sweet potato, frequently raw, with the bread and the meat, or the soup." The men were so hungry that "every scrap was eagerly devoured, sometimes raw, as it was issued." The food was as insufficient as it was unappetizing; as Helm wrote, there were often days when the prisoners were given "nothing at all to eat."[86] Even if issued every day, the rations were not adequate to sustain the lives of men subjected to the kinds of hardships being endured by the captives on Belle Isle. In October the monthly toll of prisoner deaths topped one hundred for the first time, and it would not drop below this monthly total for the remainder of the year.[87]

Put simply, the Union captives in the capital were starving. There were a number of reasons for their plight, including inadequate stocks of food and an inefficient system of distribution. But to these often-cited justifications for the failure to supply the prisoners with a viable diet, a third, more malevolent, reason must be added. In the early fall of 1863 the Confederate government, for the first time in the war, formulated and instituted an official policy that reduced rations to levels insufficient to sustain the health of prisoners. The driving force behind the adoption of that policy was the commissary general of subsistence, Colonel Lucius B. Northrop.

Northrop graduated from the United States Military Academy in 1831. He had planned on a lifelong career as an officer, but he was severely wounded in the Seminole War and in 1839 was forced to retire from active duty. Northrop had become acquainted with Jefferson Davis at West Point, and following graduation the men had been posted together as dragoon officers on the frontier. With the opening of the Civil War, Northrop volunteered his services to the Confederacy, and on 8 January 1861 Davis appointed his old friend to the position of commissary general of subsistence.[88] It was a post for which Northrop was, by temperament, uniquely unsuited. He was a blunt, combative, and secretive man, and controversy surrounded his performance as commissary general from the very first month of the war. By 1863 he had few friends or supporters in the army, and he was routinely vilified in the southern press.[89]

In August 1863, Brigadier General Alexander R. Lawton was appointed as quartermaster general of the Confederacy. Shortly after assuming his new post, he was summoned to a meeting in Secretary of War Seddon's office, where he, Northrop, and Seddon discussed the problems inherent in feeding prisoners of war. From that meeting came three decisions that would guide the provision of subsistence to captives for the remainder of the war. First, the responsibility for feeding prisoners would be transferred from the quartermaster general to Commissary General Northrop. Second, Confederate army regulations requiring prisoners to be furnished rations "the same in quantity and quality as those furnished to enlisted men in the army of the Confederacy" would be observed as far as possible, but if shortages required that southern soldiers assigned to garrison duty be provided a lower level of subsistence than those serving in the field, the rations of prisoners would be similarly reduced. Finally, and most ominously, the three men agreed that if it became impossible to provide meat to both the Confederate army and prisoners of war, rations of meat for captives would be eliminated entirely.[90]

Provisioning the Confederate army had never been an easy task, and by the middle of 1863 Northrop was finding it difficult to funnel even the most basic foodstuffs to Lee's divisions. Increasingly, he was forced to rely on unpopular measures, such as impressment. Only days after his meeting with Seddon and Lawton, he advanced his first proposal aimed at increasing the amount of food available to the southern armies by a commensurate reduction in the quantity and quality of rations issued to northern prisoners. On 12 August, Northrop suggested to Seddon that meat no longer be included in prisoner rations and that portions of oat and cornmeal gruel, pea soup, soft hominy, and bread be substituted instead. When Seddon reminded Northrop that army regulations required that prisoners were entitled to the same rations as Confederate soldiers, the commissary general retorted that the reductions were justified by the depredations of marauding Yankee armies and the mistreatment of southern captives held in northern prisons. In the past, Seddon had readily demonstrated his willingness to order acts of retaliation against prisoners, but the severity of Northrop's proposal gave even the secretary pause. Captives already weakened by their ordeal, he surely understood, would not long survive on a diet of gruel, pea soup, hominy, and bread. For the present, therefore, Seddon rejected the commissary general's suggestion.[91]

Northrop certainly required no encouragement for his attempt to slash the quantity and quality of prisoner rations, but he was not alone in attributing the prisoners' suffering to the Yankees themselves. Growing numbers of southerners were coming to embrace this idea, and the sentiment was reflected in the press. After reminding its readers of the "unspeakable horrors which our prisoners have suffered in Fort Delaware and other Yankee prisons," the *Richmond Dispatch* hastened to "say to the Yankee prisoners that if they suffer here it is not our fault, who cannot help it; but the fault of their own Government."[92]

Seddon had not invited Winder to the meeting in which Northrop had been given the responsibility for providing prisoner-of-war rations, most likely because Winder and Northrop absolutely despised each other. They had first clashed in 1862, when the commissary general had refused to fill Quartermaster Department requisitions for rations to feed prisoners in the Richmond complex.[93] Since that time the relationship between the two men had become one of the most acrimonious in the entire Confederate army, and Seddon's appointment of Northrop as the man from whom Winder would now have to obtain rations did nothing to decrease their mutual enmity.

It is thus not surprising that the amount of food provided for the captives in Richmond continued to decrease throughout the fall. Then, on 28 October, Winder was informed that no meat at all had been issued for the prisoners.[94] Shortly after receiving this news, Winder received word from the quartermaster of the prison hospitals that no meat had been received for the past twenty-four hours, and that inquiries to Northrop's department had revealed that none would be immediately forthcoming.[95] A third message, dispatched from the commander of Castle Thunder, advised Winder that prisoners in that facility were desperate for food and that the absence of meat would likely provoke an uprising. Winder quickly fired off a message to Seddon, informing him that this was "the fourth occasion upon which we have been unable to furnish the necessary rations" and warning him that unless sufficient food was provided immediately, there was no force in Richmond that would "prove adequate to the control of 13,000 hungry prisoners."[96]

Although Northrop had assumed the responsibility for feeding prisoners almost two months earlier, Seddon only now told Winder that "an arrangement between the Quartermaster-General and Commissary-General has been consummated under which the latter officer assumes the duty of feeding the prisoners of war." Beyond supplying this bit of information, the secretary did nothing to improve the flow of rations to the prisoners. On the contrary, he ordered that all purchases of food by quartermaster officers assigned to Winder's staff were to cease, and that Winder was required to submit all future requisitions for subsistence to the commissary general.[97] Winder complied, but the crisis continued to worsen, and on 9 November he again complained to Seddon of insufficient rations. Nothing was done. Only two days later Winder's supply officer notified him that there was "not one pound of meat on hand for 13,000 men." Once more Winder warned Seddon that "if these prisoners are not fed there is great danger of an outbreak."[98]

The secretary finally responded with a note to Northrop, reminding him that "such supply as is given to soldiers is by law required to be given to the prisoners," but Seddon's support of Winder remained less than enthusiastic.[99] In truth, relations between the two were becoming increasingly strained. Like his counterpart William Hoffman in the North, Winder had been considered for promotion in the spring of 1863. The recommendation had originated with the two powerful senators from Georgia, Benjamin H. Hill and Herschel V. Johnson, and it had the full support of Jefferson Davis. But the endorsement of the secretary of war was required before the nomination could be submitted to Congress for approval, and although Davis urged Seddon forward the nomination without delay, it never left the secretary's office. Seddon never offered the president an explanation for his inaction, and neither he nor Winder ever referred to the incident in correspondence. There can be little doubt, however, that Winder—proud, ambitious, and ever sensitive to such slights—deeply resented Seddon's lack of support.[100]

Personal conflicts notwithstanding, both Winder and Seddon realized that unless drastic action was soon taken, there would be wholesale starvation among the prisoners in Richmond. Political and popular pressure was also building on the Davis administration to decrease the number of prisoners held in the city.[101]

In response, Seddon determined to effect the transfer as soon as he could identify a location where the captives might be sent. On 28 October a possible solution was offered by an unlikely source—General Robert E. Lee. Citing security concerns and the numerous problems attendant in maintaining prisoners in the capital, Lee suggested that as many of the Richmond inmates as possible be transferred to Danville, Virginia, near the North Carolina border. There, Lee maintained, "wood is cheap and provisions are in abundance," and he noted that a prison would be in "little danger of any raid or attack from the enemy."[102] Seddon replied that the general's suggestion "accord[ed] entirely with [his] own previous opinions" and that preparations were already underway to send a "considerable portion" of the prisoners to Danville, where the government had access to "some large, vacant buildings" in which they would be confined.[103]

Seddon and Lee might have been confident that transferring prisoners to Danville would mitigate the challenge of feeding them, but Winder—aware of Northrop's reluctance to provision captives wherever they might be confined—was less assured. On 11 November he informed the secretary that the prisoners were being prepared for transfer as ordered, but he "begged" that "the great responsibility resting on the officers in charge of the prisoners be remembered and that a sufficient supply of provisions be insured for their maintenance."[104] His apprehensions were well placed. While the commissary general agreed that the prisoners should be removed from Richmond, he argued from the first against Danville as the site for a new prison. As Seddon later testified to a congressional committee investigating Northrop's department, "I did not understand the Commissary-General to insist exactly against the selection of Danville as a place of confinement for the prisoners, but while I was considering the propriety of sending them there he certainly urged, as a consideration against it, that it would be more difficult to subsist them, both because some of the counties around were believed to have had a deficient crop and because there was no direct railroad communication from the south; other considerations, however, left me, I thought, no other reasonable alternative, and a limited number were sent there."[105]

In fact, Seddon's "limited number" consisted of almost 4,000 prisoners. Most were enlisted men drawn from Belle Isle, but officers from the stifling rooms of Libby were also selected for transfer. On 11 November the captives were herded into rickety boxcars of the Richmond and Danville Railroad for the 145-mile trip southwest. If the men thought they would find conditions in the new prison a marked improvement over their lots in Richmond, such notions were dispelled as soon as they reached their destination.[106]

Prior to 1861, Danville had been a bustling community of 6,000 souls nestled in the heart of Virginia's tobacco-growing region. The coming of the war had wrought unhappy effects, however. Although the town had not been ravaged by opposing armies, its once-prosperous tobacco factories had been commandeered by the Confederate government and converted into supply depots and hospitals. With each month of the war, citizens found that even basic necessities were becoming increasingly difficult to obtain, and by late 1863 Danville presented, in the words of one local historian, "an appearance of general desolation."[107]

The prisoners' trip from Richmond took almost twenty-four hours, and upon arrival they were marched into the six brick or wooden tobacco factories that had been appropriated for their confinement. The buildings, designated as Prison Nos. 1 through 6, were in reality little more than shells. They had been stripped bare of all furnishings and lighting, leaving only the layers of grime that had accumulated on the rough plank floors over years of use. An average of 650 prisoners were crowded into each of the three-storied structures, and their only source of warmth during the bitterly cold nights was a pitiful assortment of smoky, inefficient, pot-bellied stoves located at one end of each of the floors. Facilities for bathing consisted of troughs filled with muddy water drawn from the Dan River, and the water was seldom changed. Soon the men were so covered with dirt and filth that the guards had trouble telling them apart.[108]

Winder's fears about insufficient rations for this sizable contingent of Yankees were quickly realized. Meat, when issued at all, was of the poorest quality; it was supplemented only by meal composed of corn and cob ground together, cabbage soup infested with bugs and worms, and rice teeming with maggots and laden with rat dung. Prisoners clever enough to catch rats readily ate them and counted themselves lucky. Moreover, the only available drinking water was obtained from stagnant pools near the prison or directly from the muddy Dan.[109]

Subjected to constant cold, denied adequate nourishment, and provided only unclean water to drink, the prisoners rapidly fell victim to a host of debilitating diseases. Chronic diarrhea and respiratory ailments were almost universal. In December the first cases of smallpox were diagnosed in the camp; it raged like wildfire through the crowded buildings, prostrating hundreds of men daily. So great had been Seddon's haste in opening the prison that no hospital had been provided, and men died by the dozen on the filthy floors where they had lived. In March, Cyrus Brannock, a young soldier from Illinois confined in Prison No. 5, wrote his uncle that the prisoners were daily exposed to "the most malignant diseases and all the privations consequent to a Prisoner's life." Brannock did not exaggerate; in January, eighty-six cases of smallpox had been diagnosed in his prison alone. Although a prison hospital was finally established, it was poorly stocked and the number of surgeons was woefully insufficient to cope with the hundreds of stricken soldiers. Day after day, wagons piled high with corpses creaked slowly to the burying ground designated for the Federal dead.[110]

Desperate to flee what seemed almost certain death, many prisoners tried to escape, and the Confederate garrison responded by tightening security at the prison. When one escape attempt proved successful, the prisoners were forced to vacate the ground floors of the buildings. This pushed the number of men crammed into the top two floors to over three hundred apiece. The only latrine facilities in the buildings were located on the ground level, and because the guards severely restricted departures from the upper floors, prisoners suffering from diarrhea and dysentery repeatedly fouled the area where they and their comrades slept.[111]

Back in Richmond, hopes of diminishing the number of prisoners confined in the capital were dashed because the constant arrival of recently captured Yankees more than exceeded the number transferred to Danville. On 17 November, 1,044 men were confined in Libby and just over 6,300 on Belle Isle.[112] In an effort to bring the number of prisoners in Libby down to a manageable level, Winder ordered the excess transferred to Castle Thunder, but the only result of this initiative was that its three buildings became overcrowded as well.

Overcrowding was only one of the grim challenges faced by the prisoners in Castle Thunder. In addition to Union prisoners of war, the facility also held Confederate deserters and convicted civilian felons. The enforcement of discipline in the prison had always been uneven, and following a series of escape attempts and threats by prisoners to blow up the buildings, Winder authorized the use of corporal punishment to restore order.[113] Captain George Alexander, the prison's commander, set to work with a vengeance. Eventually, reports that prisoners charged with even minor infractions were routinely subjected to beatings, thumb hangings, and other forms of torture became so numerous that they could no longer be ignored. The Confederate Congress appointed a committee to investigate Alexander's command, and for an entire month Yankee and Confederate inmates, prison employees, and even detectives from Winder's own staff offered chilling testimony about the brutal treatment that had become commonplace in the facility. Yet Winder steadfastly defended Alexander, claiming that his barbarous regime was necessary to maintain good order and discipline.[114] Although a majority of the investigating committee exonerated Alexander of all wrongdoing, evidence to the contrary was so overwhelming that two members, including the chairman, felt compelled to issue a minority report condemning the "barbarous and cruel" punishments authorized by Alexander and recommending that both he and Winder be removed from their posts. These removals were not effected, and as the number of prisoners confined in Castle Thunder climbed far beyond capacity in November, dark rumors of inhuman treatment within the prison's walls began to circulate through the capital once more.[115]

The effects of overcrowding also diminished the quality of medical care afforded prisoners in Richmond. On 21 November, Surgeon William A. Carrington, the chief medical officer on Winder's staff, warned the War Department that while hospital space was "barely sufficient for 800 men," there were at that moment "1,296 sick Federal Prisoners requiring hospital accommodation in this city." He pleaded that additional facilities be "opened as prison hospitals at once."[116]

Troubled by the rising mortality in prison hospitals and on Belle Isle, Winder directed Carrington to conduct a full investigation into its causes and to offer suggestions about how the health of the prisoners might be better maintained. In the course of his investigation, Carrington ascertained that prisoners were not receiving adequate medical care because overcrowding had reduced the space allotted for them in prison hospitals to half that provided sick and wounded Confederate soldiers.[117] As to the causes of the high number of deaths on Belle Isle, Carrington reported that while prisoner despondency, inadequate rations, and the lack of blankets, fuel, housing, and basic sanitation were clearly contributing factors, "most of the causes of the severity and frequency of the sickness" could be attributed to the simple fact that the men were "*too much crowded.*" The only way to improve conditions on the island, he affirmed, was to transfer "as many of the men as possible" to other locations.[118]

Winder refused to accept Carrington's conclusion. Although conceding that overcrowding was certainly a problem, he maintained that the principal causes of the escalating mortality in Richmond's prisons could be traced to prisoner malaise and a particularly virulent strain of smallpox that afflicted the captives. Given his demonstrated concern over the high number of deaths among prisoners and his ongoing battles with Seddon and Northrop to ensure that the captives in his charge were adequately provisioned, Winder's steadfast refusal to accept Carrington's findings are puzzling. He offered no explanation for rejecting the conclusions of his own inspector, which can probably be explained by the fact that he believed himself powerless to reduce the congestion in Richmond's prisons while ensuring the security of the capital. Shortages of guards and suitable structures in which to confine the ever-increasing number of prisoners had forced him to concentrate the captives, and absent a resumption of general exchanges or the transfer of large numbers of prisoners out of the city, these factors would continue to constrain his options.[119]

In November, the lot of Richmond's prisoners nonetheless improved temporarily with the delivery of blankets, food, and other supplies sent from the North. Union commissioner of exchange Sullivan Meredith, who had proposed the plan, brokered an agreement with his southern counterpart, Robert Ould, to distribute the items under the supervision of General Neal Dow, a prisoner in Libby. Dow promptly issued the supplies to the enlisted prisoners on Belle Isle, directing the officer who delivered the blankets and clothing to advise Meredith that the soldiers on Belle Isle were "suffering beyond endurance." By January, Dow predicted, they would be dying at the rate of one hundred a day. To forestall that catastrophe, he proposed that the Union government smuggle $100,000 in Confederate money through him to the prisoners. Neither Meredith nor Hitchcock responded to the general's suggestion, but when Ould agreed to allow the delivery of another 24,000 rations to the prisoners later that month, Meredith specified that they were to be distributed by officers other than Dow.[120]

Reports that food and supplies were being sent south were initially greeted with acclaim in the northern press, and the Union officers who distributed the items assured Meredith that "every facility for the inspection of the prisoners and the distribution of the clothing has been afforded . . . by the Confederate military authorities."[121] Unhappily, the future of the deliveries was immediately threatened by yet another round in the propaganda war that was perpetually raging between the two nations. On 13 November, Hitchcock had directed Meredith to notify Ould that "whatever steps may have been, or may be taken, to extend relief (to the prisoners of war in Richmond,) [they] must on no occasion be appealed to by the enemy to relieve him from the obligation to treat prisoners according to the laws of civilized warfare." Outraged at the implications of Hitchcock's instructions, Ould shot back that "until the Confederate authorities appeal to be relieved from 'the obligation to treat prisoners according to the laws of civilized warfare,' . . . it is entirely unnecessary to discuss what will be the views of your authorities." On 23 November the text of both letters appeared in the *Richmond Enquirer*, and one week later the report of the *Enquirer*, with commentary, was reprinted in the *New York Times*.[122]

The death blow to northern shipments of rations and supplies to its imprisoned soldiers was delivered on 28 November, when an "official statement" from four Union surgeons recently released from Libby prison exploded across the front page of the *New York Times*. The surgeons, all of whom had worked in Richmond's prison hospitals while confined, wrote that they considered it their "duty" to "publish a few facts that came to [their] knowledge while confined," and beneath headlines that screamed "Horrors of the Richmond Prisons," "Disease, Starvation and Death," and "Shocking Pictures of Destitution and Abject Wretchedness," they spun out their story. "For several months," the officers claimed, they had "been allowed daily access" to the hospitals where sick and wounded Union prisoners were receiving treatment. Based on their observation, they declared that "since the battle of Chickamauga the number of deaths [among captives] per diem has averaged fully fifty." The primary killers in the wards had been "diarrhea, dysentery, and typhoid pneumonia," but the surgeons reported that "of late the percentage of deaths has greatly increased—the result of causes that have been long at work, such as insufficient food, clothing and Shelter." They charged that the government rations and supplies sent south never made it to the prisoners for whom they were intended. As a result, the men were "half clad, and covered in vermin and filth, many of them too often beyond all reach of medical skill." Their condition was becoming worse daily; with the onset of winter and continued Confederate cruelties, their prognosis was grim indeed. "Judging from what we have ourselves seen and do know," the surgeons wrote, "we do not hesitate to say that, under a treatment of systematic abuse, neglect and semi-starvation, the number who are becoming permanently broken down in their conditions must be reckoned in the thousands." But if the surgeons believed that the publication of their charges would ease the suffering of prisoners in Richmond, they were sorely disappointed. In the North, the report simply added to the pressure on the Lincoln administration to conclude some sort of agreement that would bring the prisoners home. In the South, charges that relief shipments intended for the prisoners were being stolen by guards or diverted to Lee's army outraged Confederate officials. On 12 December, Ould informed Meredith that no further shipments would be allowed.[123]

Although Winder and his staff consistently denied allegations that rations intended for prisoners were being stolen or diverted, money belonging to prisoners was routinely confiscated. On 15 September, Seddon announced a policy that allowed prisoners to retain any gold they were carrying when captured, but he mandated the confiscation of all "greenbacks." Yankees who consented to "exchange" their notes for Confederate money at "the current rate" were to be permitted to use the funds to purchase available goods while confined. The Federal banknotes of captives who refused this option were also to be confiscated and held in an account in the prisoner's name.[124]

Seddon's official justification of this policy was that "Federal paper" was "not recognized as money" in the South, but the Confederate government was actually confiscating the greenbacks to fund services performed by individuals who would no longer accept rapidly depreciating Confederate notes as payment.[125] On 28 November, for example, Captain Clarence Morfit, the quartermaster officer on Winder's staff who was charged with management of the confiscated funds, advised his commander that his supply of Federal notes was rapidly being expended by the government to pay blockade runners, who would accept "northern funds" only. "The only source from which these funds [are] derived is the prisoners," Morfit complained, "and such is the scarcity of 'greenbacks' now that the brokers can not meet their orders."[126]

In short, the last seven months of 1863 saw not only a deterioration in Union and Confederate prisoner-of-war systems and a hardening of attitudes in the men who directed them; it also saw a change in the opinions of civilians in both the North and the South. Claims of prisoner neglect and abuse by the enemy had been common in both sections since the beginning of the war, but the last months of 1863 saw a growing willingness among ordinary citizens to believe that prisoners were being deliberately mistreated in order to render them unfit for further service and thus reduce the combat power of the opposing government. Correspondence from prisoners, official assessments of the state of returned captives, and increasingly lurid press accounts of conditions in enemy prisons combined to produce what historian William B. Hesseltine has characterized as a "war psychosis," which made such charges readily credible.[127]

The onset of this psychosis was evident in the increasingly vitriolic attacks on John Winder in the northern press. In 1862 the general had been commended both by northern papers and by exchanged prisoners for his efforts on behalf of captives, but by 1863 he had been transformed into the very personification of a rogue government that sanctioned unspeakable acts intended to kill or destroy the health of the prisoners under its control.[128] "Winder is . . . capable of any meanness and cruelty," a typical editorial fulminated; he was "the fit instrument of the horrible schemes of the rebel Confederacy, for undoubtedly their intention is to operate upon our Government by allowing our soldiers to rot and starve in the Richmond prisons."[129]

The psychosis was equally evident in the South. In a letter to Secretary of War Seddon, the Confederate surgeon general charged that the wretched condition of prisoners released from Fort Delaware offered ample proof that the Union was guilty of perpetrating an "unworthy attempt to subdue or destroy our soldiers by pestilence and disease." Ould echoed the prevalent opinion when he rhetorically asked Meredith if the objective of such mistreatment was to "fill our land with mourning by such means of subjugation."[130]

Reports of horrid conditions in Union prisons, coupled with the North's refusal to agree to a general exchange, continued to provide grist for the propaganda mills of the South. In his General Order No. 208, General Braxton Bragg announced that the Confederate government now "officially recognized" that "the enemy does not intend to carry out, in good faith, the cartel agreed on between his Government and the Confederate States," a fact that presented his soldiers of the Army of Tennessee with two very stark alternatives. They could allow themselves to be taken prisoner, in which case they would be "forced to languish in northern dungeons until the close of the war," or they could clearly demonstrate that they were "brave and patriotic Southern soldiers" by opting for an "*honorable death* on the field of battle, nobly fighting for the cause of freedom."[131]

In Richmond, newspapers reflected the mood of most citizens when they accused Winder of being too lenient in his treatment of the Union captives. A people guilty of holding Confederate soldiers in pens like Point Lookout and Fort Delaware, ran the common theme in the southern press, were less than human and fully deserving of like treatment. One editor, Union prisoner Warren Goss remembered, even went so far as to suggest "that dirty people required less food than people who were clean, instancing the Yankee prisoners on Belle Isle as an illustration of the truth of the assumption." Other solutions proffered by the southern press were much more ominous. "The Yankee Government . . . [is] entitled to these men," the *Richmond Examiner* offered, "and, if they will not take them, let them be put where the cold weather and scant fare will thin them out in accordance with the laws of nature."[132]

By the end of 1863 both governments had come to realize that the dreadful overcrowding in their prisons could be reduced only through the implementation of drastic measures. Since a resumption of general exchange under the cartel was out of the question, the sole remaining option was the opening of additional prisons as swiftly as possible, and in the final weeks of the year both Stanton and Seddon dispatched emissaries to search for suitable locations. Stanton instructed Hoffman to tour the states of New York, Massachusetts, Rhode Island, and Pennsylvania to determine where additional prisons might be established; in Richmond, Seddon directed Captain William S. Winder to "proceed without delay" to Georgia and select a spot where a new prison might be constructed. Winder was specifically instructed to search "in the neighborhood of Americus," where one location that quickly caught his eye was the small village of Andersonville.[133]

CHAPTER 8

"Disgraceful to All Concerned"

The Union and Confederate Prisoner-of-War Systems, 1864

BY THE WINTER OF 1863, Captain William Sidney Winder had long since abandoned any notions that service in the army of the Confederacy would bring him either fame or glory. Like most young southerners of his generation and social station, he had rushed to the colors as soon as possible after war had been declared and had been appointed to the staff of his father, General John H. Winder. In the heady days of 1861, this had seemed to offer a chance for important service that would surely be appreciated by his countrymen and rewarded by his government. But duty on his controversial father's staff had been anything but glorious, and two years of difficult and often distasteful toil had netted Sidney only one promotion.[1]

Nor did the captain have any illusions about his latest task: searching for a location where a new prison might be established. Sidney was his father's most trusted subordinate, and he had been instrumental in the occupation and administration of the Richmond prison complex. He had experienced firsthand the grueling demands that the administration of such installations placed on commanders, and he was fully aware of the challenges inherent in constructing and activating a facility capable of housing thousands of Federal prisoners in the piney woods of central Georgia.[2]

Captain Winder arrived in Americus, Georgia, on 28 November 1863, and the difficulties that he and his father had anticipated arose almost immediately. After conferring with the Commissary Department's regional agent, Winder decided to establish the new prison at Bump Head, an old camp meeting ground just west of Americus. Upon visiting the site, however, he found that it was still heavily used by local Primitive Baptists for their religious gatherings. To no one's surprise, the Bump Head faithful strongly objected to the confiscation of the land, but they were quick to suggest an alternative. Andersonville, eleven miles northwest of Americus, lay on the line of the Southwestern Railroad and had an ample supply of fresh water. The Baptists were certain that it would much better suit the government's needs.[3]

Winder journeyed to Andersonville that afternoon, where he found a ramshackle railroad depot and a hardscrabble farming community of about seventy souls. He was directed to Ben Dykes, a local speculator who owned most of the land surrounding the village. Dykes offered some acreage in the piney woods less than a mile from the depot, but Winder rejected it because it was without water. The neighboring plantation, owned by W. W. Turner, was more promising. A branch of Sweetwater Creek (a tributary of the Flint River) ran through it, and it included a clearing that Winder judged sufficient to contain a stockade. Secretary of War James Seddon's orders required that the site for the new prison be both isolated and yet easily accessible to a rail line and sufficient supplies of water and timber. Winder reckoned that a combination of Dykes's and Turner's land would satisfy these requirements. He therefore leased both parcels and set about staking out the perimeter of the stockade. The design he chose was a simple square, 750 feet on a side and bisected by the branch of Sweetwater Creek. He informed his father of his progress and asked that a quartermaster officer be sent to supervise the prison's construction.[4]

In mid-December that officer arrived in the person of yet another Winder, Sidney's cousin Richard. Sidney had originally been directed to construct a facility capable of confining six thousand captives, but Richard, mindful of the hideous overcrowding in the pens of Richmond, suggested that the stockade be enlarged to accommodate ten thousand. Sidney agreed, and the cousins went in search of the labor and materials necessary to construct the facility. They then encountered another serious problem, for they discovered that with the exception of Dykes and Turner, the Andersonville locals were not at all keen to have a prison constructed in their midst. Area slaveholders refused to lease their chattel to the Winders, only a few stockmen consented to rent out their horses and mules, and timber could not be purchased at the low fixed prices authorized by the Confederate government.[5] In desperation, Richard Winder was forced to petition Seddon for authorization to impress the necessary labor, and the secretary reluctantly granted it. On 10 January 1864 construction of the stockade finally began, but already almost two months had passed since Sidney had first arrived at the site.[6]

Other problems now arose in quick succession. Sidney found that the only physician available to care for laborers at the camp was located four miles from Andersonville, and Richard discovered that local stocks of grain and beef were entirely insufficient to feed the number of prisoners he had been told to expect. To alleviate these shortages, Quartermaster General Alexander Lawton directed that a bakery be constructed at the site and that beef be secured by driving herds up from cattle-rich northern Florida. But moving the steers to Andersonville required drivers, and when Richard asked the commander of the conscript camp at Macon to furnish draftees for this task, his request was refused. He then appealed for help from the numerous local men who had been exempted from the draft due to the machinations of Georgia's irascible governor Joseph E. Brown, but they declined to undertake the task for the low government wages offered. "It is absolutely impossible to hire exempts to drive cattle," Richard complained to General Winder in Richmond. "This class of men find speculation much more profitable than anything else, and consequently they cannot be hired; such as would be willing to perform this service are physically unable." In the end, Richard's entreaties netted only a few cripples incapable of such arduous work and five able-bodied malingerers who volunteered in order to avoid front-line service when their draft exemptions expired.[7]

Faced with the prospect of being unable to supply even half the subsistence a prisoner population of ten thousand would require, Richard sought the assistance of the commissary depot located fifty miles to the east at Columbus, Georgia. "I shall want beef, meat, flour, sugar, molasses, rice, soap, candles, &c.," he wrote to the depot commander on 3 February. Assuring the officer that the situation at Andersonville was urgent, he noted that "I shall soon have the Yankee prisoners at this post," and he begged that his request be afforded the "earliest attention." He also commissioned a civilian purchasing agent to search as far away as Atlanta to secure pots for boiling meat, even as he informed General Winder that he had been unable to procure enough baking pans, padlocks, and nails.[8]

Nor could Richard obtain lumber for construction of the prison's headquarters, hospital buildings, warehouses, and cookhouse. Trees there were aplenty, but local sawmills refused the low government rate of compensation. He considered impressing these materials, but he found that the millers were immune to such a threat because they held lucrative, government-protected contracts with the railroads. He finally persuaded a local businessman to open a sawmill and gristmill near the prison, but the output of lumber from this single source was so paltry that Winder was forced strictly to prioritize the order of construction. First priority was given to the cookhouse, with construction of the headquarters and hospital to follow. The prisoners' barracks would be built last; until they could be erected, Richard planned to quarter the captives in tents. He had been assured that the state of Georgia had surplus tents in abundance, but when he attempted to purchase them, his request was refused on orders from Governor Brown, who insisted that they be reserved for the use of Georgia state troops only.[9]

A final problem that beset the activation of Camp Sumter, as the stockade at Andersonville was officially designated by the Confederate government, concerned the selection and organization of its garrison. Adjutant General Samuel Cooper judged Sidney Winder too young and inexperienced to discharge effectively the responsibilities of camp commander. On 7 February, Secretary of War Seddon notified General Howell Cobb, the commander of the military district in which the prison lay, that the government was "about to establish a cantonment at Andersonville . . . for the safekeeping of the Federal prisoners now in [Richmond], numbering from 10,000 to 12,000," and he asked Cobb to recommend an officer from Georgia to command the post. Cobb nominated Lieutenant Colonel Alexander W. Persons, a former lawyer from Fort Valley, a town only thirty miles from the prison. Persons had the good fortune of being on leave when his entire regiment was scooped up by the Yankees in the battle of Cumberland Gap in September 1863, and he thus found himself between assignments. He was duly appointed as commander of Camp Sumter.[10]

But instead of designating Persons to direct all the operations at Camp Sumter, Seddon and Cooper determined that responsibility at the prison would be divided between three separate and distinct commanders. Persons would control operations in the area stretching from village railroad station (where the prisoners would arrive) to the walls of the stockade. Subordinate to him would be an officer who would command all garrison troops except the staff of the prison and the men specially detailed for duty at the camp. Command of the actual prison and its inmates would be the responsibility of a third officer, who would operate almost independently of Persons and the garrison commander. Within the stockade, this officer would reign supreme, but to obtain guard details for the prison or rations and supplies for the prisoners, he would be required to submit requisitions to Persons and the garrison commander. Until the camp actually became operational, Persons was permitted to assume all three commands, but this did not eliminate his problems. On 17 February, Richard Winder notified his uncle in Richmond that Persons had "not more than 100 men altogether in his command, and that those of his command who have arrived at this post as guards are without guns."[11]

As of mid-February, then, the prison at Andersonville was but a shell of an installation. Its stockade was only half completed, as were the buildings housing the camp bakery and headquarters. Construction of the prison hospital had not even begun, and there were no structures or tents of any sort to shelter prisoners. Moreover, existing arrangements for supplying subsistence were ludicrously inadequate to feed even half the projected number of prisoners, the command structure designated for the camp was hopelessly inefficient and convoluted, and the ragtag assembly of men who constituted the prison's guard force was both untrained and unarmed.

Richard and Sidney Winder had worked tirelessly to overcome these deficiencies, but the failure of the Confederacy to establish a clear and unambiguous chain of command for prisoner management ensured that their efforts would be severely hampered. Commissary officers, accountable only to Commissary General Lucius Northrop, failed to fill requisitions for rations; railroad companies, with the full support of the War Department, outbid the Winders on critical lumber contracts. The governor of Georgia refused the Winders' requests for vital supplies and equipment from the state's surplus stocks. Meanwhile, important appointments—such as the selection of a commander for the camp—were decided by the Confederate adjutant general and the military district commander with no input from General John H. Winder, the officer tasked by the secretary of war with the responsibility for establishing the post.

On 30 January 1864 General Winder had attempted to rectify these deficiencies by again recommending the appointment of a Confederate commissary general of prisoners. "I deem it necessary," Winder wrote to Seddon,

> that there should be some office having a general supervision of all that relates to prisoners of war—their management and subsistence—and where all papers connected therewith should be deposited. I would respectfully add that, unless the [War] Dept. considers it judicious to transfer the control of this subject to some other Dept., the facilities of this office are ample for the execution of the duties connected therewith without the employment of any additional clerical force, or the assignment of any other officers.[12]

As in the past, Seddon declined to make such an appointment, and the Confederate prisoner-of-war system continued to stagger along without efficient command or control.

These must have been very frustrating times for the Winder cousins. Worse—much worse—was yet to come. In early February, they received a telegram from Richmond stating, as Richard later recalled, "that it was impossible to feed the prisoners longer there, and that they must come at once to Andersonville."[13] This justification was true, as far as it went. The prisoner population in the capital had ballooned far beyond a number that General Winder and his staff could provision. Rations were becoming increasingly difficult to obtain, and Commissary General

Northrop continued to place a low priority on the replenishment of those stocks. But there were other, equally important reasons why the men who directed the Confederate prisoner-of-war system had decided to send thousands of captives to a prison they knew full well was in no way prepared to receive them.

The first of these reasons was political. Increasingly, the citizens of Richmond were coming to view the prisoners as an unnecessary drain on the strained resources of the capital, and political and public pressure was mounting on the Davis administration to reduce their rations and remove them from the city. "Are we, and we alone to suffer the penalty of their transgressions?" thundered the *Richmond Dispatch*. Its editors spoke for many in the city when they answered that the South would "be perfectly justified in stinting [the prisoners] to half or a quarter of the allowance we make to our own soldiers." If "anybody suffers," the paper maintained, "it is perfectly just that it should be they, but for whose acts, done in defiance of all the laws that regulate the proceedings of war, there would be no suffering at all."[14]

Nor were the inhabitants of Richmond the only Confederate citizens pressuring Davis to remove the Yankee prisoners from their midst. On 29 January, Seddon was presented with a petition from the "Mayor and Common Council" of Danville, "earnestly" requesting "the removal of the Yankee prisoners located amongst us to some other place." Diseased prisoners, the officials complained, had been "scattered in the most public and business places, so as to infect the whole atmosphere of the town with small Pox," and the stench from these makeshift wards had become "offensive at a distance of several hundred yards." Effluent and other filth from the prisoners' facilities, the petition continued, "runs down in small sluggish branches that run nearly through the breadth of the Town, and it is permitted to remain until a rain partially removes it, the most finding a permanent lodgment in the drains."[15] Seddon yielded to the petitioners' demands, and in March the War Department decreed that the prisoners in Danville would join the thousands of captives from Richmond already earmarked for transfer to the unfinished facility at Andersonville.[16]

The second reason that prisoners were shipped from Richmond to Andersonville before Camp Sumter was completed was the growing fear that the presence of thousands of Federal prisoners in the capital constituted a grave security risk. Lee had first raised such concerns in the fall of 1863, and apprehension over the threat posed by the captives continued to mount as 1864 opened. When the adjutant of Libby protested that the existing hospital space for the prisoners was woefully inadequate, for example, Surgeon T. G. Richardson countered that the number of hospitals then in operation could not be secured and that he "lived in fear of a breakout every night." On 12 January, Winder was notified that the prisoners in Libby had been issued no meat for four days, and that it had been eleven days since Northrop's commissary officers had delivered meat for the captives on Belle Isle. He warned Seddon and Cooper that the hungry prisoners were becoming desperate and that a massive escape or uprising was almost certain if rations did not swiftly improve. These warnings came to fruition on the night of 9 February, when 109 officers, including the infamous Colonel Abel Streight, escaped through a tunnel dug under the walls of Libby.[17]

Cooper had already directed Winder to initiate planning the transfer of as many Federals as possible out of Richmond, and two days before the Libby escape Winder had responded that preparations were underway to ship the prisoners to Andersonville at the rate of four hundred a day.[18] Now, spurred by the specter of over one hundred Yankee escapees skulking about the Confederate capital, the schedule for transferring the prisoners was accelerated. Winder notified his son and nephew to expect the first shipment of captives within ten days and to plan for subsequent arrivals at the rate of about three thousand per week. This was a stunningly ambitious rate of shipment, but on 28 February the dramatic appearance of a new and far more dangerous threat to the security of Richmond ensured that it would be met.[19]

In the winter of 1863, newspaper accounts that conditions in Libby and on Belle Isle were worsening daily and intelligence reports that Richmond was protected by only three thousand poorly trained militiamen led Union officers to plan a raid to free the captives. General Judson Kilpatrick, a reckless and impetuous cavalry commander, convinced Abraham Lincoln and Secretary of War Edwin Stanton that with a single bold stroke he could seize the Rebel capital by surprise and free the prisoners.[20] On 28 February, he struck south through the Confederate lines. Upon learning that the hard-riding raiders were fast approaching their near-defenseless city, official Richmond panicked. Seddon ordered Winder to take all possible measures to secure the prisoners, whereupon Winder ordered that a mine with a charge of two hundred pounds of gunpowder be placed in the cellar of Libby. Although he later claimed that the action was no more than a bluff, at the time he placed the mine Winder assured the captives that should they attempt to escape or in any way aid the raiders, he would not hesitate to detonate the mine and blow the prison and every one of its occupants to bits.[21]

On 1 March, columns led by Kilpatrick and his subordinate, Colonel Ulrich Dahlgren, unsuccessfully struck the outer defenses of the city. Dahlgren was killed in the attempt, and on his body searchers found papers that disclosed the intent of the raid. "We hope to release the prisoners from Belle Island first," Dahlgren had written, "and having seen them fairly started, we will cross the James River into Richmond, destroying the bridges after us, and exhorting the released prisoners to destroy and burn the hateful city, and to not allow the Rebel leader, Davis, and his traitorous crew to escape."[22] This was Richmond's worst nightmare come true, and the hysteria spawned by the raid was clearly evident in the strident calls for reprisals in the local press. "The day's sun should not go down," screamed the *Richmond Whig* in a typical editorial, "before every scoundrel taken [prisoner] in this assassin's work is blown to atoms from the mouths of cannon." There were no summary executions of prisoners, but the near-success of Kilpatrick and Dahlgren pushed Winder and Seddon to redouble their efforts to hasten the ongoing transfer of prisoners out of the capital to Andersonville.[23]

One of the Union soldiers transferred in the early shipments from Belle Isle was John Ransom, who kept a diary record of the journey that began when he and his comrades were loaded into railway cars in the middle of the night. The guards watched them closely, and "occasionally a Yank was shot" for violating their orders. For six days the train wound slowly through country that Ransom described simply as "miserable." Finally he arrived at the new prison, a facility which he characterized with equal brevity as "a dismal hole."[24]

The description was apt. The initial arrivals had reached Andersonville on 27 February, and one of the first things they noticed was that its construction was far from complete. There was no bakery, hospital, or barracks, and one end of the log stockade intended to enclose the facility still stood open. As the prisoners arrived, they were herded through this gap in the wall, where guards issued them a few cooking utensils and a meager, uncooked ration consisting of a small bit of beef or bacon, some meal, and a few sweet potatoes.[25] The guards then withdrew to the open end of the prison, where, supported by a few pieces of artillery, they formed a thin cordon to hold the prisoners inside. There was little effort to organize or instruct the captives. As there was no shelter of any sort, prisoners who were strong enough began to assemble crude huts from bits of timber that had been discarded during the erection of the stockade. Seaman Frederick James, a Union sailor captured during a coastal raid in South Carolina, recorded in his diary that he was sharing a "Chebang" with eight other men. "It is roofed with four blankets and logs for the walls at the sides," James wrote, counting himself among the fortunate at Andersonville. Prisoners too ill or too weak to provide for themselves were simply dragged to one wall of the stockade, where they were left for the attention of the few surgeons at the post. As successive groups of prisoners arrived, they were marched into the pen and left to fend for themselves. The quantity and quality of rations declined with each shipment of prisoners, and the clear stream that flowed through the camp was quickly polluted.[26]

The pattern of life and death at Andersonville had been set, and the dying began almost immediately. Many of the men shipped from Belle Isle and Danville were already gravely ill when they arrived; given the lack of shelter, inadequate medical care, and absence of sufficient rations, they succumbed in the dirt where they lay. "Can see a dozen most any morning laying around dead," John Ransom wrote shortly after arriving at the prison. "A great many are terribly afflicted with diarrhea, and scurvy begins to take hold of some."[27] The stockade had finally been completed in mid-March, and by the beginning of April over 7,500 prisoners had been herded within its walls. Of that number, 283 had already died. As there was still no hospital, the sick were gathered under tent flys in the corners of the prison. Here they lay on beds of pine straw until their conditions improved—or not. By 25 April, the number of sick who had been seen by the prison's small medical staff had risen to 2,697, and there had been 718 deaths.[28]

Richard Winder continued to work tirelessly to secure the desperately needed rations, building supplies, and equipment, but his efforts were frustrated by the low priority assigned to the shipment of these goods to the prison. On 20 February he had notified the commissary department that the rate at which rations were being provided was far too slow to provision the number of captives projected for the camp, and he urged the officer responsible to "please make some arrangement at once" that would "insure against failure." Three days later Winder informed a second commissary officer that in order to ease supply difficulties he would "gladly" feed the prisoners "offal," including "beef tongues . . . shank meat and pickled hearts," if the department would only make these items available at a reasonable price. Nonetheless, Winder's difficulties in obtaining rations only became worse, for at the end of February he received word from Richmond that the plan to feed the prisoners on cattle driven from Florida had been abandoned. This was followed by the even darker news that henceforth the responsibility for supplying rations to Camp Sumter would rest entirely with Colonel Northrop and his commissary department.[29]

Problems with timely shipments of other supplies persisted as well. On 11 April, Richard discovered that an entire trainload of lumber urgently needed to complete construction of the prison hospital had been sitting for twelve days on a siding only sixty miles from Andersonville because the quartermaster officer in Macon had taken no action to have it delivered. To illustrate the "great want and emergency" for lumber at the camp, Winder informed the officer that he had been reduced to "burying the dead without coffins," and he threatened to "report the matter to the authorities at Richmond" if the timber was not soon shipped.[30]

Significant difficulties arose within the garrison troops at the prison as well, most of which could be traced to the absence of an efficient command-and-control system for the Confederate system of prisons. General Howell Cobb, the military district commander, was responsible for finding adequate guards for Camp Sumter, but when he attempted to assign regular army troops to the prison, Governor Brown insisted that only militia and Georgia reserves be used. This group—wholly untrained and consisting mainly of old men, underage boys, and convalescents—proved entirely inadequate to the task. Overworked and underfed, the men found their duty arduous and the working conditions unhealthful. Discipline was lax, and random shootings of prisoners became so common that one of the young guards was moved to seek intervention from President Jefferson Davis. "They think the killing of a Yankee will make them great men," the soldier wrote. "They shoot prisoners, alleging they crossed the 'dead line.' I know you are opposed to such measures, and I make this statement to you to be a soldier, a statesman and a Christian." Desertions among the guards were common, discipline evaporated, and soon it became impossible for officers at the prison to control the garrison at all. While Persons was away from camp attempting to secure tools, the guards rose in a near mutiny; although order was eventually restored, they continued to be an inadequate and unstable lot.[31]

In Richmond, meanwhile, General John Winder was consumed with problems of his own. He clearly saw that the establishment of additional camps was accelerating the rate at which the flawed Confederate system of prisoner-of-war management was spinning out of control, and in a series of messages he pleaded with Adjutant General Cooper and Secretary of War Seddon to clarify the command relationships between him and the prison commanders. On 2 March, he wrote Seddon "to request that [his] position in connection with the prisons at Danville, Va., and Andersonville, Ga., may be defined." He noted that the special orders appointing Colonel Persons to command of Andersonville failed to require the colonel to report directly to his office in Richmond, placing Persons "beyond [his] control." At Danville, the case was much the same. Although Winder was held responsible for operations at that camp, the officer commanding the Danville prison reported not to him, but to the commander of the military department in which the facility was located. Clearly frustrated by this continuing confusion of the lines of authority, Winder volunteered that "if it is the wish of the Department to relieve me of the command of those prisons I offer no objections." All he sought, he assured the secretary, was "clarification," for "it would be embarrassing for me to issue orders when I had no right to do so, and it would be just as embarrassing for me to neglect to issue orders when I ought to do so."[32]

Failing to appreciate the extent of Winder's difficulties, Seddon dismissed these objections as "unnecessary" and appealed to Cooper to provide a "solution to this tangle." Cooper replied that he could "see no necessity for raising a question of difficulty in this case." Clearly revealing that he in no sense appreciated the depth and seriousness of the problems spawned by the convoluted command structure he and Seddon had instituted at Andersonville, the adjutant general sought to appease Winder by assuring him that as supervisor of the two prisons, he retained the authority to relieve the commanders at Danville and Andersonville whenever he wished. The muddled Confederate system remained in place.[33]

Even as Winder, Seddon, and Cooper continued to talk past each other, conditions in the prisons of Richmond continued to plummet. Massive transfers of captives to Andersonville failed to reverse this downward spiral, and by March 1864 the mortality among the prisoners at Belle Isle had become so alarming that Medical Director William A. Carrington ordered Surgeon G. W. Semple to conduct a thorough inspection of the facility. In his brutally straightforward assessment, the surgeon minced no words in describing how the once beautiful island had been transformed into a vast killing field. "Into the camp containing an area sufficient for the accommodation of about three thousand men, have been crowded for many months past from six to ten thousand prisoners," Semple's report of 6 March began. This chronic overcrowding had produced consequences that by this point in the war could have come as a surprise to no one in the War Department. "To prevent escape," Semple noted, the prisoners were not permitted to "visit the sinks at night," and "deposits of excrement have been made in the streets and in the small vacant spaces between the tents." Because the camp was so crowded, no effective policing of the grounds could be accomplished, and the men lived in an environment of unspeakable filth. Meat had disappeared altogether from the prisoners' daily rations, leaving them to subsist entirely on rice, peas, beans, and bread made from unbolted corn meal. Semple found the captives "badly clad and destitute of blankets"; by the time of his inspection, they had long since traded the goods they had received from the North for food. Typhoid, diarrhea, dysentery, and a host of deadly respiratory maladies were so common that the camp hospital had been completely overwhelmed, and prisoners were dying "without having been seen by, or reported to a medical officer." The only way to reduce the terrible mortality on Belle Isle, Semple concluded, was to remove as many men as possible from the island as quickly as possible.[34]

On 23 March, Carrington forwarded a copy of Semple's report to Winder. Seeking to "avoid imputation that the Medical Department could legitimately be considered as compromised by, or responsible for the existing regulations," he pointedly reminded the general that offers to transfer ill prisoners to Confederate hospitals in the capital had been rebuffed on the grounds that there were insufficient guards to secure those facilities. The mortality among the prisoners in Richmond, Carrington asserted, would continue to climb until the overcrowding in hospitals was reduced, and the medical department could not be held responsible for prisoner deaths because Winder refused to authorize the use of additional hospitals for their care.[35]

As in the past, Winder flatly refused to accept overcrowding as one of the root causes of the high rates of mortality in Richmond's prisons, preferring instead to blame smallpox and Northrop's failure to supply adequate rations. There now ensued a duel of correspondence in which Winder and officials in the Confederate medical department presented their opposing arguments to General Braxton Bragg, newly appointed to the post of special advisor to President Davis. Despite this flurry of letters and memoranda, little was done to provide Winder the additional manpower he required or to improve conditions in the prisons and hospitals. The appalling mortality continued unabated.[36]

Nor was the dying confined to the prisons of Richmond and Andersonville. At the same time that the Winders were struggling to establish the Camp Sumter stockade, the War Department determined that overcrowding in the capital could be further reduced through the establishment of an additional prison to confine captives taken in the battles in the western Confederacy. The location selected for this new facility was Cahaba, Alabama, and its structure was one of the most unusual and inadequate confinement facilities chosen by either the North or the South. The fact that it was selected at all clearly illustrates the desperation of Confederate planners at this point in the war.[37]

In 1861 a local merchant in Cahaba had commenced construction of a cotton warehouse, but he had managed to complete only the structure's brick walls when the Civil War forced him to abandon the project. The warehouse was still without a roof or a floor in January 1864; yet in spite of these deficiencies the Confederate government confiscated the building for use as a prison. At the end of its first month of operation, 256 Union officers and enlisted men were confined within this shell. Although its capacity had originally been set at 500 prisoners, by the beginning of March there were 660 Yankees held at the site.[38]

Shortly after his assignment to Cahaba, Surgeon R. H. Whitfield became so alarmed at the high rates of disease and death among the prisoners that he felt compelled to alert his superiors to the terrible conditions there. "When you know the sanitary condition of the prison," Whitfield wrote to Medical Director P. B. Scott on 31 March, "you cannot be surprised at the large number of cases reported." Recently constructed bunks in the building could "accommodate but 432 men," and because the warehouse had no floor, "228 men are forced to sleep upon the ground." The only source of heat in the open facility was a single, crude fireplace that produced far more smoke than warmth, and the latrines were not emptied or kept clean. Although the responsibility for providing rations and supplies for the prison was shared by two quartermaster officers, they had "failed to be equal to the task."[39]

By far the most glaring deficiency at Cahaba was its lack of a source of clean water for drinking, cooking, or bathing. All water, Whitfield reported, "is conveyed from an artesian well, along an open street gutter for 200 yards, thence under the street into the prison." Before it reached the prison, the water had "been subjected to the washings of the hands, feet, faces, and heads of soldiers, citizens, and negroes, buckets, tubs, and spittoons of groceries, offices and hospital, hogs, dogs, cows, and horses, and filth of all kinds from the streets and other sources." As a predictable result, the prison population had been decimated by a host of waterborne diseases.[40]

With polluted water, filthy sinks, inadequate rations, and virtually no shelter, mortality at Cahaba undoubtedly would have come to rival that of the worst Confederate camps had not the prison's existence been cut mercifully short. On 20 April, Cooper directed General Leonidas Polk, then the commander of the military department in which Cahaba was located, to transfer the prisoners and close the facility. This nonetheless spelled bad news for the Yankee captives, for Cooper's orders directed that they be sent "promptly to Andersonville."[41]

A second prison opened by the Confederacy at this time was established for the confinement of Union officers only. This facility, located at Macon, Georgia, was established after the mass escape from Libby following the Dahlgren raid; like Cahaba, it was intended to reduce the population of prisoners in Richmond and thereby enhance security in the capital. Union prisoners had been transferred out of the capital so rapidly that a number of Union officers had inadvertently been sent to Andersonville in cattle cars along with enlisted prisoners, and on 2 May 1864, Cooper moved to separate the two groups by ordering Cobb to "make proper provision for the safe-keeping of Federal officers to be sent from Andersonville to Macon, Georgia."[42]

The prison at Macon was officially designated Camp Oglethorpe after the founder of the colony of Georgia, but in no respect was the installation as grand as its name. Situated on the fairgrounds about a quarter mile southeast of the city, the facility consisted of one large building, which was designated as the hospital, and a few dilapidated sheds and filthy animal stalls that were pressed into service as makeshift barracks. These structures were surrounded by twelve-foot-high board fence with a catwalk around the outside for patrolling guards. Sixteen feet inside the prison from this wall stood a small picket fence that served as the "deadline," and any prisoner who dared cross it was liable to be shot without warning.[43]

Macon had previously served as a prison in 1862. The garrison was unprepared to receive prisoners when the facility was reactivated, and little effort was made to improve it after the first Yankees arrived. Union generals were allowed to sleep in the hospital building, but once the sheds and stalls were filled, incoming officers found that there were no barracks, tents, or shelters of any sort. On 25 May the prisoner population stood at only 170; those lucky enough to be among the early arrivals managed to cobble together makeshift hovels out of scraps remaining from the construction of the stockade. After just over a month of operation, however, the commander of the prison reported that 1,400 Union officers were confined in the prison, and most of these later arrivals were forced to live in the open or in burrows dug in the red clay.[44]

The rations at Camp Oglethorpe were more plentiful than in Libby, but the quality was dreadful. Meal for the bread consisted of corn ground with its husks, the bacon was rancid and alive with maggots, and the beans and peas were crawling with bugs. These raw rations were issued for five-day periods, and there was a dearth of cooking and storage utensils. As a consequence, prisoners were forced to store rice, meal, and beans in their woolen drawers, while bacon, when issued, had to be quickly consumed before it spoiled further. Hospital facilities at the prison were also an improvement over those in Richmond, but still the men were plagued by the diseases common to most camps. Chronic diarrhea and dysentery cut men down by the dozen, and scurvy was common.[45]

Although the hardships endured by the officers at Camp Oglethorpe were considerable, they paled to insignificance when compared to the suffering at Andersonville. Throughout the spring and summer, trains bearing hundreds of prisoners rumbled into Andersonville almost daily. After being thoroughly searched and warned of the severe penalties for attempting to escape or venturing across the camp's deadline, the new arrivals were divided into messes of thirty men each and marched from the village to the stockade. There they entered the pen through one of two gates and were left to fend for themselves. The prisoners quickly discovered they had entered a surreal world that was unorganized, chaotic, filthy, and deadly. Ezra Ripple was a naive, twenty-two-year-old private from Pennsylvania when he entered that world on 8 July 1864, and in the memoir he authored almost forty years later he recalled distinctly his horror upon first viewing the interior of the stockade. "The effect," he wrote, "was stunning and very disheartening." The prison

> resembled an immense anthill teeming with life. . . . What a sinking feeling of the heart there was when we came to realize that this was to be our home— no one knew how long—perhaps until the end of the war, whenever that might be. It was not until we passed the gate and got inside the prison that we came fully to know the dreadful lot into which the fortunes of war and the inhumanity of our captors had cast us. Filth, disease, starvation, and death were all about us in forms and shapes we had never seen or heard of before.

Ira Sampson, a prisoner who maintained a pocket diary of his wartime experiences, recorded his first impression more succinctly. "Tis horrible," he scribbled upon first entering the prison, before going in search of a few feet of empty space where he might rest.[46] He quickly discovered that space was a rare and precious commodity. The prison's planned capacity of ten thousand had been reached in April, but the trains continued to disgorge their human cargoes at Andersonville Station. In May, the number of prisoners passed fifteen thousand.[47]

As the number of prisoners at Andersonville continued to climb, the deficiencies of the faulty Confederate system of prisoner management hastened the decline of conditions at the camp. Given the triple-tiered, semi-independent command structure decreed by Cooper and Seddon, disputes over authority among the officers assigned to the camp were inevitable, and they were not long in appearing. In March, the War Department detailed the 26th Alabama for guard duty at the prison without considering the fact that Colonel Edward O'Neal, the commander of the regiment, outranked Lieutenant Colonel Persons, who exercised overall command at the post. Upon arrival, O'Neal demanded that Persons surrender command to him. Persons refused. There ensued a nasty exchange of protests and charges as both officers argued their case to the War Department, but Cooper declined to resolve the problem. O'Neal was therefore reduced to obeying orders from an officer of subordinate rank, and relations between the camp commander and the vain and sensitive Irishman were predictably terrible. Command of the prisoners was also a muddle. On 29 February, Seddon named Major Elias Griswold, a former provost marshal of Richmond, to this position, but, as was usually the case, the secretary failed to inform General John Winder of his appointment. When Griswold arrived in mid-March to assume his duties, he found that his position had already been filled by an officer selected by Winder. This necessitated yet another official inquiry in Richmond, and both officers remained in residence at the camp until 29 March, when Seddon directed Persons to appoint Winder's candidate as commander of the interior of the prison.[48]

That officer was Captain Henry Wirz, a Swiss émigré who had first worked for Winder in 1862. Winder judged Wirz to be one of the most capable and energetic officers in his command, and the zeal with which the captain attacked the staggering problems he found at Andersonville seemed to confirm this assessment. Outfitted in a small gray cap, white linen shirt, and white trousers, and armed with an enormous LeMat revolver (which, one prisoner quipped, seemed to dwarf its owner), Wirz was a constant presence in Camp Sumter, and he worked tirelessly to improve its conditions.[49]

One of the most pressing issues was the abysmal state of sanitation within the stockade. Overcrowding had forced the prisoners to convert the marshy pool formed by the creek that ran through the compound into one vast latrine, appropriately christened "the swamp" by the inmates. In an effort to clean up this open sewer, Wirz procured a few shovels and organized teams of prisoners to scoop up the excrement daily, but because the camp was so crowded, the only place to deposit the vast heaps of fecal ooze was in the lower stretches of the swamp. Wirz designed a system of locks and dams with which he hoped to flush the creek so that it might again provide a source of clean water for drinking and bathing.[50] He also sought to improve the quantity and quality of rations. Pronouncing the corn and husk meal unfit for consumption and a cause of "dysentery and other bowel complaints," he asked Persons to order the post commissary to have the meal sifted before baking. He also called the commandant's attention to the "great deficiency of buckets," without which "rice, beans, vinegar, and molasses cannot be issued to prisoners," and he advised Persons that "any number of buckets can be got from Columbus, Ga., if the quartermaster of the post would make the requisition for the same."[51]

Unfortunately, the improvements urged by Wirz were never implemented, for supplying the prison at Andersonville remained a low priority for the Confederate government. In late April, Richard Winder reminded his superiors that Camp Sumter—which by that time held ten thousand captives—still had no hospital or commissary. He at last had been authorized to impress lumber, which he had stockpiled at various locations not distant from the camp. He had also secured permission to employ prisoners with carpentry skills on construction projects. But all his entreaties to have the lumber and other necessary building supplies actually shipped to the prison continued to be either ignored or refused. As he wrote in desperation to the commander of a neighboring military district on 25 April, "I have also had great difficulty in procuring necessary working implements and nails, and am still unsupplied. If I could succeed in getting the necessary lumber, nails, and tools I could put these buildings up very rapidly, as I have no lack of mechanical force."[52]

Those supplies would not be forthcoming, because all of the available railroad cars bound for Andersonville had been dedicated to transporting Yankee prisoners to the prison as expeditiously as possible. By any standard, the magnitude of this effort was simply astounding. Just six days before Richard Winder penned his appeal, the trains delivered seven hundred prisoners to Andersonville in a single twenty-four-hour period. Nor would the pace of deliveries slacken. On 2 May, the War Department decreed that rather than concentrating the prisoners in the capital, all Yankees "captured south of Richmond" would henceforth be transported directly to Andersonville.[53]

As bad as the overcrowding at the prison was becoming, it would have been much worse without the resumption of limited exchanges of prisoners by the belligerents. These exchanges had begun in December 1863 when Union general Benjamin Butler, newly appointed by Secretary of War Edwin Stanton as special agent of exchange, had shipped 502 healthy Rebel prisoners south. Butler proposed that Confederate agent of exchange Robert Ould reciprocate in kind, leaving "all questions of difference in controversy between your authorities and my Government for the present in abeyance."[54]

Although the Confederate government was exceedingly anxious to resume exchanges, Butler's proposition presented the Rebel authorities with a dilemma. The Beast was still under Davis's sentence of death for hanging William Mumford in New Orleans, and most of the people and the press in the South supported the president's judgment.[55] To circumvent this problem, Ould was directed to ignore Butler in all official correspondence. On 28 December, Ould, working through Union assistant agent for exchange John E. Mulford rather than the Union general, passed 520 Federal prisoners through the lines. Butler, whose ego was even larger than his considerable waistline, was incensed at this slight, and for two months exchanges were suspended amid squabbles over titles and accusations regarding past violations of the cartel. Union and Confederate leaders assured their citizens that this latest suspension of exchanges was entirely justified on grounds of national pride and points of honor, and in the presses of the two nations the mood turned ugly. The editors of the *New York Times* agreed that the prisoners' release could not be purchased "at the price of such a sacrifice of justice as that on which the rebels condition a general exchange" and suggested that until such an arrangement could be negotiated, the "fifty thousand rebel prisoners now rusting and fattening in idleness" be forced into gang labor digging canals and strengthening northern defenses.[56]

These press polemics were balanced by considerable popular pressure to resume exchanges. This position was evident in resolutions passed by the General Assembly of Virginia and forwarded to Jefferson Davis on 8 February. Although the resolutions professed support for Davis's proclamation against Butler, the delegates added that they were "unwilling to attach to these exceptions, however just, an importance grave enough to be balanced against those vast and overruling considerations of humanity pleading against the condemnation." To do so would condemn "to hopeless and indefinite bondage . . . thousands of our gallant sons now pining in distant and loathsome prisons." Butler was indeed "obnoxious," the delegates conceded, and the proclamation against him should stand, but the "negotiations for a return under cartel to the exchange of prisoners of war held by both parties . . . should be resumed." Bowing to such pressure, Ould assured Mulford that the South stood ready to commence exchanges under the provisions of the cartel.[57]

Butler's proposition presented the Lincoln administration with a dilemma. Secretary of War Stanton was loath to authorize any action that would produce thousands of new parolees and lead to a replay of the debacle of 1862–1863, but he was also cognizant of the fact that the administration would not long be able to withstand the rising public clamor for a resumption of exchanges. After some deliberation, the secretary determined that what was required was a course of action that would yield a limited number of exchanges without creating parolees. The authorization of man-for-man exchanges would satisfy both of these objectives. Such an exchange, Stanton reasoned, would quiet accusations that the Lincoln government was not moving aggressively to secure the release of prisoners. It would also obviate the difficulties of managing Union parolees, for soldiers returned in this manner would immediately be declared exchanged. On 22 February, Stanton thus directed Butler to "send an experimental boat under flag of truce to City Point, Va., with 200 rebel officers, with an offer to exchange them for a like number of U.S. officers held by the rebel authorities as prisoners of war."[58]

Butler dispatched the boat as ordered, but on his own initiative he added 600 privates to the 200 officers. Ould immediately reciprocated by returning 48 Union officers and 600 privates.[59] Although this trade resulted in a Confederate deficit of 152 men, Butler was determined to continue, and on 11 March he telegraphed Commissary General of Prisoners William Hoffman to begin to consolidate up to 20,000 prisoners at Point Lookout so that they could be exchanged at the rate of 2,000 per week. This sudden thaw in exchange relations caught most in the Confederate capital by surprise. But as the *Richmond Sentinel* reported, southerners "rejoice[d]" at the news and hoped that the arrangement would be "mutually assented to and persisted in until all the prisoners on both sides shall be released."[60]

Evidencing once more his insatiable appetite for intrigue, Butler now took to corresponding with Stanton by "confidential letter" to preclude any portion of the negotiations appearing in northern newspapers before his "arrangements" were "perfected." In one such missive of 23 March, he informed the secretary that he had received "63 officers and 965 men . . . for exchange," a total larger than he had sent to Ould. "I have now got the matter of exchange to such a point that I think we may go through upon a proper basis," he boasted to Stanton, adding that he would meet with the Confederate commissioner to finalize the details.[61]

On 31 March, Butler and Ould did meet at Fort Monroe, but their discussion quickly foundered on the question of the status of black prisoners. In a dramatic concession to northern demands, Ould announced that the South would henceforth consent to exchange free black captives on the same footing as whites, but he again emphasized that under no circumstances would the Confederacy renounce its right to retain slaves captured in uniform and return them to their masters.[62] In addition to the treatment of black captives, the two men also discussed at length the ongoing dispute over how parolees were to be counted.

On 9 April, the ever-confident Butler submitted a long and detailed report of the meeting to Stanton. He opened with the stunning assertion that with the exception of issues concerning "persons of color," he could "see no reason why an agreement upon all points of difference cannot be arrived at upon just and equitable terms." In regard to enumerating and exchanging parolees, Butler wrote that "the Confederate commissioner claims nothing, so far as I can see, which he is not willing to concede to us." Nor did Butler believe that southern intransigence on the question of returning captive slaves to bondage presented an insurmountable obstacle to the resumption of exchanges. While he admitted that this "right" had been "made a *sine qua non* by the Confederates," he was confident that he had devised a strategy that would force them to abandon the policy or else provide sufficient justification for northern termination of exchanges. The United States, he advised Stanton, should resolve all past disputes over paroles and exchanges by agreeing to "declare exchanged numbers equal on either side heretofore delivered and paroled." This would leave the question of the treatment of black prisoners to "stand out alone as full justification, if not yielded by them, for setting aside the cartel, because of a gross violation of it by the Confederate authorities." The Union should then "insist that the cartel applies, as it does apply, to these colored prisoners of war, and that no further exchange can go on ... until this point is yielded, with the purpose, but not with the threat, of exact retaliation in exact kind and measure upon their men of the treatment received by ours."[63]

This was indeed a lot to consider, and before acting, Stanton asked Major General Ethan Allen Hitchcock—recently designated as commissioner for exchange of prisoners—to comment on Butler's plan. Although Hitchcock had originally suggested Butler's appointment as special agent for exchange, the two generals had been at odds almost from the start. During an earlier tiff, the acerbic Hitchcock had declared that Butler was motivated primarily by an unseemly desire to garner personal acclaim and see his name in print, a charge that anyone who knew the Beast would have readily supported. Butler always sought to enhance the importance of all his endeavors. Unbeknownst to Stanton, he had already attempted to circumvent the secretary of war's authority by secretly proposing to Lincoln that he visit the president in Washington and present his exchange proposals in person. Lincoln, preferring as always to remain discreetly distant from the potentially explosive issue of prisoners of war, instructed his personal secretary to advise Butler that he should "submit by letter or telegram to the Secretary of War the points in relation to the exchange of prisoners wherein you wish instructions," and that it was "not necessary for [Butler] to visit Washington for the purpose indicated." Never a man to be easily put off, Butler amended his request, suggesting that the president journey to Fort Monroe, where the two might meet in confidence to discuss the general's plans for breaking the exchange impasse—plans he obviously had not discussed with Stanton. For a time Lincoln humored Butler's requests, intimating that he would come to the general's headquarters. But in truth, the president was far too cagey a politician to be drawn into Butler's web. In the same cryptic language Butler loved to use, the president replied on 7 April that "Mrs. Lincoln and I think that we will visit Fort Monroe some time next week, meanwhile whatever is to be done on the business-subject will be conducted through the War Department." In fact, Lincoln had no intention of ever discussing the "business-subject" of prisoner exchanges with Butler. To do so would have betrayed his degree of knowledge and involvement in prisoner-of-war matters, which Lincoln believed was politically untenable. Accordingly, just four days later he telegraphed Butler that "Mrs. L. is so unwell that I now think that we will not make the contemplated trip this week. Will notify you in time." That notification never came.[64]

Hitchcock took a more actively negative view of Butler's initiative, maintaining that it was not only simplistic, but also detrimental to the cause of the Union. In sum, Hitchcock stated bluntly, Butler's proposal indicated that as a negotiator, he was clearly no match for "so ingenious a diplomatist as Mr. Ould."[65] Stanton then placed Butler's report and Hitchcock's rejoinder before General Ulysses S. Grant, recently promoted to command of all Union armies and currently in the process of planning a massive offensive in the eastern theater of the war. On 14 April, Grant ordered Butler to "decline all further negotiations" with Ould until the report could be fully examined.[66]

Three days later, Grant wrote Butler that he had completed a "careful examination" of the report and that he had determined that the only points requiring his approval were "the validity of the paroles of the prisoners captured at Port Hudson and Vicksburg" and "the status of colored prisoners." As to the first point, Grant ordered that "until there is released to us an equal number of officers and men as were captured and paroled at Vicksburg and Port Hudson, not another Confederate prisoner of war will be paroled or exchanged." As to the status of black prisoners, Grant insisted that "the only question" could be whether they were "at the time of their capture, in the military service of the United States." If they were, the general continued, "the same terms as to treatment while prisoners and conditions of release and exchange must be exacted and had, in the case of colored soldiers as in the case of white soldiers." He concluded that the failure of Confederate authorities to acquiesce "in both or either of these propositions will be regarded as a refusal on their part to agree to the further exchange of prisoners, and will be so treated by us."[67]

Officially, Grant's decision to terminate exchanges was predicated on disputes over past prisoner releases and the Confederacy's refusal to exchange former slaves captured while in service to the Union. In truth, his decision was intended to achieve a more direct, and decidedly military, objective. Grant journeyed to Fort Monroe for a personal meeting with Butler, at which, as Butler later recalled, the commanding general freely admitted that his primary reason for ending the exchanges was to maintain the numerical superiority of Union regiments in the field. That superiority, Grant asserted, was being seriously eroded by the rising number of desertions among conscripts and bounty jumpers, who were allowing themselves to be captured in hopes of being quickly paroled. With all possibility of exchange removed, Grant maintained, these soldiers would be more likely to remain with their regiments.[68]

Butler could not fault Grant's military logic, but his acute political sense told him that the straightforward presentation of this line of reasoning to the northern populace would prompt a firestorm of protest. He explained to Grant that the public would never support the termination of exchanges on the grounds that their sons, husbands, and brothers would not be freed because they were of more value to their country if left to suffer and die in squalid southern camps. Such a proclamation would spawn a public relations nightmare for the Lincoln administration and would play directly in the hands of Peace Democrats in the upcoming presidential and congressional elections. He also reminded Grant that the elections made it highly unlikely that Lincoln would order a resumption of the very unpopular draft before November. The recruitment of Negro regiments thus were more essential than ever to the Union cause. Should blacks in the North ever come to believe that they would be abandoned by their government if captured, "the enlistment of colored regiments would substantially cease." For all these reasons, Butler argued, the focus should be kept on the issue of the exchange of Negro prisoners. Northern citizens should be told that "the rebels stopped the exchange upon such grounds and no other," and that general exchanges of prisoners would not resume until Confederate authorities placed black captives on an equal footing with whites. In the meantime, Butler advised, public cries for a resumption of general exchanges could be substantially assuaged by permitting limited exchanges of sick and wounded prisoners.[69]

Grant accepted Butler's advice. Northern citizens would be assured that the only obstacle to the resumption of general exchanges was Confederate intransigence on the status of Negro soldiers. Regarding the exchange of invalids, Grant telegraphed Butler that he could "receive all the sick and wounded the Confederate authorities will send," but he was strictly admonished to "send no more in exchange."[70]

At this point, all hope ended that negotiations between Butler and Ould might lead to a general exchange. On 20 April, Ould declared to be exchanged all Confederate soldiers who by that point had been delivered; on 7 May, Stanton, acting on the advice of Grant and Butler, responded by declaring the same for all Union soldiers who had already come through the lines.[71] With exchange negotiations again at an impasse, Davis was forced to supply an explanation for the failure of the talks, and his reasoning was no less disingenuous than Butler's. In a message to the opening session of the Second Confederate Congress on 2 May, Davis reported that northern officials had suspended exchanges "without apparent cause," and that he had to confess his "inability to comprehend their policy or purpose." He lamented the fact that "in spite of humane care," Union prisoners were "perishing from the inevitable effects of imprisonment and home-sickness produced by the hopelessness of release from confinement."[72] In a report to Secretary of War Seddon, Ould predicted that the issue of black captives would

continue to block wholesale exchanges, but he assured the secretary that northern inquiries concerning the treatment or status of specific black prisoners would
be deflected with the response that "there was no record of any such party."[73]

The longer such political sparring went on, the worse conditions in southern
prisons became. With only a limited number of sick prisoners being sent north,
the inmate populations of Confederate prisons climbed remorselessly; with the
opening of Grant's massive Overland campaign on 4 May 1864, the number of
new captives entering southern prisons simply exploded. Only days after the
initial battles in the Wilderness, the population in Libby climbed to just over
two thousand inmates, and Belle Isle was teeming with captives. Danville, only
recently emptied, was again activated and quickly packed with captives, as were
the smaller prisons at Macon, Cahaba, Tuscaloosa, and Lynchburg.[74]

At Andersonville, conditions had descended to a level almost defying description. On 5 May, Cobb appealed directly to Cooper for relief. "There are now in
the prison about twelve thousand prisoners in an area les than eighteen acres," his
letter began. Although he was certain that "the character of the prison" was "well
understood at Richmond," he emphasized the imperative necessity for a hospital
at the site, writing, "Upon that point there cannot be two opinions among intelligent men; it ought to be done at once and such is the opinion of every sensible
man, that has examined the prison." Cobb then repeated his plea that no more
prisoners be sent to the camp. "The prison is already too much crowded and no
additional prisoners should be sent there until it can be enlarged," he admonished Cooper, closing his letter with the grim warning that if shipments were
not halted immediately, there would surely be "a terrific increase of sickness and
death, during the summer months." That prediction would come to pass with a
vengeance.[75]

On 25 May, Winder dispatched a trusted subordinate, Major Thomas P.
Turner, to follow up on Cobb's inspection. Turner found Andersonville "in a very
filthy condition," primarily because the requisitions Wirz had submitted had not
been filled. Turner also reported that the camp's confusing three-commander system had yielded predictable results. "Great confusion and serious difficulties have
existed in regard to rank among the officers . . . as to who ranks and commands,"
he noted, and those disputes tended to "disturb the good order, discipline, and
proper conduct of the post and prison." Turner suggested that precise lines of
authority be established at the camp without delay, but his recommendations
did not stop there. On his return trip to Richmond he had visited the newly
established camp at Macon, where he was shocked to discover that the Yankee
officers sent there had been forgotten as soon as they had been shipped out of

the capital. Deeply alarmed by the conditions he found at Andersonville and Macon, Turner became absolutely convinced that improvements were impossible without a drastic overhaul of the Confederate prisoner-of-war system. "Feeling an interest in the proper management of the prison department," he wrote in the conclusion of his report, "I deem it my duty to call attention to the gross mismanagement and want of system which exists at the different prisons. In my opinion there should be some head of the prison department so that rules and regulations, general and comprehensive, may be prescribed for each and all throughout the Confederacy."[76]

Even as Turner's report was on its way to Winder, a second and more emphatic recommendation for restructuring the Confederate prisoner-of-war system was placed before Adjutant and Inspector General Cooper. Cooper had directed Lieutenant Colonel Robert H. Chilton, a member of his staff, to examine the relative responsibilities of Commissioner of Exchange Ould and General Winder and supply an assessment of how well they worked together in the disposition of captives. Rather than simply composing a summary of the two officers' duties, Chilton provided a comprehensive critique of the entire Confederate prisoner-of-war system.

Chilton found that Ould had "no direct control over the prisoners, except for purposes of exchange or parole." Winder, on the other hand, was tasked with responsibility for

> all prisoners arriving here [Richmond], at Danville, and at Andersonville, Ga., and now at Macon, Ga., but has no general control over the subject. . . . With the multiplicity of duties performed by General Winder, it could not be expected that he could give that strict personal supervision to duties which of themselves are sufficient to occupy the best energies of a man of intelligence, energy, and industry, and no one can examine the records and character of service relating to the department of prisoners without being convinced of the absolute necessity for a commissary-general of prisoners. Facts have come to my knowledge respecting these prisons and the prison system which satisfy my mind fully that no effective system or organization can be secured without such an officer.[77]

Given Cooper's intimate knowledge of the terrible state of Confederate prisons and the inadequacy of the system then in place to administer them, one might reasonably expect that he would have acted swiftly on Chilton's strong and unambiguous recommendation by either appointing a commissary general of prisoners or providing reasons why he declined to establish such a post. He did neither. Instead, Cooper chose to focus on perceived problems in recording the number of prisoners confined, and on 28 May he forwarded Chilton's report to General Braxton Bragg in order to seek the presidential advisor's assistance in devising "a plan by which we may insure a more perfect record of the prisoners of the enemy in our hands than has heretofore been kept." Incredibly, it seems that Cooper's anxiety had been piqued by reports that "we have either at Danville or some other depot of prisoners east of the Mississippi 200 more prisoners of the enemy than our returns exhibit." Bragg concurred that the current system of accounting was "defective," adding his opinion that a "system of espionage" and depravities of southern soldiers who allowed themselves to be "too easily captured" were contributing to the problem. Such were the concerns of the senior officers in the Confederate system on a day when thousands of Union prisoners were confined in camps throughout the South, hundreds of whom would die of starvation and disease.[78]

Much of that dying was occurring at Andersonville. By June, the prisoner population in the camp had risen to over twenty thousand. Colonel Persons petitioned his superiors for permission to enlarge the stockade, but he received no reply. He pleaded with Cobb for an engineer to direct the expansion, but he was told that none was available. In desperation, he sought to undertake the work with materials on hand at the prison, but he quickly discovered that he possessed neither the tools nor the hardware for the job.

There was still no hospital building at Andersonville, but in the latter part of May, Chief Surgeon Isaiah H. White had relocated his patients from the squalid corner of the prison where they had been collected to a cluster of small tents and flys in an oak grove just outside the stockade. In a letter to the editor of the *Macon Telegraph*, one visitor to the prison described the new site as "a square enclosure of several acres about two or three hundred yards distant from the S.E. corner of the stockade." The makeshift wards already contained "from 500 to 600 inmates." Although a marked improvement over the earlier site, the new location held its own horrors. "Here is a world of suffering to one who has never seen it," the correspondent admitted, "and as it beggars description, I will not attempt to portray the scene, but pass on, simply remarking that from 20 to 25 die daily." The dead were hauled away by wagon to the prison burying ground, where "you will observe a detail of eight or ten stalwart Irishmen, digging trenches six feet wide, and long enough to contain one hundred corpses laid closely together. They are buried in the clothing they die in, and in many cases they are robbed by their own men of their clothing, leaving the corpse but pants or drawers and coat. On Tuesday the 28th was their heaviest work, in one day, viz: the burial of 32 dead."[79]

Colonel Persons was also having problems effectively commanding at Andersonville, since he was junior in rank to each of the commanders of the four reserve regiments assigned as guards at the post. Cobb's correspondence with Cooper about this problem produced no results, so on 2 June he telegraphed Jefferson Davis directly and asked that a senior, experienced officer be placed in command of the prison; his request was forwarded to Cooper. For some time Cooper had been contemplating transferring Winder out of the capital. Winder's stern enforcement of Richmond's wartime statutes had consistently riled many of the capital's elites, while his persistent lobbying on behalf of prisoners had long been a thorn in the side of the War Department. Cooper now saw a chance to rid himself of this problem.[80] Davis agreed that Winder should be sent to Andersonville, and on 3 June he notified Cobb that Winder would be "ordered to Andersonville as the officer best answering your requisition of those who are available." This would prove to be a very disastrous decision. Not only did it remove from Richmond the Confederate officer with the most experience in dealing with the challenges of prisoner-of-war management, but it also further confused the lines of command in the southern system of prisons. Winder was to have command of more than Andersonville, where Cooper naively believed that "his presence alone will have a beneficial effect upon the guard and the prisoners"; he was also ambiguously ordered by Cooper to "exercise a supervision over the officers' prison at Macon."[81]

Winder assumed his new command on 17 June 1864. On that date Andersonville held just over 24,000 Yankee captives, and there had been over 2,200 deaths since the prison's opening in February. The camp's thirteen surgeons were vainly struggling to attend to 2,000 patients without benefit of a serviceable hospital or adequate medicines. The water supply was hopelessly polluted by the sinks that had been placed at the edge of the camp's single stream, and the tons of feces that had piled up along this open sewer had been transformed into a fetid ooze in which maggots bred to a depth of fifteen inches. Defecations by thousands of men afflicted with chronic diarrhea and dysentery had polluted the entire interior of the stockade as well. Death had become so commonplace that the reactions of friends of those who perished was reduced to a grisly ritual. "When a person would die," prisoner Ezra Ripple remembered, "some of his comrades would prepare his body for burial by tying his two big toes together, straightening out his limbs, and folding his hands . . . and then on a scrap of paper would write his name, company, regiment and cause of death and would attach it to his collar. As the dead wagons came for them, they were tossed on them like logs of wood, twenty or more to a wagon, and were carted to the burial ground."[82]

Winder was so stunned by what he saw that he immediately dashed off a telegram to Cooper begging that he "earnestly urge upon the secretary [of war] the necessity of establishing another prison."[83] To ensure that Cooper was fully cognizant of the urgency of the situation, Winder dispatched one of his officers to Richmond three days later to deliver personally a second message to the adjutant general. "The state of affairs at this post is in a critical condition," Winder wrote. "We have here largely over 24,000 prisoners of war, and 1,205 very raw troops (Georgia Reserves), with the measles prevailing, badly armed and worse disciplined, to guard them; the prisoners rendered more desperate from the necessarily uncomfortable condition in which they are placed." Winder feared that "with the present force a raid on the post would almost of necessity be successful," and he reminded Cooper that "twenty-five thousand men, by the mere force of numbers, can accomplish a great deal." He reiterated that "another prison should be immediately established," closing his alarming assessment of his new command with a plea that "no more prisoners be sent to this post."[84]

Winder then set about trying to improve conditions at the camp. He ordered the formation of prisoner crews to clean up the swamp and the sinks, while captives with carpentry and masonry skills were set to work on the still-unfinished cookhouse and the dams proposed by Wirz. Winder also initiated plans for the construction of barracks. All these efforts were overwhelmed by the thousands of additional prisoners that continued to arrive at the Andersonville station almost daily. The crush of humanity within the stockade was so desperate that Cobb wired Davis directly to reinforce Winder's plea that no more prisoners be sent to the camp. Davis did not answer the telegram, and Cooper did not halt or even slow the shipments. Late June saw the worst overcrowding in the prison's history. When the area covered by the swamp and the strip of ground fenced off by the deadline were deducted, the stockade's sixteen acres shrank to approximately eleven. Almost 25,000 prisoners were caged in this small area, providing a ratio of about twenty square feet of ground per man. Deciding that he could wait no longer for approval or assistance from Richmond, Winder directed Persons to proceed with his plan to enlarge the compound, and on 1 July a ten-acre expansion was opened.[85]

Winder also took action to rid the camp of the brutal depredations of the "raiders," a group of Yankee thugs who had preyed upon their fellow prisoners since the prison opened. The first these raiders had arrived in the earliest shipments from Belle Isle, and their numbers and audacity had steadily grown; by June they controlled virtually all aspects of life within the walls of the stockade. Due to the small size of the Confederate guard force, Wirz had been unable to halt the robberies, beatings, and murders perpetrated by the raiders, but when the other prisoners appealed to Winder for assistance, he agreed to allow them to resolve the situation themselves. Forming into groups of "regulators," the prisoners rounded up the leaders of the raiders and, with Winder's permission, tried and hanged six of them. As John Ransom succinctly recorded in his diary, "good order" prevailed after the hangings, allowing the prisoners to "settle right down to the business of dying, with no interruption."[86]

In all of his efforts to improve conditions at Andersonville, Winder received little support from Confederate leaders in Richmond. Requested supplies arrived slowly or (in most cases) not at all, and available rations diminished steadily in both quality and quantity. Repeated requests for additional guards were also ignored. On 6 July, Cooper had one of his clerks instruct Winder to address such entreaties to Cobb rather than the War Department. Winder was also directed to expedite his search for a location for a new prison, but—as always—he was advised that in constructing the facility, obtaining guards, and transferring prisoners from Andersonville to the new site, he should expect no assistance from the War Department.[87]

One week later Winder notified Cooper that he had selected Silver Run, Alabama, as the site for the new prison. General Joseph E. Johnston—then retreating before General William Tecumseh Sherman's army north of Atlanta—had recommended that for security reasons the prisoners at Andersonville be immediately dispersed, and Winder concurred. He asked for permission to impress local labor and supplies so that he might begin construction of the new prison as soon as possible, and to ease his chronic shortage of guards he again pleaded for additional manpower for the transfer. Before either of these requests could be answered, Union cavalry raids near Silver Run forced Winder to abandon his plan. On 19 July he sent Cooper full details of the raids, along with the disappointing news that the captives would have to remain at Andersonville. Cooper and Seddon passed Winder's message to Davis, and when the president complained that he did not understand why the Silver Run option had been abandoned, Seddon—betraying either his ignorance of Winder's difficulties or, more likely, his reluctance to admit the paucity of assistance the general was receiving from Richmond—replied that he "supposed" that Winder considered the railroads too broken up to support the transfer. By now it must have been clear to Winder that Cooper and Seddon were deliberately distancing themselves from all responsibility for the hell they had created at Andersonville.[88]

Meanwhile, the situation at the prison was becoming more desperate with each passing day. While Cooper and Seddon sent little in the way of supplies and equipment to Andersonville, they were exceptionally diligent in ensuring that shipments of prisoners continued without respite. In a telegram of 18 July, Richard Winder frantically begged Treasury officer William L. Bailey for funds to pay the garrison and purchase food for the prisoners. "I am so seriously in need of funds that I do not know what I shall do," he cried. "For God's sake send me $100,000 for prisoners of war and $75,000 for pay of officers and troops stationed here. You can put in my estimates, and if you only knew what trouble I was in here for the want of funds I know you would do your very best to send me at once above amounts."[89] Unsurprisingly, sufficient funds were not forthcoming.

With each denial of support from Richmond, relations between Winder and his superiors grew increasingly adversarial. When Cooper yet again rejected Winder's request for additional guards and naively suggested that conditions at Andersonville could be ameliorated simply by enlarging the compound and ensuring the prisoners were "placed properly," Winder fired off a blistering reply: he considered Cooper's advice to be a "severe censure," and one that would not have been made if Cooper "had a clear comprehension of this post, of its wants and its difficulties." As to "placing the prisoners properly," Winder sarcastically continued, he did "not exactly comprehend what is intended by it. I know of but one way to place them, and that is to put them into the stockade, where they have between four and five square yards to the man."[90]

On 24 July, Winder submitted a report that clearly revealed the catastrophe that was unfolding at the prison. Andersonville now held 29,357 prisoners. Of that number, 1,656 were in the makeshift prison hospital; on that day alone, 59 men had died. "It will be observed that the ratio of mortality is very great," Winder concluded. "It is very necessary that another prison should be immediately established at some other point, if possible; or if that cannot be done conveniently, I will set to work immediately to build another stockade here." But food, not overcrowding, was the most critical issue facing Winder. Camp rations were issued through Columbus, Georgia, and the officer there had warned Andersonville's subsistence officer that he "should never have less than 10 day's rations on hand so as to be prepared for emergencies."[91] Provisions of all sorts continued to dwindle, however, and on 25 July, Winder reached the absolute bottom of the barrel. "There are 29,400 prisoners, 2,650 troops, 500 negroes and other laborers," Winder telegraphed Cooper, "and not a ration at the post. I have ordered that at least ten days' rations should be kept on hand, but it has never been done."[92]

Cooper forwarded Winder's telegram to Lucius Northrop. As was usually the case when the performance of his department was challenged, the commissary general of subsistence exploded in indignation. Control of "everything relating to subsisting [the prisoners]," Northrop blustered, rested exclusively with his office, and Winder had "no right to give any orders on the subject." Had the commissary officer servicing Andersonville complied with Winder's order to maintain sufficient rations, Northrop fumed, he would have personally countermanded it; even as Winder was demanding a ten-day reserve, Lee's army was restricted to maintaining only a single day's rations on hand. "If General Winder thinks that the subsistence of the prisoners has been or is critical, he can communicate with the Commissary General on the subject if he pleases," Northrop concluded, adding that he "will receive from the Commissary-General such information which will satisfy him that the prisoners will be duly cared for and not suffer until the army is pinched."[93]

In sum, the response was vintage Northrop. Due to a combination of incompetence and a criminal lack of concern, his department had failed in its responsibility to provide adequate subsistence to Andersonville. As a result, there were now over 24,000 helpless captives confined at a prison where there was not a single ration. But instead of moving quickly to forestall additional misery and death at the camp, Northrop chose to attack Winder's authority to issue orders to commissary department officers. Contrary to Northrop's assertions, the captives were obviously not being "duly cared for." Confederate army regulations directed that prisoners receive rations comparable to those provided Confederate soldiers. As Northrop himself had reported to Seddon, subsistence provided Lee's soldiers during the first half of 1864 reached its lowest level in June, but the daily ration still included bread, a third of a pound of beef, coffee, sugar, and fresh vegetables.[94] Even more damning was the fact that Johnston's Army of Tennessee, then engaged in operations only 150 miles from the gates of Andersonville, was, by Johnston's own account, being well supplied with staples procured locally by his commissary officer and with fresh beef from cattle driven up from Florida by Charles Munnerlyn's famed "Cow Cavalry."[95]

Could Northrop have secured adequate subsistence for the prisoners at Andersonville had he chosen to do so? Evidence clearly indicates that the answer is yes. When Lee requested that a stockpile of rations be established north of Richmond in May 1864, for example, Northrop quickly created a supply point at Beaver Dam Station. To this location he dispatched two trains laden with over half a million rations of bread and almost a million rations of meat. At the same time that this huge cache was being assembled, prisoners were starving at Belle Isle, only forty miles to the south.[96]

Northrop had never attempted to conceal his reluctance to supply adequate rations to prisoners, and his response to Winder's message was predictable. Far more astonishing is the fact that Confederate authorities in Richmond allowed to pass without comment Northrop's assertions that the level of subsistence at Andersonville was not yet "critical" and that Federal prisoners were not suffering. President Davis, Secretary of War Seddon, and Adjutant General Cooper were all fully aware of the terrible suffering at Andersonville and other Confederate prisons. Reports submitted by prison commanders and inspectors dispatched by the War Department and Medical Department had clearly and repeatedly stated that the high mortality in Confederate prisons was due, in large part, to Northrop's failure to provide adequate rations. Davis and his subordinates knew that Yankee prisoners were starving, yet they took no action to compel Northrop to provide rations as required by army regulations.

Winder's reports nonetheless finally convinced Seddon that no more captives should be sent to Andersonville. "I do not consider it advisable to send more prisoners just now," the secretary advised Cooper on 24 July. Unfortunately, the secretary's message had no effect whatever on operations in Cooper's office, and trains bearing hundreds of additional prisoners continued to pull in to the Andersonville station. Meanwhile, Winder kept looking for a suitable location for a new prison; but even as his search was in progress, Sherman's advancing army compelled him to initiate the transfer of the prisoners in Macon. "Charleston is the only place where accommodations can be had," he informed Cooper, and in the last week of July he began preparations to evacuate other prisons as the military situation worsened.[97]

This transfer to Charleston would not be the first for the prisoners in Macon. Yankee batteries on Morris Island were shelling Charleston quite heavily throughout the spring of 1864, and in an effort to halt the bombardments General Sam Jones, the commander of Confederate forces in the area, requested that the War Department transfer fifty officer prisoners from Macon to Charleston, where they would be placed in the open under the fire of their own guns. Upon learning that they were shelling their own men, Jones reasoned, the Yankees would cease their bombardment of the city. This use of prisoners was obviously illegal under the accepted rules of war, but such technicalities had never slowed Seddon, and on 9 June he directed that the prisoners be transferred as Jones requested. General J. G. Foster, the Union commander on Morris Island, protested vehemently upon learning of the scheme, whereupon Jones piously insisted that the arrival of the prisoners had nothing to do with the shelling of the city. Foster accepted this explanation, and the correspondence between the two officers eventually led to a limited agreement under which the fifty captive officers were exchanged.[98]

So things stood when Winder ordered that the camp at Macon be emptied. Six hundred of the captives were sent initially to Savannah, but the camp there was so overcrowded that after only a short stay they were shipped on to Charleston, which was still suffering daily bombardment from Morris Island. Despite Confederate protests to the contrary, the six hundred new arrivals were convinced that they were being used as human shields in a diabolical plan to end the shelling of the city. Over on Morris Island, General Foster agreed. Outraged that the Rebels had once again deliberately placed Federal prisoners in harm's way, he retaliated by requesting that six hundred Confederate officers be immediately transferred from Fort Delaware to Morris Island. As soon as the Rebels arrived, the general assured the newspaper correspondents covering the story, he would place them in tents he had already erected so that "no delay may be occasioned as to the matter of getting them under fire."[99]

Both the Union and Confederate captives remained confined in their makeshift pens in Charleston and on Morris Island until mid-October, when they were transferred to other camps. The conditions of confinement for those unfortunate enough to have been caught up in this latest round of retaliation were terrible, and although no prisoners were killed in the shelling, exposure, poor food, and neglect exacted a dreadful toll at both locations. The plight of the captives was closely reported in the northern and southern press, and because the prisoners were all literate officers, the episode produced a plethora of polemic and highly imaginative personal narratives penned by the survivors after the war.[100]

With the management of captives becoming ever more complex, Seddon at long last moved to revamp the lines of command and control in the Confederate prisoner-of-war system. That was the good news. The bad news was that his action served only to make a very confused situation worse. Rather than appointing a single officer as commissary general of prisoners, Seddon divided the responsibility between Winder and Brigadier General William M. Gardner, a former military district commander with almost no experience in the complexities of prisons or prisoner-of-war management. Winder was "assigned to the command of the military prisons in the States of Georgia and Alabama," while Gardner was to command the "military prisons in the other States east of the Mississippi River." The order further stipulated that "in all matters relating to prisons and prisoners," both officers were to "communicate directly with and receive orders from the Adjutant and Inspector General." The ultimate authority for resolving all prisoner-of-war issues, in other words, would continue to reside with Cooper and Seddon in Richmond.[101]

In the end, Seddon's edict did absolutely nothing to clarify the lines of responsibility and authority in the Confederate prisoner-of-war system. It failed, for example, to assign responsibility for Camp Ford, which had been established in 1863 near Tyler, Texas, and which was the largest Confederate camp west of the Mississippi.[102] Nor did the order provide Gardner or Winder any explanation of the extraordinary responsibilities they had been assigned. Gardner seems to have been completely surprised by his appointment, and he was totally confused by the order's provisions. "The vague indorsement . . . placing me in charge of all the prisons, does not inform me what prisons exist," he telegraphed Cooper on the same day the order was published, "nor does it name those which are excepted from its operation and left in charge of General Winder, though some such are excepted."[103]

Winder, for his part, was so absorbed in his efforts to improve security and upgrade conditions at Andersonville that he took little notice of the order. Vegetables had been absent from the prisoners' diet since early spring, and by August scurvy was rampant in the camp. Sympathetic local civilians collected a small amount of food for the prisoners, but Winder, fearful that his guard force would be overwhelmed by the riot that would surely result when not all the captives received a share, refused to have it issued. But while some civilians sympathized with the prisoners' plight, the majority of the region's residents had a decidedly different opinion. One typical letter from a visitor to the camp sought "to impress upon the proper authorities the importance of a strong guard of disciplined troops of the regular Confederate service." As the writer warned, "It will be too late to cry wolf, when they shall have made their escape and are sacking every smokehouse in the country, cutting telegraph wires, burning government stores, destroying railroad bridges, killing stock, etc." The editors of the *Macon Telegraph* agreed that the Yankees constituted a security threat, and they offered a solution to the problem. "The large number of Federals who have been captured lately," editorial proclaimed in early August,

has increased the number of prisoners at Andersonville to over thirty thousand and the cry is 'still they come.' What are we going to do with this large army of unarmed Yankees in our midst? The amount of food they daily consume is alone of great importance, while their presence keeps several thousands of our soldiers occupied. We really do wish that the government would make some arrangements by which we can get rid of these men, and send them back to their own country. Our men would infinitely prefer to fight than to feed and guard them.[104]

Winder took little notice of such complaints, preferring to concentrate on improving conditions in the camp. Renovations of the bake house and hospital were nearing completion, and he had finally secured enough lumber to begin construction of barracks for the prisoners. The structures were low, narrow, two-story affairs designed to house 270 men each, and Richard Winder reckoned he had enough materials to raise five of them by the end of August.[105]

As always, the War Department had supplied little in the way of men or materials to assist Winder in these endeavors. What Cooper did send was yet another inspector to report on conditions at the prison, and this time the man he selected for the task was not just another bureaucrat from Richmond. He was Lieutenant Colonel Daniel T. Chandler, and he came to Andersonville looking for trouble.

Historians have argued that Chandler, an officer in the U.S. army before the war, had already concluded that the Confederacy would lose the war and that his findings at Andersonville were aimed at currying favor with Yankee brass, who would surely seek vengeance for the suffering of their comrades incarcerated there.[106] Such may very well have been the case. In a letter seeking to obtain his release from prison after the war, Chandler assured Union secretary of war Edwin Stanton that he had accepted an assignment in the Confederate War Department only to avoid conscription and that he had always intended to return to service in the U.S. army as soon as possible.[107] Whatever his motives, Chandler's inspection was, by all accounts, cursory, and charges that he was predisposed to issue as negative a report as possible seemed to gain weight when the first stop on his tour of inspection was not Winder's office, but the home of Ambrose Spencer, Andersonville's notorious and highly "imaginative" Unionist.[108]

The real mystery surrounding Chandler's inspection is why he was sent to Andersonville at all. Cooper's orders directed Chandler to "proceed to Andersonville, Ga., and make a careful and minute inspection of the prison there established for Federal prisoners." He was to devote special attention to "shelter, police, prison discipline, and proper security of the prisoners, having due consideration for their health and comfort, and their subsistence and sanitary condition within the prison enclosure." Further, he was to assess the "management" of the prison hospital, the "strength and character of the guards employed, the competency of their officers," and the measures that had been instituted to protect the facility from Union raids. What is most puzzling about these instructions is that comprehensive reports addressing each of these areas of concern were being furnished to Cooper by Captains Richard Winder and Henry Wirz, Lieutenant Colonel Alexander Persons, and General John Winder on a continuing basis. For months, these reports had unanimously documented a situation that was terrible and becoming worse every day, and through all that time Cooper and his staff had refused to provide the food, medical supplies, and other equipment required to stave off a humanitarian catastrophe at Andersonville.[109]

Chandler was further directed to report whether the prison should be removed to "some other more eligible location." If he judged the guard force too "insufficient," he was to notify Governor Brown or General Cobb of the fact and "urge upon them an immediate increase of this force." Again, Cooper's instructions are perplexing. Winder had been calling for the establishment of a new prison since the day he arrived at Andersonville, and for months he had been unsuccessfully petitioning Cobb and Cooper to reinforce the camp's inadequate guard force.[110]

Finally, and most interesting, Chandler was directed by Cooper to "require lists of all officials, officers, agents, and employees under General Winder, setting forth the authority under which they were assigned and the duties performed by each," and he was granted the authority to "order," in Cooper's name, "such measures as your inspection here may suggest as necessary to be immediately adopted."[111] Any investigation of the command structure in place at Andersonville would reveal that it was hopelessly convoluted, redundant, and designed to foster disputes among the camp's officers. That structure had been established by Seddon and Cooper themselves, and although suggestions as to how it might be "promptly corrected" had been offered by Persons, Wirz, and General Winder, they had been routinely ignored in Richmond.

Why, then, did Cooper order an inspection that was sure to highlight glaring deficiencies that he already knew full well existed at the Andersonville? To suggest that he sincerely wished to be appraised of conditions at the prison so that he might direct improvements would be to accept the notion that the authorities in Richmond were ignorant of the deplorable state of affairs in the camp and that they had received no recommendations as to how conditions might be improved. Such was manifestly not the case. Wirz, for example, had notified Chandler himself of shortages in equipment and supplies only one week before the inspector arrived at the camp. Similarly, Isaiah White, the camp's chief surgeon, had informed Surgeon General S. P. Moore on 1 July that the health of the prisoners at Andersonville was rapidly deteriorating because of difficulties in obtaining even the most basic medicines and other hospital supplies.[112]

Why did Cooper send Chandler to Andersonville? The most plausible explanation is that having chosen not to act on the numerous reports and recommendations submitted by General John Winder and his subordinates, Cooper and Seddon sought to fix responsibility for the horror of Andersonville on its commanding officer. Chandler's report did just that. In the main, the report was a recounting of the terrible conditions at the camp, but the politic Chandler astutely avoided mention of the fact that Winder had repeatedly reported those conditions to both Cooper and Seddon, or that the desperate requests for assistance from the general and his staff had generated little interest or support from the War Department.[113]

Chandler's most polemical findings were contained not in his original assessment, but in an "additional report" that he composed after he returned to Richmond. In this addendum he praised the efforts of Wirz and Richard Winder but closed with a vicious personal attack on General Winder's competency and motives. "My duty requires me," Chandler wrote, "respectfully to recommend a change in the officer in command of the post, Brig. Gen. J. H. Winder, and the substitution in his place of some one who unites both energy and good judgment with some feelings of humanity and consideration for the welfare and comfort (so far as is consistent with their safe-keeping) of the vast number of unfortunates placed under his control." Chandler charged that Winder "deliberately and in cold blood" had "advocate[d] the propriety of leaving them in their present condition until their number has been sufficiently reduced by death to make the present arrangements suffice for their accommodation." Moreover, Winder "consider[ed] it a matter of self-laudation and boasting that he has never been inside the stockade, a place the horrors of which it is difficult to describe, and which is a disgrace to civilization." Had he but wished, Chandler asserted, Winder could have "considerably improved" conditions at the prison through "the exercise of a little energy and judgment, even with the limited means at his command," but he had chosen instead to let the prisoners die by the hundreds.[114]

Quite predictably, Chandler's report was received with righteous indignation and profuse declarations of astonishment by the same War Department officials who had long been aware of conditions at the prison and the deficiencies in the Confederate prisoner-of-war system. Colonel Robert Chilton, who had warned Cooper back in May that Winder had been assigned a scope of responsibility far beyond "the best energies of a man of intelligence, energy, and industry" and who had urged the appointment of a commissary general of prisoners, now pronounced the conditions at Andersonville a "reproach to us as a nation" and concurred in Chandler's findings.[115] R. B. Welford, a legal advisor to Seddon, found the "discomforts and sufferings of the prisoners" as described by Chandler "almost incredible," making no mention of the fact that Winder's repeated requests for sufficient supplies at the post had gone unfilled. Welford did concede that "no effectual remedy for all these evils seems available so long as the numbers are in such large excess over that for which the prison was designed," but he opted not to comment on the fact that Cooper had deliberately chosen to ignore Winder's request that shipments to the prison be halted. Assistant Secretary of War John A. Campbell, a Seddon confidant who had long been aware of the problems at the prison, now proclaimed that "these reports show a condition of things at Andersonville which calls very loudly for the interposition of the Department in order that a change may be made," offering no explanation of why Winder's numerous pleas for War Department "interposition" had been largely ignored.[116]

Shortly after receiving Chandler's report, Seddon sent for Robert Ould and advised him of its contents and recommendations. The secretary informed Ould that although he was inclined to dismiss Winder as Chandler had advocated, he could not do so without a hearing, and that a copy of the report had been sent to Winder so that he might prepare a defense.[117] But if the secretary seriously intended to relieve Winder, he did not tell the general. Nor, in spite of what he told Ould, did he forward Chandler's report to Winder. Indeed, Winder was never informed of Chandler's recommendation that he be relieved; nor was he provided a copy of that portion of the inspection report. What Winder did receive was a selection of "extracts" of the report, sent to him on Cooper's instructions with the ludicrous directive that Winder "take measures to correct the abuses" noted by Chandler. Without a massive infusion of rations, medical supplies, building materials, and other equipment, absolutely nothing could be effected; and as had been the case in the past, no such infusion would be forthcoming from Richmond.[118]

In his rebuttal of Chandler's findings, Winder assembled a prodigious collection of reports and testimony from his staff which detailed their many fruitless requests for assistance, but this had little impact in the War Department. Winder's assertion that Chandler had come to Andersonville "determined to report unfavorably of everything he saw or heard" was also dismissed by Cooper and his staff. Chandler's report had firmly fixed responsibility for the horror of Andersonville on Winder, and Seddon and Cooper were determined to make it stick. Winder's charge that Chandler had deliberately misrepresented the facts, Chilton snapped, simply proved that the general was "an officer who seems to be as careless and indifferent respecting the honor of another's reputation as he is reported to be to the dictates of humanity."[119]

Even as he was attempting to clear his name and respond to Chandler's findings, Winder continued his search for a location where a new prison might be constructed to relieve the congestion at Andersonville. On 30 July he informed Cooper that he had dispatched Captain Sidney Winder and another officer to reconnoiter a possible site at Millen, Georgia. As he wired Richmond, it was "very important to build as soon as possible," for in spite of Seddon's order that shipments to the prison be halted, the number of prisoners had risen to over 32,000 by July, and in that single month almost 2,000 had died.[120]

During the first months of 1864 the number of prisoners confined in the North fluctuated, much as they did in the South. Northern prisons held 35,549 Rebels when the year opened, but this number had dropped by almost 2,000 by the end of April, largely as a result of the exchanges initiated by Butler.[121] Yet this decrease did not end the overcrowding in the Federal network of prisons, nor did it result in a significant improvement to the terrible conditions that existed in the camps at the end of 1863.

At Rock Island, the smallpox epidemic that had flared in December 1863 continued to rage without respite. In January, the disease claimed 231 prisoners; in February, another 346 died. Because Commissary General of Prisoners William Hoffman had decreed that the prison be constructed without a hospital, the sick were placed in ten of the camp's barracks, an arrangement that newly assigned camp surgeon William Watson found totally unsatisfactory. As Watson wrote to departmental medical director Charles S. Tripler on 29 March, the makeshift wards suffered from overcrowding and a "great want of cleanliness." Prison medical director A. M. Clark visited the post in February and was disgusted by what he saw. "To speak plainly," he wrote to prison commander Colonel A. J. Johnson, "I was horrified to find on my inspection yesterday 38 cases of pox laying in the prison." Clark knew that treatment of the sick at Rock Island would not improve until a hospital was constructed at the site. Accordingly, he authorized the immediate construction of a 560-bed facility. The work went well until Hoffman heard of the plans and ordered the construction halted immediately. Watson explained to Tripler that Hoffman had decided that the high rates of sickness and death among the prisoners at Rock Island were mainly due the presence of smallpox and were therefore "of a temporary character." When seen in this light, a new hospital was clearly an unwarranted extravagance; but as a result, Watson was forced to crowd 485 smallpox cases into a space adequate for only 240 patients.[122] In March, another 283 men died at Rock Island, and Tripler forwarded Watson's report to the War Department with a recommendation that construction of the hospital be resumed immediately. Finally, on 4 April, Hoffman notified the commander of the prison that the War Department had approved the hospital. But with an eye toward thrift as always, Hoffman qualified the approval with instructions that all building expenses were to be paid from the prison fund and that the work was to be accomplished "observing the closest economy in all things."[123]

Smallpox was also rampant in other Federal prisons during the spring of 1864. Like Rock Island, the prison at Alton, Illinois, still had no hospital. Prisoners infected with smallpox were moved to a makeshift pest house on a nearby island in the Mississippi River, where the care provided them by Union surgeons was uneven at best. By March, prisoner Griffin Frost recorded in his diary, the pest house was filled to bursting with "poor Southern men . . . lying at the point of death, with this terrible disease, having no one to care for them except the rough soldier nurse detailed from the prisoners."[124]

Gratiot Street Prison in St. Louis was yet another Union facility where smallpox patients remained with uninfected prisoners in overcrowded rooms until the disease was well advanced. The inevitable result was a staggering rate of infection and death. On 14 March 1864 a city newspaper reported that of the 1,800 captives confined in the prison, 1,100 were either in the hospital or sick in quarters. A visiting Federal inspector found the filth and neglect so appalling that he urged Hoffman to shut down the prison immediately and transfer the prisoners to another camp, but Hoffman, who had earlier refused to allow a renovation of the prison hospital on the grounds that Gratiot Street was a temporary facility, declined to authorize the move.[125]

Smallpox was only one of the grim realities of daily life at the Point Lookout and Fort Delaware prisons. By the spring of 1864, both of these facilities had developed into the true prison depots Hoffman had envisioned. Records maintained at Point Lookout indicate that by March the prisoner population had dropped by almost 2,000 due to "exchange," and in April the count remained stable at just over 6,000 men. In May, however, the termination of exchanges and the commencement of Grant's Overland campaign combined to boost the total to twice that number, and at the end of the month 12,027 Rebels were confined in the 23-acre compound.[126] Rations were so skimpy that prisoners were driven to supplement their diets by catching and eating the large wharf rats that swarmed throughout the prison, and by mid-June the facility was so overcrowded that camp surgeon James H. Thompson was moved to "most respectfully protest against the reception of additional numbers of prisoners." As Thompson advised his superiors in the district adjutant general's office, the prisoner population had swelled to over 14,000, a number far too great to be humanely confined within the "limited area" of the stockade. Further increases, he maintained, would surely lead to "an epidemic that will decimate . . . the ranks of prisoners," since the medical facilities at the prison were already stretched far beyond capacity. Because his earlier request for an enlargement of the hospital had not been granted, Thompson wrote, he had been forced to billet two hundred sick prisoners among the general population, a practice that was certain to fuel the smallpox and typhoid fever already ravaging the camp. Furthermore, the prison water supply was of such "insufficient quantity and injurious quality" that it was primarily responsible for the increasing number of deaths due to chronic diarrhea and dysentery, and there was an alarming rise in cases of scurvy, due mainly to the fact that the prisoners' diet was terribly deficient in fresh vegetables.[127]

This absence of vegetables presented something of a mystery, for garrison officers at the facility had long insisted that sufficient quantities of vegetables were being purchased from the prison fund, and records of expenditures supported this claim.[128] The solution to this puzzle emerged when an audit of the abnormally large prison fund revealed that $500 allegedly expended for vegetables had in fact been used by the post's enterprising supply officer to purchase mackerel, which he then passed to the camp sutler, who sold the fish to prisoners at a tidy profit. When Hoffman was informed of the scam, he reminded the camp commander that such purchases were "irregular." He did not, however, censure the officer for failing to make sure that prisoners were receiving vegetables or for allowing the prison fund to grow so large that it attracted the attention of Federal inspectors. Instead, he congratulated the commander for the "judicious management of the issues and savings of rations" that had allowed the fund become "very large," and he assured the officer that any concern from Washington was prompted solely by a desire to ensure that future revenues "be so accumulated that any inquiries which may be made may be very satisfactorily answered."[129]

Throughout the spring of 1864 Hoffman continued to petition Secretary of War Stanton for increased control over all aspects of the Union prisoner-of-war system. In particular, Old Huffy sought additional authority over the departmental commanders who outranked him and who often defied his instructions concerning prisoner management. He told Stanton that there continued to be "some want of uniformity of practice and some want of understanding by department commanders in regard to the control of prisoners of war." Only through enhancement of the powers of the commissary general of prisoners could this problem be corrected. Stanton agreed. On 3 May, Hoffman's expanded authority was formalized in the publication of General Orders No. 190. Earlier orders had granted him the "supervision" of enemy captives, but under the provisions of this new directive "the commanders of depots and other places at which prisoners may be assembled" would be "directly accountable for [the prisoners] to the Commissary-General of Prisoners, from whom they will receive orders direct, and to whom they will report directly in all matters relating to prisoners." Hoffman was further authorized to request from commanders of military departments "such assistance in the execution of his duties as the case may demand." Although senior in rank, department commanders were required to furnish as many guards as Hoffman deemed necessary, and they were prohibited from relieving or transferring those guards without first notifying the commissary general of prisoners.[130]

Hoffman had been very busy in the early months of 1864, addressing a number of specific problems in camps where conditions had become clearly intolerable. In January, he relieved the bungling commander of Johnson's Island and ordered that the camp's deplorable sanitation be improved through the construction of new latrines. When Medical Inspector A. M. Clark reported that the horrendous smallpox epidemic at Rock Island was being perpetuated because there were no uncontaminated uniforms to issue soldiers infected with the disease, Hoffman ordered replacement clothing furnished "at once." At Point Lookout he temporarily authorized the delivery of "boxes containing nothing hurtful or contraband sent to prisoners of war by their families of friends," and when guards at the facility became too trigger-happy, he issued revised and more stringent instructions limiting the use of deadly force against prisoners.[131]

Near the end of April, the orders issued by Hoffman and Secretary of War Stanton took a decidedly darker turn. At first glance, these pronouncements appear to be simply a continuation of the harsh policies mandated by the secretary in the summer and fall of 1863. Such was not the case. In fact, the orders signaled nothing less than the advent of a new and far more determined effort to develop and implement a policy of successive rounds of retaliation, deliberately designed to lower conditions in the camps and increase immeasurably the suffering of prisoners. In supplying the fuel to fire this new call for harsher treatment of prisoners, those who directed the Union prisoner-of-war system would work in concert with a group of powerful and equally determined allies—the members of the Joint Committee on the Conduct of the War.

In the fall of 1861, the humiliating Union reversals at Manassas, Wilson's Creek, and Ball's Bluff led Radical Republicans in Congress to question both the loyalty of Democratic generals and Lincoln's ability successfully to direct military operations.[132] The Radicals believed that the war effort was deficient in both direction and vigor; only the institution of close congressional oversight would lead to a Union victory. In December, Senator John Sherman called for the establishment of a joint committee invested with broad powers to investigate all aspects of "the general conduct of the war." Sherman's fellow congressmen approved the idea, and on 10 December 1861 the Joint Committee on the Conduct of the War was born. Republican Senator Benjamin F. Wade of Ohio chaired the new committee, which immediately assumed a decidedly Radical cast.[133] Because Stanton was a Democrat and had served as U.S. attorney general in the Buchanan administration, many Democrats expected that he would act to counter the growing influence of the Radicals in Congress. They were disappointed, however. From the start, the secretary established close ties with Wade and his committee. "He agreed with us fully," committee member George Julian remembered, adding that "we were delighted with him."[134]

Wade was convinced that the secret of the Confederacy's military success lay in the superior morale of Rebel soldiers—a quality which, the congressman maintained, was derived from the consuming hatred that southerners felt toward their northern foes. Accordingly, the chairman and his colleagues embarked upon an effort to instill a comparable degree of loathing in the hearts of Union soldiers and civilians. Ably assisted by Stanton, they devoted their substantial abilities and vast powers of subpoena and investigation to accomplishing this mission. In the hands of these men, retaliation—a practice heretofore employed primarily to secure humane treatment for captives—was redirected to ensure the prosecution of a hard war against the Rebels and a radical reconstruction of the South after the war.

The committee's first investigation was prompted by accusations that Confederate soldiers had committed horrible atrocities against the Union dead at Manassas and were brutally mistreating the prisoners of war they had shipped to Richmond.[135] In February 1862 the committee was instructed by Congress to inquire into these allegations. Wade personally directed the collection of testimony, and the manner in which he released the investigation's results revealed much about his objectives. The findings of the committee were initially prepared not as an official report for submission to Congress, but in pamphlet form for release to the northern press and public. Seizing upon the most lurid accounts while rejecting a sizable amount of testimony to the contrary, Wade informed northerners that the "fiendish rebels" had desecrated the bodies of "heroic" Union dead by boiling down their remains to obtain finger bones for trinkets and skulls from which to drink their hellish southern brews. Helpless Yankee wounded had been gleefully bayoneted by the "barbarous" enemy, and their mutilated and naked corpses had been left unburied on the field.[136]

Wade's accounts of the treatment of Union prisoners of war were no less sensational or damning. Wounded prisoners were consigned to the care of youthful and inexperienced southern surgeons who "seemed to delight in hacking and butchering" their patients. Prisoners who survived these encounters were transported to the squalid prisons of Richmond, where they were denied food, clothing, shelter, and medical care while being subjected to a routine regimen of torture and murder.[137]

Wade and the committee did their work well. The report was reprinted across the North in dozens of newspapers, as well as in popular news magazines such as *Frank Leslie's Illustrated Newspaper* and *Harper's Weekly*.[138] Because the report was released as an official summary of findings by a congressional committee, the northern public accepted it as factual and well-substantiated, and they were outraged by its contents. The Radicals quickly moved to capitalize on their success. Shortly after the report was released, George Julian rose in the House to demand that southern atrocities be answered by swift and severe retaliation against the Rebels held in Union prisoner-of-war camps.[139]

While seemingly straightforward, Julian's demand was calculated to evoke responses on a number of different levels. Most obviously, the target of Union retaliation was the Confederate government, and its objective was to secure better treatment for Union prisoners. But there were other, more complex targets and objectives as well, the first of which was the president of the United States. Radicals had long been dissatisfied with Lincoln's reluctance to institute measures such as the immediate emancipation of slaves and the confiscation of Rebel lands, and they were particularly incensed by his unwillingness to implement a systematic program of retaliation against Confederate prisoners.[140] The president had rejected such reprisals because he feared that retaliation would only beget retaliation by the enemy and thus spiral beyond control. To the members of the committee, however, this reticence was simply one more sign of Lincoln's weakness, and they now hastened to use his refusal to retaliate to force him to accede to their demands for the prosecution of a harsher war.

For Congress, as well as for the assembled members of the press, Julian's address offered a grisly review of the atrocity testimony collected by the committee. The Rebels, Julian charged, "give arsenic to our soldiers, mock at the agonies of the wounded," and "boil the dead bodies of our soldiers in cauldrons." With his audience hanging in rapt attention on his every word, Julian closed his speech by censuring the president personally for allowing such acts to go unpunished. The Union had been too soft in its treatment of traitors, Julian thundered; as a result, outrages like those committed on the field at Manassas and in the prisons of Richmond would inevitably continue until the Lincoln administration adopted a vigorous policy of retaliation.[141]

The president was not the only target of Radical calls for retaliation. Their demands for retribution for the "savage deeds" perpetrated at Manassas and in

Richmond were also aimed at the soldiers and the civilian populace of the North. Wade's conviction that Union soldiers were suffering defeats because they did not sufficiently loathe their foes was reinforced when committee members investigated the Fredericksburg debacle in December 1862. General Ambrose Burnside informed committee members that his army had been defeated because his soldiers did not "adequately hate" their enemy. As Julian remembered, the general "urged me to breathe into the hearts of the people . . . a spirit of righteous indignation and wrath towards the Rebels." In speeches to soldiers and civilians across the North during the spring of 1863, committee members took every opportunity to demonize southerners whenever possible. Confederates, they told their audiences, routinely committed atrocities on the battlefield and in their prisons, and a people capable of perpetrating such heinous crimes were deserving of stern and unrelenting retaliation. Northerners were thus completely justified in exacting such retribution, even against Rebels confined as prisoners of war.[142]

While the Radicals hoped such calls for retaliation would garner public support for a more vigorous prosecution of the war, their ultimate objective was even more ambitious and far-sighted. The conduct of the Rebels, Wade wrote in the official report on Manassas, should "arouse the horror and disgust" of civilized people everywhere and steel the citizens of the loyal states to "renewed exertions to protect our country from the restoration to power of such men." Already in 1862, the Radicals were anticipating the reconstruction that would follow the war, and their message was clear: men who would order the desecration of Union dead and the murder of Union prisoners were completely undeserving of positions of leadership in a reconstructed South.[143]

Both Hoffman and Stanton had earlier demonstrated that they were more than willing to execute the policy of retaliation sought by the Radicals. When a Confederate officer had complained to Hoffman of mistreatment by his keepers at Camp Chase, for example, Hoffman had replied that the guards were simply exacting just retribution for the "innumerable outrages which have been committed on our people." In late 1863, Stanton had sanctioned this attitude with his declaration that Confederate prisoners were to receive "precisely similar treatment" to that allegedly being inflicted upon Union prisoners in the South.[144] Execution of the secretary's mandate had been postponed by Commissioner for Exchange Ethan Allen Hitchcock, but beginning in April 1864 a series of events combined to ensure the implementation of Stanton's wished-for policy of systematic retaliation.

The first of these events occurred on the morning of 12 April, when the Union garrison at Fort Pillow, Tennessee, was surrounded and overwhelmed by Confederate cavalry under the command of General Nathan Bedford Forrest. Precisely what happened following the capitulation remains a topic of intense controversy, but most historians agree that Forrest's men were guilty of perpetrating numerous atrocities against the black soldiers and Tennessee Unionists who surrendered.[145] Accounts of a massacre of Federal soldiers quickly circulated in the northern press, and with each retelling the conduct of Confederates became more barbarous and the calls for retribution more strident. "Let the action of the Government be as prompt and horrible as it will be final," screamed *Harper's Weekly* in a typical editorial. Lincoln, while refusing to act hastily, clearly felt pressed to accede to such demands. Speaking at a Sanitary Fair rally in Baltimore on 18 April, he assured his audience that an investigation was ongoing and that should allegations of a massacre be "conclusively proved . . . retribution shall as surely come."[146]

On the same day, the Senate passed a resolution directing the Committee for the Conduct of the War to investigate the massacre. After meeting with Lincoln and receiving from Stanton a directive placing the full resources of the War Department at their disposal, Wade and his fellow committee member, Representative Daniel W. Gooch of Massachusetts, departed for Fort Pillow.[147] Yet Stanton was not willing to delay retribution pending substantiation of the charges, and on his instructions Hoffman issued a War Department circular on 20 April reducing prisoner rations. This publication of this order was significant, for it was the initial directive in what would become a comprehensive and systematic Union policy of retaliation toward captives.[148]

Upon arriving at Fort Pillow, Wade and Gooch began to take testimony from witnesses. On 27 April, Gooch, employing a tactic used often by the committee, leaked a report to the radical press claiming that the atrocities committed by Forrest's cavalry far exceeded even the most lurid charges.[149] Meanwhile, even as the investigation was ongoing, Stanton was laying plans to ensure that this time Lincoln would be compelled to follow through on his promise to authorize retaliation against southern prisoners. The secretary's opportunity to force the president's hand came on 3 May, when Lincoln called a cabinet meeting to solicit opinions about the best response to the massacre. Secretary of the Navy Gideon Welles began by deeming the idea of retaliation "barbarous." The relationship between Welles and Stanton had always been cold and distant. From his first day in office, Stanton had dismissed the Navy Department as being of little importance in the overall war effort, and he routinely excluded Welles from high- level discussions. Welles naturally resented these slights, and he harbored a deep personal enmity toward Stanton. He also resented the close relationship between Stanton and Lincoln, and he was deeply suspicious of the motives and objectives of the secretary of war and his Radical associates in Congress. On being informed of the Fort Pillow allegations, Welles therefore urged caution. He conceded that there was "probably something in these terrible reports" of the massacre, but he also distrusted congressional committees because, as he tersely warned Lincoln, "they exaggerate."[150]

On 6 May the full cabinet convened a second time, and Lincoln asked each member to submit a written recommendation of the course of action the administration should pursue. All agreed that the Rebels should be afforded an opportunity to disavow the actions of Forrest's men and issue assurances that black captives would henceforth receive the same treatment as whites; but on the question of the proper response should such assurances not be forthcoming, the cabinet split along ideological lines. The moderates—Welles, Postmaster General Montgomery Blair, and Attorney General Edward Bates—were repelled by the prospect of retaliation, contending that it would be detrimental to efforts aimed at improving conditions in southern prisons. Bates, who had earlier had warned Lincoln to beware of the "extreme men in Congress" and who feared that the president "lack[ed] the nerve" to control Stanton, argued that retaliation was no more than a "compact . . . for mutual slaughter," which, if implemented, would yield only "blood and murder." Cabinet hardliners—Stanton, Secretary of State William Seward, Secretary of the Treasury Salmon P. Chase, and Secretary of the Interior John P. Usher—were of a very different mind. They recommended that Rebel officers equal in number to the Federal soldiers allegedly murdered at Fort Pillow be immediately placed in close confinement pending a response from the Confederate government. Should authorities in Richmond refuse to disavow the massacre or decline to issue specific assurances that such acts would not be repeated in the future, man-for-man retaliation against the prisoners would begin immediately. Stanton presented Lincoln with a six-point plan detailing the manner in which the retaliation should proceed, and soon after the meeting Chase—in a statement clearly intended to spur the president to action—told a newspaper reporter that he "trust[ed] that the slaughter at Fort Pillow will not be permitted to go unpunished." Lincoln yielded to the Radicals' demands, promising that if the charges of a massacre were substantiated, he would "enforce the most energetic measures of retaliation."[151] Before the joint committee's report on Fort Pillow could be released, however, new charges of Rebel atrocities against prisoners of war surfaced.

Throughout the spring of 1864 Confederate authorities had continued to ship sick and wounded prisoners north in accordance with the agreement reached between Ould and Butler. In late April, they announced that they would release 32 officers and 363 sick and wounded Union prisoners who had been confined at Belle Isle and other prisons. Union ships were dispatched to transport the prisoners to medical facilities at Annapolis, Maryland. On 29 April, Hoffman informed Stanton that although he had received no substantiated reports of mistreatment of the captives on Belle Isle, accounts submitted by recently released Union parolees left "little doubt" that prisoners were confined there under unspeakable conditions. He suggested the solicitation of "the testimony of some of the most intelligent paroled prisoners recently arrived." If it confirmed the reports of the paroled prisoners, Hoffman recommended that severe retaliation be exacted on the Confederate officers confined at Johnson's Island. Specifically, he proposed that the officers "be allowed only half-rations; that their clothing be reduced to what is only sufficient to cover their nakedness, and that they be denied the privilege of purchasing the articles allowed to other prisoners."[152]

Stanton agreed, and on 2 May he ordered Hoffman to be present when the transports arrived at Annapolis so that he might personally assess their condition. Accordingly, Hoffman was on the wharf when the flag-of-truce boat *New York* berthed. He was so outraged by the pitiful condition of the returnees that he immediately telegraphed the secretary to "respectfully urge that retaliatory measures be at once instituted by subjecting the [southern] officers we now hold as prisoners of war to a similar treatment."[153] While the returning Union officers were "in generally good health," Hoffman reported, the enlisted men were "in a very sad plight, both mentally and physically." Most of them were "wasted to mere skeletons," and many had "scarcely life enough remaining to appreciate that they were now in the hands of their friends." Hoffman estimated that fewer than one third of the men could be nursed to a "convalescent state" within ten days; the others, if they survived at all, would recover their health only after prolonged hospitalization. There could be no doubt that Union prisoners were being "starved to death," Hoffman charged, dismissing Rebel assurances that prisoners in their hands were receiving the same rations as Confederate soldiers. "Can an army keep the field," he asked indignantly, "and be active and efficient on the same fare that kills prisoners of war at a frightful percentage? I think not; no man can believe it."[154]

Sensing yet another opportunity to advance the Radical agenda, Stanton forwarded Hoffman's report to Wade with the recommendation that the committee investigate "the enormity of the crime committed by the rebels" and present their findings to the country. Wade readily concurred, and committee members traveled to Annapolis on 6 May and began to gather testimony from the returned

prisoners, completing their work in only three days. Following the pattern established with earlier reports, they released their findings in sensational press notices
and thousands of pamphlets, which were distributed throughout the North.[155]

The testimony gathered by the committee was indeed shocking. Although
Wade conceded that evidence indicated that the treatment of prisoners confined
in locations other than the Confederate capital was "far more humane," he carefully focused the report on the accounts of returnees from camps in Richmond.
"Your committee," he wrote in the preface to the report, "are unable to convey
any adequate idea of the sad and deplorable condition of the men they saw in the
hospitals they visited." Although now under the care of Union surgeons, many of
the prisoners were "dying daily, one of them being in the very throes of death as
your committee stood by his bed-side and witnessed the sad spectacle there presented." The committee heightened the report's effect by including eight graphic
lithographs of the most emaciated and enfeebled prisoners. Wade insisted that
the committee's report provided incontrovertible proof that the prisoners were
the victims of a "predetermined policy . . . of the rebel authorities . . . to reduce
our soldiers in their power . . . to a condition that those who survive shall never
recover." He again demanded that the nation exact the sternest retaliation for
these "inhuman acts."[156]

Newspapers across the North accorded the report front-page status. The photographs of the living cadavers were published in both *Harper's Weekly* and *Leslie's
Illustrated Newspaper,* and outraged editors assailed Lincoln for not acceding to
Radical demands for retaliation. Wade also ordered twenty thousand copies of
the report to be prepared in pamphlet form for nationwide distribution, and its
effect among ordinary citizens was galvanic. "It is horrible, atrocious!" wrote one
reader in typical disgust. "History records no instances of such deliberate ferocity.
Let Lincoln send a copy of this book into every home."[157]

Lincoln did not do so, but in the wake of the report he could no longer
refuse to implement the plan of retaliation advocated by Stanton. On 17 May
he directed the secretary to notify Rebel authorities that a number of Confederate officers had been "set aside" and were being held in close confinement. If
assurances that all Federal captives would be fairly treated as prisoners of war
and that there would be no repeat of the Fort Pillow massacre were received in
Washington by 1 July, there would be no retaliation against the officers. If no such
assurances were tendered by that date, the U.S. government would assume that
"captured colored troops shall have been murdered or subjected to Slavery," and
that the "said government will, upon said assumption, take such action as may
then appear expedient and just."[158]

With the publication of this proclamation, it seemed that Stanton and the Radicals had finally gained the presidential action they had been demanding. Unlike Davis, however, Lincoln had always been leery of personally issuing orders for retaliation against prisoners. He knew that a substantial portion of the electorate in the North—both Republican and Democrat—continued to favor a resumption of exchanges. The butcher's bill run up during the first two months of Grant's Overland campaign had been horrendous; thousands more Union boys were now dying in squalid pens across the South. Even as the Radicals cried for harsher retaliation, calls for a general exchange were again swelling to a crescendo. By July 1864 Lincoln correctly sensed that his chance for reelection that November might become yet one more casualty of the hell of the Wilderness; in August he told his stunned cabinet that he would likely lose the election. The president had previously distanced himself from retaliatory directives issued by his secretary of war, and Stanton knew that Lincoln would not risk alienating a significant portion of the electorate by issuing such orders now. The secretary suspected—quite correctly, as it turned out—that the 1 July deadline of the president's ultimatum would pass without either Confederate acquiescence or presidential action. But this time, Stanton would not be put off.[159]

In a telegram to the secretary of war on 19 May, Hoffman had suggested that prisoner rations could be "considerably reduced" beyond the cuts imposed on 20 April. Although he was fully aware that scurvy was already decimating prisoners in northern camps, he proposed a 50 percent cut in vegetables, which he asserted could be made "without depriving [the prisoners] of the food necessary to keep them in health." Major General Henry Halleck, eager as always to curry favor with Stanton, sniffed the mood of the moment and proposed that the prisoners' daily ration be slashed even further. "Why not dispense with tea, coffee, and sugar and reduce the ration to that issued by the rebel Government to their own troops!" he added enthusiastically. This suggestion was blocked when the acting surgeon general advised that rations of tea, coffee, and sugar to the sick and wounded should continue. Stanton approved of Hoffman's proposal, and on 1 June the commissary general of prisoners ordered that the new round of reductions be instituted immediately. Correctly perceiving that these deep cuts would yield an enormous surplus for his beloved prison fund, Hoffman also supplied instructions for the disposition of the money that would be saved by feeding prisoners less. "The difference between the ration as above established and the ration allowed by law to soldiers of the U.S. Army," he advised the camp commanders, "constitutes the 'savings' from which is formed the 'prison fund.'"[160]

Although this retaliation was debilitating to the health of captives throughout the Union system of prisons, nowhere were its effects more evident or devastating than at the newest of the Federal camps, Elmira. On 19 May, Hoffman had advised Stanton that all of the camps in the Union system of prisons were swiftly filling far beyond capacity and that the capability to confine additional captives was rapidly being exhausted. He estimated that five thousand more prisoners might be squeezed into the depot at Point Lookout, but that Fort Delaware could accommodate no more enlisted prisoners and only "a few" more officers. The Overland campaign was now well underway, and the ferocious combat was yielding scores of prisoners daily. Grant's termination of the Butler exchanges was indeed depleting the strength of Confederate regiments, but it was also speeding the day when the existing network of Federal prisoners would be unable to accept any further captives. Hoffman knew that the near-continuous combat of the Wilderness and Grant's policy of refusing exchanges would combine to push the numbers of Rebel prisoners coming north to levels never before experienced, and he thus proposed that a new prison be established at the "draft rendezvous camp" at Elmira, New York. The camp, he informed Stanton, was readily accessible through a combination of steamship and rail, and fencing off one section of the post's barracks would provide accommodation for "8,000 or possibly 10,000 prisoners." Stanton approved the recommendation immediately, and Hoffman wired Lieutenant Colonel Seth Eastman, the commander at Elmira, to "set apart the barracks on the Chemung River at Elmira as a depot for prisoners of war." Although Hoffman admitted he was "unable to say how soon the barracks will be required," he directed Eastman to be prepared for the first shipment "within ten days."[161]

Hoffman's instructions to convert Elmira into a massive prisoner-of-war camp came as a complete surprise to Eastman, and in his reply he questioned the wisdom of the decision. Elmira's barracks could accommodate only four thousand prisoners "without crowding," he informed Hoffman, and no more than an additional thousand captives could be billeted in tents. Feeding the prisoners would also present a significant problem, for the post kitchen could prepare rations for only five thousand men daily. Most ominously, Eastman reminded Hoffman that "there is no hospital at these barracks, hence hospital tents will have to be used for the sick."[162]

The camp's prison enclosure was also problematic, for it could not have been located in a more unhealthful spot. The site encompassed thirty acres, all situated below the level of the muddy Chemung River, which bordered the camp. One acre within the proposed stockade was perpetually flooded by Foster's Pond, a brackish, stagnant backwater of the river. Furthermore, the barracks the prisoners would occupy were actually no more than shells. They had been hastily constructed of green lumber and lacked both ceilings and foundations. The workmanship was exceptionally poor, and in only a few weeks the cracks that opened between the planks as they dried were so large that the walls and the floors provided little protection from either the wind or the rain.[163]

Hoffman had made his decision, however, and on 30 June the commander of Point Lookout was directed to initiate the transfer of two thousand prisoners to the new camp. The men were shipped to New York City in the hold of an aging Federal transport and then transported inland by train; the first contingent reached Elmira early on the morning of 6 July. As one witness to their arrival noted, the Rebels were indeed a pitiful lot. "They wore all sorts of nondescript uniforms," the observer recalled, and "some had nothing on but drawers and shirts." They were "pale and emaciated, hollow-eyed and dispirited in every act and movement," and because they had been vaccinated with a contaminated batch of smallpox vaccine before leaving Point Lookout, many of the men were afflicted with "great sores, big enough, it seemed to put your arm through."[164]

By the end of July there were over 4,400 prisoners crammed into the camp on the Chemung, and another 3,000 were en route from Point Lookout. The first arrivals had scrambled to secure a place in the rickety barracks, and later arrivals had to seek shelter in an assortment of dilapidated tents. These were soon full as well, forcing hundreds of men to sleep in the open without blankets. By mid-August the number of captives had climbed to 9,600—so many, Eastman reported to Hoffman, that there were not enough hours in the day to feed them because of the camp's inadequate cooking and eating facilities. The greatest problem at the post, however, was an almost total lack of sanitation. Garbage from the kitchen and fecal matter from the latrines was simply dumped into Foster's Pond. As one Union surgeon with an obvious flair for statistics noted, this was further exacerbated by the fact that "seven thousand men will pass 2,600 gallons of urine daily," all of which was going into the pond as well.[165]

Given such conditions, men succumbed to disease by the hundreds. The first prisoner died on 27 July, one of eleven Confederates who died that month. In August, that number skyrocketed to 115; in September, 385 men died. Abysmal sanitation and overcrowding contributed to this horrific mortality, as did the weakened physical condition of the men when they were transferred from other northern prisons. The provision of an adequate and nutritious diet would certainly have ameliorated the sickness and suffering of the captives, but rations were yet another of Elmira's problems. Camp cooking and dining facilities were so overtaxed that prisoners could be fed only twice daily, and the nutritional value of the provisions was insufficient to sustain the prisoners' health. The Union inspector tasked to assess the quality of the meat furnished the prisoners, for example, reported that less than half of it was edible.[166]

Indeed, the quantity and quality of rations at Elmira was the most debilitating blow to the prisoners' health. For men already weakened by months in other prisons and then exposed to the unhealthy environment of Elmira, the progressive cuts in the amounts and nutritional value of rations were devastating. In desperation, prisoners attempted to stave off starvation by eating rats and fighting over the rancid leavings in the cook's bone cart.[167] John King, a Confederate infantryman who arrived at Elmira on 1 August 1864, remembered well the agony of slow starvation. "Many men, once strong, would cry for something to eat," he recalled, adding, "I know from experience."[168]

Moreover, the paltry amount of vegetables in the prisoners' diet resulted in an outbreak of scurvy at the prison. The first cases of this painful and deadly disease appeared less than two months after the camp opened; by mid-September, camp surgeons reported that 1,870 prisoners had been stricken.[169] John King was a robust twenty-two-year-old when he arrived at Elmira, but within weeks chronic diarrhea brought on by poor diet and living in filth had reduced him to a mere skeleton. He was also one of the early victims of the scurvy epidemic, and in his case the disease was so severe that he discovered to his horror that his teeth and gums "could be removed with the fingers." Still his illness worsened, and eventually John King went blind.[170]

Because the camp had no hospital, eight of the unfinished barracks buildings were set aside as makeshift wards. Like all the other barracks at Elmira, they had no ceilings and were brutally cold in the winter. In October, Eastman urgently asked that straw be provided for the beds in the hospital, but he received no answer to his request. Later, the camp commander petitioned Hoffman for permission to install ceilings in the makeshift hospital wards, but the commissary general refused to authorize the construction.[171] On 16 October the captain who served as camp inspector reported that there were 588 prisoners "in hospital" and another 1,021 "receiving medical treatment." The captain also noted that in the four days prior to his report, 44 Confederate soldiers had died. "The cause of this amount of sickness and death," he assured his superiors, "is a matter of deep interest."[172]

Confronted with the terrible overcrowding and appalling rates of sickness and mortality raging in the Union camps by mid-1864, Hoffman finally authorized a number of rudimentary improvements to prisoner-of-war facilities. Additional tents were sent to Point Lookout, where a new prison hospital was erected. Tents were also shipped to Johnson's Island to shelter prisoners who could not find space in the prison's barracks, and the facility's ramshackle water supply system was improved. The level of sanitation at Camp Douglas was upgraded, and the opening of a new prison compound reduced the overcrowding at Camp Chase.[173]

In every case, however, the improvements were very limited and implemented at far too slow a pace to ameliorate the rapidly escalating crisis. By August, for example, the prisoners' lack of fresh vegetables had produced frightful epidemics of scurvy in most Union camps. When surgeons and camp commanders appealed for permission to increase the amount of vegetables given the prisoners, Hoffman responded by reminding them that they were authorized to purchase antiscorbutic drugs from the prison fund. Unfortunately, these potions were often not effective in curbing the disease. When the number of new scurvy cases at Elmira continued to rise, Eastman petitioned Hoffman directly for permission to allow the prisoners to purchase fresh vegetables from the camp sutler. Faced with the brutal fact that there were then 793 cases of scurvy in the camp, the commissary general of prisoners reluctantly gave his assent, but he admonished Eastman that the practice was to be allowed only until the disease abated. In response to a similar request from the commander of Camp Douglas, Hoffman granted permission to resume issues of fresh vegetables, but he ordered that the additional costs incurred were to be defrayed by commensurate reductions in the amount of meat provided to the prisoners.[174]

Even as conditions in northern prisons plummeted, Stanton and Hoffman continued to maintain that Rebel prisoners were being treated humanely and that the conditions found in Union prisons were far superior to those in South. In the fall of 1864, support for these claims was provided by a very unlikely source—the U.S. Sanitary Commission. Previous inspections of prisons by the commission had been remarkably even-handed; commission inspectors had not hesitated to fault Union management of prisoner-of-war camps, as they had done in the Swalm report on conditions at Point Lookout in late 1863.[175] In June 1864, a committee from the commission solicited Hoffman's assistance in preparing a comparison of prisoner treatment in Union and Confederate prisons, but Stanton—remembering the negative reports penned by commission inspectors in the past—replied that Wade's report on the condition of the Annapolis returnees had already provided such a comparison, and he denied the request. Undeterred, the committee decided to proceed anyway. The manner in which they began to gather facts for their report, however, quickly indicated that their findings would be neither accurate nor unbiased. Rather than actually inspecting Union prisons, they submitted to Hoffman a list of questions concerning the treatment of Rebel prisoners. Hoffman alone was to provide an assessment of whether prisoner rations, clothing, housing, and medical care were adequate. To the surprise of absolutely no one, his answers were favorable in every instance. To them he appended the schedule of rations he had issued on 20 April, carefully omitting any mention of the subsequent reductions he had recommended and Stanton had approved since that date.[176]

Hoffman presented northern prisons as models of efficiency and order in which Rebel prisoners, no matter how sullen or unrepentant, were treated with the utmost humaneness. Clean, modern hospitals ministered to the sick, and convalescent prisoners were encouraged to improve their minds through the use of well-stocked camp libraries. Prison food was nutritionally balanced, and it was provided in such abundance that the surplus was maintained in a fund from which prisoners purchased luxury items from a variety of merchants who served the camps.

When preparing their assessment of the treatment of Union captives in southern prisons, the Sanitary Commission committee relied on the Annapolis report authored by Wade and the Committee on the Conduct of the War, as well as the most damning testimony they could obtain from interviews with returned prisoners. All of the outrageous atrocity stories that had been circulating in the North since the beginning of the war were recounted as absolute truth, and the document left no doubt where the blame for these crimes should be placed. Accounts of robbery, starvation, confinement in "filthy rooms or unsheltered encampments . . . disease without care or medical treatment and of deaths without number" were presented in detail; and while the commission protested that it would impose no "inferential statements," it also darkly concluded that "certain known effects" were inextricably linked to "certain known causes." Commission reports had always been models of diligence and objectivity, and they would return to a level of unbiased accuracy before the end of the war. Why this inaccurate and biased account was released at this time is still debated. Perhaps, as William Hesseltine suggests, commission directors were utilizing the prevailing war psychosis in the North to boost donations.[177]

Even as the Sanitary Commission report was being proclaimed as gospel by the northern press, other inspectors were providing the War Department with a more accurate assessment of the worsening conditions in Union prisons. At Camp Douglas the number of sick climbed to 167 in June, when there were 34 deaths. In October, the total of sick prisoners approached 400, and 123 prisoners died. On 14 October a panel of Washington surgeons proclaimed that the condition of the men confined at Elmira was "disgraceful to all concerned," and by the end of the month conditions in the camp were such that the commander offered the chilling prediction that if the mortality rate for August and September was sustained, all of the prisoners would be dead within a year.[178]

Conditions in southern prisons were equally dreadful. The prisoner population at Andersonville had peaked at just over 33,000 in August. Almost 3,000 prisoners died there in that terrible month, 103 of them in a single day. Although the prison at Cahaba had been closed temporarily when Andersonville was established, the ceaseless influx of prisoners into the Confederate system had forced its reopening in less than a month. By October, the cotton warehouse held 2,151 men, more than quadruple its capacity.[179] In Richmond, both Libby and Belle Isle had again filled far beyond capacity, and Confederate surgeons reported that prison hospitals in the capital were overcrowded with patients, understocked with medical supplies, and undermanned with competent physicians.[180] In Danville, the city fathers learned that the respite gained when prisoners were transferred from their midst to Andersonville would be only temporary. On 26 July, Cooper notified Lee that Andersonville could accept no more prisoners and that captured Yankees were to be confined among the citizens of Danville.[181]

All these problems were daunting enough, but beginning in August 1864 the men who directed the southern prisoner-of-war system were forced to react to a new threat. Union offensives were slicing into the Confederacy from all sides, forcing the War Department to initiate a massive transfer of Federal prisoners away from the encroaching blue columns. As Sherman continued his drive south through Georgia, Seddon became increasingly concerned that the Yankees would launch a raid to free the captives at Andersonville. Those prisoners, he became convinced, had to be moved immediately to more secure locations. His efforts to effect this transfer set in motion a chain of events that ensured that camps already filled to bursting would be inundated with new waves of prisoners.

On 25 August, Seddon frantically telegraphed Winder to "hasten to the utmost the preparation of other prisons." Winder responded that the camp under construction at Millen was not yet complete, whereupon the secretary ordered that transfers from Andersonville commence at once to Savannah and Charleston instead. When notified of the secretary's decision, the commanders at those two locations vehemently protested the order. The commander at Savannah notified Winder that he was struggling to manage the number of prisoners already confined in his facility, and he pleaded that no additional Federals be sent. Winder was fast running out of options, however, and he was compelled to reply that the secretary's order stood. The Savannah garrison, he telegraphed the distraught commander, should prepare for the arrival of between 5,000 and 10,000 prisoners within one week.[182]

On 5 September, the transfers from Andersonville began. Private Francis Marion Blaloch was one of the Confederate soldiers detailed as a guard on one of the trains carrying the prisoners away. According to his account, the Yankees were marched from the stockade to the station and herded up ramps into cattle cars. When the cars could hold no more men, the doors were locked and the guards mounted the tops of the cars for the trip south. Although a hardened veteran, young Blaloch was struck by the pitiful condition of the filthy and emaciated captives. "Many were sick to death with a deadly disease called scurvy," he recalled. When the cars were opened in Charleston or Savannah, many of the northern boys had died.[183]

Some soldiers were so ill that they could not be moved from Andersonville. One of these was Frederick James, a seaman captured on the coast of South Carolina. In June, James had entered the prison a robust young man, but his diary entries clearly and poignantly chronicle the deterioration of his health—a progress that was common to thousands of Andersonville internees. The rations of raw rice, unbolted corn meal, and raw beans had wrecked his digestive system. "My bowels are a little out of tune," James wrote on 16 June. Three days later he penned a prayer asking God to "grant a speedy deliverance to us all," but his conditioned worsened. By 22 August he was too weak to walk or even wash out his underclothes. All he could do was lie in his own filth and eat "some raw potato" to relieve the scurvy that ravaged his body. The end came on 15 September. Frederick Augustus James lasted less than four months at Andersonville. Along with the daily entries, his diary included bits of poetry and free verse. One of these, entitled "St. Patrick's Day," contained one of the stinging indictments of the Lincoln administration that were very common among Federal prisoners by this point in the war:

> Who shall bear the brunt of this great crying evil?
> Is it Jefferson Davis? Or his privy Counselor the devil?
> Or shall the weight of it, in truth, be laid upon,
> The policy of our Government at Washington?[184]

Meanwhile, Winder continued to receive desperate messages from Richmond urging the earliest possible opening of the camp at Millen. On the same day that he initiated shipments from Andersonville, Cooper ordered Winder to "push forward the completion of the prison" and suggested that "part" of the camp be occupied before "completion of the whole prison grounds." Winder again protested that the stockade was far from ready, but he prepared to begin rail shipments as Cooper had directed.[185]

John Ransom was one of the prisoners transferred from Andersonville to Millen, and he recalled that the boxcar in which he traveled was "very crowded with sick prisoners." During the overnight journey, two of them died. When he arrived at Millen, Ransom was surprised that construction of the prison had still not been completed. Nonetheless, prisoners continued to arrive at a frantic pace; within days, the camp held 10,299 men. Food was initially more plentiful than at Andersonville, Ransom noted, adding that in other ways his new abode was much the same. There was little shelter available, and because the camp had been occupied before a hospital was constructed, little could be done to treat the hundreds of weak and desperately ill prisoners entering the compound daily. As a result, 486 men died in the camp's first month of operation. The horror ended when the encroachment of Sherman's army forced the abandonment of the camp only six weeks after Ransom and his comrades arrived. In that short time, it is estimated that Millen claimed the lives of over 700 men.[186]

Prisoners from Andersonville were also transferred to Florence, South Carolina, where, as at Millen, the initial shipments arrived before preparations at the site were completed. Marched into an open field, the Yankees were guarded until a crew of slaves finished building a rough stockade. The enclosure was not completed until mid-October, by which time the prison held nearly thirteen thousand men. There was no shelter for the captives, and the camp "hospital," an inspecting officer reported, was no more than a collection of "boughs of trees" that afforded "very little protection from the rain." The "emaciated and sickly" prisoners were ravaged by "scurvy and diarrhea," a combination that "carr[ied] off from twenty to fifty per day." Given such conditions, Winder predicted that the rate of mortality at Florence would exceed even Andersonville's, and he was correct. Sherman's advance forced the closing of Florence after only four months of operation, but by that time 2,802 of its 12,000 prisoners had died.[187]

The worst suffering that resulted from the closing of Andersonville, however, was borne by the prisoners who were shipped to Salisbury Prison in North Carolina. The inmate population at Salisbury had remained low since the initiation of exchanges in 1862, but that situation rapidly changed for the worse after the shuttering of the Georgia camp. When the number of captives confined at Belle Isle and Libby began yet another precipitous climb, the War Department ordered Major Thomas Turner, the commander of prisons in Richmond, to begin shipping excess Federals to Salisbury as quickly as possible. Turner attempted to comply, but the transfer was a nightmare from the start. Due to a combination of haste and poor planning, the initial trainloads of prisoners were sent from the capital without a single ration, and they remained without food for the three days of their journey. Their situation improved only slightly when they arrived at their destination. Rations had been adequate for the few hundred prisoners who had been confined at Salisbury during the first nine months of 1864, but they were quickly exhausted by the flood of new arrivals. Major John H. Gee commanded at Salisbury; having been warned in September to prepare for "a very large number of prisoners," he had immediately begun to enlarge the camp's stockade and dig additional wells.[188] These projects were scarcely underway when the first wave of captives arrived on 5 October. Over the next eight weeks, 10,321 Yanks were shipped to Salisbury, and Gee and his staff were completely overwhelmed. Most of the prisoners arrived clad in rags, and replacement clothing could be provided only by stripping the dead before burial. The available barracks space was sufficient for barely half of the captives, and although this was supplemented by three hundred tents of varying sizes, almost four thousand of Salisbury's new inmates secured protection from the elements only by burrowing holes in the earth or constructing crude shelters from scraps of lumber and bits of blankets.[189]

In order to supply one meal daily for this multitude of prisoners and the Confederate garrison, Captain Abram Myers, the post commissary officer, had to procure 13,000 rations every twenty-four hours. Myers earnestly attempted to satisfy this staggering requirement by instituting a ferocious plan of impressment and commandeering local mills to grind the corn and wheat he took from farmers, but the supply of food he amassed could not keep pace with the demand. Meat virtually disappeared from the prisoners' diet, daily rations of bread grew ever smaller, and often the men were issued only unbolted cornmeal to eat. Under such conditions, the prison yards at Salisbury were transformed into a surreal world of starving savages, where the strongest prisoners stole the rations of the weak and infirm. Men nearly mad from hunger raided garbage piles in search of discarded bones; they killed and devoured rats and the few dogs and cats that strayed into the camp and consumed raw acorns that fell from the trees bordering the stockade.[190]

The number of patients in the camp hospital climbed from 100 at the beginning of October to 600 at the end of the month. In that single month there were 267 deaths, more than had been recorded in the previous three years of the prison's history; in November, 969 more prisoners died. Most fell victim to the effects of prolonged exposure and malnutrition. Diarrhea, pneumonia, and scurvy were the greatest killers. Faced with death from starvation, the prisoners became desperate: on 26 November thousands of them rushed the prison gates in a futile bid for freedom. The guards cut them down with a volley of musketry and point-blank artillery fire, "killing," the commander of the guard noted, "between forty and fifty." After this single blast, the officer assured his superiors, "everything then quieted down." For the prisoners, the dying continued, and in December another 1,164 succumbed.[191]

Before the fall of 1864, the dead at Salisbury were given funerals and interred in individual graves, but after October all such trappings of civilization vanished. One prisoner who served on a burial detail in November recalled that after being stripped of all serviceable clothing, the dead were piled up "like hogs" and then simply heaved into mass graves, where they were "covered with a few shovelfuls of dirt." A local minister who viewed the spectacle shamefully recorded that "they throw them in the graves like dogs."[192]

Union boys were not the only casualties of this frantic period in the history of southern prisons. On 10 October, General William Gardner, the officer designated by Seddon to share with Winder the responsibility for prisons in the eastern theater, angrily notified Cooper that he wished to be relieved of duty. "I find that I am unequal to a proper administration of affairs relating to Federal prisoners scattered over the country," he protested. Gardner complained that prisoners in his area of responsibility were being moved about without his knowledge, and while he admitted that the transfers might have been necessary given "the exigencies of the times," the War Department's confusion and lack of coordination had rendered his job impossible. As an example, he wrote that he learned of the decision to transfer thousands of prisoners from Andersonville to Florence only when he read of it in the newspaper. In the final paragraph of his letter, he recommended that "some officer should be placed in sole control of this branch of service." And he cautioned Cooper that this individual should be very carefully selected, for "the condition of prisoners requires the attention of an active, capable, and energetic commanding and administrative officer."[193]

Cooper referred Gardner's recommendation to Seddon. At first the secretary attempted to retain the cumbersome and ineffective dual system of control and responsibility he had initially instituted, but after six weeks of searching in vain for a "proper officer to relieve General Gardner," he at long last adopted the course of action that had been urged on him for almost two years. On 21 November 1864 Seddon appointed General John Henry Winder as commissary general of prisoners. The appointment was officially announced with the publication of General Orders No. 84, the provisions of which were sweeping indeed. Winder was to assume responsibility for "the custody and care of all prisoners of war and the discipline and general administration of such prisons east of the Mississippi River," and "all officers and men on duty at the several military prisons" in that vast region were placed under his direct command. Commanders of posts "in the vicinity of these military prisons" were "made subordinate" to the general "in all matters necessary for the security of the prisoners," and officers at all levels were "required not to interfere with the prisoners, the prison guard, or the administration of the prisons."[194]

Sadly, the appointment came too late for Winder or any other officer to exercise effective command and control over the Confederate prisoner-of-war system. By this stage in the war, the South had been reduced simply to reacting to the hammer blows delivered by encircling Union armies, and Winder lacked both the resources and the time to institute the changes so desperately required in the system of prisons he now directed. Given the military situation in the winter of 1864, he could do little but continue to confine Union prisoners in the existing camps of the South and hope for the renewal of exchanges.

On 10 August, exchange negotiations between the bellicose governments were reopened when Colonel Ould surprised northern authorities by suddenly agreeing to the man-for-man exchange that Butler had proposed back in April. In a letter of explanation to Union assistant agent of exchange John E. Mulford, Ould acknowledged that although the plan had been repeatedly rejected by Confederate authorities in the past, "the very large number of prisoners now held by each party and the suffering consequent upon their continued confinement" had compelled the Davis administration to reassess its position. "I now consent to the . . . proposal," Ould wrote Mulford, "and agree to deliver to you the prisoners held in captivity by the Confederate authorities, provided you agree to deliver an equal number of Confederate officers and men." As Butler had proposed, prisoners who had been held the longest would be the first to be freed, and as equal numbers of captives were received by each side, they would be declared exchanged.[195]

Mulford forwarded Ould's letter to Butler with a request that instructions for implementing the exchanges be swiftly issued, but for Butler the issue was not that simple. On the one hand, he still desperately craved the public acclaim and boost to his postwar political fortunes that securing the release of suffering prisoners would bring; on the other hand, he had promised Grant that his specific instructions prohibiting such exchanges would be "implicitly obeyed." To the surprise of no one familiar with Butler's priorities, he resolved his dilemma by telegraphing Mulford immediately to fill the flag-of-truce boat *New York* with "wounded" Confederate officers and one Rebel general designated for special exchange and to transport the lot with all speed to City Point. And he elected not to inform Grant of his plan, probably hoping that the exchange could be concluded before the commanding general discovered what was afoot.[196]

Butler's scheme might have succeeded had not the *New York* anchored within sight of Grant's headquarters at City Point. It did, however, and as soon as Grant saw the ship he correctly deduced that Butler was once again attempting to circumvent his orders prohibiting exchanges. "I see the *New York* has arrived," Grant telegraphed Butler on 18 August. "Is she going to Aiken's Landing or elsewhere under flag of truce?" His subterfuge now discovered, Butler scrambled to justify his scheme by claiming that all he intended was to conclude a few "special exchanges" and set a new meeting date to discuss the treatment of prisoners with Ould. Grant knew Butler too well to be fooled by such rhetoric, and he fired back a message pointedly directing that "no flags of truce be sent to the enemy nor any arrangements or agreements entered into with him without my first being fully advised of what is being done and yielding my consent to it." The *New York,* Grant continued, "will not be permitted to proceed to Aiken's Landing until I receive a report of the full object of the mission and the load she now has on board."[197]

Butler again protested that he had never intended to disobey Grant's orders, but at the same time he sent a telegram to Major General Ethan Allen Hitchcock in Washington, in which he sought the commissioner's support in doing just that. Noting that he had received "one or two endorsements" from Hitchcock that seemed to support a resumption of exchanges, Butler wrote that the only obstacle to securing it remained the question of the colored troops. He advised Hitchcock that Grant remained adamantly opposed to exchanges, but promised that he would again meet with Ould to determine if a compromise could be reached.[198]

Butler sent Grant a copy of his message to Hitchcock. Grant agreed to allow the meeting with Ould to proceed, but he hastened to add that "on the subject of exchange, I differ from General Hitchcock." In support of his objection, he supplied the most detailed justification of his position offered to date: "It is hard on our men held in Southern prisons not to exchange them, but it is humanity to those left in the ranks to fight our battles. Every man we hold, when released on parole or otherwise, becomes an active soldier against us at once either directly or indirectly. If we commence a system of exchange which liberates all prisoners taken, we will have to fight on until the whole South is exterminated. If we hold those caught they amount to no more than dead men."[199] This was indeed a hard policy. Most historians of the period maintain that it originated with Grant and that in supporting it, the general stood alone. But such was not the case. In his advocacy of a policy of no general exchanges, Grant could count on the support of a powerful ally—Secretary of War Edwin M. Stanton.

Shortly after Grant assumed overall command of the Union armies in March 1864, Stanton prepared a confidential memorandum maintaining that the Confederacy was benefitting disproportionately from exchanges. Paroles and exchanges, Stanton argued, only prolonged the war and should be terminated, regardless of the suffering that would result in the camps. When Stanton later met with Grant, he was delighted to discover that the general was in perfect agreement. Indeed, across the bottom of a memorandum the secretary scrawled that Grant "presented the same argument to me before I could advance it to him."[200]

Finally accepting that Grant was not going to allow a resumption of exchanges, Butler shifted from attempting to sidestep his commander's policy to crafting a defense that would render it acceptable to the northern public. In a meeting with Grant, Butler again maintained that while his superior's reasoning was militarily sound, it would never be accepted by northerners and would likely destroy Lincoln's chances of reelection. Butler urged that the North insist upon conditions for exchange that the South would never accept, thereby placing the onus for the failure of negotiations squarely on the Davis administration. To accomplish this objective, Butler proposed to send Ould a letter setting forth "in the most offensive form possible" Union insistence that any exchange include Negro prisoners, which should be simultaneously released for publication in the northern press. In the very unlikely event that the South should accede to this demand, Butler suggested a back-up plan that would absolutely guarantee "the wishes of the lieutenant-general that no prisoners of war should be exchanged." He would—"as a last resort, to prevent exchange"—demand that the charges of "outlawry" against him "be formally rescinded" and that he receive a public apology from the Confederate government before he would "further negotiate the exchange of prisoners."[201] Grant and Stanton approved of the scheme in full. On 27 August, Butler dispatched a letter containing the objectionable conditions to Ould; on 6 September, the letter appeared in northern newspapers. As expected, Butler never had to implement his back-up plan. As he later wrote, "the Confederacy never offered to me afterward to exchange the colored soldiers who had been slaves."[202]

In spite of such efforts to retain public support, pressure for a resumption of exchanges continued to increase in the North. This was the late summer of 1864, and the war was going very badly for the Union. In Virginia, Grant's offensive had resulted in thousands of killed or captured Yankee soldiers without yielding the destruction of Lee's army, and although Sherman was steadily advancing against Joe Johnston in Georgia, a decisive Union victory in that theater seemed no closer than when the campaign had begun. But in large measure, the growing demand to resume exchanges did not stem from military successes or failures. Rather, it was an unintended consequence of the efforts of the very group who wished most ardently to see exchanges blocked—Senator Benjamin Wade's Committee on the Conduct of the War.

Ironically, Wade and the members of the Committee had done their work too well. The Radicals' ceaseless claims of southern atrocities and their calls for retribution had became so strident that they had created an effect quite the opposite of what they sought. Bombarded with increasingly graphic descriptions of the horrid conditions in Confederate camps, northern churchmen, civic leaders, and even senior army officers began to appeal to Lincoln for a renewal of exchanges. Even the president's most loyal supporters warned that a failure to do so would prove disastrous in the fall elections. In a typical letter, one backer from Ohio wrote Lincoln that the administration's policy would "affect our coming elections" in November. "Our enemies," he informed the president, were "making use of this with effect," while "good and influential men" had been pushed to the "deliberate conclusion that their noble sons are the victims of a heartless, cruel neglect." The petitioner left no doubt where the blame for such neglect was being laid. "All hold you responsible," he warned Lincoln, adding that the failure to approve exchanges was "crushing the patriotism out of the poor prisoners and embittering hundreds of thousands of their friends. We know you can have them exchanged if you give your attention to it," he closed. "It is simple murder to neglect it longer."[203]

Adding to this chorus of pleas for exchange were dozens of poignant letters and petitions penned by northern soldiers suffering in southern camps. These missives were addressed not only to family members and friends but to congressmen and northern newspapers as well. In them, the prisoners decried their abandonment by the Lincoln administration because of southern refusals to release black captives. On 28 September the prisoners in Savannah held a mass meeting in which they composed a petition to be sent to Lincoln "in the hope that he might take such steps as in his wisdom he might think necessary for our speedy exchange or parole." Although the petitioners assured the president that they had "suffered patiently and were still willing to suffer if by so doing we can benefit the country," they warned that they were "not willing to suffer to further the ends of any party or clique to the detriment of our honor." Similar declarations from within the stockades at Macon and Andersonville assumed a darker and more malevolent tone. The prisoners in those camps attributed the administration's refusal to authorize exchanges to the cold machinations of Stanton, and their hatred of the secretary was so virulent that they formed organizations sworn to assassinate him upon their release.[204]

Major northern newspapers were also calling for a resumption of exchanges. The *New York Times,* for one, had long been pushing for a shift in the Lincoln administration's policy. "The Government," the paper's editors had insisted near the close of 1863, "ought at once to take measures to bring about a general exchange." Disputes over the operation of the cartel should be set aside, for it could "hardly be maintained that it is better to let twelve thousand of our soldiers be starved to death than to give way." These demands reached a crescendo eight months later, when the *Times* charged that the Lincoln administration's exchange policy was flawed because it failed to "embrace other considerations besides those of strict military expediency." The editors drove home this assertion by publishing in full a letter from a reader who angrily charged that Butler's refusal to yield on the question of "a few colored soldiers" meant that "many thousands of brave [white] men" were "being immolated by adherence to a mere abstraction."[205]

With public pressure becoming unbearable and Lincoln's reelection clearly imperiled, Stanton directed Butler to propose an exchange of sick and wounded prisoners. Such a course of action, the secretary reasoned, would quiet demands for exchanges without compromising his and Grant's agreed-upon exchange strategy. Accordingly, Butler wrote Ould on 9 September to propose that "waiving all other questions," the two governments should "exchange all sick and invalid officers and men who from wounds or sickness shall, in the judgment of the party holding them, be unfit for duty and likely to remain so for sixty days." Moving quickly to capitalize on the northern groundswell of support for resuming exchanges, Ould answered that the South would ship men north immediately.[206]

Ould's swift agreement stemmed in part from his realization that the Confederacy would likely never again possess a large enough number of prisoners to coerce Union acceptance of a general exchange. It was also prompted by a growing conviction among Confederate leaders and ordinary citizens that the only course of action remaining for the South was to release large numbers of prisoners, regardless of whether the North reciprocated or not. The motivations of this group were diverse. Some, like J. H. Stillwell, were moved by simple humanity. A farmer who lived near Andersonville, Stillwell had seen its horrors at first hand, and he admonished Davis to follow the Biblical example of the "King of Israel" who magnanimously freed his captives. "Send the prisoners at Andersonville home on their parole," Stillwell wrote in September 1864, "before the cold proves more destructive of their lives than the heat has been in the open and unshaded pen your officers provided for them."[207]

Others, like Winder and his subordinates, argued that the debilitating drain on southern resources could be lessened if all Yankee officers and men whose terms of enlistment had expired were passed through the lines. A third group maintained that a massive repatriation of prisoners would result in a substantial propaganda victory and political gains for the South. Politician-turned-general Howell Cobb, for example, complained to Seddon that the Yankees confined in Georgia were "eating up our subsistence," and he proposed to reduce this drain on resources by sending north all prisoners who were opposed to Lincoln and swore to vote against him in the November election. Seddon nonetheless remained adamantly opposed to any unilateral release, and he responded to all such suggestions with a proposal that was as draconian as Cobb's was innovative. He proposed to Cobb that the number of Yankee prisoners in the South should be thinned through summary executions of a select group of Union officers. "As to the white officers serving with negro troops," Seddon added, "we ought never to be inconvenienced with such prisoners."[208]

Surprisingly, one group of military prisoners was entirely exempt from this wrangling over releases. At the end of August 1864 the Union and Confederate secretaries of the navy had entered into bilateral negotiations that had yielded an agreement for the full exchange of all captured sailors and marines, man-for-man, regardless of race. An examination of the facts surrounding the negotiation and execution of this remarkable agreement clearly illuminates the true motives and objectives of Stanton and Lincoln. Stanton, it seems, had not informed Lincoln that the naval secretaries were even corresponding; as Gideon Welles recorded in his diary, when the president learned of the negotiations in early October, he "called upon me to inquire respecting arrangements for a proposed exchange of naval prisoners which was making some disturbance at the War Department and with General Butler."[209]

For almost fifteen months, Welles explained to Lincoln, naval personnel had been confined in Rebel prisons while exchange negotiations languished. The captives had sent him "appeals earnest and touching," informing him that they were being held under horrible conditions—some "in irons and in close confine-ment"—and notifying him that in the limited exchanges of sick and wounded prisoners arranged by the War Department, "no naval prisoners were embraced." This "omission from exchanges, whether from neglect or design," was "justly causing dissatisfaction" among the captives, and Welles appealed to Stanton for relief. "For more than year," Welles told Lincoln, he had "at various times made inquiry of the Secretary of War and at the War Department, generally oral, but sometimes by letter, and received evasive answers, of difficulties on account of remoteness, of unusual prisoners, of refusal by the Rebels to exchange Negroes, but with assurances that matters would soon be adjusted." After several months,

Welles decided to act. He authorized his assistant, Gustavus V. Fox, to initiate an "informal correspondence" with Confederate naval officials to determine whether an agreement for exchange might be reached. As soon as Confederate secretary of the navy Stephen Mallory heard of the Yankee inquiry, he wrote Welles directly to propose, as Welles related to Lincoln, "to exchange all naval prisoners." After some discussion with his staff, Welles agreed to commence the exchanges at Fort Monroe, but when Butler heard of the agreement, he protested against it vociferously to both Lincoln and Stanton.[210]

On 5 October 1864, the day following Lincoln's meeting with Welles, the president summoned Seward, Stanton, Hitchcock, Halleck, and Welles to Stanton's office. Lincoln told the group that he wished the naval exchanges to go forward if possible, whereupon Stanton objected. The secretary of war, Welles recorded in his diary, was in a particularly bad humor because of the president's support of the naval initiative. He denied that he had received any communication from Welles concerning Union contacts with the Confederate navy, and he insisted that exchange negotiations should be conducted by the army alone. Stanton was opposed to the navy plan because of the Confederate refusal to exchange blacks, and he chastised Welles for recognizing Mallory as the "Confederate Secretary of the Navy" in correspondence. Welles countered that he had carefully avoided assigning Mallory any official title and that in the course of the negotiations "no question as regards color had ever come up." Hitchcock then spoke, agreeing with Stanton that all exchanges should remain under army control. Lincoln declared that he still wanted the exchanges to proceed but that he would leave the final decision to Grant.[211] He promptly wrote the general, conceding that the agreement between Welles and Mallory had occasioned "some uneasiness" in Washington but stating that it remained his desire that the sailors be exchanged. "The numbers to be exchanged," he wrote, "are small, and so much has already been done to effect the exchange I hope you may find it consistent to let it go forward."[212]

The exchanges did go forward. Despite their endless protests to the contrary, the fate of captive black soldiers had never been the primary concern of either Lincoln, Stanton, or Grant. Their primary concern, as Grant had very plainly stated to Butler, was the reduction of the combat strength of the Confederate armies in the field—an objective that Lincoln supported completely. But in the agreement negotiated between Welles and Mallory, the president recognized a unique opportunity to answer the northern public's demand that some action be taken to free Union captives without raising the strength of Confederate land forces. He thus recommended that Grant approve the exchange, and for these reasons, Grant did.[213]

Ever attuned to the political ramifications of military decisions and furious that the naval exchanges would net him no personal gain among his constituents, Butler vigorously condemned the agreement. Bypassing Grant yet again, he telegraphed Stanton that "our soldiers will not be too well pleased to hear that sailors can and soldiers cannot be exchanged," but his objections were in vain. Stanton replied that the agreement was to be implemented, and on 15 October, Grant ordered Butler to "get the naval prisoners on hand through the lines."[214]

The exchanges of sick and wounded prisoners arranged by Butler and Ould in September had also begun, but this operation was far from flawless. Thousands of Confederate invalids from Johnson's Island, Alton, Rock Island, and Camps Chase, Morton, and Douglas were hastily consolidated, only to languish in collection pens because Mulford was unable to obtain the trains and ships required to move them to the points of exchange. When transportation finally became available, Hoffman controlled the transfer; and, as always, the instructions he provided his subordinates were quite detailed. Prisoners were to be issued cooked rations to sustain them during the trip. Each man was also to be provided with one army blanket, which was to be "taken from them at the point of delivery" and returned to government control. Hoffman also cautioned camp surgeons carefully to select for exchange only captives who were so infirm that they would "not be able to perform service in the field within sixty days," but who were "not too feeble to endure the fatigues of the journey." The surgeons obviously encountered some difficulty in satisfying both these requirements; many captives were so near death that they did not survive their journey to freedom. "Nearly 30 died out of 500 in the last load," Butler wrote to Hoffman of one shipment. "The occurrence," the general noted astutely, "does not speak well either for the Government or its officials."[215]

Prisoners were exchanged at City Point in Virginia. With a small fleet of ships assembled by Butler, Mulford transported an initial shipment of almost four thousand Rebels to Savannah, where he had arranged to trade them for Union captives held in the southernmost Confederate camps. Ould promised that if he could not assemble an equal number of Yankee invalids, he would make up the difference in healthy prisoners, adding that should this become necessary, only men whose terms of enlistment had expired were to be exchanged. When Sherman's advance rendered Savannah untenable as a point of exchange, operations were shifted further up the coast to Charleston. From these two points, Mulford was able to ship away almost twelve thousand Union prisoners by the end of November.[216]

Northerners responded to news of the resumption of exchanges with joyous approval. "The great exchange of prisoners has begun," proclaimed the

National Intelligencer on 21 November, giving anxious northern readers details of how the Rebels to be exchanged had been embarked aboard ships at Point Lookout for the trip south. On 26 November, the *New York Times* announced that "about ten thousand" Union captives were on their way north from Savannah, and the paper's correspondent supplied details of exactly how the exchange was effected.[217]

In a message to Butler from Savannah, Mulford reported with surprise that although the Union prisoners were clothed in tatters and filthy beyond description, their physical condition was "rather better than expected." Perhaps unsurprisingly, the newspaper correspondents accompanying him offered more sensational assessments. The prisoners, reported one newspaper, were in "a deplorable condition." Another newspaper featured interviews in which returnees railed against the "unparalleled vindictiveness of the South" and supplied gruesome accounts of the horrific conditions in which they had been confined. Readers were told how "men in the last stages of emaciation from chronic diarrhea received no nourishment whatever," while "others, suffering from gangrene and ulcers, were compelled to fester in putridity without even sufficient water to cleanse their loathsome sores." Furthermore, as one correspondent reported, the prisoners "generally believe that they have been abandoned by our Government."[218]

Responses to these new accusations of Rebel barbarities varied, but many in the North believed that they simply offered further proof that the Lincoln administration's policy of approving only limited exchanges had failed and should, at long last, be discarded. A *New York Times* headline proclaimed that a "loud demand for an immediate and sweeping exchange" had seized the country, and the paper cautioned that although calls for swift and severe retaliation were being received in its offices, "common justice and common humanity alike" demanded that general exchanges of white prisoners resume, regardless of the problems attendant with securing the return of black captives. As in the past, much of the blame for the government's failure to conclude a general exchange was heaped upon Stanton. On 21 December, the House of Representatives responded to the anger and frustration of its constituents by ordering the secretary to provide a copy of "all communications in reference to the exchange of prisoners not heretofore published."[219]

As the fourth year of the Civil War drew to a close, conditions in the prisons of the Union and Confederacy plunged to the lowest levels yet seen. From the northern public, calls for a resumption of general exchanges were becoming ever more insistent; in Congress, the demands of Wade and the Radicals for harsher measures of retaliation were becoming increasingly strident. In Federal prisons the punitive reductions in rations ordered by Stanton and Hoffman were producing a ghastly toll of starvation, disease, and death among Rebel captives, and even deeper cuts were being planned.

In the South, the long overdue appointment of a commissary general of prisoners had come too late to bring order and efficiency out of the chaotic southern system of prisons. The quality and quantity of rations issued to prisoners by Northrop's commissary department had sunk to levels insufficient to prevent mass starvation. Even the most rudimentary medical care for captives was a thing of the past, and Grant's advancing armies were threatening to overrun prisons on every front. The situation had become so desperate that by the last day of the year General John Winder was forced to tell his superiors in Richmond that after months of frantically shifting prisoners first to one location and then to another, he now knew of no place in the entire Confederacy where he could safely confine the Yankees in his charge.[220]

CHAPTER 9

"Too Sad to Be Patiently Considered"
The End and Afterlife of the Prison Systems

IN JANUARY 1865, Lieutenant Colonel A. S. Cunningham, a staff officer in the Confederate adjutant and inspector general's department, was ordered to Danville, Virginia, to conduct an inspection of the military prisons located there. Life for the Yankee captives at Danville had always been grim, but in the winter of 1864–1865 conditions in the town's prisons had taken a decided turn for the worse. By that point, there were over 4,500 souls crowded into Danville's six prisons (formerly tobacco factories); as Cunningham discovered, the captives' daily existence had been reduced to a desperate struggle simply to remain alive. The prisons were "dirty" and "filled with vermin," and the Yankees were suffering mightily. The winter had been so severe that the Dan River had completely frozen over, and the captives were ill supplied to ward off the numbing cold. Union major George Putnam estimated that only 70 of the 350 officers who shared his floor in Prison No. 3 had even a scrap of a blanket. Prisoners who still possessed shoes were forced to guard them carefully from thieves, and the men's blue uniforms were so tattered that most were nearly naked.[1]

Cunningham's inspection confirmed Putnam's dreadful assessment. The prisoners, he reported, had "almost no clothing, no blankets, and a very small supply of fuel." Sanitation was almost nonexistent. Water for washing, when available, was drawn from the muddy and polluted Dan, and this same source supplied the soldiers' drinking water. Not surprisingly, the death rate in the camp was alarming: the Danville undertaker who serviced the prison buried 130 prisoners in November 1864, 140 prisoners in December, and another 103 prisoners in January 1865. Scurvy, smallpox, and chronic diarrhea ravaged the men. But perhaps the primary cause of the high mortality at Danville, Cunningham related, was the "insufficiency of food ... the ration entire being only a pound and a half of corn bread per day." The method of ration distribution consisted simply of dumping the captives' food on the prison's filthy floors and then leaving the starving men to fight over the crusts and crumbs like wild animals. The bulk of the food was always taken by the stronger men, leaving the sick and infirm to grow weaker still. "This state of things is truly horrible, and demands the immediate attention of higher authorities," Cunningham wrote. "It is a matter of surprise that the prisoners can exist."[2]

One higher authority who could not have been surprised by Cunningham's report was Confederate secretary of war James Seddon. In the three months since his appointment as commissary general of prisoners, General John Winder had repeatedly apprised Seddon and Adjutant and Inspector General Samuel Cooper of the worsening state of southern prisons, and he had been tireless in his efforts to improve conditions within them. He had undertaken a grueling schedule of prison inspections, and he continued to search for locations where new facilities might be opened. Winder had also imposed regulations requiring bimonthly reports from camp commanders, and he repeatedly petitioned his superiors in Richmond for additional supplies and manpower. Realizing that clothing for prisoners was becoming increasingly difficult to obtain in the South, he suggested to Cooper that the Federal government be allowed to send replacement uniforms through the lines. In an effort to improve the dismal state of medical care in the prisons, he appointed surgeon and longtime subordinate Isaiah White to the position of chief medical officer, and he supported White's efforts to procure medical supplies and civilian physicians for the camps. White managed to institute a number of improvements in the medical care of the prisoners, but overall conditions in the camps remained abysmal. Winder also took action to preclude the assignment of prisoners to dangerous details, which he considered a violation of the accepted rules of war. When General P. G. T. Beauregard asked that captives be employed to clear unexploded shells and torpedoes from a siding on the West Point and Atlanta Railroad, for example, Winder responded that such labor was not "legitimate work for prisoners of war" and denied the request.[3]

With the Confederacy collapsing around him, Winder had been forced to relocate his headquarters three times in as many months. Initially he had established operations at Millen, but enemy advances had forced him first to Augusta and then to Columbia, South Carolina. There he began to plan for the establishment of a new prison at Killian's Mills, fourteen miles from the city, but by mid-January the military situation in the Confederacy had become almost hopeless. Advancing Union troops were now closing on the prison at Florence, and Winder was at last forced to concede that he had simply run out of places to transfer captives. "I am at a loss to know where to send prisoners from Florence," he telegraphed Cooper. "In one direction the enemy are in the way. In the other the question of supplies presents an insuperable barrier." As Winder saw it, his possible options had shrunk to only two: the South could either allow the prisoners to starve or free them unconditionally. The course he favored was clear. "I again urge paroling the prisoners and sending them home," he begged, as he had done before; but once again his request was refused.[4]

The situation only continued to deteriorate. An inspector at the prison in Columbia sent word that although the efforts of Winder and White had resulted in an improvement in medical care and accountability for the stockade's 7,538 captives, "the ration issued daily amounts almost to starvation." There had "been but two issues of meat in the last two months," and even the provision of syrup had become a rarity. On the same day, the commander at Florence reported that the daily ration at his camp had shrunk to "one pound of meal, one-third pound of peas, [and] three pounds of salt per 100 rations per day," an amount which he judged to be "totally insufficient for the sustenance of the prisoners." As in the past, Winder blamed Commissary General of Subsistence Lucius Northrop for the lack of provisions. "I find that where we have to depend upon the staff officers of the posts we can get nothing but what is forced out of them," Winder telegraphed Cooper on 28 January, repeating his plea for the appointment of commissary officers accountable to his department alone.[5]

The manner in which Winder's urgent request for rations was handled by the War Department is instructive, for it clearly illustrates not only the bureaucratic muddle that existed in Richmond, but also the fact that the Confederacy's failure to provide sufficient rations for prisoners resulted from a deliberate choice rather than an inability to do so. The request went first to Lieutenant Colonel Robert H. Chilton, assistant adjutant and inspector general, who forwarded it to Adjutant General Cooper with an endorsement conceding that "it is quite probable that the assignment of a commissary may be the means of bettering the condition of the prisoners at Florence, S.C." Following this second assessment by the adjutant and inspector general's office, Winder's request was passed to Northrop at the Bureau of Subsistence. Ever true to form, Northrop replied that unless he received additional money, "it [would] be impossible to continue to issue the present ration to prisoners of war, much less to increase it." From Northrop's office, the request was submitted to Assistant Secretary of War John A. Campbell, who then queried Treasury Secretary George A. Trenholm about the availability of additional funds. Trenholm replied that "the means at his command [were] very limited," and that at present the priority of his department was to "supply the necessary funds for the pay of our returned prisoners." On 18 February the request was returned to the secretary of war's office. Ultimately, neither Campbell nor Seddon directed that funds be reallocated to combat the starvation in the camps.[6]

For sixteen days, then, Winder's desperate plea for immediate assistance in feeding starving prisoners had been passed from office to office in the Confederate government, garnering a total of seven endorsements. In all this verbiage and bureaucratic shuffling, not a single official challenged Winder's assessment that the prisoners were starving; yet there was not one offer of assistance. This lack of action does not mean that no decision had been reached. When presented with ample and incontrovertible evidence that captives in their charge were starving, the men who directed the Confederate prisoner-of-war system decided to do nothing to save them. No reallocation of funds from the Confederate treasury was ordered, Winder's proposal to free all prisoners who could not be fed was denied, and Northrop's assertion that further ration reductions were required went unchallenged.

Winder would never learn that this latest request for assistance, like most he had submitted to Richmond over the past year, had been denied. On the bitterly cold morning of 6 February he had set out by train from Columbia to conduct yet another inspection of the prison at Florence. Staff officers at the camp had been charged with cheating and abusing prisoners, and Winder intended to sack the offenders on the spot if the allegations were substantiated. He was now just two weeks short of his sixty-fifth birthday. The trials and frustrations of his work had taken their toll, and he was old and haggard beyond his years. It was late in the day when he reached Florence, and shortly after entering the compound he clutched his chest and fell to the ground, the victim of a massive heart attack. A doctor was summoned, but to no avail. John Henry Winder was dead.[7]

On the following day, Cooper was notified of Winder's death in a terse telegram from Florence that stated simply, "General John H. Winder died suddenly on arriving here last night." News of the general's death quickly circulated among the prisoners. Most believed him responsible for their suffering, and they rejoiced at his passing. One rumor among the Yankees held that with his last gasp he had ordered, "Cut off the molasses, boys"; another maintained that his final words had been, "My faith is in Christ; I expect to be saved. Be sure and cut down the prisoners' rations." At least one person saw the hand of divine providence in Winder's passing. "Well," famed Confederate diarist Mary Boykin Chesnut recorded, "Winder is safe from the wrath to come."[8]

Although it had taken almost four years for Confederate leaders finally to decide to establish the position of commissary general of prisoners, Jefferson Davis and Secretary of War Seddon now moved swiftly to ensure that the post did not long remain unfilled. Perhaps they acted with too much haste, for Winder's replacement, Brigadier General Gideon J. Pillow, was a disaster from the first. Pillow was almost sixty years of age, and his record of service was anything but sterling. He was roundly despised and distrusted by his fellow officers. As punishment for abandoning his command at Fort Donelson he had been officially reprimanded and relegated to recruiting and conscription enforcement duties in his native state of Tennessee. Nonetheless, he was Davis's choice. In a 10 February message lauding Pillow's "known patriotism, intelligence, and capability to conduct an important branch of the public service," Cooper notified the general of his new post and asked that he assume his duties with the "least practicable delay."[9]

One of Pillow's most pressing challenges was securing adequate rations and supplies for the prisoners in his charge, and for a brief moment in early 1865, a solution to that problem seemed to be at hand. General Winder's brother, William H. Winder, had not cast his lot with the South during the war, but had, quite amazingly, remained a prosperous businessman in the North. In August 1864 he had written Union secretary of war Edwin Stanton with a remarkable proposition based on the method of dealing with prisoners that had been adopted by the Americans and the British during the War of 1812. Appealing to the secretary's "best judgment and sense of humanity," William Winder suggested that the Union and Confederate governments assume responsibility for provisioning their own prisoners of war. The Federal government would provide the Confederate prisoners in northern camps with "all necessary supplies of clothing, &c." A Confederate officer would "attend to the delivery and receipting and certify to their correctness," and the South would then pay for the supplies obtained "in cotton at a specified price." The Union, in turn, would "be allowed to send supplies to the Federal prisoners, to be distributed by a Federal officer." When asked by Stanton for his opinion of the proposal, General Ethan Allen Hitchcock responded that in the past the Rebels had "systematically refused to relieve or suffer us to relieve our soldiers," and would likely do so again. Stanton agreed, and for the moment Winder's suggestion was shelved.[10]

When public demands for some measure of relief for northern prisoners rose in the fall of 1864, however, Stanton was moved to reconsider Winder's idea. On 31 October, Butler thus directed Colonel John E. Mulford, the Union assistant agent for exchange, to ask his Confederate counterpart, Robert Ould, whether the South would agree to a plan of mutual supply of captives. Under this revised proposition, the Union would deliver food, clothing, medical supplies, shelter, and fuel to Federal captives in the South. The Confederacy would be permitted to purchase the same supplies for its soldiers from the United States and to pay for the goods in cotton shipped to the port of New York. Accounting and distribution of the supplies would be overseen by a board of three paroled officers selected by each government from the captives at each prison. Ould backed the idea. Although Union naval assaults against southern ports delayed implementation of the plan, 830 bales of cotton were finally loaded aboard the U.S. transport *Atlanta* at Mobile, and on 24 January 1865 the ship steamed into New York Harbor.[11] General William N. R. Beall, the senior distribution agent for the South, reported to Ould that after selling the cotton at market price he was able to purchase 16,930 blankets, 16,216 coats, 19,888 pairs of pants, 19,000 shirts, 5,984 pairs of drawers, 10,140 pairs of socks, and 17,000 pairs of shoes for Rebel prisoners. Meanwhile, the shipment of supplies to Yankee prisoners in the South had begun. It appeared that the belligerents had at last hit upon a solution that would ensure that all prisoners would be well fed and supplied. Ould petitioned General Ulysses S. Grant for permission to ship another 1,500 bales of cotton north, and Grant, noting that the agreement did not violate his central criterion of permitting no action that put additional Confederate soldiers in the field, recommended to Stanton that the arrangement be continued.[12]

But while the agreement might not have violated Grant's stipulations, it did run counter to Stanton's policy of harsh treatment for southern captives. Loath to surrender even the smallest measure of control over the treatment of Rebel prisoners, Stanton opposed the mutual resupply plan from the first. Although public pressure had forced him to yield to the cotton-for-supplies deal, he was determined to terminate the agreement as soon as he could craft a plausible justification for doing so. That justification was not long in coming. On 17 February, Major General Henry Halleck, citing the patently absurd charge that the Rebels were using the arrangement to secretly "purchase and carry back the means of fitting out their own men for the field," notified Grant that "under these circumstances the Secretary of War is not disposed to sanction the admission of any more cotton on the same terms."[13]

As a result, an end to the prisoners' suffering again depended on the conclusion of a negotiated exchange, and no such agreement seemed likely. In January the daily ration for Union prisoners at Salisbury shrank to a ladle of rice or pea soup and twenty ounces of bread per man. The blankets and clothing that prisoners had obtained from the North had been quickly sold or traded for additional food, and "muggers" among the captives stole from fellow prisoners who were too weak or too ill to fend them off. On 1 February, North Carolina governor

Zebulon B. Vance wrote prison commander General Bradley T. Johnson that "distressing accounts" of the "suffering and destitution" of the prisoners at Salisbury had reached his office. "If the half be true," Vance admonished Johnson, "it is disgraceful to our humanity and will provoke severe retaliation." Sadly, the reports the governor had received were much more than half true. Of the 10,321 prisoners who had entered Salisbury since 5 October 1864, over one third—3,479 men—had died. This placed the prison's mortality rate at 34 percent, higher than that of Andersonville or any other Confederate prison.[14]

In northern camps, the situation was little better. At Elmira, the rates of sickness and death spiked sharply in the opening months of 1865. Temperatures hovered below zero, and the prisoners—bereft of blankets, warm clothing, or serviceable shoes—added frostbite to the array of afflictions they faced. The suffering during these months was horrific. The shoes that prisoner John King had been wearing when captured had long since fallen apart. While in the barracks, King recalled, "I wrapped my feet in old rags which kept them warm, but in the late winter we were compelled to stand in the snow every morning for roll call, consequently my feet and shins were badly frozen."[15] Only after repeated requests to Commissary General of Prisoners William Hoffman was the commander at Elmira able to obtain two stoves for use in each of the drafty and uninsulated barracks, but these were pitifully small and far too inefficient to warm the men. "Imagine, if you can," Rebel cavalryman John Opie later wrote, "with the weather ten to fifteen degrees below zero, 100 men trying to keep warm by one stove." Every morning, the half-frozen men would crawl out of their bunks to scuffle for a place near the fire. "God help the sick or the weak," Opie lamented, "as they were literally left out in the cold." Feeble, freezing, and suffering from malnutrition, the men at Elmira were easy prey for smallpox, scurvy, and other diseases that plagued the camp. In February, 1,398 of the prison's 8,996 captives were reported sick; of that number, 426 died. "If there was ever a hell on earth," one captive avowed, "Elmira prison was that hell." Statistics support this conclusion. Almost 3,000 of Elmira's 12,123 prisoners died there. With a mortality rate of 24 percent, "Helmira" joined Salisbury in eclipsing Andersonville in this grisly category.[16]

Records of the other major prisons of the North and the South reveal that the worsening conditions and rising rates of sickness and death at Salisbury and Elmira were not anomalies. Put simply, the longer the war continued, the more terrible the camps of the Union and the Confederacy became. Early in 1865, tens of thousands more prisoners in blue and gray seemed destined for early graves. In February, however, discussions concerning a resumption of exchanges took a dramatic turn.

Sizable exchanges of sick and wounded prisoners had been ongoing since November; but rather than assuaging public insistence for a general exchange, as Stanton had hoped, press reports describing the deplorable state of returnees served only to heighten demands for a general exchange. Stanton was also pressed to respond to a 21 December resolution by the House of Representatives, which demanded that he supply legislators with copies of all exchange communications "not heretofore published"—a clear indication that Congress had come to question not only the wisdom of the Lincoln administration's policy, but also the degree to which the secretary had been completely forthright in keeping them informed.[17]

On 21 January, Stanton forwarded to Speaker of the House Schuyler Colfax hundreds of exchange documents and messages dating back to 1862. In a clever move to deflect the public and congressional criticism aimed at him, the secretary added that since 15 October 1864, not he but Grant had been directing all activities and correspondence concerning exchanges.[18] The general had been invested with "full authority to take any steps he might deem proper to effect the release and exchange of our soldiers," and he had been "instructed that it was the desire of the President that no efforts consistent with national safety and honor should be spared to effect the prompt release of all soldiers and loyal persons in captivity to the rebels as prisoners of war." Stanton assured Colfax that "in order to afford every facility for relief," special exchanges of the sick and wounded had been effected whenever "permitted by the rebel authorities." He concluded with the optimistic assessment that recent communications from Grant gave reason to believe that "a full and complete exchange of all prisoners will speedily be made."[19]

Stanton's response to the Speaker was true as far as it went, but—as often was the case in the secretary's communications with Congress—it was also notable for what it did not say. Technically, Grant had indeed been in charge of exchange negotiations since October. But the ultimate control of Union prisoner-of-war policy had always rested with Stanton. Although Grant had favored continuing the agreement under which each belligerent would supply its own prisoners, for example, Stanton had overruled him, and the scheme had been swiftly terminated. In other words, Grant was permitted to direct the course of exchange operations as long as his decisions did not run counter to Stanton's objectives; but when they did, the secretary had the final say.

Stanton was truthful in his assertion that Grant was moving closer to approval of a general exchange. Back in September, Ould had proposed that "all prisoners of war on each side be released from confinement (close) or irons, as the case may be, and either placed in the condition of other prisoners of war or sent to their respective homes for their equivalents." At the time, Grant and others in the Union War Department had summarily dismissed the suggestion. On 13 January, however, Grant unexpectedly telegraphed Colonel Mulford that he now viewed the proposal to be "equally fair and beneficial to both sides," and he ordered Mulford to inform Ould "without delay" that the United States was ready to implement the suggested exchange. Ould heard the news with delight, and the exchange of this class of prisoners began immediately.[20]

Grant's order must have come as something of a shock to Mulford, for in the past the general had been adamant in his demands that only the most feeble and infirm prisoners be exchanged. Even more surprising, this order was only the first in a flurry of directives Grant would dispatch that spring, each of which expanded the categories of prisoners to be freed. At first glance, this must have appeared to constitute an abrupt and sweeping change of Union policy. But although Grant did come to support the resumption of large-scale exchanges, he never altered either his motive in doing so or his insistence that exchanges be structured so that the balance of forces on the battlefield remained unchanged.

The exchanges authorized by Grant in the spring of 1865 were initiated to ease the unrelenting public pressure on the Lincoln administration to secure the release of Union captives. This pressure had taken the form of letters to politicians and the press from private citizens, editorials in national newspapers and magazines, and a formal resolution from the increasingly hostile U.S. Congress. In late January, a quite unexpected voice was added to the chorus of those demanding a change in exchange policy—that of General Benjamin Butler.

Grant, long vexed by Butler's military bungling and endless scheming, had removed the Beast from command of Fortress Monroe on 7 January 1865, sending him home to Massachusetts.[21] Butler's service as special commissioner for exchange was also unceremoniously terminated. Yet Butler was not a man who would passively submit to such rough handling, and the pugnacious general came back swinging. In an effort to salvage his tattered reputation and shaky political future, Butler took to the lecture circuit to convince the people of his state that the war would have gone much better if his ideas and initiatives had been adopted by the War Department. Addressing a large crowd in Lowell in late January, he insisted that at the time of his relief, he had removed all obstacles blocking a general exchange and was on the verge of freeing all the Union prisoners when he received orders from his superiors that precluded him from doing so. Butler never identified the source of these orders—in fact, his assertion was pure bunk—but the speech received wide play in the press and added to the pressure on Lincoln to bring the prisoners home.[22]

Butler's fulminations dovetailed with Grant's increasing realization that the Rebel armies were tottering on the brink of collapse. By judiciously designating the categories of prisoners to be sent south, Grant could answer the public cries for exchanges without enhancing the combat capabilities of Rebel regiments. In a telegram of 2 February, he informed Stanton that he was "endeavoring to make arrangements to exchange about 3,000 prisoners per week," which would stem the demands for the resumption of large-scale exchanges. But in order to ensure that no advantage accrued to southern arms, Grant specified that only invalids who had been recruited from areas of the South already under Union control were to be sent through the lines. "I would like disabled troops (troops from Missouri, Kentucky, Arkansas, Tennessee, and Louisiana) sent first," Grant telegraphed Stanton, "as but few of these will be got in the ranks again."[23]

As these men were being collected, a completely unexpected challenge arose. Prison commanders discovered that large numbers of southern captives did not wish to be exchanged at all. Confederate prisoners had long been given the option of "swallowing the eagle," or swearing allegiance to the Union, and the reasons why some opted to do so varied. At Point Lookout, prisoner J. B. Stamp remembered, some were lured by offers of better housing, additional rations, or the promise of release and assignment as "galvanized Yankees" to Federal posts on the western frontier. As Stamp wrote, such men were "at all times regarded with contempt by the other prisoners." In his reminiscences, John King proudly proclaimed that he always refused the oath and that those who took it were scorned even by their Union guards. "These fellows looked like they had stolen something and been caught with it," prisoner John Copley wrote of one such group at Camp Douglas. "The ground had a special attraction for their eyes."[24]

In the spring of 1865, one category of Confederates began "swallowing the eagle" for a very different reason. In large measure, these men hailed from regions of the South that were already occupied by Union troops. They knew that if they were exchanged, the Richmond government would never allow them to return to their homes or their former regiments. Instead, they would likely be ordered into one of the polyglot units composed of recent conscripts and other returned prisoners. Understanding that the end of the war was imminent, they had no desire to be forced to serve in a regiment of strangers and again placed in harm's way. But they also knew that further confinement in the deadly prisons of the North placed them at great risk of death from disease and starvation. Thus, many men who had heretofore resisted the oath of allegiance now opted to take it. Under the provisions of Lincoln's Proclamation of Amnesty and Reconstruction of 8 December 1863, they could then remain in the North until the war ended.[25]

The numbers of these men were truly astonishing. Colonel A. A. Stevens reported that of the 1,882 prisoners from occupied portions of the South held at Camp Morton, "1,516 express freely their desire to remain in prison until such time as they can be released by taking the oath as prescribed in the President's proclamation." From Camp Douglas, Hoffman received word that fully one third of the Rebels would refuse to be exchanged if they were assured that they would be "released within a reasonable time," while Colonel A. J. Johnson, the commandant at Rock Island, reported that "thirteen hundred and thirty prisoners decline to be exchanged." From Elmira, Colonel B. F. Tracy informed Hoffman that "the number who do not wish to be exchanged will depend very much upon the treatment those who refuse are to receive after the exchange is perfected." If he were free to offer assurances of immediate release or even "greater liberty than is now extended to them," Tracy wrote, "I think one-half of this camp would refuse to be exchanged, but if they are to choose between being exchanged or confinement in prison for an indefinite period, I think very few will decline to be exchanged." The commander at Johnson's Island concurred with Tracy's opinion. In response to this flood of refusals, Stanton ordered that "those who do not wish to be exchanged be retained at camp until further orders."[26]

When informed that thousands of Rebel prisoners were willing to swear allegiance to the United States if promised they would be released and not sent south, Halleck advised Stanton that they be accommodated. It was "contrary to the usages of war," Halleck opined, "to force a prisoner of war to return to the enemy's ranks." He argued that prisoners who declined to return home were considered to be deserters, and desertion was always to be encouraged. "The President's proclamation," he continued, was designed to motivate Rebels to "leave their ranks and resume their allegiance to the United States"; to compel them to return home, where they would be swiftly reincorporated into the Confederate army, "would not only be a violation of the usages of war, but an abandonment of the policy of the President's proclamation." Most of the prisoners who did not wish to be returned were from "States now in or about to return to the Union," and Halleck maintained that "to force back into the rebel ranks such of their citizens as wish to be loyal would be unjust to these States as well as to the individuals themselves." Halleck was convinced that if Grant would only undertake a "full consideration" of the question, he too would support retaining the men in the North, for it was surely "much cheaper to feed an enemy in prison than to fight him in the field."[27]

Grant did carefully consider the question; but whereas Halleck had based his argument to Stanton on the "usages of war" and notions of what constituted "just" and "unjust" treatment of Rebel prisoners, the commanding general remained completely focused on the possible military ramifications. Given that criteria, it is not surprising that Grant's proposal was exactly the opposite of Halleck's. "Those who do not wish to go back are the ones whom it is most desirable to exchange," the general argued in a message to Hitchcock. If they were not sent south, no Union prisoners would be returned for them. But if they were sent for exchange, Confederate authorities would be required to return a like number of Union soldiers. Moreover, given the fact that the Rebels had asked to remain in the North, there was very little danger they would again become effective soldiers. As Grant saw it, "if they do not wish to serve in the rebel army they can return to us after exchange and avoid it."[28]

On 2 February, Grant ordered Mulford to "make arrangements for exchanging 3,000 prisoners per week, or as many as can be delivered on each side." The man-for-man exchanges were to commence immediately and continue "until the party having the fewest prisoners is exhausted of all on hand." Reflecting the Confederacy's desperation to rid itself of its Federal prisoners, Ould informed Grant on 11 February that he was prepared to deliver one thousand prisoners a day to Wilmington, North Carolina, and Cox's Wharf on the James River, and he urged that the exchanges begin "as early . . . as practicable." Five days later, General Cooper notified the commanders of the prisons at Florence, Salisbury, and Charlotte that "a general exchange of prisoners has been agreed upon," and he directed them to be prepared to complete the "entire exchange . . . in as short a time as possible."[29]

Things were now moving very swiftly indeed. Grant was corresponding directly with Ould, and Mulford had assumed operational control of the actual exchanges. Initially, there appeared to be a danger that Hoffman would be left behind in this swirl of activity. For a time, in fact, he had been absent from the eastern theater. In October 1864 he had at last received a brevet promotion to brigadier general, but shortly after his advancement Stanton decided to divide the duties of the commissary general of prisoners between an eastern and a western office. Under orders published on 11 November 1864, Hoffman was assigned as commissary general "for the region west of the Mississippi." Responsibility for prisons and prisoners east of the river was transferred to Brigadier General Henry W. Wessells, an officer who had himself been a prisoner of war for a short time in 1864. Dividing responsibility for prisoners in this manner had already proved totally unworkable in the South, and a host of similar problems very quickly arose in the North. In the end, the arrangement survived less than three months. On 1 February the two offices were reconsolidated, and Hoffman again became the nation's single commissary general of prisoners.[30]

Soon thereafter, Hoffman was directed by Hitchcock to prepare to send prisoners south as soon as the operational details governing the exchanges were finalized. Prisoners in eastern camps would be sent directly to City Point for exchange, while prisoners in the western theater were consolidated at Point Lookout. On 18 February, Hoffman directed the commander of Point Lookout to ensure that the captives were maintained "in readiness to be forwarded whenever called for by Colonel Mulford." It was well that Hoffman ordered these preparatory measures, for when the calls for shipments began, they came in rapid succession.[31]

To Grant fell the responsibility of disposing of all Union prisoners exchanged, and on 16 February he warned Halleck that "our prisoners in the South will probably be delivered to us as fast as they can be got through without reference to the number received from us." Realizing that these returnees would likely not be fit for duty with their regiments before the war ended and mindful of Stanton's insistence that there be no replay of the parolee debacle of 1862–1863, Grant directed that returnees were to be given their back pay and furloughed to their homes as quickly as possible.[32]

In early March, Grant told Hoffman that, as expected, "the enemy are putting all their returned prisoners into the ranks of the Eastern Army without regard to the organization to which they belong." Yet even this act of southern desperation failed to slow the fevered pace of exchanges. Grant cleverly countered this Confederate strategy by ordering Hoffman to exchange only men "unfit for duty" until all of that "class" held in the North had been traded. In February, just over 10,000 Confederate prisoners were exchanged; in March, an additional 13,573 were sent through the lines.[33]

Freedom for the Yankee prisoners of war came in a variety of ways. At Salisbury, the prison commander, Major John Gee, mounted the sentinel's wall at noon on 22 February to inform the prisoners that a general exchange was about to commence. At the conclusion of his address, 2,871 prisoners were formed into a column almost three miles long for the march to Wilmington and freedom. Benjamin F. Booth had been captured at Cedar Creek in 1864, and he had survived the worst period in the prison's history. "I went out from Salisbury Prison in a condition that would have been a lasting disgrace to a third class tramp of our day," he recorded in his diary, adding that "no tongue or pen [could] describe the joy and happiness" he experienced when the gates of the prison were thrown wide and he and his comrades shuffled through. Soon after leaving Salisbury, hundreds of the weaker and more emaciated prisoners began to straggle badly, but their Rebel escorts were unconcerned. After the first night on the road, in fact, the Yankees were guarded hardly at all, and they frequently strayed from the column to forage for food. On 25 February, Booth and his fellows reached Goldsboro, where they were loaded on trains for the remainder of their journey. When they arrived in Wilmington, they found that it was already inundated by thousands of captives from Florence and other prisons in the Deep South. On 2 March, to the strains of "Home Sweet Home" played by an army band, Booth and a crush of prisoners walked beneath a banner proclaiming, "We welcome you home, our brothers," and were officially exchanged. For many of the prisoners, the experience was emotionally overwhelming. As the reality that they were free took hold, Booth remembered, they "fell down by the side of the road and wept like children."[34]

The first shipment of prisoners from Danville occurred on 18 February, when a group of gaunt, filthy inmates from Prison No. 3 moved haltingly across the Dan River bridge to the town's railroad depot. Many were so weak that they could walk only with the aid of their friends; others, unable to stand at all, were borne to the station in the arms of stronger comrades. The agonizingly slow trip from Danville to City Point in rickety, overcrowded boxcars in freezing weather supplied a final trial for the emaciated captives. But as one of the prisoners explained to his keepers, "We are willing to endure that and even more if by so doing we may put distance between us and Danville."[35]

Daniel Reynolds was a mere sixteen when he enlisted in the Eleventh Michigan Cavalry, and after only nine months' service he was captured and confined in Libby Prison, where he maintained a diary of his time in captivity. By December 1864 death had become so commonplace in the prison that the passing of friends hardly merited elaboration. "Rations grow smaller, and we have . . . cold, chilly weather," he cryptically recorded at the beginning of the month. "Comrades dying from want of care also from cold and hunger."[36] Reynolds had become convinced that he too would perish in the squalor of Libby, but at the end of January 1865 he received the glorious news that he was to be among the initial group of captives sent from Richmond in the exchange. Shortly thereafter, he and his comrades were ordered to assemble for the mile-long march to the docks, where they would board flag-of-truce boats for the short voyage to City Point. "Some were so weak that comrades had to hold them up," he later wrote, but nonetheless they staggered along, determined not to miss what would probably be their final opportunity for life and freedom. No sooner had the men boarded the steamers, however, than their hopes were crushed by news that the trip had been canceled due to ice jams in the James River. They were marched back to Libby, where they sat for days, anxiously observing the James. Finally, a heavy tide split the jams, and Reynolds and his fellows were again embarked on the ships. After a voyage of only a few hours, the Yankees reached City Point, where they were exchanged and placed aboard waiting Union hospital ships for transport to the medical facilities at Annapolis. Union surgeons assured the men that they would soon be fed, but as Reynolds later admitted, he and his friends "were so starved that we couldn't wait for rations and stole the corn that was for the mules."[37]

Indeed, the Yankees' last days of captivity were anything but easy. The administrative reforms and improvements in the care of captives that had been instituted by Winder during his brief stint as commissary general of prisoners died with him, and Gideon Pillow proved as inept a commissary general of prisoners as he had a field commander. On 27 February, after less than a month, he was abruptly relieved and subsequently assigned the make-work task of rounding up absentees from the army of General Joe Johnston. On 24 March, Brigadier General Daniel Ruggles, yet another poor performer who had been relegated to staff positions because of incompetence in the field, was named as Pillow's successor.[38]

Oddly, Pillow seems not to have been informed that he had been sacked. For almost a month the hapless general continued to roam the South, visiting prisons, issuing orders, and thoroughly befuddling the Union and Confederate officers with whom he corresponded. On the very day that Ruggles was appointed as commissary general of prisoners, Pillow was busily notifying the Union commander in Jacksonville, Florida, that he had decided to "deliver a portion of the Andersonville prisoners" to that city because he had determined that "the route of travel to that point will be less fatiguing to the Federal prisoners than any other at present open." And, in a line clearly confirming that he had absolutely no grasp of the fact that southern camps had long ago reached the bottom of the barrel in rations and supplies of all categories, Pillow blithely assured the Yankee commander that he would personally "make every necessary preparation for the comfort of the prisoners during the trip"[39]

This bizarre missive was eclipsed by a message Pillow dispatched directly to Hoffman on 26 March. Assuming a chatty style, Pillow admonished Hoffman that it was the "high christian duty of governments to treat prisoners of war with kindness and to make them as comfortable as the hardships of war will allow." It was high time, Pillow insisted, that he and Hoffman brushed aside past disputes and adopted a "mutual system of kind treatment to prisoners of war." He explained that shortages of supplies and the uncivilized depredations of lawless Yankee raiders had prevented adequate provisioning of Union prisoners. Although the North had seized upon these issues as justification for unwarranted retaliation against innocent southern captives, at this late stage it would be "productive of no good result to attempt to discuss the question of responsibility." As he continued, "I am now persuaded that both governments would be pleased with a change of practice." To that end, he proposed that each government henceforth "stipulate" to "select healthy localities for Military prisons," confine prisoners in "comfortable barracks," issue them "the same rations, in kind and quantity (to be agreed upon hereafter by the Commissary Generals of Prisoners)," and provide "such articles of clothing, blankets, hats and shoes as may be necessary." To defray the cost of issuing these goods to Federal captives, Pillow suggested that the South be allowed to ship cotton to the markets of the United States or other foreign markets; furthermore, to ensure the timely and uninterrupted delivery of the supplies, he proposed that the Federal government promise to refrain from breaking up southern railways or interfering in any way with their operation.[40]

It is highly unlikely that Pillow consulted anyone in the Confederate government before he composed and dispatched this remarkable letter; not surprisingly, there is no record of any response by Hoffman. When Confederate secretary of war James Seddon became aware that Pillow was continuing to function as the commissary general of prisoners, he inquired of the Adjutant and Inspector General's Department whether the general had been informed of his removal. Receiving no satisfactory answer, he quickly directed that another copy of the relief order be dispatched to the general.[41]

One very likely reason for the confusion surrounding Pillow's relief was that daily operations within the Davis administration were becoming increasingly more difficult and chaotic. The destruction of the Army of Tennessee under General John B. Hood, General William Tecumseh Sherman's campaign in Georgia and South Carolina, and the worsening supply situation throughout the Confederacy had prompted an investigation into the direction of the war by a joint committee of the Confederate Congress. While the lawmakers were unsparing in their criticism of President Jefferson Davis and his cabinet, the bulk of their invective was directed at Secretary of War James Seddon. In mid-January the Virginia congressional delegation adopted resolutions calling for his dismissal, and on 19 January Seddon submitted his resignation. Davis was initially opposed to his departure, but when the Congress threatened a vote of no confidence, the president was forced to accept the inevitable. On 6 February, Davis nominated General John C. Breckinridge as Seddon's replacement.[42]

Time had also finally run out for Lucius B. Northrop. From the moment Breckinridge had assumed office, Richmond had been abuzz with rumors that he would relieve Northrop as promptly as possible; and Northrop, never more than a step away from controversy, was not long in providing the new secretary with ample justification for doing just that. For almost two years the Confederate government had tolerated Northrop's failure to provide adequate rations for prisoners, and in 1865 his fulfillment of that responsibility sank to new lows. On 2 January he had written Seddon to complain that the 13,000 prisoners then held at Salisbury were "being subsisted from a section of country which should, at this juncture, be wholly tributary to General Lee's army," suggesting that the captives be "removed" to a location where provisions were more abundant. Like most of Northrop's answers to complex problems, this solution, while simple and straightforward, was also woefully unrealistic and impractical. When asked for comment, General John Winder had reminded Seddon that Yankee incursions had rendered most areas of the shrinking Confederacy unsuitable for confining captives, and that for the present the prisoners at Salisbury and other camps in the eastern theater would have to remain where they were. When informed that the captives would not be relocated, Northrop implemented yet another of his overly simplistic solutions—he stopped feeding them.[43]

On 31 January, Lieutenant Colonel John F. Iverson, the commander of the camp at Florence, notified Winder that "large numbers [of prisoners] are dying daily, and I am satisfied it is from not being properly fed." Iverson had first notified the commissary officer at Florence of the problem, but he had been informed that there were "not . . . sufficient stores to warrant . . . increasing the ration." The commissary officer was apparently bound by instructions from Northrop, which ordered that the "present scarcity of meat requires that prisoners be wholly subsisted on sorghum when practicable, and not on meat and sorghum," as had been previously issued. Commanders at a few camps might be able to supplement prisoners' rations with food purchased locally or by allowing sales by post sutlers, Iverson explained to Winder, but at Florence and most other southern prisons, this was not the case. "If the Government is really not able to give these prisoners more to eat, then no blame can be attached to anyone," he argued, hastening to add that "if they are, then I must think that the fault lies at the door of the Subsistence Department."[44]

Winder forwarded Iverson's message to Cooper, "earnestly requesting that a remedy be immediately applied." On 11 February, the message was referred to Northrop for comment. His response could well have served as a summary of the philosophy that had guided his actions as commissary general of prisoners. "The state of the commissariat will not allow the issue of a full ration to our own troops in the field, much less to prisoners of war," Northrop retorted. "It is just as well that the men who caused the scarcity shall be the first to suffer from it." He concluded with a chilling warning that even worse was yet to come, informing Cooper that "present appearances indicate the prospective necessity of a still greater reduction of the ration." Northrop's reply might have been predictable, but it is telling that neither Cooper nor anyone else in the Confederate war office challenged the commissary general's refusal to supply rations to starving prisoners. Cooper and his subordinates justified their inaction with the assertion that because a general exchange of prisoners would probably soon commence, no action was required. Iverson's desperate plea was ordered "filed" and promptly forgotten.[45]

Such a "file and forget" response sufficed for Yankee prisoners, but it would not do when southern soldiers began to go hungry. On 8 February, Lee reported that his men in the trenches at Petersburg had been "without meat for three days, and all were suffering from reduced rations," as well as exposure to "cold, hail and sleet." War Bureau chief Robert G. H. Kean and Northrop were with Breckinridge when he received Lee's message, and Kean reported that when Breckinridge pressed Northrop for an explanation of the shortages, Northrop was as condescending and abrasive as ever. "It is just what I predicted long ago," the commissary general retorted. When Breckinridge asked him for a plan to remedy the shortages, Northrop snapped that he had no solution. Rather, Kean recalled, he insisted yet again that "if his plans had been carried out instead of thwarted," the crisis could have been averted.[46]

Exasperated, Breckinridge forwarded Lee's distressing report directly to Jefferson Davis, who was outraged by it. "This is too sad to be patiently considered, and cannot have occurred without criminal neglect or gross incapacity," Davis asserted, ordering that adequate supplies be promptly obtained "by purchase, or borrowing, or other possible mode." To emphasize the imperative for immediate action, he quickly sent a second note to Breckinridge, directing that "meat and whiskey must be borrowed, or impressed, and should be sent over before the commissary officers slept that night." As Kean recorded in his diary, "This too Colonel Northrop saw, but coolly laid aside, remarking to [Quartermaster General] Lawton *sotto voce* that it was 'sensational'; to the Secretary that he could not borrow because he had already borrowed more than could be returned, nor impress because by the law money had to be tendered; that it was partly General Lee's fault, and wholly Mr. Seddon's etc. And no suggestion of any means of relief was so much as offered by him."[47]

With this response, the colonel had finally gone too far. By 1865, Davis was Northrop's only supporter in the Confederate government; without his backing, the commissary general's fate was sealed. To spare Northrop the shame of being relieved, Breckinridge allowed him to resign. On 16 February the secretary appointed General Isaac M. St. John, then director of the Nitre and Mining Bureau, in his place.[48]

St. John, a Yale graduate trained both as a civil engineer and an attorney, had already established a name as an innovative and resourceful officer, and as commissary general of subsistence he quickly demonstrated that this reputation was fully deserved. Like his predecessor, St. John knew that sufficient stocks of rations and forage could be secured only through a direct appeal to the people. But whereas Northrop had been imperious and heavy-handed in his dealings with the public, St. John earnestly implemented an ingenious plan that played to southerners' patriotism. Rather than employing threats, St. John implored each farmer, planter, and mill owner to contribute enough supplies to provision one soldier for six months. The response was overwhelming. Food of every description poured into commissary depots across the South. But St. John was just beginning. He next appealed to governors to release for general distribution all the rations and supplies they had been stockpiling for issue to the soldiers of their states alone; similarly, turning his attention to the government bureaus that had maintained independent reserves of food, he ordered the consolidation of these stocks into a single account from which his department could draw. At every point St. John's entreaties met with stunning success. By 10 March, less than a month after replacing Northrop, he was able to report to that he had collected enough food to provide a ten-day reserve of bread and meat for Lee's army. Furthermore, as he assured Breckinridge, "a sufficient surplus remains within the Confederate lines in Virginia, North Carolina, upper South Carolina, and East Tennessee to subsist the Confederate forces operating therein until the next crop can be made available." Nor would the South's larders go empty in the future, for St. John told the secretary that "with adequate military protection in the more exposed localities, and with a prompt supply of suitable funds, the officers and agents of this service can keep the depot full in anticipation of all arrangements of the Quartermaster's Department to remove and forward." Unfortunately, St. John's appointment came too late to help the prisoners.[49]

The commissary department was not the only Confederate agency engaged in frantic activity that spring. Between drafting no-confidence motions and debating such monumental questions as voluntary manumission and the recruitment of blacks as combat soldiers, the days of the members of the Confederate Congress had also been quite full. It is thus surprising that the legislators found time to compose and issue a major report—and one that was one of the most astounding documents by either of the belligerents during the entire war. The South had been stung not only by the findings of the U.S. Sanitary Commission's report on the treatment of Union captives, but also by the report of Senator Benjamin Wade's Joint Committee on the Conduct of the War, which contained the inflammatory testimony and photographs of returned prisoners at Annapolis. The Confederate solons were determined to answer the charges contained in these documents. Accordingly, on 9 January 1865, with their country literally collapsing around them, the Confederate Congress appointed a select committee of three senators and five representatives "to investigate and report upon the condition and treatment of the prisoners of war respectively held by the Confederate and United States Governments, and also upon the causes of their detention and refusal to exchange."[50]

On 3 March, barely one month before Appomattox, the committee released its findings in a preliminary report that, like the two Union documents it was intended to refute, was pure propaganda. The report asserted that far from being "intended for the humane purpose of ameliorating the condition of the unhappy prisoners held in captivity," the two northern reports had been "designed to inflame the evil passions of the North" and should be taken no more seriously than the "yellow covered novels" that crowded the shelves of sleazy Yankee bookstalls. The photographs of prisoners represented a "disingenuous attempt . . . to produce the impression that these sick and emaciated men were fair representatives of the general state of the prisoners held by the South, and that all their prisoners were being rapidly reduced to the same state, by starvation and cruelty, and by neglect, ill-treatment, and denial of proper food, stimulants, and medicines in the Confederate hospitals." In fact, the report maintained, the men in the photographs were members of a small group of prisoners who were "suffering not only with excessive debility, but with 'nostalgia,' or homesickness, whose cases were regarded as desperate, and who could not live if they remained, and might possibly improve if carried home. Thus it happened that some very sick and emaciated men were carried to Annapolis, but their illness was not the result of ill-treatment or neglect." On the contrary, northern prisoners in southern hospitals had been afforded "everything that humanity could dictate." Their food was "the best that could be procured for them." Indeed, the sick were supplied with "such articles as milk, butter, eggs, tea, and other delicacies when they were required by the condition of the patient."[51]

The report slammed the Union charge that the Confederate government had pursued a policy of deliberately starving prisoners as "false in fact and design," assuring its readers that the rations furnished captives held by the South were "never less than those furnished to the Confederate soldiers who guarded them, and have at some seasons been larger in quantity and better in quality than those furnished to Confederate troops in the field." Any "scarcity of meat and of breadstuffs" had been the result of the "savage" Union policy of "burning barns filled with wheat or corn, destroying agricultural implements, and driving off or wantonly butchering hogs and cattle." Charges that men had frozen to death on Belle Isle, the report declared, were "but a clumsy daub, founded on the fancy of the painter," for "tents were furnished sufficient to shelter all the prisoners" and "a fire was furnished in each of them." Only one captive had succumbed to the elements, the report insisted, and his death had resulted from the cruelty of his fellow prisoners, who "thrust him out of the tent in a freezing night because he was infested with vermin."[52]

In contrast to this rosy picture, the report asserted that Confederate prisoners in the North had "suffered from insufficient food" and were routinely "subjected to ignominious, cruel, and barbarous practices, of which there is no parallel in anything that has occurred in the South." Southern boys had been starved, beaten, deliberately infected with smallpox, and deprived of even the most basic medical care. But the Union's greatest crime had been its rebuff of the South's repeated entreaties for a "prompt and fair exchange of prisoners." Exchanges under the cartel would have continued uninterrupted, the report claimed, if the Lincoln government had not adopted a policy of "seducing negro slaves from their masters, arming them and putting white officers over them to lead them against us." The implementation of this putatively irresponsible and illegal policy had forced the Confederacy to consider the "grave question" of "whether men who encouraged insurrection and murder could be held entitled to the privileges of prisoners of war under the cartel." But even this deplorable act "ought never to have interrupted the general exchange." In summary, the committee members reassured southerners that the facts clearly demonstrated that the responsibility for the termination of exchanges rested squarely with the government of the United States alone, and that in consequence, "every groan of suffering, every heart broken by hope deferred among these 80,000 prisoners, will accuse them in the judgment of the just."[53]

This astounding piece of work would serve as the foundation for postwar Confederate justifications of the treatment of Union prisoners. It was one of the very last documents produced by the Confederate Congress, for the war in the eastern theater was fast rushing toward its inevitable conclusion. As the recently appointed commissary general of prisoners, there was little Daniel Ruggles could do but ensure that the massive exchanges begun in February continued at a swift pace. Exchanges at City Point were halted temporarily when Grant launched his final major offensive on 1 April, but they were resumed as soon as the Union armies struck off to the west in hot pursuit of Lee's desperately fleeing remnant. On 3 February, Grant ordered Hoffman to transfer his operations to City Point so that the exchange process might be expedited further still. By 9 April, Grant had Lee cornered near Appomattox, and on that same day Ould notified the Union general that he and four of his staff officers had entered U.S. lines near the village under a flag of truce. Ould carried with him the records of the Confederate Bureau of Exchange, and he said he was prepared to answer "any questions connected with the delivery and exchange of prisoners." Those questions would have to wait, however. Even as Ould dispatched his message, Grant was accepting the surrender of the Army of Northern Virginia.[54]

Although the Union prisoners' release was now assured, most of them had just begun their journey north to family and friends. Sadly, the tribulations of these men did not end with exchange. Many of the sick had passed beyond any hope of recovery by the time they were released, and those poor souls survived only a short time after they were freed. Others were by no means immune to the cold grasp of disaster and death, and in no instance was this sad fact more clearly illustrated than in the tragedy of the steamboat *Sultana*. The ship, touted in advertisements as a "large and commodious passenger steamer," had traveled down the Mississippi from St. Louis to New Orleans during the third week of April. Along with its more mundane cargo, the vessel carried the news of Lincoln's assassination to cities along the river as it steamed south. After a short stay in the Crescent City, Captain J. Cass Mason nosed the 660-ton ship into the river for the long trip back north. The Mississippi, swollen by spring rains and an unusually heavy snow melt, was running particularly strong, and progress against the current was a struggle from the start. The vessel had barely gotten underway when one of its four boilers developed a serious leak. Because the ship had experienced such problems twice before, the engineer advised that the leak be immediately repaired. Mason agreed and informed the passengers and crew that the *Sultana* would be putting in at Vicksburg.[55]

What Mason did not know was that the environs for miles around Vicksburg had been transformed into a sprawling camp where thousands of Rebel and Yankee prisoners, formerly held in the pens of the western theater, were being exchanged at a feverish pace. On 21 February, harried Union and Confederate exchange officers had agreed to establish a jointly administered area where prisoners of both sides would be collected and subsisted on Union rations while being processed for exchange. The site, designated Camp Fisk, ran along the banks of the Big Black River, and by 14 April it held 4,700 Federal prisoners who had been shipped to Vicksburg from as far away as Macon and Andersonville. The majority of the Yankees at Camp Fisk had been confined at Cahaba, and most could scarcely believe they had survived the experience. Life had always been hard at Cahaba, but death rates had risen precipitously after starving inmates had rioted on the morning of 20 January. Rations had been suspended completely for a period following the riot, and the commanding general had ordered that if the episode was repeated, "the Guard shall instantly fire upon the mutineers and if necessary the whole body of prisoners until perfect order is restored."[56]

There had been no further disturbances, and the Cahaba prisoners had been duly transported to Camp Fisk for exchange. By the time Mason put in for repairs, many of the camp's former inhabitants had already begun their journey north on other boats, but a sizeable number of ex-prisoners still remained. Upon learning that the *Sultana* had berthed, the officer in charge of scheduling transportation ordered the camp emptied by loading all the remaining prisoners aboard the recently arrived vessel. Unfortunately, he had not actually counted the men awaiting shipment. Although the maximum capacity for the *Sultana* was 376 passengers and crew, an estimated 2,300 men were crowded aboard when the vessel steamed slowly away from Vicksburg in the early morning hours of 24 April. The load was so great that the ship's deck bowed downward and probably would have collapsed had not the chief mate quickly hammered in reinforcing beams to support its weight. As the *Sultana* passed Helena, Arkansas, a photographer set up his camera to capture the moment, and the ship almost capsized when hundreds of men surged to the railing to ensure they would be in the photo.[57]

Around two in the morning on 27 April, the *Sultana* was churning past Paddy's Hen and Chickens about eight miles north of Memphis when one of its boilers exploded. This deafening initial blast was followed by a second thunderous roar as two of the remaining boilers exploded almost simultaneously. The eruptions ripped the ship from prow to stern, and dozens of men and tons of debris were blasted hundreds of feet into the air. Those who were not hurled into the river were scalded to death by escaping jets of steam or incinerated by the flames that quickly consumed the ship. The Mississippi was soon choked with over two thousand men. Some survived by clinging to bits of wreckage, but many were too burned or broken to remain afloat, and one by one they sank beneath the inky water. The wreck of the *Sultana* remains the greatest marine disaster in U.S. history. The death toll was placed at 1,238, but because no one knew exactly how many men had crowded aboard the vessel at Vicksburg, the exact number of deaths will never be known. Estimates run as high as 1,800, with 1,585—more than the total number of soldiers killed at First Manassas—being the figure most commonly cited. For over a month, blue-clad corpses bobbed to the surface at ports downstream, and riverboat captains were compelled to exercise special caution so that the bloated bodies would not become fouled in the paddles of their vessels.[58]

Although no such disaster was visited on southern prisoners, their release and return home was somewhat more protracted. In the final months of the war, Hoffman was still busy establishing new prisoner-of-war camps at Hart's Island in Long Island Sound and at Newport News, Virginia. But with the termination of hostilities, Grant was eager to extend to prisoners the same magnanimity that he had shown Lee's army at Appomattox. "By going now," he reasoned, "they may still raise something for their subsistence for the coming year and prevent suffering next winter." Accordingly, War Department orders issued on 8 May directed that "all prisoners of war, except officers above the rank of colonel, who before the capture of Richmond signified their desire to take the oath of allegiance to the United States and their unwillingness to be exchanged be forthwith released upon their taking the said oath, and transportation furnished them to their respective homes." Hoffman proposed to Grant that the order be implemented by releasing fifty men daily from each prison, beginning with captives below the rank of general who had no charges pending against them. Since northern prisons then held about 50,000 men, sixty days would be required to empty the camps. Grant approved the plan, but Hoffman was forced to abandon it on 20 June, when he learned that President Andrew Johnson had ordered the immediate release of all prisoners except those captured with Jefferson Davis and those in a small number of other special categories. Hoffman began the mass releases immediately, and by the end of the month only 2,381 Rebels were still imprisoned.[59]

As the number of Confederate prisoners declined, Hoffman moved to close prisons and eliminate the need for guards wherever possible. Ever mindful of economy, the commissary general assured Stanton that the public property at closed facilities would be sold at auction and the proceeds transferred to the U.S. Treasury. By the first week of July, Hoffman was able to report that Point Lookout, Rock Island, Elmira, Newport News, Alton, and Camps Morton and Chase had been emptied except for a small number of invalids who had been transferred to the Federal hospitals at those posts. By 1 August, only 165 men remained incarcerated in northern prisons; by the end of October, that number had shrunk to only four.[60]

Hoffman's duties and responsibilities were rapidly diminishing, but he had one more important task to complete. As the camps closed, he ordered the money remaining in the prison and hospital funds of all Union prisons to be forwarded to him for consolidation. In 1864, as Stanton had repeatedly slashed the prisoners' rations, the money in these accounts had grown rapidly. Although army regulations specified that these assets were to be expended to improve conditions in the camps, Hoffman never required commanders to spend the funds as intended. He authorized and in some cases directed that the funds be used to purchase items such as iron doors, manacles, leg irons, and security locks, and he lavishly praised and rewarded subordinates who amassed large sums in their accounts rather than spending the money. As one historian has noted, by 1864 the primary objective of the prison and hospital funds was simply to raise money.[61]

For prisoners, the combination of Stanton's successive ration cuts and Hoffman's refusal to expend prison and hospital funds had been devastating. The fund maintained at Elmira, for example, could have done much to relieve the suffering of prisoners in the wake of the ration reductions ordered at the camp during the last six months of 1864. Official prison records indicate that just over $150,381 had been deposited in the prison fund. From July to December 1864, however, expenditures from the fund totaled a paltry $32,117, leaving a one-year "savings" of $118,264 to be returned to Hoffman.[62] The full extent to which prison funds had been misused during the war became clear in October 1865, when Hoffman submitted the savings to the War Department. Records reveal that although camp commanders collected over $3 million, less than half of it was spent for the relief of prisoners. The remainder—over $1.8 million—Hoffman proudly returned as evidence of the strict economy with which he had operated the Union system of prisons.[63]

The return of these funds would be one of Hoffman's last official acts. On 3 November, the War Department issued Special Orders No. 581, relieving him of duty as commissary general of prisoners and directing him to "proceed to join his regiment in the Military Division of the Mississippi." Brigadier General William Hoffman's service as warden for the Union was at an end.[64]

Meanwhile, the former Union and Confederate prisons were being put to new uses. The tobacco factories at Danville and Cahaba were used to store harvested crops in the years immediately following the war. The cemetery where the Union dead were buried at Danville became a national cemetery, and the bodies of the Federal dead at Cahaba were exhumed and moved to a newly designated national cemetery at Marietta, Georgia. Following the departure of the last prisoners from Salisbury, the Confederate War Department planned to hold the facility in readiness for "such purposes of the Government as circumstances may render most urgent," but these notions went up in smoke when General George Stoneman and his Yankee cavalry put the main building of the Rowan cotton factory to the torch on 12 April 1864. Most of the prison's records were consumed in the conflagration. The land on which it had stood was seized by the Federal government and sold to local residents in 1866. The remaining structures returned to service as mills; a short time later, some of them were converted for use as a private school. Salisbury's sprawling prisoner graveyard was designated as a national cemetery in 1868, and in 1876 permanent headstones and a monument to the Union dead were erected there.[65]

Many of the Confederate prisons occupied during the war had few, if any, permanent buildings. The stockade of the Florence pen was dismantled and the land was put back into crops at the war's end. Eventually the grounds became a city park, while the graves of the thousands of Yankee boys who did not survive the camp's brief but terrible existence were incorporated into a national cemetery. The few structures that had been erected at Millen were destroyed by fire shortly after the prison was vacated, and the stockade grounds were converted to farmland. Andersonville also initially went under the plow, and the site might have been lost forever if the government had not purchased the land from Ben Dykes in 1875. Today, the fields where the prison stood have been converted into a national historic site, and the trenches where the thousands of Andersonville's dead were buried are now maintained as part of a national cemetery. The site also contains the graves of the prisoners who died at Millen.[66]

In Richmond, Belle Isle was developed as a postwar industrial site, and its Union dead were reinterred in a national cemetery that had been established in the former capital. Most of the warehouses that had been converted into prisons reverted to their former use, but a special fate was reserved for the infamous ship chandlery of Libby and Son. In an act prompted more by revenge and symbolism than security, Libby served as the primary location where Confederates apprehended in the Richmond area were detained while Union officials pondered their fate. Among those who were afforded the opportunity to see the facility in this entirely new light was Richard Turner, the former commandant of the prison. None of the Rebels held in the structure were ever brought to trial, and after the last was released, the building became a storage facility of the Southern Fertilizer Company. Given Libby's widespread notoriety in the North, however, it was almost inevitable that capitalism would come calling, and in the late 1880s William H. Gray of the Knights Templar Assurance Association of Chicago developed a plan to have the structure disassembled and transported to the Windy City for conversion into a museum. Gray and his group of entrepreneurs purchased the building for $23,000, and in December 1888 the dismantling began. Every brick, timber, nail, and shingle was numbered to ensure faithful reconstruction, and the entire lot was transported north by train. In Chicago, Libby was reassembled and outfitted at the then-princely cost of $200,000, and in December 1889 the Libby Prison War Museum opened to the public. Displays included tools used in escape attempts, personal papers and official documents, and the timbers upon which hundreds of prisoners had carved their names. The enterprise was initially profitable, but by 1899 the museum had lost its drawing power and the investors ordered it demolished. Bricks from the building were preserved as part of the north wall of the Chicago Historical Society's Civil War Room, and the famous timbers were purchased by a farmer from La Porte, Indiana, who used them in the construction of a barn. In 1980 a plaque was dedicated in Richmond indicating the original location of the facility.[67]

On the Union side, Camps Chase, Douglas, Morton, and Elmira all reverted once more to Federal troop depots, where thousands of Union soldiers were demobilized. The Confederate cemetery at Camp Chase was deeded to the Federal government, while at Camps Douglas, Morton, and Elmira, sections of local cemeteries were set aside for the reburial of former prisoners. In St. Louis, the buildings that had housed the Gratiot and Myrtle Street prisons were pulled down; their dead were reburied at Jefferson Barracks National Cemetery. Alton Penitentiary was returned to the control of the state of Illinois. Its Rebel cemetery was ceded to the Federal government, but the bodies that had been buried near the pest house on Tow Head Island were washed away and lost forever. The graves on Johnson's Island also remained under Federal control, but the site of the former prison was quickly transformed into farmland and summer residences.[68]

Forts Delaware, Warren, and Lafayette, as well as the other government installations, once more became part of the nation's coastal defense system, while the part of the Rock Island complex that had been set aside for prison use passed under the control of the island's Federal arsenal. In some instances, the burial grounds at these facilities were incorporated into the national cemetery system; in other places, the bodies were exhumed and reinterred at national cemeteries already in operation nearby. The lone exception was Point Lookout, where grounds that had once held almost 52,000 prisoners were converted for use as farmland and summer resorts. The bodies of the thousands of Confederates buried in the prison's cemetery were thus exhumed, transported inland, and summarily reinterred in mass graves on Federal land.[69]

Although most of the prisons seemed destined to pass quietly into the mists of memory in the years immediately following the war, activities by a number of groups in both the North and the South ensured that the prisoners' experiences would not be so quickly forgotten. The first and most prominent of these groups was that of the prisoners themselves. Prisoner accounts began appearing even before the war ended, and literally hundreds of these narratives were published after 1865. The former prisoners had varied reasons for making their stories public. Some simply sought to guarantee that neither their families nor the nation for whom they had given so much would forget the story of their suffering and sacrifice. Ex-prisoner John King was moved to compose his memoirs of captivity at Elmira and Point Lookout for the edification of his "own children and grandchildren" and to satisfy a "great desire that the world be better informed regarding the treatment of prisoners during the war." Ezra Hoyt Ripple penned his account of captivity at Andersonville in the hope that it would help northerners to "appreciate the sacrifice" made by prisoners and to spur parents to "teach their boys and girls their duty in preserving this Union for which their lives were so freely given."[70] Other prisoners had more immediate and quantifiable objectives in mind. Some wrote to substantiate claims of war-related disabilities in applications for veterans' pensions; others sought to justify their own conduct while confined or to charge their captors or fellow prisoners with wrongdoing.

A second group that kept the experiences of prisoners alive was the clergy of both sections. In sermons delivered before and during the war, pastors had lauded the righteousness of the northern or southern way of life while demonizing the practices and beliefs of the opposing section. As the fighting drew to a close, the message emanating from most northern pulpits was one of forgiveness and reconciliation. President Lincoln's assassination dramatically changed the tone of many sermons, however. To many northern clergymen, the murder of the president was simply one more heinous incident perpetrated by a people who had delighted in mistreating the prisoners in their care. As Pastor Robert Lowry proclaimed to his Brooklyn flock on Easter Sunday, 1865, John Wilkes Booth's act was evidence of the same malevolent southern spirit that had "starved our unhappy prisoners in the pens of Andersonville . . . froze our veterans to death on Belle Island" and "crowded our officers in the damp dungeons of Richmond, till you could gather the mold from their beards by the handful!"[71]

A third group that perpetuated the memory of the sacrifices of prisoners was the veterans' organizations that proliferated after the war. The largest and most powerful of these were the Grand Army of the Republic (GAR) for northern veterans and the United Confederate Veterans (UCV) in the South. The GAR was founded in 1866 and reached its peak membership in 1890, when more than 400,000 men belonged to its posts scattered across the North. Local reunions of Confederate units were common in the years immediately following the war as well. Concerns that reuniting large numbers of Confederate veterans might spark trouble delayed the founding of the UCV until 1889; it reached its peak in 1903, when 80,000 members were recorded on its rolls. A women's auxiliary, the Women's Relief Corps, supplemented posts of the GAR, while chapters of the UCV were aided by the United Daughters of the Confederacy.[72]

The activities of these veterans' groups and their auxiliaries were numerous and varied. They sponsored reunions, provided opportunities for members to recount campaign histories and personal experiences, and lobbied politicians for pensions, soldiers' homes, and the maintenance of veterans' graves. They also exerted a powerful influence on the shaping of the nation's collective memory of the conflict by promoting the adoption of textbooks espousing their particular interpretations of the war.[73] In each of these activities, they were particularly careful to recall and preserve the experiences of prisoners, for in many ways the suffering of captive soldiers epitomized the veterans' sacrifices for their countries. The UCV solicited prisoner accounts for publication in journals such as the *Confederate Veteran* and the *Southern Historical Society Papers,* and these articles often contained gruesome depictions of the conditions in northern camps, leveling bitter indictments against those who directed the Union system of prisons.[74]

In terms of both passion and grim realism in the memorialization of the suffering of prisoners, nothing exceeded the induction ceremony of the GAR. On the appointed night each recruit, or candidate for induction, was blindfolded before entering the post meeting room. His jacket and hat were taken from him, and in their place he was provided only the shredded remnant of an army blanket. The recruit was then led into the post room, which had been readied according to detailed instructions: "The camp is prepared by placing a box, six feet in length and three in width, and two in depth in the centre of the room, labeled upon the lid, in a conspicuous manner, with the name and regiment of some soldier who died in Andersonville Rebel Prison. On the centre of the box will be placed an open Bible and crossed swords, with the American flag draped in mourning." The candidate was first led around the room to the strains of "slow solemn music." He was then forced to kneel before the mock coffin, where, with one hand on the Bible, he was required to swear to uphold the ideals of the organization and to "sustain . . . at all times the citizen Soldier of the Republic." The prisoner-of-war imagery in the ceremony served to remind the recruit that just as the helpless captive had depended on the assistance of his comrades to survive Rebel prisons, veterans must protect and aid each other in the harsh postwar world. The entire service, as one historian of the GAR has noted, was very much "a pact with the dead against the living."[75]

A final group that worked to guarantee that the travails of prisoners would not be soon forgotten was the politicians of the North and the South. While politicians had traded allegations concerning the mistreatment of prisoners throughout the war, the charges and countercharges did not cease with the fighting. In the weeks after Appomattox, many Confederate military and civilian officials were arrested and confined on allegations that they had participated in the mistreatment of Federal prisoners. Only Captain Henry Wirz, the former commander of the stockade at Andersonville, was ever brought to trial. He was charged with "maliciously, willfully and traitorously . . . combining, confederating and conspiring . . . to injure the health and destroy the lives of soldiers in the military service of the United States." Yet even the most cursory examination of the record of his trial reveals that the entire proceeding was a sham—and a poorly executed sham at that. Witnesses for the prosecution were shamelessly coached and then led through their testimony to ensure they delivered the most damning evidence possible. Conversely, witnesses for the defense were threatened by government operatives with arrest and imprisonment; if they were judged to be potentially damaging to the prosecution's case, they were ordered to be dismissed before they could even testify. Wirz's initial defense team withdrew in protest shortly after the trial opened, and the two unpaid lawyers appointed in their place were helpless in the face of the overwhelming resources marshaled by the Federal government. In reality, the Wirz affair was no trial at all. It was merely one more propaganda exercise orchestrated by Stanton and the Radicals, and their work was made easier by the wave of anger and the demand for vengeance that swept through the North in the wake of Lincoln's assassination. The government insisted that Wirz would receive a fair hearing before nine members of a military commission, but its impartiality was betrayed when the commission's findings were published as yet another polemical report of the House of Representatives. In sum, as one scholar has accurately noted, the trial was no more than "a shameless charade," and Wirz was "a dead man from the start."[76] He was convicted, and on 10 November 1865 he was hanged.

The Committee on the Conduct of the War was dissolved at the war's end, but even as Wade and his colleagues departed, they delivered a final report that was intended to sustain the popular hatred of the South they had labored so hard to create. Issued in May 1865, this parting blast of Radical propaganda admonished northerners that while they were right to extend enthusiastic welcomes to their returning heroes, they should never forget the thousands of Union boys who had "fallen victims to that savage and infernal spirit which actuated those who spared not the prisoners at their mercy."[77]

Surprisingly, none of the members of the Committee on the Conduct of the War were appointed to the powerful Joint Committee on Reconstruction that was formed by Congress in December 1865; but the objectives and methods of Wade and his colleagues lived on nonetheless. When the Radicals became dissatisfied at the pace and direction of presidential Reconstruction under Andrew

Johnson, they revived the tactic of issuing a lengthy and biased congressional report, the intent of which was to remind northerners that the very men the president was allowing to assume positions of authority in the South were the same ones who had starved and murdered Union prisoners during the war. As the report thundered, "The evidence points with unerring finger to the highest as well as the subordinate officers of the confederacy as the great criminals, guilty of atrocities for which Wirz suffered on the gibbet, and for whose like punishment every principle of justice and violated law is to-day speaking in thunder-tones from the voices of history."[78]

CHAPTER 10

"The Real Cause of the Suffering"

Testimony, Evidence, and Verdict

THE JUSTIFICATIONS FOR and rationalizations of prisoner-of-war management began long before the guns went silent at Appomattox. Both the North and the South insisted that its own prisoner-of-war system guaranteed humane conditions in the camps, and both charged that the enemy's system had been deliberately designed and operated to ensure that if prisoners survived at all, they would return home physically and mentally broken.

By the early years of the twentieth century, a spirit of national reconciliation had combined with the passage of time to soften these polarizing charges. In the main, historians documenting the prisoner-of-war experience echoed this more conciliatory stance. Scholars argued that the terrible loss of life in the camps had resulted from factors beyond the control of the belligerents. Neither the North nor the South, they insisted, was guilty of systematically or intentionally mistreating prisoners. Writing in the first years of the new century, Edward Channing concluded that each side cared for its prisoners just about as well as it cared for its own soldiers, while in his 1937 history of the Civil War, J. G. Randall ascribed the high numbers of deaths in the camps to the fact that Union and Confederate military and civilian leaders were simply overwhelmed by the magnitude of the prisoner-of-war challenge. The same line of reasoning also prevailed in later studies. In his 1968 history of Andersonville, Ovid Futch concluded that although the Confederate government should have done more to improve conditions in the camp, the "root of much prisoner suffering" could be found in "contentious officials, gross mismanagement and inadequate organization."[1]

Historians continue to offer such explanations. James M. McPherson finds that although conditions in all prisons were "usually bad," there was "no evidence to support Northern charges of deliberate Confederate cruelty to prisoners—except for captured black soldiers." In their biography of Jefferson Davis,

Herman Hattaway and Richard Beringer maintain that "neither side actually had any systematic policy of maltreatment." Charles P. Roland is even more pointed, asserting that "no objective Civil War scholar today believes that either group of authorities was guilty of following a policy of deliberate cruelty toward [prisoners]."[2] These conclusions fly in the face of overwhelming evidence to the contrary. Although organizational incompetence and the absence of resources certainly contributed to the horrors in the camps, the roots of Civil War prisoners' suffering and death lay in decisions and directives that were deliberately chosen and implemented by Union and Confederate leaders.

For over a decade after the war ended, Republicans continued to employ the tactic that became known as "waving the bloody shirt" to stifle meaningful discussion about Reconstruction. This was aimed not only at southerners but also at limiting the growth and impact of the Democratic Party in the North. John Logan, a Republican politician and national commander of the GAR, repeatedly took to the stump to remind voters that the Democratic Party had been the party of Rebels and Copperheads during the Civil War. As such, he argued, it should have no part in the nation's postwar affairs.[3]

The Confederacy's most comprehensive defense of its treatment of prisoners appeared well after the war ended. As former Confederates returned to Congress, they took up the fight to refute Republican charges that Union prisoners had been deliberately mistreated in southern prisons. These heated confrontations came to a boil during debate over the Amnesty Bill of 1876, which proposed the return of full political rights to southerners who had held high office in the Confederacy. In January 1876, Maine congressman and presidential aspirant James G. Blaine proposed an amendment to the bill that called for the continued exclusion of Jefferson Davis. This was not because Davis had been the highest of all Confederate officeholders, but rather because, as Blaine reminded the House, he had been "the author, knowingly, deliberately, guiltily and willfully, of the gigantic murders and crimes of Andersonville." Although the Confederate president had been "thoroughly informed as to the condition of affairs" at the prison, he had done nothing to mitigate the plight of "35,000 poor, helpless, naked, starving, sickened, dying men."[4] Representative Benjamin Hill of Georgia rose to defend both Davis and the Confederacy, arguing that the former president did not know of the conditions at Andersonville and that the suffering of Union captives there or at any other southern camp was attributable primarily to the North's refusal to agree to a general exchange. The debate rapidly turned personal when Representative James Garfield of Ohio questioned Hill's veracity, and Hill retaliated with the accusation that Blaine acted for the "obvious partisan purpose of exciting . . . bitter sectional discussion, from which his party, and perhaps himself, may be the beneficiary."[5]

As a means of excluding Davis from again enjoying the full rights of citizenship, Blaine's proposed amendment proved unnecessary. The former president had vowed that he would never seek or accept amnesty, and he never did. Nevertheless, the Hill–Blaine debate was tremendously important, for in its wake Davis and others who had served in positions of leadership in the Confederacy were spurred to compose their own versions of the history of Civil War prisons and prisoner treatment. These contrasting histories, one northern and one southern, decisively shaped the national memory of Civil War prisons.[6]

The lead in the defense of Confederate policies and actions was assumed by the Southern Historical Society, an association composed largely of former Confederate officers dedicated to the publication of articles and texts that furthered a decidedly southern interpretation of the history of the war. In an effort to counter the accusations leveled by Blaine, the society devoted two full articles of its initial volume of the *Southern Historical Society Papers* to the question of the treatment of prisoners. The articles, authored by Reverend J. William Jones, a former general officer and the secretary of the society, were intended to "prove, before any fair tribunal," six "points" in defense of the Confederacy. Jones's "proof" reveals the essence of the argument that defenders of the Confederate prisoner-of-war system have employed from that day to this.[7]

Jones began by asserting that "the Confederate authorities *always* ordered the kind treatment of prisoners of war, and if there were individual cases of cruel treatment it was in violation of positive orders." In support of this claim, he offered a review of the 21 May 1861 congressional statute that provided for the "safe custody and sustenance" of captives, as well as the "testimony of leading Confederates"—including Jefferson Davis, Robert E. Lee, and Robert Ould—who predictably insisted that they had had no knowledge of any cruelties to Yankee prisoners.[8]

Yet even members of the Confederate Congress characterized the barbarous treatment instituted by Captain George Alexander and his thugs in Castle Thunder as "cruel," and the wholesale execution of captured black soldiers at Fort Pillow stands as another well-known example of Confederate cruelty to Union prisoners.[9] Equally cruel was General Samuel Cooper's decision to continue shipping prisoners to Andersonville in spite of John Henry Winder's warning that it would result in thousands of deaths. Equally cruel was the Confederate War Department's refusal to institute and enforce even the most rudimentary standards of cleanliness and field sanitation in the camps. Importantly, these and many other instances of cruelty were not perpetrated "in violation of positive orders."

Contrary to Jones's assertions, they were carried out with the full knowledge and support of leaders in the highest echelons of the Confederate government.[10]

In his second point, Jones turned to refuting specific charges, the first of which was that the South had failed to provide its prisoners with sufficient rations. But before he could launch his rebuttal, he was forced to amend earlier defenses of the southern record on the issue. In its March 1865 report, the Confederate Congress had insisted that "the evidence proves that the rations furnished to prisoners of war ... have been *never* less than those furnished to the Confederate soldiers who guarded them, and have at some seasons been larger in quantity and better in quality than those furnished Confederate troops in the field."[11] The reams of official Confederate correspondence detailing ration shortages and the publication of scores of Union "starvation narratives" obviously rendered such claims untenable, but Jones retreated no further than necessary. He maintained that "the orders were to give prisoners the same rations that our own soldiers received, and if rations were scarce and of inferior quality, it was through no fault of the Confederacy."[12] In his memoirs, Jefferson Davis adopted this explanation and expanded upon it, contending that Confederate leaders "did the best we could do for those whom the fortune of war placed at our mercy." Any shortages of rations were due to the depredations of the Yankees, who "devastated our fields, destroyed our crops, broke up our railroads, and thus interrupted our means of transportation, and reduced our people, our armies, and consequently their soldiers, who were our prisoners, all alike, to the most straitened condition for food."[13]

The justifications offered by Jones and Davis rest on the assumption that food would have been provided to Union prisoners of war if it had been available. As James M. McPherson writes in his critically acclaimed *Battle Cry of Freedom*, most historians have fully accepted this rationalization. Modern scholars, McPherson writes, "concur with contemporary opinions ... that a deficiency of resources and the deterioration of the Southern economy were mainly responsible for the sufferings of Union prisoners. The South could not feed its own soldiers and civilians; how could it feed enemy prisoners?"[14]

The critical question thus becomes whether food was obtainable. Were Confederate stocks of food exhausted by 1864? The answer is no. Food was available throughout the South during the final eighteen months of the war. For ample evidence supporting this fact, one need search no further than the official records of the Confederate government. They reveal that in 1864 and 1865—when the number of prisoner-of-war deaths from starvation was highest—the commissary department collected vast quantities of food, stockpiling it in depots across the South. Commissary General of Subsistence Lucius B. Northrop demonstrated an ability to amass tons of food on short notice, caching half a million rations of bread and almost a million rations of meat at Beaver Dam Station for Lee in May 1864, and Northrop's accomplishments were eclipsed by the near-miraculous feats of his successor, General Isaac M. St. John.

The tons of food collected by St. John and his commissary officers were stockpiled in locations that had been serving as ration depots since the early months of the war.[15] Confederate commissary reports indicate that as of 1 April 1865, there were over 300,000 rations of bread and meat stored in Richmond. Further to the west, a depot in Danville contained 1.5 million rations of meat and 500,000 rations of bread, while a similar facility in Lynchburg held another 180,000 rations of the same items. Commissary warehouses in Greensboro, North Carolina, contained an additional 1.5 million rations of meat and bread. Salisbury boasted by far the largest stockpile of food, much of which had been transferred there from warehouses in Columbia, South Carolina. The astounding dimensions of the Salisbury cache were revealed when Union general George Stoneman's cavalry captured the town on 12 April 1865. Federal officers who inspected the Confederate warehouses near the prison reported that the buildings contained 100,000 bushels of corn, 60,000 pounds of bacon, 100,000 pounds of salt, 20,000 pounds of sugar, 27,000 pounds of rice, 50,000 pounds of wheat, 30,000 pounds of cornmeal, and 100,000 pounds of flour.[16]

Nor were the War Department's ration depots the only storage facilities for immense stocks of food. Other Confederate agencies, such as the Nitre Bureau and the Navy Department, also maintained substantial reserves of food and clothing. By 1864, Secretary of the Navy Stephen Mallory and his officers had stockpiled between four and eight months' supply of all key commodities at every naval base in the Confederacy. Even larger quantities of the same items were available for issue from the navy's main supply depots in Charlotte, Montgomery, Charleston, and Augusta.[17]

The fact that so much food was available at these sites substantially weakens the argument that Union prisoners went hungry because there was no food to issue them. The case against those who directed the Confederate system of prisons is rendered infinitely more damning, moreover, by the fact that without exception, these vast quantities of food were stockpiled either within or closely adjacent to the same cities and towns that also contained the South's major prisons. When considered from a national security standpoint, this made perfect sense. Ideally, ration depots were placed in areas secure from enemy action yet easily accessible by rail and roads; the same characteristics determined the locations of prisons. Those seeking to justify the policies of the Confederate government have argued that these rations were not issued to prisoners because they were earmarked for Rebel armies in the field. That might have been the case, but it is a very different argument from the argument that Union prisoners starved because the Confederate government had no food to issue them.

In postwar defenses of their actions, James Seddon, Jefferson Davis, and other senior Confederate leaders often insisted that in the last year of the war southern soldiers suffered as much as Yankee captives from hunger. As historian Bell I. Wiley noted years ago, Johnny Reb was often compelled to endure short rations, and no one familiar with accounts of the conditions in the southern trenches around Petersburg can doubt that "Lee's Miserables" were perpetually hungry during the last months of the war.[18]

But while southern soldiers might have been underfed, they were not dying by the score from the effects of starvation, as were prisoners at Danville, Salisbury, Florence, Millen, and other camps during those same months. The southern soldier was certainly forced to endure many days when no rations were issued, but he was able to obtain food from a variety of alternative sources. Johnny Reb was an accomplished forager, not above raiding the orchards or hen houses of nearby farmers, and he often received food from home or from sympathetic civilians residing nearby. The prisoner had no access to supplemental food sources. Only a very few camps allowed captives to make purchases from sutlers or local merchants, and those meager supplements were not sufficient to sustain health and life.[19]

If food was available, then perhaps the problem, as Davis often maintained, was that the enemy had "broken up" the Confederate railroad system, thus interrupting the means by which rations might have been transported to the prisons. As Robert C. Black demonstrated in his seminal study, the Confederate railroad network, never a robust or particularly efficient system, was indeed progressively degraded by overuse, Yankee assaults, and the parochial demands of states'-rights governors throughout the war.[20] Yet there is ample evidence that southern railroads never lost the capacity to support adequate deliveries of food and other needed supplies to the prisons. Studies by logistical historian James Doster demonstrate that military and civilian transportation managers in the South were exceptionally adept at repairing damaged roads, and in his landmark study of Confederate supply, Richard Goff argues that the condition of the southern rail net in the spring of 1864 was "by no means desperate, for the trains continued to distribute both war materials and civilian goods around the country and into Virginia."[21]

The same trains also continued to transport prisoners. As earlier noted, thousands of Yankees were transferred from Richmond and Danville to Andersonville by train in the spring of 1864, and when Andersonville was closed in the late summer, its prisoners were shipped—again by rail—back to Virginia, to other prisons in Georgia, and to camps in North Carolina, South Carolina, and Alabama. In fact, the wholesale movement of prisoners by rail throughout the South continued up to the resumption of exchanges in February 1865. The rail lines that transported these thousands of captives passed through the richest agricultural regions of the Confederacy. Without question, the trains that carried this unending stream of men from prison to prison could just as easily have delivered rations and supplies.

Nor were railroads the only means that might have been employed to transport food to southern prisons. Confederate logistical planners had repeatedly demonstrated their ability to move huge volumes of supplies by wagon early in the war; they did so once again in 1864, when rail traffic was interdicted during the siege of Petersburg. In the case of the prisons at Richmond, Danville, and Salisbury, which had supply depots close at hand, no great skill or effort would have been necessary to feed the prisoners. All that would have been required was a decision to allocate part of the stockpiled food to feed men who were starving. But this was a decision that neither Davis nor any of his lieutenants chose to make.[22]

A final justification often heard for the failure to provision adequately the southern camps is that the leaders of the nascent Confederate nation simply did not possess the organizational ability efficiently to staff, administer, and supply the complex of prisons they established. As historian and organizational theorist Carl L. Romanek contends in one example of this argument, "The prisoners at Andersonville suffered and died because their captors were unable to recognize and solve the organizational problems that confronted them." Northrop biographer Thomas R. Hay agrees. While admitting that "food in quantity was available in depots in North Carolina, Georgia, Alabama, and elsewhere" during the last year of the war, Hay argues that the commissary department was never able to solve "the problem of getting it to Richmond and Lee's troops."[23] Although there were clearly problems in transporting rations to the Confederate armies, the simple fact that there was no mass starvation in southern regiments strongly suggests that Romanek and Hay overstate their case. Obviously, the men who directed the Confederate commissary and quartermaster departments managed to overcome the daunting challenges inherent in supplying large armies on the move, and had they wished, they could have done the same for the prisons.

So much for the second part of Reverend J. William Jones's defense of the Confederate treatment of Union prisoners of war. Jones's third point addressed the issue of medical care afforded Union prisoners. He asserted that Confederate prison hospitals were "put on the same footing precisely" as the facilities in which southern soldiers were treated. All shortages of medical supplies could be attributed to the fact that Federal authorities had declared such items "contraband of war" and had "refused to accept the Confederate offer to allow Federal surgeons to come to the prisons with supplies of medicines and stores."[24] Here, Jones was being considerably less than honest. While both prisoners and Rebel soldiers suffered because of Yankee contraband declarations, Jones's claim of parity in prison hospitals and hospitals that treated Confederate soldiers is pure nonsense.

Medical care for prisoners in the South had been shabby since First Manassas; as the war dragged on, it became absolutely disgraceful. In the Richmond complex, the central problem was overcrowding. Yankee patients might have been administered the same medicines as their southern counterparts, but they were given less than half the hospital space per man, and the results were devastating. In a typical report submitted on 14 March 1864, inspectors T. G. Richardson of the Medical Department and Colonel George W. Brent of General Cooper's staff noted that although the combined capacity of the capital's three prison hospitals was 500 patients, just over 1,100 men were crowded into the buildings on the day of the inspection. "The wards contain therefore more than twice the number prescribed by orders, and such is the crowded condition that in some instances, two patients were found on a single bunk," the officers wrote angrily. Sick and wounded Yankees were dying at the rate of 26 per day, and the ratio of deaths per 1,000 patients hospitalized had rocketed to 244. Nor was an end in sight. As Brent and Richardson warned, "The ratio is rapidly increasing, and compared with that of the Hospitals of our own sick and wounded, the mortality in which for the same period did not in any case exceed 20 per 1000 . . . is truly frightful."[25]

In other southern camps, conditions for the sick and wounded were much, much worse. Thousands of Union boys died because Andersonville, Florence, and Millen were opened with no hospitals at all. At Salisbury a prisoner recorded that "very little medicine" was provided in the hospital, which was so overcrowded that the sick were laid in "tightly packed rows . . . on the dampness and filthiness of the dirt floor."[26] At Danville, guards conceded that the drinking water supplied to the sick was so polluted that it stank, while the camp surgeons' failure to remove smallpox cases from wards crowded with noninfected patients quickly transformed the prison hospital into a charnel house. So much for Jones's contention that the standards of medical care in hospitals treating Union prisoners were the same as in hospitals that cared for Confederate soldiers.

The Reverend Jones went on to tender his own explanation for the stunning number of prisoner deaths in southern camps—one which would quickly become a staple excuse for Confederate apologists. The "great mortality among the prisoners," Jones insisted, "arose from epidemics and chronic diseases which our surgeons had not the means of preventing or arresting." As a "strong proof" of this claim, he asserted that "*nearly as large a proportion of the Confederate guard at Andersonville died as of the prisoners themselves.*"[27]

This claim, like most made by Jones, did contain a grain of truth. The efforts of Confederate physicians to combat sickness in the camps had indeed been impeded by a scarcity of hospital supplies. In the last months that the Salisbury prison was operational, for example, a visiting southern clergyman criticized the available hospital supplies as "meager and irregular." But the absence of adequate quantities of medicines, blankets, and serviceable replacement clothing in the camps does not mean that these items were not available. When Stoneman's troopers burned the Salisbury depot in April 1865, their commander recorded that among the items put to the torch were "100,000 suits of . . . clothing, 250,000 army blankets . . . and medical supplies, valued by the rebel medical director at $100,000 in gold."[28]

Even if one accepts the fact that medicines and hospital supplies were limited, this in no way explains why the men who directed the southern system of prisons tolerated—and in many instances actually created—the conditions in which sickness and disease flourished. Why did prison commanders not insist that basic standards of field sanitation be maintained and that the camps be properly policed? As historian Stewart Brooks writes in his study of Civil War medicine, the connection between sanitation and disease was well known in both armies. The link between prolonged exposure to the elements and the onset of deadly pulmonary diseases was equally well understood, while the relationship between health and nutrition was considered by physicians to be so important that "most illness was looked upon as being directly or indirectly tied up with . . . 'scorbutic diathesis,' a fancy bit of Civil War nomenclature applied to scurvy or malnutrition."[29]

Yet there was little effort to maintain even the most rudimentary standards of cleanliness in southern camps. As a result, diarrhea, dysentery, and typhoid fever—all diseases contracted as a consequence of poor field sanitation—cut men down by the thousands. Because most of the major southern camps afforded captives little or no shelter from the elements, prisoners fortunate enough to avoid death from fluxes and fevers were easy targets for pneumonia in the winter or heat injuries in the broiling southern summers. And the perpetual overcrowding in Confederate camps led to frequent outbreaks of deadly eruptive fevers such as smallpox, measles, scarlet fever, and erysipelas. The failure of prison commanders to provide competent care or to institute basic isolation measures guaranteed that when these epidemics struck, they would be exceptionally virulent and long-lived.

Even with an ample supply of medicines, Confederate physicians could have done very little for prisoners because of preexisting conditions in the camps. The diseases that ravaged the camps were all killers, and as histories of mid-nineteenth-century medical care attest, contemporary drug therapies could do little once a deadly illness had taken hold. Still, many lives could have been saved if officials in the Davis administration and the War Department had insisted upon measures to upgrade sanitation, reduce overcrowding, and improve the prisoners' diet. These improvements could have been undertaken regardless of the Yankee blockade or contraband decrees, but they were not.

Jones's assertion that the level of mortality among prisoners was no greater than that experienced by the guards at the camps is another mantra often intoned by Confederate apologists. The claim, most often applied in defense of conditions at Andersonville, is cited as additional proof that prisoners were not treated cruelly and that their water, food, and medical care were the same as that of the guards. Equal mortality rates among guards and prisoners, especially in a hellhole like Andersonville, would unquestionably give pause; but, in fact, the number of deaths was not equal. In no southern prison did guards sicken and die at the same appalling rate as prisoners. At Andersonville, the percentage of deaths among captives was almost six times greater than among guards. Comparisons of the causes of deaths among prisoners and guards at Andersonville are equally revealing. The most comprehensive and detailed examination conducted by the Confederate medical department was the "pathological investigation" conducted by Surgeon Joseph Jones in September 1864. It concluded that the chief cause of death among guards was typhoid and other communicable diseases, which were common in Civil War armies. In contrast, the greatest killers among prisoners were "diarrhea, dysentery, scurvy and hospital gangrene." Deaths from gangrene were due to inadequate care in the prison hospital, but the report concluded that deaths from diarrhea, dysentery, and scurvy were the direct results of "the long continued use of salt meat, and of coarse, unbolted corn bread, and improperly cooked food, and . . . the foul emanations from the all-abounding filth and excrements." If the guards had been issued the same deficient diet, subjected to the same inadequate medical care, and forced to live in the same unspeakable filth as the prisoners, the causes of death at Andersonville would have been the same. The fact that they were not explodes the myth that the two groups lived under the same conditions.[30]

Jones concluded his articles in the *Southern Historical Society Papers* with a pair of accusations that have served to underpin virtually all defenses of the South's treatment of prisoners. The first was that although Confederate captives were confined in "a land flowing with plenty," they were "famished with hunger." Furthermore, they were treated in prison hospitals that were so far below the standards of Union army hospitals that they "died by thousands from causes which the Federal authorities *could* have prevented." Second, Jones charged that the blame for the misery and death among Yankee prisoners ultimately lay with the Yankees themselves. "The real cause of the suffering on both sides was the stopping of the exchange of prisoners," he maintained, "and for this the *Federal authorities alone* were responsible. The Confederates kept the cartel in good faith. It was broken on the other side."[31]

To support his contention that the North alone was responsible for the termination of exchanges, Jones offered the personal reminiscences of Davis and other Confederate political leaders, as well as dozens of pages of official wartime correspondence between Ould and northern agents of exchange. Notably absent in all this verbiage is any acknowledgment that Confederate leaders violated the terms of the cartel by refusing to exchange black soldiers, or the obviously illegal declarations by which Ould repeatedly returned southern parolees to full duty. These and similar issues were dismissed with a few sentences and the admonition that they "ought never to have interrupted the general exchange."[32]

Once more, Jones's assertions contain elements of truth. The history of Confederate prisons would certainly have been brighter if the South had been required to care for hundreds rather than thousands of prisoners during the last years of the war. But unhappily, it was. So yet again the question is reduced to why the Confederacy did not do more to improve prison conditions as they actually existed. The Confederacy had food, clothing, and medical supplies that its officials might have issued Yankee prisoners; its failure to do so was not due to the inevitable consequences of broken railroads or bureaucratic bungling. In the end, the fundamental reason for the appalling state of the camps was that although senior officials in the Confederate government knew that hundreds of Union prisoners were dying daily from the effects of starvation, exposure, and disease, they declined to make decisions or initiate actions that would have improved the conditions under which the prisoners were held.

There is no doubt that the horrors of the camps were well known at the highest levels of the Confederate War Department. When the war began, officials had been caught unawares by the demands of caring for thousands of prisoners, and only the implementation of exchange under the Dix–Hill cartel prevented a catastrophe in the camps in 1862. After these exchanges were terminated in the summer of 1863, General John Winder went to extraordinary lengths to keep both Secretary of War Seddon and Adjutant and Inspector General Cooper informed of the steadily worsening situation in the expanding Confederate prison system. As we have seen, his repeated pleas came to naught. Instead, the querulous and parsimonious Lucius Northrop was appointed as commissary general of subsistence. Sent to Andersonville in July 1864, Winder was soon faced with an utter paucity of rations with which to feed prisoners.

Nor were Winder's travails unique. Prison commanders all over the South reported to the War Department that prisoner deaths from disease and starvation were spiraling to grisly heights. Without swift and substantial assistance from the capital, catastrophe was inevitable. Inspecting officers dispatched from Richmond reinforced these predictions. In detailed reports they clearly described the deplorable state of the camps and offered workable solutions to improve conditions and stem the dying. Seldom were these recommendations heeded. In the end, the dying in southern camps ceased only when exchanges were resumed in the spring of 1865.

What part did Jefferson Davis play in the history of the Confederate prison system? It is clear that from the beginning of the war, Davis was insistent in his demands that southern prisoners be treated humanely; he was quick personally to authorize acts of retaliation if they were not. And while he pushed relentlessly for the exchange of prisoners under the terms of the Dix–Hill cartel, he was not above violating the terms of that agreement when he thought that doing so served his nation. But it is less clear why Davis took no action to improve conditions in Confederate prisons. As his country's chief executive and commander-in-chief, Davis had both the power and the authority to shape and direct prisoner-of-war policy, and he readily intervened in prisoner affairs when he wished. He denied the demands of southern governors that they retain control of Yankees captured within their states, and in spite of repeated pressure from congressmen and members of his own cabinet, he refused to fight the war "under the black flag" or order the execution of Union prisoners in retaliation for alleged Federal atrocities. But the question remains: why did he not improve conditions within the camps?[33]

In seeking an answer to this question, one must first determine what Davis knew and when he knew it. Biographers of the president have remained largely silent on this subject. The most recent biography, for example, devotes only one paragraph to the topic. Defenders of the president have gone to extraordinary lengths to insist that he had no knowledge of the suffering of Yankee prisoners. In crafting their argument, Davis's apologists have focused on whether or not he ever saw the scathing report submitted by Colonel David T. Chandler following his inspection of Andersonville in August 1864. Confederate War Department records indicate that when Chandler's report reached Richmond, it was forwarded to Seddon. There is no evidence that the secretary ever passed it on to the president, and Davis always denied having seeing it. Northern politicians and journalists of the time argued otherwise, and academics and veterans' groups both North and South continued the debate into the early years of the twentieth century. Northern historian James Ford Rhodes asserted that Davis had seen the report and simply had declined to act on it, while southern scholars, led by Louisiana State University's Walter L. Fleming, countered that the president did not know of the document until after the war.[34]

Although interesting, there is much less to this dispute than meets the eye. Regardless of whether Davis saw the Chandler report or not, there can be no doubt that he was fully aware of the high mortality rate in southern camps. In his message to the opening session of the Second Confederate Congress on 2 May 1864, he acknowledged that he had been informed that Union prisoners were "perishing from the inevitable effects of imprisonment and homesickness."[35] Moreover, the prisoners' miserable existence was an inescapable fact of life for residents of Richmond. Davis, like all the capital's citizens, could not have avoided seeing the endless lines of gaunt, filthy Yankees being herded through the streets toward Libby and other pens. Out in the James River, the horrors of Belle Isle were on full display daily.

The most compelling evidence that Davis knew of the desperate plight of the Yankee prisoners, however, was supplied by the president himself. "We all knew of the disease and fatalities among the prisoners at Andersonville," he wrote to a confidant ten years after the war. As always, he ascribed the high mortality to "the climate and the corn meal diet, and the absence of the proper medicine for such diseases as existed." But Davis never attempted to offer a satisfactory explanation of why more was not done to provide additional food, medical care, and necessary supplies for the prisoners. To the end of his days, he insisted that the South did all it could and should have done for the prisoners and that the high number of deaths was unavoidable due to the lack of a general exchange. Davis, like most Confederate leaders, seems to have relied completely on a resumption of exchanges to end the suffering in the camps, and when this was not forthcoming, neither he nor anyone else felt obligated to develop and implement alternative solutions that might have slowed the dying. "The fact is," Davis once told a friend, "as a general proposition, we showed humanity, and though we could not provide for the prisoners as we would have wished to do, we did the best we could."[36]

Although no individual or group in the North was moved to author a comprehensive postwar defense of the Union treatment of Confederate prisoners, the official Federal position was encapsulated by the House of Representatives'

Report No. 45, released four years after the conflict ended. The report, completed at the urging of Radicals seeking to retain control of the course of Reconstruction, directly confronted the charge that northern refusal to consent to a general exchange after 1863 was the primary cause of the suffering and death in both the Union and Confederate prisoner-of-war camps. Its testimony promised a "full, complete and convincing refutation of these excuses and charges," while demonstrating that the "loyal administration of Abraham Lincoln, and the army and navy of the United States, are wholly and entirely exculpated from any responsibility for these great sufferings and crimes."[37] Unsurprisingly, many in the South contested the findings of Report No. 45, agreeing instead with Jones's charges that "Confederate prisoners ... were starved in a land of Plenty ... frozen where fuel and clothing were abundant" and "suffered untold horrors for want of medicines, hospital stores and proper medical attention."[38]

In their evaluations of these conflicting interpretations, modern historians have generally sided with the authors of Report No. 45. Union camps, they acknowledge, were plagued by mismanagement, overcrowding, and occasional shortages of food and supplies; but scholars contend that the men who directed the northern system of prisons were not guilty of systematically and deliberately mistreating prisoners. Sadly, the truth lies nearer the charges leveled by Jones.

It was not simply overcrowding or poor management that led to the worsening of prison conditions in the North during the last half of 1863. Rather, it was a hardening of the attitudes of those charged with directing the Union prisoner-of-war system. Secretary of War Edwin Stanton was in the vanguard of this movement, repeatedly denying the desperate entreaties of Union prison commanders seeking improvements in their prisons. To justify his refusals, Stanton cited the terrible conditions under which Union prisoners were being held in southern camps. The introduction of this justification signaled the beginning of a decidedly more brutal era in the northern camps.[39]

In pursuing this harder line, Stanton found a powerful ally in the Joint Committee on the Conduct of the War, led by Senator Benjamin Wade and dominated by Radical Republicans. The committee advocated a policy of systematic retaliation against southern prisoners, and Stanton implemented this policy with increasing severity. As he and the Radicals insisted, the Rebels had caused the war; moreover, they were guilty of unspeakable crimes in their prisons. They were thus fully deserving of harsh treatment while confined in the North and completely undeserving of positions of leadership in a reconstructed South.

If Stanton found allies among Wade and the Radicals, he found a willing, capable, and niggardly subordinate in Commissary General of Prisoners William Hoffman. Stanton's progressively harsher treatment of prisoners fit well with Hoffman's obsession for economy. As the commissary general soon learned, exceptionally large sums of money could be saved if the quantity of the prisoners' rations was reduced at the same time that expenditures from the prison and hospital funds were severely constrained. Hoffman's biographer maintains that the colonel was driven by a simple desire to conserve funds, but the commissary general of prisoners was motivated by more than mere fiscal considerations.[40] There was a darker side to William Hoffman, and in the last months of 1863 his treatment of prisoners became progressively more oppressive and cruel. It was in 1864, however, that he and Stanton instituted the measures that would result in the greatest amount of suffering and death in northern camps. Rations were repeatedly cut, as were the amounts of clothing, blankets, and other supplies. As a result, conditions in the camps reached new lows in the winter of 1864, and the number of prisoners requiring medical attention rose precipitously. Union prison hospitals, never adequately staffed or provisioned under Hoffman, could not keep pace with the crisis, and thousands of prisoners died without ever receiving medical attention.

Although the Union's refusal to continue general exchanges under the terms of the cartel in no way justified the appalling conditions in southern camps, Confederate leaders were correct in their assertion that northern leaders could have resumed exchanges any time they wished to do so. As official and private correspondence between Generals Benjamin Butler and Ulysses S. Grant clearly reveals, the Union claim that exchanges were halted because the South refused to return black soldiers along with whites was no more than a sop thrown to the restive northern press and public. The reason the North refused to renew exchanges, as Grant very clearly and repeatedly stated, was to preclude exchanged Rebels from reentering southern regiments and boosting Confederate combat strength in the field. Although a death sentence for many Union captives, Grant's position was militarily sound, and in adopting it Grant enjoyed the full and enthusiastic support of Secretary of War Stanton.

Surprisingly, few historians have addressed the question of how much Lincoln knew about the operation of northern camps or the treatment of Confederate prisoners of war. Those that have nonetheless consistently argue that Lincoln exerted a moderating influence in prisoner-of-war affairs. But a close examination of the president's record indicates that he was not always so benevolent.[41] He remained silent as Stanton ordered successive reductions of prisoner rations and essential supplies, and he voiced no objection to Grant's policy of severely constraining prisoner exchanges in 1864. And, as historian Mark E. Neely has demonstrated, he fully supported such questionable practices as imprisoning Confederate civilians as hostages.[42]

Lincoln was much more circumspect than Davis in his personal involvement in the controversial question of prisoner treatment. His assassination precluded the composition of memoirs, which might have revealed the depth of his knowledge of conditions in the camps or else served as a defense of Union prisoner-of-war policies. Ever the consummate politician, Lincoln fully appreciated the explosive nature of the prisoner-of-war issue, and he went to extraordinary lengths to avoid anything that would directly implicate him in the formulation of policies or decisions that determined the day-to-day operation of the camps. But the scarcity of documents demonstrating Lincoln's direct involvement in prisoner-of-war policy should not be construed to suggest that he had no knowledge of the terrible conditions in the camps or that he had no part in determining the manner in which enemy captives would be treated. In fact, Lincoln was very much aware of the conditions in the Union camps. For clues as to how he influenced the formulation of prisoner policy and sanctioned the mistreatment of captives in northern camps, one need only examine his working relationship with Secretary of War Edwin Stanton and the manner in which he dealt with the Radicals on the Committee on the Conduct of the War.

It would have been impossible for Lincoln to remain ignorant of the deplorable state of affairs in Union prisons. The newspapers of towns adjacent to camps frequently featured articles describing the shocking conditions under which Confederate prisoners were held. On 21 November 1864, for example, the editor of the *Rock Island Argus* accurately reported that although the North was "abundantly able to furnish all they really need," prisoners at Rock Island were being denied adequate food, clothing, and medical care. The policy constituted no less than the "deliberate and willful torture" of helpless men, the editor charged, and Union leaders from Lincoln down to the camp commander were thus "guilty of a great crime." Far from denying the accusations, the camp commander responded with a letter assuring the editor that if he had the power, he would slash rations and medical care even further and confine the Rebels under conditions equal to those at Andersonville.[43] Lincoln also read firsthand accounts of prison conditions in letters from southern prisoners who petitioned him for release. Reports chronicling the terrible plight of the Confederate captives poured into the War Department from dozens of Union military and civilian inspectors, as did hundreds of telegrams in which Federal camp commanders described in gruesome detail the overcrowding, sickness, and death that were a part of daily prison operations. As all Lincoln biographers agree, the president closely monitored messages received in the War Department's telegraph office. Given the political sensitivity of the prisoner-of-war issue, it is very unlikely that he would have allowed the headstrong Stanton to formulate and implement national policies without presidential direction and approval.

Many members of Congress and the president's cabinet feared that Lincoln was too much controlled by Stanton, but biographers of both men agree that such was not the case. Historian Philip Shaw Paludan suggests that Lincoln "knew the value of having a subordinate who could take the heat for actions the president desired but did not wished to be blamed for," and that subordinate was Stanton. The secretary was allowed free rein as long as he served Lincoln's purpose, but the president never hesitated to overrule him when necessary. In his role of the president's point man on controversial issues, Stanton frequently became the target of public outrage and condemnation. He was unjustly singled out for his opposition to general exchanges in 1862, and he bore the brunt of public condemnation for the Union parolee debacle.[44]

Evidence of the subtle manner in which Lincoln influenced Union prisoner-of-war policy may also be found through examining his relationship with the Radicals on the Committee on the Conduct of the War. This link has long been a subject of inquiry by scholars, and assessments vary greatly about the degree to which one influenced the actions of the other. T. Harry Williams, who characterized the committee as the "unnatural child of lustful radicalism," maintains that Wade and his fellow members forced Lincoln to implement disastrous policy decisions he would not otherwise have considered.[45] Hans L. Trefousse contends that Lincoln employed the committee as a sort of congressional attack dog to prod reluctant Union officers like George B. McClellan to action.[46] In a third interpretation, Bruce Tap argues that although the consequences of certain committee investigations were clearly more important to the president than others, Wade and his fellows constituted a force which Lincoln could never afford to ignore.[47]

An assessment combining elements of each of these interpretations is probably closer to the mark. As Williams maintained, the committee did often act as a malevolent force, ruining the careers of a number of good officers and firing public demands for retaliation against helpless prisoners. Equally sound is Trefousse's conclusion that the actions of the committee often presented the president with precisely the outcome he wished. Likewise, Tap's assertion that Wade and his minions were a power Lincoln never took lightly has been well documented.

But while the president knew that he could not ignore the will of the committee, he did not hesitate to refuse the Radicals' demands when he thought best. The most telling example of this resistance is the fact that Lincoln never did accede to the Radicals' continued insistence that he personally decree and direct a policy of retaliation against Confederate prisoners. Following the Fort Pillow massacre, Lincoln correctly judged that public support for retaliation was overwhelming. He thus finally agreed to issue an ultimatum threatening the Rebel government with the plan of retaliation urged by Stanton and the committee. As in the past, however, the president remained leery of personally ordering acts of retaliation, and he ultimately he took no action. Confederate prisoners of war wound up bearing the brunt of Union wrath. Instead of issuing a presidential decree, Lincoln gave free rein to Stanton, who promptly directed Hoffman to initiate reductions in prisoner rations, essential equipment, and medical care. As a result, prisoners in camps across the North sickened and died by the hundreds of malnutrition, exposure, and disease. It must again be emphasized that these deaths occurred precisely because Stanton and his generals, with the enthusiastic support of Wade and the Committee on the Conduct of the War and the full knowledge of President Lincoln, coolly and deliberately chose to withhold food, supplies, and medical care—all of which were readily available.

As historians have correctly maintained, the president did not possess the authority to interfere directly with the official investigations of Wade and his committee. Nor could he silence their cries for retaliation.[48] At any time, however, Lincoln could have instructed Stanton to rescind the orders that were causing the deaths of prisoners, and he could have directed that a policy of humane treatment be instituted in the camps. He chose otherwise. And although it is quite true that there is no extant record of the president personally ordering acts of retaliation or other sorts of mistreatment of prisoners of war, it is equally true that there is no evidence that he ever expressed outrage or even dismay at the obvious fact that in camps across the North helpless prisoners were suffering and dying because of the policies of his administration and the actions of his subordinates.

Lincoln's failure to improve the lot of captives is even more damning when one considers that he did not hesitate to intervene directly into prisoner affairs when he perceived a personal or political benefit to be gained from doing so. Such was the case on 18 March 1864, when he wrote Stanton seeking relief from the "intolerable pressure" he was receiving about the disposition of prisoners whose homes, by that point in the war, lay within Union lines. Large numbers of such prisoners had asked that they be allowed to take the oath of allegiance and be discharged to their homes rather than be exchanged. Driven by public opinion, Lincoln reluctantly backed this course of action, and Stanton acceded to the president's wishes.[49]

Nor did Lincoln shy away from intervening directly into the minutiae of exchange operations when it would improve the fortunes of the Republican Party.

On most occasions, his interventions took the form of presidential correspondence ordering that an exchange be arranged for specific Union prisoners with politically powerful kin. A typical example of this sort occurred on 19 March 1864, when Lincoln ordered Butler to "find a Captain among the rebel prisoners . . . and exchange for Capt. T. Ten Eyck . . . now a prisoner at Richmond." The imprisoned Union captain was the son of New Jersey senator John C. Ten Eyck, and neither the president nor the senator balked at privately arranging the younger Ten Eyck's freedom even as they publicly professed support for the official administration policy prohibiting such exchanges. On another occasion Lincoln was so desperate to obtain the release of Major Harry White, a senator in the Pennsylvania legislature deemed essential to the continued Republican control of the state, that he directed Hitchcock to offer a Confederate brigadier general in exchange.[50] But despite all this involvement and interaction, not a single case exists in which the president intervened to upgrade conditions in the camps or reverse the directives that were resulting in so much misery and death. In the end, Abraham Lincoln must be held as accountable as his subordinates for the shameful history of the Union prisoner-of-war system.

Years ago, historian Ovid Futch suggested that it was "illogical to argue that since exchange would have saved lives, refusal to exchange caused deaths." Men who survived the prisons and were returned to the ranks through exchange, Futch maintained, might very well have fallen in battle or been struck down by disease.[51] Perhaps. But while Futch's argument posits only possibilities, the statistics from the camps present a grim and inescapable reality. The brutal fact is that in places like Elmira, Andersonville, and a score of other Union and Confederate prisons, it was common for young men who were perfectly healthy when confined to sicken and die within the space of a few weeks. These soldiers were never afforded the opportunity to risk death on the battlefield. Because they were prisoners of war, they died far from the ravages of shot and shell or chance exposure to some fatal illness. Indeed, there was little at all that was random in their passing. Their lives ended in a tightly controlled, closely guarded environment. They died from the effects of overcrowding, poor sanitation, inadequate medical care, starvation, and needless exposure to the elements and contagious diseases, and the causes of their deaths were manifestly clear to those who confined them.

It is impossible to know the number of deaths that could have been prevented. What is clear, however, is that tens of thousands of captives would not have suffered and died as they did if the men who directed the prison systems of the North and the South had cared for them as their own regulations and basic humanity required. Yet this was something that they very deliberately chose not to do. The failure to treat prisoners humanely, young Sabina Dismukes had warned back in 1864, would "most surely draw down some awful judgment"; and at long last, that verdict must be rendered. For both the Union and the Confederacy, the treatment of prisoners during the American Civil War can only be judged "a most horrible national sin."[52]

Notes

ANHS	Andersonville National Historical Site
CWH	*Civil War History*
CWTI	*Civil War Times Illustrated*
GPO	Government Printing Office
GSA	Government Services Administration
LC	Library of Congress
NA	National Archives
OR	U.S. War Department. *The War of the Rebellion: A Compilation of the Official Records of the Union and Confederate Armies,* 128 vols. in 2 ser. Washington, D.C.: GPO, 1880–1901.
SHSP	*Southern Historical Society Papers*

INTRODUCTION

1. Bell I. Wiley, *The Life of Billy Yank: The Common Soldier of the Union* (Baton Rouge: Louisiana State University Press, 1991), 124; Bell I. Wiley, *The Life of Johnny Reb: The Common Soldier of the Confederacy* (Baton Rouge: Louisiana State University Press, 1990), 244. For an excellent summary of the impact of disease, see also James M. McPherson, *Ordeal by Fire: The Civil War and Reconstruction,* 3rd ed. (New York: McGraw-Hill, 2001), 416.

2. Sabina Dismukes to Jefferson Davis, 12 October 1864, in "A Statement of the Evidence Found in the Archive Office of the War Department Relating to the Treatment of Union Prisoners," Papers Relating to Confederate Camps and Other Places Where Federal Prisoners Were Confined during the Period 1861–1865, RG 109, Entry 464, Box 1, NA.

CHAPTER 1

1. James M. McPherson, *Battle Cry of Freedom: The Civil War Era* (New York: Oxford University Press, 1998), 238, 333.

2. The exact number of soldiers who became prisoners during the Civil War and the number of men who died in captivity will never be known. In 1866 Major General E. A. Hitchcock, the Union commissary general of prisoners, provided totals of 220,000 Confederates, of whom 26,436 died, and 126,952 Union soldiers, of whom 22,576 died. In 1930 historian William B. Hesseltine raised the number of captives to 220,000 Union and 220,000 Confederate. The most commonly accepted figures are those of General F. C. Ainsworth, chief of the U.S. Record and Pension Office. In 1903, Ainsworth made public various documents indicating that 194,743 Union soldiers and 214,865 Confederates were held for various periods of time, of which Union deaths totaled 30,218, or 15.5 percent, and Confederate deaths totaled 25,976, or 12.1 percent. William B. Hesseltine, *Civil War Prisons: A Study in War Psychology* (Columbus: Ohio State University Press, 1930), 2; McPherson, *Ordeal by Fire*, 486; *OR*, ser. 2, vol. 8, 946–48.

3. William E. S. Flory, *Prisoners of War: A Study in the Development of International Law* (Washington, D.C.: American Council on Public Affairs, 1942), 15, 17. Under the terms of the treaty, prisoners were to be released without ransom at the close of a war.

4. Charles G. Metzger, *The Prisoner in the American Revolution* (Chicago: Loyola University Press, 1971), 283; Larry G. Bowman, "The Pennsylvania Prisoner Exchange Conferences, 1778," *Pennsylvania History* 45, no. 3 (July 1978): 257.

5. Robert Leckie, *George Washington's War: The Saga of the American Revolution* (New York: Harper Collins, 1992), 332; Larry G. Bowman, *Captive Americans: Prisoners during the American Revolution* (Athens: Ohio University Press, 1976), 12–13, 17–19.

6. John C. Miller, *Triumph of Freedom, 1775–1783* (Boston: Little, Brown, 1948), 166; Emerson W. Reck, "Living Death on the Old *Jersey*," *American History Illustrated* 11, no. 3 (1976): 23.

7. Metzger, *Prisoner in the American Revolution*, 154.

8. Continental Congress, *Journals of the Continental Congress, 1774–1789*, 34 vols. (Washington, D.C.: GPO, 1904–1937), 9:939, 1009.

9. Thomas Fleming, *Liberty! The American Revolution* (New York: Viking Books, 1997), 296; Gerald O. Haffner, "The Treatment of Prisoners of War by the Americans during the War of Independence" (Ph.D. diss., Indiana University, 1952), 26.

10. Haffner, "Treatment of Prisoners," 187; Leckie, *George Washington's War*, 417.

11. Metzger, *Prisoner in the American Revolution*, 3–4; Haffner, "Treatment of Prisoners," 245; Claude Halstead Van Tyne, *The Loyalist in the American Revolution* (New York: Macmillan 1902), 274.

12. Bowman, *Captive Americans*, 97–99.

13. *Journals of the Continental Congress*, 21:830; Flory, *Prisoners of War*, 43; Bowman, *Captive Americans*, 81.

14. George Washington to General Thomas Gage, 20 August 1775, in *The Writings of George Washington*, 39 vols., ed. John C. Fitzpatrick (Washington, D.C.: GPO, 1931–1944), 3:416–17, 430–31.

15. Haffner, "Treatment of Prisoners," 151–54.

16. Bowman, *Captive Americans*, 84.

17. Ibid., 84–85.

18. *Journals of the Continental Congress*, 18:1028.

19. Bowman, *Captive Americans*, 103–4.

20. Metzger, *Prisoner in the American Revolution*, 222.

21. Ibid., 113–15.

22. Anthony G. Dietz, "The Prisoner of War in the United States during the War of 1812" (Ph.D. diss., American University, 1964), 9–11, 18–20.

23. Ibid., 27; Flory, *Prisoners of War,* 116–17.

24. Dietz, "Prisoner of War in the United States," 24, 29.

25. Donald R. Hickey, *The War of 1812: A Forgotten Conflict* (Urbana: University of Illinois Press, 1989), 177.

26. U.S. Congress, "Cartel for the Exchange of Prisoners of War between Great Britain and the United States of America," in *New American State Papers, Naval Affairs,* 10 vols., ed. Jack Bauer (Wilmington, Del.: Scholarly Resources, 1981), 8:13–21.

27. Dietz, "Prisoner of War in the United States," 51, 58.

28. Ibid., 61.

29. Ibid., 160–61.

30. Hickey, *War of 1812,* 177.

31. Steven A. Channing, *Crisis of Fear: Secession in South Carolina* (New York: W. W. Norton, 1974), 21.

32. Dietz, "Prisoner of War in the United States," 114.

33. Hickey, *War of 1812,* 154.

34. Dietz, "Prisoner of War in the United States," 115–16.

35. *American State Papers: Foreign Relations,* 6 vols. (Washington, D.C.: GPO, 1832–1859), 3:635.

36. Ibid., 640–41.

37. Ibid., 636; Hickey, *War of 1812,* 178.

38. Ralph Robinson, "Retaliation for the Treatment of Prisoners in the War of 1812," *American Historical Review* 49 (October 1943–July 1944): 70; Dietz, "Prisoner of War in the United States," 300.

39. U.S. Congress, "Cartel for the Exchange of Prisoners," in *New American State Papers,* ed. Bauer, 8:13–21.

40. Dietz, "Prisoner of War in the United States," 150–51.

41. Ibid., 151–52.

42. Justin H. Smith, *The War with Mexico,* 2 vols. (New York: Macmillan, 1919), 2:50.

43. John S. D. Eisenhower, *Agent of Destiny: The Life and Times of General Winfield Scott* (New York: Free Press, 1998), 256; Smith, *War with Mexico,* 2:58.

44. Winfield Scott, *Memoirs of Lieut.-General Scott, LL.D.,* 2 vols. (1864; reprint, Freeport, N.Y.: Books for Libraries Press, 1970), 1:441; Joseph E. Chance, "Prisoners of War: Mexican Prisoners," in *The United States and Mexico at War: Nineteenth-Century Expansionism and Conflict,* ed. Donald S. Frazier (New York: Macmillan, 1998), 333.

45. Smith, *War with Mexico,* 2:353 n. 30; T. Michael Parrish, "Taylor's Armistice," in *United States and Mexico at War,* ed. Frazier, 407.

46. Flory, *Prisoners of War,* 18; Bruce Winders, "Prisoners of War: U.S. Prisoners," in *United States and Mexico at War,* ed. Frazier, 335; U.S. Congress, House, *Mexican War Correspondence. Message of the President of the United States, and the Correspondence Therewith Communicated, between the Secretary of War and Other Officers of the Government upon the Subject of the Mexican War.* 30th Cong., 1st sess., 1848, House Ex. Doc. No. 60, 983.

47. Chance, "Prisoners of War: Mexican Prisoners," in *United States and Mexico at War,* ed. Frazier,

334; James M. McCaffrey, *The Army of Manifest Destiny: The American Soldier in the Mexican War, 1846–1848* (New York: New York University Press, 1992), 194–95.

48. McCaffrey, *Army of Manifest Destiny,* 194.

49. W. A. Croffut, ed., *Fifty Years in Camp and Field: Diary of Major General Ethan Allen Hitchcock, U.S.A.* (New York: G. P. Putnam's Sons, 1909), 305, 307. For a more sympathetic account of Scott's imposition of military government, see Ralph H. Gabriel, "American Experience with Military Government," *American Historical Review* 49 (October 1943–July 1944): 634–37.

CHAPTER 2

1. *OR,* ser. 1, vol. 1, 2, 108.

2. Ibid., 109.

3. Ibid.; Emory M. Thomas, *The Confederate Nation, 1861–1865* (New York: History Book Club, 1979), 68.

4. J. J. Bowden, *The Exodus of Federal Forces from Texas, 1861* (Austin: Eakin Press, 1986), 3.

5. *OR,* ser. 1, vol. 1, 579–80.

6. Ibid., 580; Bowden, *Exodus of Federal Forces,* 37.

7. Bowden, *Exodus of Federal Forces,* 33.

8. *OR,* ser. 2, vol. 1, 25.

9. Ibid., 26.

10. Hesseltine, *Civil War Prisons,* 2; *OR,* ser. 2, vol. 1, 22.

11. *OR,* ser. 2, vol. 1, 1–2.

12. Ibid., ser. 1, vol. 1, 503–4, and ser. 2, vol. 1, 32–35.

13. Bowden, *Exodus of Federal Forces,* 62.

14. *OR,* ser. 2, vol. 1, 2, 6.

15. Ibid., 31.

16. Ibid.

17. Bowden, *Exodus of Federal Forces,* 56.

18. *OR,* ser. 1, vol. 1, 581; Bowden, *Exodus of Federal Forces,* 39.

19. *OR,* ser. 2, vol. 1, 9–10; *New York Times,* 9 June 1861.

20. *OR,* ser. 2, vol. 1, 12.

21. Bowden, *Exodus of Federal Forces,* 105; *OR,* ser. 1, vol. 1, 623.

22. Bowden, *Exodus of Federal Forces,* 101.

23. William H. Powell, *Powell's Record of Living Officers of the United States Army* (Philadelphia: L. R. Hamersley, 1890), 67; *OR,* ser. 2, vol. 1, 102, 87.

24. *OR,* ser. 2, vol. 1, 56.

25. Earl Van Dorn to Emily Van Dorn, in Emily Van Dorn Miller, *A Soldier's Honor* (New York: n.p., 1902), 52.

26. Stephen Schwartz, *Twenty-Two Months a Prisoner of War* (St. Louis: F. Nelson, 1891), 74–75.

27. *OR,* ser. 2, vol. 1, 106.

28. Ibid., ser. 1, vol. 1, 670.

29. Hesseltine, *Civil War Prisons,* 6; *OR,* ser. 2, vol. 1, 106–8.

30. *OR,* ser. 2, vol. 1, 108.

31. Abner Doubleday, "From Moultrie to Sumter," in *Battles and Leaders of the Civil War,* 4 vols. (1888; reprint, Secaucus, N.J.: Castle, 1982), 1:48.

32. Bowden, *Exodus of Federal Forces,* 89; Lonnie Speer, *Portals to Hell: Military Prisons of the Civil War* (Mechanicsburg, Pa.: Stackpole Books, 1997), 4.

33. *OR,* ser. 2, vol. 1, 1.

34. Jefferson Davis, *The Rise and Fall of the Confederate Government,* 2 vols. (New York: D. Appleton, 1881), 2:582; Confederate States of America, *A Digest of the Military and Naval Laws of the Confederate States, from the Commencement of the Provisional Congress to the End of the First Congress under the Permanent Constitution* (Columbia, S.C.: Evans and Cogswell, 1864). For an example of northern coverage of Davis's actions, see the *New York Times,* 18 April 1861.

35. Kenneth J. Hagan, *This People's Navy: The Making of American Sea Power* (New York: Free Press, 1991), 16; Allan R. Millett and Peter Maslowski, *For the Common Defense: A Military History of the United States of America* (New York: Free Press, 1994), 112.

36. *New York Times,* 16 June 1861.

37. Davis, *Rise and Fall,* 2:582.

38. Ivan Musicant, *Divided Waters: The Naval History of the Civil War* (New York: Harper Collins, 1995), 50; *OR,* ser. 2, vol. 3, 13; Hesseltine, *Civil War Prisons,* 8.

39. *OR,* ser. 2, vol. 3, 4.

40. James D. Richardson, ed. and comp., *The Messages and Papers of Jefferson Davis and the Confederacy, Including Diplomatic Correspondence, 1961–1865,* 2 vols. (New York: Chelsea House–Robert Hector, 1966), 1:115–16.

41. *OR,* ser. 2, vol. 3, 689.

42. Confederate States of America War Department, *Laws for the Army and Navy of the Confederate States* (Richmond, Va.: Ritchie and Dunnavant, 1861), 80–81.

43. Richardson, ed., *Messages and Papers of Jefferson Davis,* 1:115–16.

44. Roy P. Basler, ed., *The Collected Works of Abraham Lincoln,* 9 vols. (New Brunswick, N.J.: Rutgers University Press, 1953–1955), 4:332.

45. Don E. Fehrenbacher, ed., *Abraham Lincoln: Speeches and Writings, 1859–1865* (New York: Library of America, 1989), 257; David H. Donald, *Lincoln* (London: Jonathan Cape, 1995), 302; Basler, ed., *Collected Works,* 4:421–41.

46. *New York Times,* 26 June 1861.

47. John D. Gordon III, "The Trial of the Officers and Crew of the Schooner 'Savannah,'" *Yearbook—Supreme Court Historical Society* (1983): 40.

48. James G. Randall, *Constitutional Problems under Lincoln,* rev. ed. (Urbana: University of Illinois Press, 1964), 93.

49. Ibid., 94; Carl Sandburg, *Abraham Lincoln: The War Years,* 4 vols. (New York: Harcourt Brace, 1939), 1:287.

50. Donald, *Lincoln,* 302.

CHAPTER 3

1. Shelby Foote, *The Civil War: A Narrative,* vol. 1, *Fort Sumter to Perryville* (New York: Vintage Books, 1986), 71; William C. Davis, *Battle at Bull Run: A History of the First Major Campaign of the*

Civil War (Norwalk, Conn.: Easton Press, 1996), 74–77.

2. McPherson, *Ordeal by Fire,* 212; Davis, *Battle at Bull Run,* 252.

3. Emory M. Thomas, *The Confederate State of Richmond: A Biography of the Capital* (Austin: University of Texas Press, 1971), 61.

4. William H. Jeffrey, *Richmond Prisons, 1861–1862, Compiled from the Original Records Kept by the Confederate Government, Journals Kept by Union Prisoners of War, Together with the Name, Rank, Company, Regiment, and State of the Four Thousand Who Were Confined There* (St. Johnsbury, Vt.: Republican Press, 1893), 7–8.

5. Thomas, *Confederate State of Richmond,* 59–60.

6. J. L. Burrows, "Recollections of Libby Prison," *SHSP* 11 (February–March 1883): 83–84.

7. *OR,* ser. 2, vol. 3, 691.

8. Confederate States of America War Department, *Laws for the Army and Navy of the Confederate States,* 61.

9. *Richmond Enquirer,* 30 July 1861.

10. B. B. Vassal and W. A. Abbott to William H. Jeffrey, May 1890, quoted in Jeffrey, *Richmond Prisons,* 89–90, 97–98.

11. Alfred Ely, *Journal of Alfred Ely, A Prisoner of War in Richmond,* ed. Charles Lanman (New York: D. Appleton, 1862), 4; Speer, *Portals to Hell,* 23.

12. Jeffrey, *Richmond Prisons,* 9.

13. Arch Frederic Blakey, *General John H. Winder, C.S.A.* (Gainesville: University of Florida Press, 1990), 14–25.

14. Hickey, *War of 1812,* 199–201.

15. While a number of Winder's contemporaries asserted that he perceived slights concerning the Bladensburg episode where none existed, other evidence suggests that his sensitivity might have been well justified. In his very first reference to Winder, for example, John B. Jones, the oft-quoted war clerk and diarist of Richmond, referred to him as the son of the man who "unfortunately permitted the City of Washington to fall into the hands of the enemy." See John B. Jones, *A Rebel War Clerk's Diary,* ed. Earl Schenk Miers (Baton Rouge: Louisiana State University Press, 1993), 31.

16. Blakey, *Winder,* 7.

17. Ibid., 7–8.

18. Ibid., 29, 45.

19. Thomas, *Confederate State of Richmond,* 36–39; Blakey, *Winder,* 50.

20. Jones, *Diary,* 39–40; *Richmond Examiner,* 2 October 1861.

21. Blakey, *Winder,* 51–52, 56.

22. Hesseltine, *Civil War Prisons,* ix. For similar examples of this argument, see Blakey, *Winder,* 57, and Reid Mitchell, "'Our Prison System, Supposing We Had Any': The Confederate and Union Prison Systems," in *On the Road to Total War: The American Civil War and the German Wars of Unification, 1861–1871,* ed. Stig Förster and Jörg Nagler (Washington, D.C.: German Historical Institute, 1997), 566.

23. Sandra V. Parker, *Richmond's Civil War Prisons* (Lynchburg, Va.: H. E. Howard, 1990), 3.

24. *OR,* ser. 2, vol. 3, 756.

25. Papers Relating to Confederate Camps and Other Places Where Federal Prisoners Were Confined during the Period 1861–1865, Record Group (hereafter cited as RG) 109, Entry 464, Box 1, NA; *OR,* ser. 2, vol. 3, 732.

26. *OR*, ser 2, vol. 3, 734.

27. Benjamin to Clark, 4 November 1861, Papers Relating to Confederate Camps and Other Places Where Federal Prisoners Were Confined during the Period 1861–1865, RG 109, Entry 464, Box 1, NA.

28. Burton Craige to Benjamin, 27 November 1861, ibid.

29. Louis A. Brown, *The Salisbury Prison: A Case Study of Confederate Military Prisons, 1861–1865* (Wendell, N.C.: Avery Press, 1980), 2; Speer, *Portals to Hell,* 32. The commander, a man of the cloth by training and therefore unfamiliar with things military, nonetheless proved a quick study of the politics of command. Within two weeks he was petitioning Benjamin to authorize an increase in the size of his force and a promotion for himself. Trinity College is today Duke University.

30. Henry T. Clarke to Benjamin, 2 November 1861, Papers Relating to Confederate Camps and Other Places Where Federal Prisoners Were Confined during the Period 1861–1865, RG 109, Entry 464, Box 1, NA.

31. Benjamin to A. B. Moore, 25 October 1861, ibid.

32. *OR,* ser. 2, vol. 3, 745.

33. Ibid., 757–58.

34. Ibid., 733–34.

35. *Charleston Mercury,* 14 September 1861.

36. Speer, *Portals to Hell, 30; OR,* ser. 2, vol. 3, 723.

37. Lynda Lasswell Crist, ed., *The Papers of Jefferson Davis,* vol. 7, *1861* (Baton Rouge: Louisiana State University Press, 1992), 261.

38. Richard D. Goff, *Confederate Supply* (Durham, N.C.: Duke University Press, 1969), 17–18.

39. Blakey, *Winder,* 61; Ely, *Prisoner of War,* 69, 100.

40. Ely, *Prisoner of War,* 69; Hesseltine, *Civil War Prisons,* 59.

41. Ely, *Prisoner of War,* 101.

42. Blakey, *Winder,* 62.

43. Brown, *Salisbury Prison,* 46.

44. Jeffrey, *Richmond Prisons,* 87–88.

45. Ibid., 131.

46. Speer, *Portals to Hell,* 24.

47. Thomas, *Confederate State of Richmond,* 61.

48. *Richmond Enquirer,* 17 and 20 September 1861.

49. Blakey, *Winder,* 64.

CHAPTER 4

1. U.S. War Department, *Revised Regulations for the Army of the United States, 1861* (Philadelphia: J. G. L. Brown, 1861), 107.

2. *OR,* ser. 2, vol. 3, 9–10.

3. Lawrence Sangston, *The Bastilles of the North* (Baltimore: Kelly, Hedian, and Piet, 1863), 23; Francis K. Howard, *Fourteen Months in American Bastilles* (Baltimore: Kelly, Hedian, and Piet, 1863), 18, 22.

4. John A. Marshall, *American Bastille: A History of the Illegal Arrests and Imprisonment of American Citizens during the Late Civil War* (Philadelphia: Thomas W. Hartley, 1869), vi; Richard F. Hammerlein, *Prisons and Prisoners of the Civil War* (Boston: Christopher Publishing House, 1934), 26.

5. Howard, *Fourteen Months,* 17–30; Speer, *Portals to Hell,* 37–38.

6. Speer, *Portals to Hell,* 39–40; Hammerlein, *Prisons and Prisoners,* 26.

7. *OR,* ser. 2, vol. 3, 47.

8. Hesseltine, *Civil War Prisons,* 36; *OR,* ser. 2, vol. 3, 45–46.

9. *OR,* ser. 2, vol. 3, 47.

10. Hesseltine, *Civil War Prisons,* 36–37; *OR,* ser. 2, vol. 3, 45.

11. *OR,* ser. 2, vol. 3, 10.

12. Speer, *Portals to Hell,* 45.

13. Constance M. Green, *Washington: Village and Capital, 1800–1878* (Princeton: Princeton University Press, 1962), 252.

14. Margaret Leech, *Reveille in Washington, 1860–1865* (New York: Harper and Brothers, 1941), 106.

15. Minor H. McLain, "The Military Prison at Fort Warren," in *Civil War Prisons,* ed. William Hesseltine (Kent, Ohio: Kent State University Press, 1962), 34; *OR,* ser. 2, vol. 2, 120.

16. *OR,* ser. 2, vol. 2, 110–11.

17. Sangston, *Bastilles of the North,* 65–66; *OR,* ser. 2, vol. 2, 110; McLain, "Fort Warren," 34.

18. McLain, "Fort Warren," 34, 35.

19. Ibid., 35.

20. Theodore B. Hassel to his cousin, 13 April 1864, in McLain, "Fort Warren," 40.

21. Sangston, *Bastilles of the North,* 72.

22. J. Thomas Scharf, *History of St. Louis City and County, from the Earliest Periods to the Present Day* (Philadelphia: Louis H. Everts, 1883), 404; William B. Hesseltine, "Military Prisons of St. Louis," *Missouri Historical Review* 23, no. 3 (1929): 381.

23. Scharf, *History of St. Louis,* 417–18; *Missouri Republican,* 1 June and 27 December 1861.

24. *OR,* ser. 2, vol. 3, 169.

25. Hesseltine, *Civil War Prisons,* 37; *OR,* ser. 2, vol. 3, 216.

26. *OR,* ser. 2, vol. 3, 185–86.

27. Ibid., ser. 1, vol. 7, 40; Leslie G. Hunter, "Warden for the Union: General William Hoffman (1807–1884)" (Ph.D. diss., University of Arizona, 1971), 20.

28. Phillip R. Shriver and Donald J. Breen, *Ohio's Military Prisons in the Civil War* (Columbus: Ohio State University Press, 1964), 7–8.

29. *OR,* ser. 2, vol. 3, 48.

30. Shriver and Breen, *Ohio's Military Prisons,* 7–8; *OR,* ser. 2, vol. 3, 136.

31. Blakey, *Winder,* 64; Russell F. Weigley, *Quartermaster General of the Union Army: A Biography of M. C. Meigs* (New York: Columbia University Press, 1959), 165.

32. Hunter, "Warden for the Union," 1; *OR,* ser. 2, vol. 3, 8.

33. Blakey, *Winder,* xv; OR, ser., 1, vol. 51, pt. 2, 482.

34. *OR,* ser. 2, vol. 3, 32.

35. Ibid., 48.

36. Hunter, "Warden for the Union," 15.

37. Ibid., 11; *OR,* ser. 1, vol. 1, 517–18.

38. *OR,* ser. 2, vol. 1, 43–44.

39. Ibid., 58.

40. Hunter, "Warden for the Union," 13–14.

41. *OR,* ser. 2, vol. 1, 73.

42. Hunter, "Warden for the Union," 14; *OR,* ser. 2, vol. 1, 81–82.

43. *OR,* ser. 2, vol. 3, 121.

44. Ibid., 49.

45. Hunter, "Warden for the Union," 22; *OR,* ser. 2, vol. 3, 54–56.

46. Hesseltine, *Civil War Prisons,* 38; *OR,* ser. 2, vol. 3, 56.

47. *OR,* ser. 2, vol. 3, 55–58.

48. Ibid., 57.

49. Shriver and Breen, *Ohio's Military Prisons,* 30; *OR,* ser. 2, vol. 3, 122–23.

50. Hunter, "Warden for the Union," 29–30.

51. *OR,* ser. 2, vol. 3, 32.

52. Hunter, "Warden for the Union," 31–32.

53. Shriver and Breen, *Ohio's Military Prisons,* 29–30; *OR,* ser. 2, vol. 3, 169.

54. Shriver and Breen, *Ohio's Military Prisons,* 30; Alan A. Kurnat, "Prison Life at Johnson's Island," *Western Reserve Magazine* 6 (September–October 1981): 30.

55. Hunter, "Warden for the Union," 34–35.

56. Ibid., 35.

57. *OR,* ser. 2, vol. 3, 169.

58. *New York Times,* 31 October 1861.

CHAPTER 5

1. Basler, ed., *Collected Works,* 5:86.

2. See, for example, McPherson, *Battle Cry of Freedom,* 791–92; Randall, *Constitutional Problems under Lincoln,* 64; Stephen W. Sears, *To the Gates of Richmond: The Peninsula Campaign* (New York: Ticknor and Fields, 1992), 161.

3. Basler, ed., *Collected Works,* 4:426, 441.

4. McPherson, *Battle Cry of Freedom,* 184.

5. Davis, *Rise and Fall,* 2:13–14.

6. Phillip Shaw Paludan, *The Presidency of Abraham Lincoln* (Lawrence: University Press of Kansas, 1994), 80–81.

7. *New York Times,* 26 June 1861.

8. Blakey, *Winder,* 62–63; Ely, *Prisoner of War,* 212; Davis, *Rise and Fall,* 2:10.

9. Ely, *Prisoner of War,* 212, 213; *OR,* ser. 2, vol. 3, 738–39.

10. Michael Corcoran, *The Captivity of General Corcoran* (Philadelphia: Barclay, 1862), 13–14.

11. See, for example, the *New York Times,* 11 August 1861.

12. Thomas, "Prisoner of War Exchange," 56; Corcoran, *Captivity,* 27, 50, 61, 89.

13. *OR,* ser. 2, vol. 3, 265.

14. Hesseltine, *Civil War Prisons,* 19; *OR,* ser. 2, vol. 3, 246.

15. *New York Times,* 1 and 5 August 1861.

16. Ely, *Prisoner of War,* 68.

17. Jeffrey, *Richmond Prisons*, 44–45.

18. Ely, *Prisoner of War*, 68.

19. *OR*, ser. 2, vol. 3, 160, 126.

20. John Y. Simon, ed., *The Papers of Ulysses S. Grant* (Carbondale: Southern Illinois University Press, 1970), 3:39n.

21. *OR*, ser. 2, vol. 1, 526–27.

22. David Donald, ed., *Inside Lincoln's Cabinet: The Civil War Diaries of Salmon P. Chase* (New York: Longman's, Green, 1954), 48–49.

23. *OR*, ser. 2, vol. 3, 152–53.

24. State of Michigan, Senate, *Resolutions of the Legislature of Michigan in Favor of the Adoption of Measures for the Exchange of Prisoners*. 34th Cong., 2d sess., 1862, Misc. Doc. 23; *OR*, ser. 2, vol. 3, 211.

25. *OR*, ser. 2, vol. 3, 157.

26. Ibid., vol. 1, 560–61.

27. Hesseltine, *Civil War Prisons*, 16–17; *OR*, ser. 2, vol. 3, 155–56.

28. Lieutenant William Biggs to Colonel Justin Dimick, 21 January 1862, Union Provost Marshal's File, Rolls of Confederate Prisoners, Purchased May 3, 1879, RG 109, Entry 199, Box 1, NA; *OR*, ser. 2, vol. 3, 128–29.

29. *OR*, ser. 2, vol. 3, 137.

30. Ibid., 51–52.

31. Ibid., 128, 753.

32. Ibid., 157.

33. Ibid., vol. 1, 69–70.

34. Hesseltine, *Civil War Prisons*, 18; *OR*, ser. 2, vol. 3, 175, and ser. 1, vol. 9, 353.

35. *National Intelligencer*, 21 January 1862.

36. *OR*, ser. 2, vol. 3, 191–92.

37. Ibid., 774.

38. Ibid., 777.

39. Hesseltine, *Civil War Prisons*, 19–21; *OR*, ser. 2, vol. 3, 212.

40. Hesseltine, *Civil War Prisons*, 20–21; *OR*, ser. 2, vol. 3, 213, 222–23, 230.

41. *OR*, ser. 2, vol. 3, 778–79.

42. Ibid., 248–50.

43. Ibid., 254.

44. *New York Times*, 15 February 1862; *OR*, ser. 2, vol. 3, 261.

45. *OR*, ser. 2, vol. 3, 302.

46. Hesseltine, *Civil War Prisons*, 24–25; *OR*, ser. 2, vol. 3, 302, 322.

47. Hesseltine, *Civil War Prisons*, 26.

48. *OR*, ser. 2, vol. 3, 333.

49. Hesseltine, *Civil War Prisons*, 25–26; *OR*, ser. 2, vol. 3, 811, 376, 460–61.

50. *OR*, ser. 2, vol. 3, 266.

51. Hattie Lou Winslow and Joseph R. H. Moore, *Camp Morton, 1861–1865, Indianapolis Prison Camp* (Indianapolis: Indiana Historical Society, 1940), 253; *OR*, ser. 2, vol. 3, 269, 274.

52. *OR*, ser. 2, vol. 3, 269.

53. Hunter, "Warden for the Union," 47; *OR*, ser. 2, vol. 3, 268.

54. *OR,* ser. 2, vol. 3, 277.

55. Hoffman to Meigs, 24 February 1862, Office of the Commissary General of Prisoners, Letters Sent, RG 249, NA.

56. *OR,* ser. 2, vol. 3, 316–17.

57. Winslow and Moore, *Camp Morton,* 255–56.

58. *Indianapolis Journal,* 20 February 1862.

59. *OR,* ser. 2, vol. 3, 515.

60. James E. Paton, "The Civil War Journal of James E. Paton," *Register of the Kentucky Historical Society* 61 (1963): 228.

61. Winslow and Moore, *Camp Morton,* 256; Speer, *Portals to Hell,* 77.

62. Winslow and Moore, *Camp Morton,* 256, 275; *OR,* ser. 2, vol. 3, 516–17.

63. Winslow and Moore, *Camp Morton,* 256; *OR,* ser. 2, vol. 3, 375.

64. Hunter, "Warden for the Union," 53; *OR,* ser. 2, vol. 3, 386–87.

65. George Levy, *To Die in Chicago: Confederate Prisoners at Camp Douglas, 1862–1865* (Gretna, La.: Pelican, 1999), 41; Speer, *Portals to Hell,* 71–72.

66. Levy, *To Die in Chicago,* 45; *OR,* ser. 2, vol. 3, 297, 301.

67. *OR,* ser. 2, vol. 3, 312.

68. Hunter, "Warden for the Union," 4; *OR,* ser. 2, vol. 3, 297, 299.

69. *OR,* ser. 2, vol. 3, 361; Levy, *To Die in Chicago,* 56.

70. Ibid.

71. *OR,* ser. 2, vol. 3, 383, 386.

72. Levy, *To Die in Chicago,* 68; *OR,* ser. 2, vol. 4, 106; Speer, *Portals to Hell,* 72.

73. Levy, *To Die in Chicago,* 68, 73; *OR,* ser. 2, vol. 4, 106.

74. *OR,* ser. 2, vol. 4, 129.

75. Speer, *Portals to Hell,* 73; *OR,* ser. 2, vol. 5, 379.

76. *OR,* ser. 2, vol. 3, 364.

77. Ibid., 363; Hoffman to quartermaster, 10 March 1862, Office of the Commissary General of Prisoners, Letters Sent, RG 249, NA.

78. *Illinois State Register,* 10 March 1862; Speer, *Portals to Hell,* 74.

79. Camilla A. C. Quinn, "Forgotten Soldiers: The Confederate Prisoners at Camp Butler, 1862–1863," *Illinois Historical Journal* 81, no. 1 (Spring 1985): 38.

80. *OR,* ser. 2, vol. 4, 245.

81. Ibid., vol. 3, 384.

82. Ibid., 448.

83. Shriver and Breen, *Ohio's Military Prisons,* 33–34.

84. *OR,* ser. 2, vol. 3, 280.

85. Ibid., vol. 4, 198; Shriver and Breen, *Ohio's Military Prisons,* 10–11.

86. Speer, *Portals to Hell,* 80.

87. *OR,* ser. 2, vol. 3, 499–500.

88. Ibid., 337.

89. Shriver and Breen, *Ohio's Military Prisons,* 14.

90. *OR,* ser. 2, vol. 4, 195–208.

91. Lazelle to Commander, Camp Chase, 14 July 1862, Letters, Telegrams, Orders, and Circulars

Received from the Commissary General of Prisoners Relating to Paroled Federal Prisoners and to Confederate Prisoners of War, 1862–1865, RG 249, Entry 167, NA; *OR*, ser. 2, vol. 4, 195–208.

92. *OR*, ser. 2, vol. 4, 197.

93. Ibid., vol. 3, 471.

94. Nancy Travis Keen, "Confederate Prisoners at Fort Delaware," *Delaware History* 13 (1968): 1–2.

95. Hoffman to Stanton, 15 June 1862, and Hoffman to Captain A. A. Gibson, 15 June 1862, Office of the Commissary General of Prisoners, Letters Sent, RG 249, NA; *OR*, ser. 2, vol. 4, 23.

96. *OR*, ser. 2, vol. 4, 120.

97. Hoffman to Commander Fort Columbus, 16 June 1862, and Hoffman to Stanton, 17 June 1862, Office of the Commissary General of Prisoners, Letters Sent, RG 249, NA.

98. See, for example, Hoffman to the commander of Camp Butler, *OR*, ser. 2, vol. 3, 363.

99. *OR*, ser. 2, vol. 3, 8.

100. Ibid., 156.

101. Ibid., 327.

102. Hoffman to Meigs, 19 March 1862, Office of the Commissary General of Prisoners, Letters Sent, RG 249, NA; *OR*, ser. 2, vol. 3, 389–90.

103. *OR*, ser. 2, vol. 3, 390.

104. Ibid., 417–18.

105. Hoffman to Meigs, 2 April 1862, Office of the Commissary General of Prisoners, Letters Sent, RG 249, NA; *OR*, ser. 2, vol. 4, 30.

106. *OR*, ser. 2, vol. 4, 196.

107. Hoffman to Meigs, 5 June 1862, Office of the Commissary General of Prisoners, Letters Sent, RG 249, NA.

108. Brown, *Salisbury Prison*, 22: *OR*, ser. 2, vol. 3, 766; *New York Times,* 9 July 1862.

109. *OR*, ser. 2, vol. 3, 142.

110. Robert W. Waitt Jr., *Confederate Military Hospitals in Richmond* (Richmond, Va.: Richmond Civil War Centennial Committee, 1964), 8, 14–17.

111. Parker, *Richmond's Prisons*, 9; Blakey, *Winder,* 155.

112. *New York Times,* 6 November 1863.

113. Parker, *Richmond's Prisons,* 11.

114. Sallie Brock Putnam, *Richmond during the War: Four Years of Personal Observation* (New York: G. W. Carlton, 1867), 154; Thomas, *Confederate State of Richmond,* 97; Blakey, *Winder,* 138.

115. *OR*, ser. 2, vol. 4, 777, 779.

116. Parker, *Richmond's Prisons,* 14–15; Blakey, *Winder,* 156; *Richmond Enquirer,* 11 July 1862.

117. Parker, *Richmond's Prisons,* 15.

118. *OR*, ser. 2, vol. 3, 401.

119. Ibid., 883.

120. Hesseltine, *Civil War Prisons,* 29; *OR*, ser. 2, vol. 3, 884.

121. Hesseltine, *Civil War Prisons,* 28–29; *OR*, ser. 2, vol. 3, 881–86.

122. Hesseltine, *Civil War Prisons,* 29; *OR*, ser. 2, vol. 3, 886.

123. U.S. Congress, House, *Exchange of Prisoners of War.* 37th Cong., 2d sess., 1862, H. Ex. Doc. 124, 4–6; *OR*, ser. 2, vol. 3, 654.

124. *OR,* ser. 2, vol. 3, 663, 666.

125. U.S. Congress, House, *Exchange of Prisoners of War.* 38th Cong., 2d sess., 1865, H. Ex. Doc. 20, 8:1–3.

126. *New York Times,* 9 July 1862.

127. Ibid.; Ely, *Prisoner of War,* 279.

128. Ibid.

129. *New York Times,* 9 July 1862; *OR,* ser. 2, vol. 4, 53, 797–98.

130. *OR,* ser. 2, vol. 4, 168, 210.

131. Basler, ed., *Collected Works,* 5:380–81, 7:42; William C. Davis, *Lincoln's Men: How President Lincoln Became Father to an Army and a Nation* (New York: Free Press, 1999), 124; Ely, *Prisoner of War,* 279.

132. See James M. McPherson, *Abraham Lincoln and the Second American Revolution* (New York: Oxford University Press, 1990), 66, and Donald, *Lincoln,* 392.

133. *Illinois State Register,* 10 March 1862.

134. See Randall, *Constitutional Problems under Lincoln,* 154–55, and Davis, *Lincoln's Men,* 123–24.

135. Lincoln to Halleck, 9 April 1862, and Lincoln to Officer in Charge of Confederate Prisoners at Camp Chase, Ohio, John G. Nicolay Papers, Box 12, Manuscript Division, LC.

136. Basler, ed., *Collected Works,* 5:403, 6:522.

137. Ibid., 5:264–65.

138. Benjamin P. Thomas and Harold M. Hyman, *Stanton: The Life and Times of Lincoln's Secretary of War* (New York: Alfred A. Knopf, 1962), 371; *OR,* ser. 2, vol. 4, 174.

139. *OR,* ser. 2, vol. 4, 266–68.

140. Ibid.

141. Ibid., 268; Bauer, ed., *New American State Papers,* 8:21.

142. *New York Times,* 13 July 1862; *Richmond Dispatch,* 16 and 25 July 1862.

CHAPTER 6

1. *Richmond Dispatch,* 16 August 1862; Holland Thompson, ed., *The Photographic History of the Civil War,* vol. 4, *Prisons and Hospitals* (1911; reprint, Secaucus, N.Y.: Blue and Gray Press, 1987), 109; Hesseltine, *Civil War Prisons,* 69–70. The full title of Corcoran's work—*The Captivity of General Corcoran, the Only Authentic and Reliable Narrative of the Trials and Sufferings Endured during his Twelve Months' Imprisonment in Richmond and Other Southern Cities, by Brig. General Michael Corcoran, the Hero of Bull Run*—was almost as long as his period of captivity!

2. Edward Younger, ed., *Inside the Confederate Government: The Diary of Robert Garlick Hill Kean* (1957: reprint, Baton Rouge: Louisiana State University Press, 1993), 27; Stewart Sifakis, *Who Was Who in the Civil War* (New York: Facts on File, 1988), 281.

3. Hoffman to Major S. Pierson, 15 June 1862, Letters, Telegrams, Orders, and Circulars Relating to Paroled Federal Prisoners and to Confederate Prisoners of War, 1862–1865, RG 249, Entry 167, NA; *OR,* ser. 2, vol. 4, 291.

4. *OR,* ser. 2, vol. 4, 365, 414.

5. Hoffman to Ekin, 22 August 1862, and Hoffman to Lazelle, 22 August 1862, Office of the Commissary General of Prisoners, Letters Sent, NA.

6. Hoffman to Brevet Brigadier General Richardson, 7 March 1862, Letters, Telegrams, Orders, and Circulars Received from the Commissary General of Prisoners Related to Paroled Federal Prisoners

and to Confederate Prisoners of War, 1862–1865, RG 249, Entry 167, NA.

7. Joe Barbiere, *Scraps from the Prison Table, at Camp Chase and Johnson's Island* (Doylestown, Pa.: W.W.H. Davis, 1868), 268–76.

8. Hoffman to Allison, 31 July 1862, Letters, Telegrams, Orders, and Circulars Relating to Paroled Federal Prisoners and to Confederate Prisoners of War, 1861–1865, RG 249, Entry 167, NA.

9. Hunter, "Warden for the Union," 111.

10. "Roll of Prisoners of War," Papers of General William Hoffman, 1862–1867 (hereafter Hoffman Papers), RG 249, NA.

11. Blakey, *Winder,* 154, 157, 159.

12. Hoffman to Lazelle, 12 June 1862, Hoffman Papers, RG 249, NA.

13. Aiken's Landing quickly proved too underdeveloped and isolated to serve as the eastern point of exchange, and operations were transferred to City Point, Virginia, thirteen miles north of Petersburg.

14. Hoffman to Stanton, 24 July 1862, Hoffman Papers, RG 249, NA; Hoffman to Stanton, 27 November 1862, Office of the Commissary General of Prisoners, Letters Sent, RG 249, NA.

15. Blakey, *Winder,* 157; Brown, *Salisbury Prison,* 2; *OR,* ser. 2, vol. 4, 413.

16. Notations of William S. Winder, Adjutant, Correspondence, Circulars, and Orders of the Confederate Military Prison at Richmond, Virginia, Relating to Federal Prisoners of War, RG 249, Entry 135, NA; Blakey, *Winder,* 159.

17. Hoffman to James A. Ekin et. al., n.d., Hoffman Papers, RG 249, NA; *OR,* ser. 2, vol. 4, 223, 307; Hunter, "Warden for the Union," 107.

18. *OR,* ser. 2, vol. 4, 393.

19. Thomas, "Prisoner of War Exchange," 94–95; Lincoln to Johnson, 4 June 1862, and Johnson to Lincoln, 5 June 1862, in Basler, ed., *Collected Works,* 5:260. Lincoln emphasis in original.

20. Circular, 7 July 1862, Letters, Telegrams, Orders, and Circulars Received from the Commissary General of Prisoners Relating to Paroled Federal Prisoners and to Confederate Prisoners of War, 1862–1865, RG 249, Entry 167, NA.

21. Ibid.

22. Ibid.

23. Ibid.

24. Ibid.

25. Hunter, "Warden for the Union," 94–95.

26. Papers Relating to Confederate Camps and Other Places Where Federal Prisoners Were Confined during the Period 1861–1865, RG 109, Entry 464, Box 1, NA; Joseph T. Helm, "Prison Life at Belle Isle," *The Cosmopolitan* n.v. (May 1893): 48.

27. Blakey, *Winder,* 157; Papers Relating to Confederate Camps and Other Places Where Federal Prisoners Were Confined during the Period 1861–1865, RG 109, Entry 464, Box 1, NA.

28. *OR,* ser. 2, vol. 4, 911; Blakey, *Winder,* 158.

29. Blakey, *Winder,* 156; *OR,* ser. 2, vol. 4, 821–22.

30. *OR,* ser. 2, vol. 4, 901.

31. Ibid., 821.

32. Ibid., 875; Blakey, *Winder,* 158.

33. *OR,* ser. 2, vol. 4, 30; Blakey, *Winder,* 159.

34. Davis, *Rise and Fall*, 2:314.

35. *Richmond Dispatch*, 1 August 1862; *OR*, ser. 2, vol. 4, 829.

36. *OR*, ser. 2, vol. 4, 830–31; *Richmond Dispatch*, 4 August 1862; Confederate States Army War Department, *General Orders from Adjutant and Inspector General's Office, Confederate States Army, in 1862* (Charleston, S.C.: Evans and Cogswell, 1863), 66–68. Hereafter referred to as *General Orders in 1862*.

37. *OR*, ser. 2, vol. 4, 830–31.

38. *Richmond Dispatch*, 5 July 1862; *OR*, ser. 2, vol. 4, 835, 329–30; William J. Cooper, *Jefferson Davis, American* (New York: Alfred Knopf, 2000), 407.

39. *OR*, ser. 2, vol. 4, 362; Herman Hattaway and Richard E. Beringer, *Jefferson Davis, Confederate President* (Lawrence: University Press of Kansas, 2002), 191.

40. Richardson, ed., *Messages and Papers of Jefferson Davis*, 1:234; *OR*, ser. 2, vol. 4, 854–55.

41. Confederate States Army War Department, *General Orders in 1862*, 72–73.

42. *OR*, ser. 2, vol. 4, 827–28.

43. Ibid., 306–7.

44. Hesseltine, *Civil War Prisons*, 84; *OR*, ser. 2, vol. 4, 346.

45. Barbiere, *Scraps from the Prison Table*, 130.

46. *OR*, ser. 2, vol. 4, 603.

47. Ibid., 621–22; Hesseltine, *Civil War Prisons*, 84.

48. *OR*, ser. 2, vol. 4, 94.

49. Ibid., 295–300.

50. Ibid., 297.

51. Ibid., 298; Hesseltine, *Civil War Prisons*, 75.

52. *OR*, ser. 2, vol. 4, 298.

53. Ibid., 250.

54. Hesseltine, *Civil War Prisons*, 75; *OR*, ser. 2, vol. 4, 242.

55. *OR*, ser. 2, vol. 4, 250–51.

56. Ibid., 288.

57. Ibid., 30.

58. Ibid., 689–690; S. C. Sears to "Friend Thomas," 20 February 1863, Drawer 3, Folder V973.772, Camp Parole, Maryland, ANHS.

59. *OR*, ser. 2, vol. 4, 698; Hunter, "Warden for the Union," 115–16.

60. *OR*, ser. 2, vol. 4, 696.

61. Ibid., 727.

62. Hoffman to Sangster, 21 November 1862, Office of the Commissary General of Prisoners, Letters Sent, RG 249, NA; *OR*, ser. 2, vol. 4, 771.

63. *OR*, ser. 2, vol. 4, 548.

64. Ibid., 545–46.

65. Ibid., 546.

66. Ibid., 360.

67. Ibid., vol. 5, 194.

68. Ibid., vol. 4, 499.

69. Ibid; Hesseltine, *Civil War Prisons*, 77.

70. *OR,* ser. 2, vol. 4, 519, 522.

71. Ibid., 563.

72. Basler, ed., *Collected Works,* 5:432.

73. *OR,* ser. 2, vol. 4, 569–71; Hesseltine, *Civil War Prisons,* 79.

74. *OR,* ser. 2, vol. 4, 571.

75. Ibid., 295.

76. Ibid., 594, 586, 620, 638–39, 749.

77. Hesseltine, *Civil War Prisons,* 79; *OR,* ser. 2, vol. 4, 562.

78. *OR,* ser. 2, vol. 4, 529; Foote, *Civil War,* 1:680.

79. *OR,* ser. 2, vol. 4, 542, 546–47, 596; Hesseltine, *Civil War Prisons,* 79.

80. Levy, *To Die in Chicago,* 92.

81. *OR,* ser. 2, vol. 4, 600; Levy, *To Die in Chicago,* 92.

82. Levy, *To Die in Chicago,* 94–95; *OR,* ser. 2, vol. 4, 645.

83. Levy, *To Die in Chicago,* 96.

84. Hesseltine, *Civil War Prisons,* 81; *OR,* ser. 2, vol. 4, 652–53.

85. *OR,* ser. 2, vol. 4, 937–38.

86. Ibid., vol. 5, 20.

87. Richardson, ed., *Messages and Papers of Jefferson Davis,* 1:271.

88. *Richmond Dispatch,* 24 December 1862.

89. Confederate States Army War Department, *General Orders in 1862,* 158; Richardson, ed., *Messages and Papers of Jefferson Davis,* 1:274.

90. *OR,* ser. 2, vol. 4, 892.

91. Ibid., 945–46.

92. Ibid., 954.

93. Hesseltine, *Civil War Prisons,* 85.

94. *OR,* ser. 2, vol. 5, 128.

95. U.S. Congress, *Journal of the Congress of the Confederate States of America, 1861–1865.* 7 vols. (Washington, D.C.: GPO, 1904–1905), 6:17 (hereafter *Journal of Congress);* Wilfred Buck Yearns, *The Confederate Congress* (Athens: University of Georgia Press, 1960), 164; *OR,* ser. 2, vol. 5, 807–8.

96. *OR,* ser. 2, vol. 5, 178, 186.

97. Yearns, *Confederate Congress,* 164.

98. Hesseltine, *Civil War Prisons,* 89.

99. *OR,* ser. 2, vol. 5, 394.

100. Ibid., 397.

101. Ibid., 398.

102. Ibid., 431.

103. Ibid., 469; Hesseltine, *Civil War Prisons,* 90.

104. *OR,* ser. 2, vol. 5, 306–7.

105. Confederate States of America, *A Digest of the Military and Naval Laws of the Confederate States, from the Commencement of the Provisional Congress to the End of the First Congress under the Permanent Constitution* (Columbia, S.C.: Evans and Cogswell, 1864), 172.

106. Papers Relating to Confederate Camps and Other Places Where Federal Prisoners Were Confined during the Period 1861–1865, RG 109, Entry 464, Box 1, NA.

107. Ibid.; *OR,* ser. 2, vol. 5, 691. For an account of the selection and treatment of the two Union hostages, see James Goldy, "I Have Done Nothing to Deserve this Penalty," *Civil War Times Illustrated* 25, no. 10 (February 1987): 17–21. The hostages were not executed.

108. *OR,* ser. 2, vol. 5, 703; Hesseltine, *Civil War Prisons,* 94.

109. *OR,* ser. 2, vol. 5, 946–47, 955–56, 960–69, 701–4.

110. Francis Lieber, *Contributions to Political Science* (Philadelphia: J. B. Lippincott, 1880), 268–69.

111. *OR,* ser. 2, vol. 5, 670–71.

112. Hesseltine, *Civil War Prisons,* 95; *OR,* ser. 2, vol. 5, 767.

113. OR, ser. 2, vol. 5, 691.

114. Ibid., 457.

115. Ibid., vol. 6, 69.

116. Richardson, ed., *Messages and Papers of Jefferson Davis,* 1:340–41.

117. *OR,* ser. 2, vol. 6, 78–79.

118. Ibid., 92–93; Hesseltine, *Civil War Prisons,* 100.

119. Hesseltine, *Civil War Prisons,* 100; *OR,* ser. 2, vol. 6, 112.

120. *OR,* ser. 2, vol. 6, 112, 126.

121. Ibid., 226.

122. Ibid., 224, 206, 218.

123. Ould to Meredith, 11 September 1863, Secretary of War, Schedule of Papers in the Archive Office Referring to the Exchange and Treatment of Prisoners of War in Southern Prisons, 1861–1865, RG 109, Vol. 245, Chap. 9, p. 29, NA; *OR,* ser. 2, vol. 6, 295.

124. *OR,* ser. 2, vol. 6, 305–7, 300.

125. See, for example, the *New York Times,* 10 November 1863.

126. *OR,* ser. 2, vol. 6, 457.

127. Ibid.

128. Ibid., 594.

129. Thomas, "Prisoner of War Exchange," 201.

130. *OR,* ser. 2, vol. 6, 505, 686.

131. *New York Times,* 2 December 1863; *OR,* ser. 2, vol. 6, 594–600.

132. Ibid.

133. *OR,* ser. 2, vol. 6, 527–28; Thomas, "Prisoner of War Exchange," 202–3.

134. Hesseltine, *Civil War Prisons,* 112; *OR,* ser. 2, vol. 6, 527–28, 532–34.

135. *OR,* ser. 2, vol. 6, 528.

136. *National Intelligencer,* 2 December 1863.

137. *New York Times,* 11 December 1863.

138. *OR,* ser. 2, vol. 6, 639.

139. Ibid., 691.

140. Ibid., 659, 691; Hesseltine, *Civil War Prisons,* 113.

141. *OR,* ser. 2, vol. 6, 711–12.

142. Ibid., 647–48.

143. President's Message on the Subject of Exchange of Prisoners, General Records of the Government of the Confederate States of America, Records Pertaining to Prisoners of War, RG 109, Entry 445, Box 3, NA; Richardson, ed., *Messages and Papers of Jefferson Davis,* 1:375–77.

CHAPTER 7

1. Speer, for example, contends that the "tragic period" of the camps should be dated from the opening of Elmira Prison in the North and Andersonville in the South, and Charles P. Roland's explanation of conditions at Andersonville and Elmira is presented with no discussion of the camps established earlier in the war. Speer, *Portals to Hell,* 241; Charles P. Roland, *An American Iliad: The Story of the Civil War* (New York: McGraw-Hill, 1991), 108–9.

2. Hunter, "Warden for the Union," 132; *OR,* ser. 2, vol. 6, 61.

3. *OR,* ser. 2, vol. 6, 61, 70, 113, 191–92; Speer, *Portals to Hell,* 134.

4. *OR,* ser. 2, vol. 6, 150–51; Hunter, "Warden for the Union," 134.

5. Levy, *To Die in Chicago,* 138.

6. *OR,* ser. 2, vol. 6, 200.

7. Ibid., 206.

8. Levy, *To Die in Chicago,* 141.

9. Hunter, "Warden for the Union," 153–54.

10. Hoffman to Stanton, 19 September 1863, Hoffman Papers, RG 249, NA; *OR,* ser. 2, vol. 6, 314.

11. *OR,* ser. 2, vol. 6, 434–35.

12. Ibid., 315; Hesseltine, *Civil War Prisons,* 184.

13. Lieber, *Contributions to Political Science,* 258, 261.

14. *OR,* ser. 2, vol. 6, 363.

15. Ibid., 371–74.

16. Ibid.

17. Ibid.

18. Ibid., 434.

19. Ibid., 374; Levy, *To Die in Chicago,* 162.

20. *OR,* ser. 2, vol. 6, 417.

21. Ibid., 315.

22. Ibid., 417, 315.

23. Lieber, *Contributions to Political Science,* 261.

24. Ibid.; Milton Asbury Ryan, "Experience of a Confederate Soldier in Camp and Prison in the Civil War, 1861–1865." http://www.izzy.net/~michaelg/ma-ryan.htm (accessed 24 December 2004).

25. *OR,* ser. 2, vol. 6, 637.

26. Ibid., 234.

27. T. R. Walker, "Rock Island Prison Barracks," in *Civil War Prisons,* ed. William B. Hesseltine (Kent, Ohio: Kent State University Press, 1962), 48–49.

28. *OR,* ser. 2, vol. 6, 196; Walker, "Rock Island Prison," 49, 50.

29. Walker, "Rock Island Prison," 49.

30. *OR,* ser. 2, vol. 6, 848; Walker, "Rock Island Prison," 50.

31. Richard A. Blondo, "A View of Point Lookout Prison Camp for Confederates," *Magazine of History* 8, No. 1 (Fall 1993): 30.

32. *OR,* ser. 2, vol. 6, 132.

33. Ibid., 577.

34. Blondo, "Point Lookout," 30; *OR,* ser. 2, vol. 6, 140, 183.

35. *OR,* ser. 2, vol. 6, 368.

36. Speer, *Portals to Hell,* 152–53; *OR,* ser. 2, vol. 6, 390.

37. *OR,* ser. 2, vol. 6, 422.

38. Ibid., 473, 489.

39. Blondo, "Point Lookout," 33; *OR,* ser. 2, vol. 6, 489.

40. Blondo, "Point Lookout," 33.

41. Jane Turner Censer, ed., *The Papers of Frederick Law Olmsted,* vol. 4, *Defending the Union: The Civil War and the U.S. Sanitary Commission, 1861–1863* (Baltimore: Johns Hopkins University Press, 1986), 684.

42. *OR,* ser. 2, vol. 6, 575–80.

43. Ibid.

44. Ibid.

45. Ibid., 585, 643.

46. Blondo, "Point Lookout," 34; *OR,* ser. 2, vol. 6, 705–6.

47. Censer, ed., *Papers of Frederick Law Olmsted,* 4:684.

48. *OR,* ser. 2, vol. 6, 585.

49. Ibid., 554, 763.

50. Shriver and Breen, *Ohio's Military Prisons,* 15; *OR,* ser. 2, vol. 6, 636.

51. *OR,* ser. 2, vol. 6, 356.

52. Ibid., 389–90.

53. Ibid., 479–80; Speer, *Portals to Hell,* 138.

54. *OR,* ser. 2, vol. 6, 19–20; Winslow and Moore, *Camp Morton,* 325; *OR,* ser. 2, vol. 5, 2, 741, 762.

55. Winslow and Moore, *Camp Morton,* 330; *OR,* ser. 2, vol. 6, 424–26.

56. *OR,* ser. 2, vol. 6, 424–26.

57. Ibid., 442–43.

58. *Indianapolis Sentinel,* 17 October 1863; *OR,* ser. 2, vol. 6, 468.

59. *OR,* ser. 2, vol. 6, 474–75.

60. See, for example, the *National Intelligencer,* 11 and 20 November 1863.

61. *OR,* ser. 2, vol. 6, 485.

62. Ibid., 486.

63. *Indianapolis Sentinel,* 1 January 1864.

64. Winslow and Moore, *Camp Morton,* 337; *OR,* ser. 2, vol. 6, 504–5.

65. *OR,* ser. 2, vol. 6, 504–5.

66. Ibid., vol. 5, 457.

67. Nancy Travis Keen, "Confederate Prisoners of War at Fort Delaware," *Delaware History* 13 (1968): 4; *OR,* ser. 2, vol. 7, 990.

68. *OR,* ser. 2, vol. 6, 88; Keen, "Fort Delaware," 4.

69. Quoted in Speer, *Portals to Hell,* 144.

70. Decimus U. Barziza, *The Adventures of a Prisoner of War, 1863–1864,* ed. R. Henderson Shuffler (Austin: University of Texas Press, 1964), 89; Keen, "Fort Delaware," 7.

71. *New York Times,* 11 July 1863; Hesseltine, *Civil War Prisons,* 182.

72. Censer, ed., *Papers of Frederick Law Olmsted,* 4:684.

73. *OR,* ser. 2, vol. 6, 359.

74. Ibid., 517.

75. Ibid., 235, 281, 359, and vol. 8, 992.

76. Ibid., vol. 6, 1039–40.

77. *Richmond Whig,* 9, 10 March 1863.

78. Younger, ed., *Inside the Confederate Government,* 41.

79. Putnam, *Richmond during the War,* 209.

80. Thomas, *Confederate State of Richmond,* 119–20.

81. *OR,* ser. 1, vol. 18, 958; *Richmond Whig,* 6 April 1863.

82. Thomas, *Confederate State of Richmond,* 118; Jones, *Diary,* 185; Putnam, *Richmond during the War,* 211; Parker, *Richmond's Prisons,* 43.

83. *Richmond Whig,* 30 October 1863.

84. Frank L. Byrne, "A General behind Bars: Neal Dow in Libby Prison," in *Civil War Prisons,* ed. William B. Hesseltine (Kent, Ohio: Kent State University Press, 1962), 61; Speer, *Portals to Hell,* 122.

85. William M. Armstrong, "Libby Prison: The Civil War Diary of Arthur G. Sedgwick," *Virginia Magazine of History and Biography* 71 (1963): 453–54.

86. Helm, "Prison Life at Belle Isle," 49–50, 75.

87. Blakey, *Winder,* 170; *OR,* ser. 2, vol. 6, 587–88.

88. Thomas Robson Hay, "Lucius B. Northrop, Commissary General of the Confederacy," *Civil War History* 9, no. 1 (March 1963): 5–6.

89. Jerrold Northrop Moore, *Confederate Commissary General: Lucius Bellinger Northrop and the Subsistence Bureau of the Southern Army* (Shippensburg, Pa.: White Mane Publishing, 1996), viii–ix; Mark M. Boatner III, *Civil War Dictionary* (New York: David McKay, 1959), 601.

90. Moore, *Northrop,* 226–27; *OR,* ser. 2, vol. 6, 281–82; Confederate States War Department, *Laws for the Army and Navy,* 61.

91. Jones, *Diary,* 256–57.

92. *Richmond Dispatch,* 13 November 1863.

93. Blakey, *Winder,* 158.

94. Burnham to Turner, 28 October 1863, Correspondence, Circulars, and Orders of the Confederate Military Prison at Richmond, Va., Relating to Federal Prisoners of War, 1887, RG 249, Entry 135, NA.

95. Simmons to Turner, 28 October 1863, ibid.

96. Winder to Seddon, 28 October 1863, Secretary of War, Schedule of Papers in the Archive Office Referring to the Exchange and Treatment of Prisoners in Southern Prisons, 1861–1865, RG 109, Vol. 245, Chap. 9, NA; *OR,* ser. 2, vol. 6, 439.

97. *OR,* ser. 2, vol. 6, 456.

98. Ibid., 498.

99. Ibid., 497.

100. Blakey, *Winder,* 148–49.

101. See, for example, the *Richmond Dispatch,* 30 October 1863.

102. *OR,* ser. 2, vol. 6, 438–39.

103. Ibid., 455–56.

104. Ibid., 502.

105. Ibid., 821.

106. James I. Robertson Jr., "Houses of Horror: Danville's Civil War Prisons," *Virginia Magazine of History and Biography* 61 (1961): 329; *OR,* ser. 2, vol. 6, 527.

107. Robertson, "Houses of Horror," 330.

108. Ibid., 332, 336.

109. Ibid., 336–37.

110. Ibid., 333; Cyrus Brannock to Banard Van Deren, 27 March 1864, Catalog Number 133–150, File Box 4-A, ANHS.

111. Robertson, "Houses of Horror," 334–35.

112. Papers Relating to Confederate Camps and Other Places Where Federal Prisoners Were Confined during the Period 1861–1865, RG 109, Entry 464, Box 1, NA.

113. Blakey, *Winder,* 145.

114. Parker, *Richmond's Prisons,* 28–30; Blakey, *Winder,* 144–45

115. *OR,* ser. 2, vol. 5, 894, 901, 919–24; Parker, *Richmond's Prisons,* 28–33.

116. Carrington to Pegram, 21 November 1863, Correspondence, Circulars, and Orders of the Confederate Military Prison at Richmond, Va., Relating to Federal Prisoners of War, 1887, RG 249, Entry 135, NA.

117. Wilkins to Carrington, 21 November 1863, ibid.

118. Carrington to Winder, 27 November 1863, ibid. Underlining in original.

119. Blakey, *Winder,* 171.

120. *OR,* ser. 2, vol. 6, 482–83, 503–26.

121. See, for example, the *National Intelligencer,* 11 and 20 November 1863; *OR,* ser. 2, vol. 6, 643.

122. *New York Times,* 4 December 1863.

123. Ibid., 28 November 1863; *OR,* ser. 2, vol. 6, 686.

124. Morfit to Winder, 6 October 1863, Secretary of War, Letters Sent, Richmond, Va., Relating to Prisoners, 1863–1865, RG 109, Vol. 232, Chap. 9, NA; *OR,* ser. 2, vol. 6, 292.

125. Ibid.

126. Morfit to Winder, 28 November 1863, Secretary of War, Letters Sent, Richmond, Va., Relating to Prisoners, 1863–1865, RG 109, Vol. 232, Chap. 9, NA.

127. Hesseltine, *Civil War Prisons,* viii, 172–73.

128. For accounts supporting Winder, see Ely, *Prisoner of War,* 24, 53, 96, and Corcoran, *Captivity of General Corcoran,* 29.

129. *New York Times,* 15 November 1863.

130. *OR,* ser. 2, vol. 6, 181.

131. General Order No. 208, Headquarters, Army of Tennessee, as printed in the *New York Times,* 4 December 1863. Italics in original.

132. Virginia State Library, "Belle Isle," *Virginia Cavalcade,* n.v. (Winter 1955): 13; *Richmond Examiner,* 30 October 1863, as reported in the *National Intelligencer,* 11 November 1863.

133. Benton McAdams, *Rebels at Rock Island: The Story of a Civil War Prison* (DeKalb: Northern Illinois University Press, 2000), 58; *OR,* ser. 2, vol. 6, 687–88, 558; William Marvel, *Andersonville: The Last Depot* (Chapel Hill: University of North Carolina Press, 1994), 14.

CHAPTER 8

1. Blakey, *Winder,* 48.

2. Marvel, *Last Depot,* 12–14.

3. Ovid L. Futch, *History of Andersonville Prison* (Gainesville: University of Florida Press, 1968), 3; John W. Lynn, *Eight Hundred Paces to Hell: Andersonville, A Compilation of Known Facts and Persistent Rumors* (Fredericksburg, Va.: Seargent Kirkland's Museum and Historical Society, 1999), 3. Numerous histories of Andersonville refer to the village by its earlier designation of "Anderson," and even locals used both designations. Confederate War Department correspondence always referred to the place as "Andersonville," however, and that designation will be employed here.

4. Marvel, *Last Depot,* 15–16.

5. Futch, *Andersonville,* 4; Marvel, *Last Depot,* 17.

6. *OR,* ser. 2, vol. 6, 965; Marvel, *Last Depot,* 18.

7. *OR,* ser. 2, vol. 6, 885–86, 965; Marvel, *Last Depot,* 19.

8. *OR,* ser. 2, vol. 6, 914, 1000.

9. Ibid., vol. 8, 732.

10. Cooper to Cobb, 7 February 1864, Papers Relating to Confederate Camps and Other Places Where Federal Prisoners Were Confined during the Period 1861–1865, RG 109, Entry 464, Box 1, NA.

11. Marvel, *Last Depot,* 23; *OR,* ser. 2, vol. 6, 966.

12. Winder to Seddon, Papers Relating to Confederate Camps and Other Places Where Federal Prisoners Were Confined during the Period 1861–1865, RG 109, Entry 464, Box 1, NA.

13. *OR,* ser. 2, vol. 8, 731.

14. *Richmond Dispatch,* 22 December 1863.

15. Mayor and Common Council of Danville to Seddon, 29 January 1864, General Records of the Government of the Confederate States of America, Records Pertaining to Prisoners of War, RG 109, Entry 445, Box 1, NA.

16. Confederate States War Department to Major G. C. Cabell, 5 March 1864, Papers Relating to Confederate Camps and Other Places Where Federal Prisoners Were Confined during the Period 1861–1865, RG 109, Entry 464, Box 1, NA; *OR,* ser. 2, vol. 7, 36.

17. Blakey, *Winder,* 172; *Richmond Whig,* 12 February 1864; Thomas, *Confederate State of Richmond,* 157. For Dow's account of how the prisoners escaped, see Byrne, "General behind Bars," 70.

18. *OR,* ser. 2, vol. 6, 926.

19. Blakey, *Winder,* 177.

20. For an account of the raid and other raucous exploits of Kilpatrick, see Samuel J. Martin, *Kill-Cavalry: The Life of Union General Hugh Judson Kilpatrick* (Mechanicsburg, Pa.: Stackpole Books, 2000).

21. Byrne, "General behind Bars," 74; Blakey, *Winder,* 173; *New York Times,* 12 March 1864.

22. Lengthy reports examining press coverage of the raid in the *Richmond Examiner,* the *Richmond Whig,* and the *Richmond Dispatch* were printed in the *New York Times,* 10 March 1864.

23. Blakey, *Winder,* 173. The *Whig* editorial was republished in papers across the North. See the *National Intelligencer,* 11 March 1864. For an account of the treatment of the prisoners captured at the time Colonel Dahlgren was killed, see *OR,* ser. 1, vol. 33, 218. Union authorities quickly claimed that

the "Dahlgren Papers" were forgeries planted by the Confederates, and the debate on their authenticity continues to this day.

24. John Ransom, *John Ransom's Diary* (1883; reprint, New York: Berkley Books, 1963), 51, 53. Some historians have challenged the truthfulness and accuracy of Andersonville diarists like Ransom and his fellow prisoner John McElroy, but if employed judiciously and corroborated by other sources, these accounts can supply insights into the prisoner experience not available elsewhere.

25. *OR,* ser. 2, vol. 7, 731.

26. Frederic Augustus James, *Frederic Augustus James's Civil War Diary: Sumter to Andersonville,* ed. Jefferson J. Hammer (Rutherford, N.J.: Fairleigh Dickinson University Press, 1973), 78; Marvel, *Last Depot,* 27–28; Blakey, *Winder,* 177.

27. Ransom, *Andersonville Diary,* 60.

28. *OR,* ser. 2, vol. 7, 89.

29. Ibid., vol. 6, 977, 985, 996.

30. Ibid., vol. 7, 40.

31. Private James E. Anderson to Davis, 23 June 1864, in Lynda L. Crist, ed., *The Papers of Jefferson Davis* (Baton Rouge: Louisiana State University Press, 1999), 10:481; Blakey, *Winder,* 178; *OR,* ser. 2, vol. 7, 63–64.

32. *OR,* ser. 2, vol. 6, 1041–43.

33. Ibid.

34. Semple to W. A. Carrington, 6 March 1864, Correspondence, Circulars, and Orders of the Confederate Military Prison at Richmond, Va., Relating to Federal Prisoners of War, 1887, RG 249, Entry 135, NA.

35. Carrington to Winder, 23 March 1864, ibid.

36. See, for example, Surgeon T. G. Richardson to Bragg, 11 April 1864, ibid.

37. William O. Bryant, *Cahaba Prison and the Sultana Disaster* (Tuscaloosa: University of Alabama Press, 1990), 20–21.

38. Captain Howard A. M. Henderson, Report of Federal Prisoners Confined, Papers Relating to Confederate Camps and Other Places Where Federal Prisoners Were Confined during the Period 1861–1865, RG 109, Entry 464, Box 1, NA.

39. Whitfield to Scott, 31 March 1864, Letterbook, Jefferson Davis Papers, RG 109, Entry 1, NA.

40. Ibid.; Peter A. Brannon, "The Cahawba Military Prison, 1863–1865," *Alabama Review* 3, no. 3 (July 1950): 165–66.

41. Cooper to Polk, 20 April 1864, Papers Relating to Confederate Camps and Other Places Where Federal Prisoners Were Confined during the Period 1861–1865, RG 109, Entry 464, Box 1, NA.

42. Cooper to Cobb, 2 May 1864, ibid.; *OR,* ser. 2, vol. 7, 106.

43. Hesseltine, *Civil War Prisons,* 159–60; Speer, *Portals to Hell,* 266.

44. Turner to Winder, 25 May 1864, Papers Relating to Confederate Camps and Other Places Where Federal Prisoners Were Confined during the Period 1861–1865, RG 109, Entry 464, Box 1, NA; Hesseltine, *Civil War Prisons,* 160; *OR,* ser. 2, vol. 7, 418.

45. Hesseltine, *Civil War Prisons,* 160.

46. Ezra Hoyt Ripple, *Dancing along the Deadline: The Andersonville Memoir of a Prisoner of the Confederacy,* ed. Mark A. Snell (Novato, Calif.: Persidio Press, 1996), 18; Marvel, *Last Depot,* 55.

47. *OR,* ser. 2, vol. 7, 524–25, 546.

48. Ibid., vol. 6, 1041–43, and vol. 7, 169–70; Marvel, *Last Depot,* 34–35, 44.

49. John McElroy, *Andersonville: A Story of Rebel Prisons* (Washington, D.C.: National Tribune, 1899), 142–43. Many captives, including McElroy, charged that Wirz was a cruel martinet who delighted in their suffering, and testimony in the sham trial staged by the U.S. government after the war was carefully orchestrated to support this assessment. The record of his actions at Andersonville suggests otherwise, and a more balanced view of his career is offered in Marvel, *Last Depot,* and Hesseltine, *Civil War Prisons.*

50. *OR,* ser. 2, vol. 7, 136.

51. Ibid., 207.

52. Ibid., 89.

53. Ibid., 90; Marvel, *Last Depot,* 53; Adjutant and Inspector General's Office, General Orders No. 45, 2 May 1864, Papers Relating to Confederate Camps and Other Places Where Federal Prisoners Were Confined during the Period 1861–1865, RG 109, Entry 464, Box 1, NA.

54. *OR,* ser. 2, vol. 7, 754–55.

55. See, for example, the call for sustaining the sentence against Butler in the *Richmond Whig,* 19 January 1864, and the report of the depth of the South's hatred of Butler in the *New York Times,* 3 February 1864.

56. *OR,* ser. 2, vol. 6, 769; Hesseltine, *Civil War Prisons,* 211; *New York Times,* 3 February 1864.

57. *OR,* ser. 2, vol. 6, 934–35.

58. Ibid., 754, 769, 921, 978.

59. Butler to Stanton, 8 March 1864, Benjamin F. Butler Papers, Container 27, Telegrams, 1–31 March 1864, Manuscript Division, LC.

60. Butler to Hoffman, 11 March 1864, ibid., Container 26, 11–15 March 1864, Manuscript Division, LC; *Richmond Sentinel,* 7 March 1864, as reported in the *National Intelligencer,* 11 March 1864.

61. *OR,* ser. 2, vol. 6, 1033, 1082; Butler to Stanton, 23 March 1864, and Butler to Ould, 29 March 1864, Benjamin F. Butler Papers, Container 27, 1–31 March 1864, Manuscript Division, LC.

62. *OR,* ser. 2, vol. 6, 1121–22.

63. Ibid., vol. 7, 29–34.

64. John Hay to Butler, 6 April 1864, and Lincoln to Butler, 7 April 1864, Edwin M. Stanton Papers, Microfilm, Reel 7, Manuscript Division, LC; Basler, ed., *Collected Works,* 7:289, 293.

65. *OR,* ser. 2, vol. 7, 46–50.

66. Grant to Butler, 14 April 1864, Benjamin F. Butler Papers, Container 28, 11–15 April 1864, Manuscript Division, LC.

67. Grant to Butler, 17 April 1864, ibid.; Ulysses S. Grant, *Memoirs and Selected Letters: Personal Memoirs of U. S. Grant, Selected Letters 1839–1865,* ed. John Y. Simon (New York: Library of America, 1990), 1048.

68. Benjamin F. Butler, *Butler's Book* (Boston: A. M. Thayer, 1892), 594; Hesseltine, *Civil War Prisons,* 220.

69. Butler, *Butler's Book,* 596.

70. Grant to Butler, 20 April 1864, Benjamin F. Butler Papers, Container 28, 16–20 April 1864, Manuscript Division, LC.

71. *OR,* ser. 2, vol. 7, 108, 126; Butler to Stanton, 2 May 1864, Benjamin F. Butler Papers, Container 30, 1–5 May 1864, Manuscript Division, LC.

72. Richardson, ed., *Messages and Papers of Jefferson Davis,* 1:445.

73. *OR,* ser. 2, vol. 7, 103, 105.

74. Henry P. Beers, *The Confederacy: A Guide to the Archives of the Government of the Confederate States of America* (Washington, D.C.: National Archives and Record Administration, 1986), 250–58; Blakey, *Winder*, 183.

75. Cobb to Adjutant General Cooper, 5 May 1864, Andersonville Vertical File, Section 2, American Prisoners of War, Letters Written by Howell Cobb and R. J. Hallett, ANHS.

76. *OR*, ser. 2, vol. 7, 168.

77. Ibid., 172–73.

78. Ibid., 173–74.

79. *Macon Telegraph*, 8 June 1864; Edwin C. Bearss, *Andersonville National Historic Site: Historic Resource Study and Historical Base Map, Sumter and Macon Counties, Georgia* (Washington, D.C.: National Park Service, 1970), 122–74.

80. Crist, ed., *Papers of Jefferson Davis*, 10:142.

81. Cobb to Davis, 2 June 1864, and Davis to Cobb, 3 June 1864, in ibid., 10:444; Blakey, *Winder*, 183; Bearss, *Andersonville National Historic Site*, 87; *OR*, ser. 2, vol. 7, 192, 213, and ser. 1, vol. 39, pt. 2, 634.

82. Blakey, *Winder*, 184; Marvel, *Andersonville*, 84–85; Ripple, *Dancing along the Deadline*, 22.

83. Winder to Cooper, 21 June 1864, Papers Relating to Confederate Camps and Other Places Where Federal Prisoners Were Confined during the Period 1861–1865, RG 109, Entry 464, Box 1, NA.

84. *OR*, ser. 2, vol. 7, 393, 410–11.

85. Marvel, *Andersonville*, 101; Cobb to Davis, 24 June 1864, in Crist, ed., *Papers of Jefferson Davis*, 10:482.

86. Ripple, *Dancing along the Deadline*, 27–28; Ransom, *Andersonville Diary*, 105–17.

87. *OR*, ser. 2, vol. 7, 445–46.

88. Ibid., 463, 476; Crist, ed., *Papers of Jefferson Davis*, 10:547.

89. *OR*, ser. 2, vol. 7, 458, 473.

90. Winder to Cooper, 21 July 1864, Papers Relating to Confederate Camps and Other Places Where Federal Prisoners Were Confined during the Period 1861–1865, RG 109, Entry 464, Box 1, NA; *OR*, ser. 2, vol. 7, 480.

91. Major M. A. Allen to Captain J. W. Armstrong, 12 June 1864, Catalog Number 442–454, ANDE File Box 4-A, ANHS.

92. *OR*, ser. 2, vol. 7, 493; Winder to Cooper, 25 July 1864, Papers Relating to Confederate Camps and Other Places Where Federal Prisoners Were Confined during the Period 1861–1865, RG 109, Entry 464, Box 1, NA.

93. *OR*, ser. 2, vol. 7, 499–500.

94. Ibid., ser. 1, vol. 36, pt. 3, 899.

95. Joseph E. Johnston, *Narrative of Military Operations* (New York: D. Appleton and Sons, 1874), 351; Moore, *Northrop*, 259, 267.

96. *OR*, ser. 1, vol. 51, pt. 2, 909–10. The official report of the Commissary Department itemized the rations stockpiled at Beaver Dam as 915,000 rations of meat and 504,000 rations of bread. This cache was burned by Sheridan's cavalry on 9 May 1864. For accounts of the action, see Douglas Southall Freeman, *Lee's Lieutenants*, vol. 3, *Gettysburg to Appomattox* (New York: Charles Scribner's Sons, 1944), 414, and Shelby Foote, *The Civil War: A Narrative*, vol. 3, *Red River to Appomattox* (New York: Vintage Books, 1986), 225.

97. *OR*, ser. 2, vol. 7, 490, 463.

98. Hesseltine, *Civil War Prisons,* 163; *OR,* ser. 2, vol. 7, 185, 216–17, 371 , and ser. 1, vol. 35, pt. 2, 135.

99. Hesseltine, *Civil War Prisons,* 164; *OR,* ser. 2, vol. 7, 418, 472; *New York Times,* 23 August 1864.

100. The best known and most often quoted of these narratives is Major J. Ogden Murray, *The Immortal Six Hundred: A Story of Cruelty to Confederate Prisoners of War* (Winchester, Va.: Eddy Press, 1905). See also W. T. Baldwin, "In a Federal Prison: Interesting Career of Lieutenant W. W. George of Echols' Brigade," *SHSP* 29 (1901): 229–39, and Junius Lackland Hempstead, "How Long Will This Misery Continue," ed. Bess Beaty and Judy Caprio, *CWTI* 19, no. 10 (February 1981): 20–23; *OR,* ser. 2, vol. 7, 597–98.

101. *OR,* ser. 2, vol. 7, 501–2.

102. Hesseltine, *Civil War Prisons,* 163. From the time of its creation, Camp Ford operated beyond the control of Gardner, Winder, or any of the authorities in Richmond, and for that reason it is not a subject of this study. For a history of its operation, see F. Lee Lawrence, *Camp Ford, C.S.A.* (Austin: Texas Civil War Centennial Advisory Committee, 1964), and Leon Mitchell Jr., "Camp Ford Confederate Military Prison," *Southwestern Historical Quarterly* 66 (1962–1963): 1–16. An interesting account of archeological activities at the camp may be found at the installation website, http://www.texasbeyondhistory.net/ford (accessed 24 December 2004).

103. *OR,* ser. 2, vol. 7, 490–91.

104. *Macon Telegraph,* 21 May and 8 August 1864; Andersonville Vertical File, Section 2, American Prisoners of War, Newspaper Articles, Ande., Oglethorpe, Elmira (*Macon Telegraph*), ANHS.

105. Marvel, *Andersonville,* 192; *OR,* ser. 2, vol. 8, 603.

106. See Marvel, *Andersonville,* 166, and Hesseltine, *Civil War Prisons,* 148.

107. Hesseltine, *Civil War Prisons,* 253; Blakey, *Winder,* 192.

108. Blakey, *Winder,* 190; Marvel, *Andersonville,* 166–70.

109. Cooper to Chandler, July 1864, Papers Relating to Confederate Camps and Other Places Where Federal Prisoners Were Confined during the Period 1861–1865, RG 109, Entry 464, Box 1, NA; *OR,* ser. 2, vol. 7, 429–30.

110. Ibid.

111. Ibid.

112. *OR,* ser. 2, vol. 7, 521; White to Surgeon General Moore, 1 July 1864, Correspondence, Circulars, and Orders of the Confederate Military Prison at Richmond, Va., Relating to Federal Prisoners of War, 1887, RG 249, Entry 135, NA; H. H. Cunningham, *Doctors in Gray: The Confederate Medical Service* (Gloucester, Mass.: Peter Smith, 1970), 104.

113. *OR,* ser. 2, vol. 7, 546–50; Hesseltine, *Civil War Prisons,* 154.

114. Inspection Report 1–C–5, 5 August 1864, Papers Relating to Confederate Camps and Other Places Where Federal Prisoners Were Confined during the Period 1861–1865, RG 109, Entry 464, Box 1, NA; *OR,* ser. 2, vol. 7, 552. Appropriately, Chandler's report returned to haunt Seddon after the war, when Federal officials used it during the Wirz trial in an effort to charge the former secretary of war with complicity in the crimes committed at Andersonville. See Younger, ed., *Inside the Confederate Government,* 227–30.

115. *OR,* ser. 2, vol. 7, 172–73, 550; U.S. Congress, House, *Report on the Treatment of Prisoners of War by the Rebel Authorities during the War of the Rebellion,* 40th Cong., 3d sess., 1869, H. Rept. 45, 133.

116. U.S. Congress, House, *Report on the Treatment of Prisoners of War,* 133, 143.

117. Younger, ed., *Inside the Confederate Government,* 228.

118. Blakey, *Winder*, 191; *OR*, ser. 2, vol. 7, 755.

119. *OR*, ser. 2, vol. 7, 756–62; Blakey, *Winder*, 191.

120. *OR*, ser. 2, vol. 7, 514; Hesseltine, *Civil War Prisons*, 152.

121. Hunter, "Warden for the Union," 209.

122. McAdams, *Rebels at Rock Island*, 55–56, 60.

123. Walker, "Rock Island Prison," 52; McAdams, *Rebels at Rock Island*, 60–61; *OR*, ser. 2, vol. 7, 12–13, 16.

124. Griffin Frost, *Camp and Prison Journal* (Quincy, Ill.: Quincy Herald Book and Job Office, 1867), 113.

125. *(St. Louis) Daily Missouri Democrat*, 14 March 1864; Hesseltine, "Military Prisons of St. Louis," 393.

126. Blondo, "Point Lookout," 30; *OR*, ser. 2, vol. 7, 995–96.

127. *OR*, ser. 2, vol. 7, 399–400.

128. Speer, *Portals to Hell*, 188–89; *OR*, ser. 2, vol. 7, 399.

129. *OR*, ser. 2, vol. 6, 1116–17.

130. Ibid., vol. 7, 5, 106.

131. Shriver and Breen, *Ohio's Military Prisons*, 38; *OR*, ser. 2, vol. 7, 26, 37, 177; Hoffman to Brigadier General G. Marston, Commanding Depot Prisoners of War, Point Lookout, Md., 11 March 1864, Office of the Commissary General of Prisoners, Letters Sent, RG 249, NA.

132. Bruce Tap. *Over Lincoln's Shoulder: The Committee on the Conduct of the War* (Lawrence: University Press of Kansas, 1998), 16–17.

133. *Congressional Globe*, 37th Cong., 2d sess., 16–17, 29–32, 40; Tap, *Over Lincoln's Shoulder*, 24.

134. George W. Julian, *Political Recollections, 1840–1872* (Chicago: Jansen, McClurg, 1884), 204.

135. Julian, *Political Recollections*, 225; T. Harry Williams, "Benjamin F. Wade and the Atrocity Propaganda of the Civil War," *Ohio Archaeological and Historical Quarterly* 48 (1939): 34; Hans L. Trefousse, *Benjamin Franklin Wade: Radical Republican from Ohio* (New York: Twayne, 1963), 177.

136. U.S. Congress, *Reports of the Joint Committee on the Conduct of the War, Reports*, 8 vols. (Washington: GPO, 1863–1866), 3:451–77.

137. Ibid., 3:449–65, 485–90.

138. Articles featuring the report were carried in *Harper's Weekly*, 5 April, 17 May, and 7 June 1862, and *Frank Leslie's Illustrated Newspaper*, 22 November 1862. See W. Fletcher Thompson Jr., *The Image of War: The Pictorial Reporting of the American Civil War* (New York: Thomas Yoseloff, 1960), 45–46.

139. Trefousse, *Wade*, 184; T. Harry Williams, "The Committee on the Conduct of the War: A Study in Civil War Politics" (Ph.D. diss., University of Wisconsin, 1937), 401–2.

140. Williams, "Committee on the Conduct of the War," 329; Tap, *Over Lincoln's Shoulder*, 29, 192.

141. Tap, *Over Lincoln's Shoulder*, 25; George Julian, *Speeches on Political Questions, 1850–1868*, ed. Lydia Maria Child (1872; reprint, Westport, Conn.: Negro University Press, 1970), 7; Williams, "Committee on the Conduct of the War," 402.

142. Williams, "Committee on the Conduct of the War," 402–3; Julian, *Speeches*, 83.

143. U.S. Congress, *Reports of the Committee on the Conduct of the War*, 3:449–50.

144. *OR*, ser. 2, vol. 5, 487, and vol. 6, 485.

145. For balanced accounts of the affair, see Tap, *Over Lincoln's Shoulder*, 194–95; James M. McPherson, *The Negro's Civil War: How American Blacks Felt and Acted during the War for the Union* (New York:

Ballentine Books, 1991), 220–27; Albert Castel, "The Fort Pillow Massacre: A Fresh Examination of the Evidence," *CWH* 4 (1958): 37–50; and John Cimprich and Robert C. Manifort Jr., "The Fort Pillow Massacre: A Statistical Note," *Journal of American History* 76 (1989): 930–37.

146. *Harper's Weekly,* 30 April 1864; Basler, ed., *Collected Works,* 7:303.

147. Stanton to Officers Commanding Military Posts, 18 April 1864, Benjamin F. Wade Papers, Vols. 9–10, Microfilm, Reel 5, Manuscript Division, LC.

148. *OR,* ser. 2, vol. 7, 73.

149. *Congressional Globe,* 38th Cong., 1st sess., 1662–1665, 1673, 2108; Tap, *Over Lincoln's Shoulder,* 196. The Gooch leak appeared in the *Chicago Tribune,* 27 April 1864.

150. Gideon Welles, *Diary of Gideon Welles,* ed. John T. Morse, 3 vols. (Boston: Houghton Mifflin, 1911), 2:23–24; John Niven, *Gideon Welles: Lincoln's Secretary of the Navy* (New York: Oxford University Press, 1973), 402.

151. Howard K. Beale, ed., *Diary of Edward Bates, 1859–1866* (Washington, D.C.: GPO, 1933), 365; Mark E. Neely Jr., *Abraham Lincoln Encyclopedia* (New York: McGraw-Hill, 1982), 116, 287; Thomas and Hyman, *Stanton,* 373; Williams, "Committee on the Conduct of the War," 330–31; Tap, *Over Lincoln's Shoulder,* 200–1.

152. *OR,* ser. 2, vol. 7, 81.

153. U.S. Senate, Joint Committee on the Conduct and Expenditures of the War, *Report on Returned Prisoners,* 38th Cong., 1st sess., 9 May 1864, S. Rept. 68, 4–5.

154. Ibid.; *OR,* ser. 2, vol. 7, 110–11.

155. U.S. Senate, JCCW, *Returned Prisoners,* 4; Tap, *Over Lincoln's Shoulder,* 203.

156. U.S. Senate, JCCW, *Returned Prisoners,* 3–4.

157. *Harper's Weekly,* 18 June 1864, 385, 387; *Leslie's Illustrated Newspaper,* 18 June 1864, 193; Donald, *Lincoln,* 477; Williams, "Atrocity Propaganda of the Civil War," 42; U.S. Senate, JCCW, *Returned Prisoners,* 1.

158. Basler, ed., *Collected Works,* 7:345–46.

159. For a discussion of the connection between the election of 1864 and Lincoln's hesitancy to order acts of retaliation, see Tap, *Over Lincoln's Shoulder,* 206.

160. *OR,* ser. 2, vol. 7, 150–51, 183–84.

161. Michael P. Gray, *The Business of Captivity: Elmira and Its Civil War Prison* (Kent, Ohio: Kent State University Press, 2001), 2; *OR,* ser. 2, vol. 7, 152.

162. Gray, *Business of Captivity,* 3–4; *OR,* ser. 2, vol. 7, 157.

163. James I. Robertson Jr., "The Scourge of Elmira," in *Civil War Prisons,* ed. William B. Hesseltine (Kent, Ohio: Kent State University Press, 1962), 82, 84; Clay W. Holmes, *The Elmira Prison Camp: A History of the Military Prison at Elmira, New York, July 6, 1864 to July 10, 1865* (New York: G. P. Putnam's Sons, 1912), 119.

164. *OR,* ser. 2, vol. 7, 424; Robertson, "Scourge of Elmira," 82; Holmes, *Elmira,* 27–29, 84, 294, 307–8.

165. Gray, *Business of Captivity,* 19, 27; *OR,* ser. 2, vol. 7, 467, 604.

166. Robertson, "Scourge of Elmira," 89; *OR,* ser. 2, vol. 7, 1093, 1185.

167. See Anthony M. Keiley, *Prisoner of War, or Five Months among the Yankees* (Richmond, Va.: West and Johnston, 1865), 87–88.

168. John R. King, *My Experience in the Confederate Army and in Northern Prisons* (Clarksburg,

W.Va.: United Daughters of the Confederacy, 1917), 46, 37; Philip Burnham, "The Andersonvilles of the North," *Military History Quarterly* 10, no. 1 (Autumn 1997): 49; Gray, *Business of Captivity,* 29.

169. Robertson, "Scourge of Elmira," 88.

170. King, *My Experience,* 48–49.

171. Robertson, "Scourge of Elmira," 90–91; *OR,* ser. 2, vol. 7, 1093–94, 1134–36, 1157, 1173.

172. *OR,* ser. 2, vol. 7, 996–97.

173. Hesseltine, *Civil War Prisons,* 201; *OR,* ser. 2, vol. 7, 440, 448–50, 162, 182–84, 200, 369, 382.

174. Robertson, "Scourge of Elmira," 88; *OR,* ser. 2, vol. 7, 666, 683, 785; Hesseltine, *Civil War Prisons,* 203.

175. Censer, ed., *Papers of Frederick Law Olmsted,* 4:684.

176. *OR,* ser. 2, vol. 7, 387–88, 398.

177. U.S. Sanitary Commission, *Narrative of Privations and Sufferings of United States Officers and Soldiers in the Hands of Rebel Authorities, Being the Report of a Commission of Inquiry Appointed by the United States Sanitary Commission, with an Appendix, Containing the Testimony* (Boston: Littells Living Age, 1864), 12–13; Ann Fabian, *The Unvarnished Truth: Personal Narratives in Nineteenth-Century America* (Berkeley: University of California Press, 2000), 129; Hesseltine, *Civil War Prisons,* 196–200.

178. Robertson, "Scourge of Elmira," 85; *OR,* ser. 2, vol. 7, 997.

179. Blakey, *Winder,* 192; Marvel, *Last Depot,* 169; Bryant, *Cahaba Prison,* 32, 167–68, 171.

180. Reports of Inspections, Richmond Hospitals, Correspondence, Circulars, and Orders of the Confederate Military Prisons at Richmond, Va., Relating to Federal Prisoners of War, 1887, RG 249, Entry 135, NA.

181. Cooper to Lee, 26 July 1864, Papers Relating to Confederate Camps and Other Places Where Federal Prisoners Were Confined during the Period 1861–1865, RG 109, Entry 464, Box 1, NA.

182. Blakey, *Winder,* 193–94; *OR,* ser. 2, vol. 7, 678.

183. "Account of Francis Marion Blaloch," Drawer 1, Section 2, American Prisoners of War, Civil War, Confederate Soldiers' Accounts, Civil War, ANHS.

184. James, *Civil War Diary,* 81–94.

185. *OR,* ser. 2, vol. 7, 773.

186. Ibid.; Ransom, *Andersonville Diary,* 160, 163; Speer, *Portals to Hell,* 279.

187. *OR,* ser. 2, vol. 7, 973; Blakey, *Winder,* 197.

188. *OR,* ser. 2, vol. 7, 982; Speer, *Portals to Hell,* 210; Brown, *Salisbury Prison,* 27, 117.

189. Brown, *Salisbury Prison,* 113, 108, 110.

190. Ibid., 96–97.

191. Ibid., 169–70; J. Caldwell to General Richard Ewell, 26 November, Records of the Commissary General of Prisoners, Records Relating to Individual Prisoners of War, Miscellaneous Rolls and Related Records of Federal Prisoners of War, 1861–1865, RG 249, Nos. 547–654, Box 7, NA.

192. Brown, *Salisbury Prison,* 132; Blakey, *Winder,* 198.

193. *OR,* ser. 2, vol. 7, 963–64.

194. Blakey, *Winder,* 196–97; *OR,* ser. 2, vol. 7, 964, 1150.

195. Butler, *Butler's Book,* 597; *OR,* ser. 2, vol. 7, 578–79.

196. Butler, *Butler's Book,* 597.

197. *OR,* ser. 2, vol. 7, 606; Hesseltine, *Civil War Prisons,* 225.

198. Butler, *Butler's Book,* 599; *OR,* ser. 2, vol. 7, 606.

199. Butler, *Butler's Book,* 598; *OR,* ser. 2, vol. 7, 606–7. Grant reiterated his position on exchanges in a letter to Secretary of State Seward on 19 August. See also Grant, *Memoirs and Selected Letters,* ed. Simon, 1066. For a discussion of Grant's reasoning and examples of his refusal to allow other subordinates to engage in exchanges, see McFeely, *Grant,* 183.

200. Thomas and Hyman, *Stanton,* 374.

201. Butler, *Butler's Book,* 599, 605.

202. Ibid., 605; *New York Times,* 6 September 1864.

203. D. C. Anderson to Lincoln, 4 September 1864, *OR,* ser 2, vol. 7, 767–68.

204. *Richmond Examiner,* 8 October 1864; Hesseltine, *Civil War Prisons,* 222–23. For other examples of letters sent by imprisoned Union officers and enlisted men, see *OR,* ser. 2, vol. 7, 616–22.

205. *New York Times,* 10 November 1863, 23 August and 8 September 1864.

206. *OR,* ser. 2, vol. 7, 793.

207. J. H. Stillwell to Davis, 7 September 1864, "A Statement of the Evidence Found in the Archive Office of the War Department Relating to the Treatment of Union Prisoners," Papers Relating to Confederate Camps and Other Places Where Federal Prisoners Were Confined during the Period 1861–1865, RG 109, Entry 464, Box 1, NA.

208. *OR,* ser. 2, vol. 7, 783, 1304; Cobb to Seddon, 9 September 1864, Letterbook, Jefferson Davis Papers, RG 109, Entry 1, NA; Hesseltine, *Civil War Prisons,* 226, 221– 22 n. 44; *OR,* ser. 2, vol. 7, 189–91, 203.

209. Howard K. Beale, ed., *Diary of Gideon Welles, Secretary of the Navy under Lincoln,* vol. 2, *April 1, 1864–December 31, 1866* (New York: W. W. Norton, 1960), 168.

210. Ibid., 170; Crist, ed., *Papers of Jefferson Davis,* 10:624.

211. Beale, ed., *Diary of Gideon Welles,* 2:171.

212. Ibid.; *OR,* ser. 2, vol. 7, 661, 790, 924.

213. Butler, *Butler's Book,* 604; Basler, ed., *Collected Works,* 8:36; *OR,* ser. 2, vol. 7, 914.

214. Butler, *Butler's Book,* 606; *OR,* ser. 2, vol. 7, 989.

215. *OR,* ser. 2, vol. 7, 907, 872.

216. Hesseltine, *Civil War Prisons,* 228; Butler, *Butler's Book,* 608–9; *OR,* ser. 2, vol. 7, 1101.

217. *National Intelligencer,* 21 November 1864; *New York Times,* 26 November 1864.

218. *National Intelligencer,* 26 November 1864; *New York Times,* 26 November 1864; Butler, *Butler's Book,* 1046.

219. *New York Times,* 16 and 26 November, 16 and 23 December 1864; *OR,* ser. 2, vol. 7, 1257.

220. *OR,* ser. 2, vol. 7, 1304.

CHAPTER 9

1. Report of Inspection, 8 February 1865, Papers Relating to Confederate Camps and Other Places Where Federal Prisoners Were Confined during the Period 1861–1865, RG 109, Entry 464, Box 1, NA; Robertson, "Houses of Horror," 340–41.

2. Ibid.

3. Blakey, *Winder,* 198, 200; *OR,* ser. 2, vol. 8, 49, 135.

4. Winder to Cooper, 20 January 1865, Papers Relating to Confederate Camps and Other Places Where Federal Prisoners Were Confined during the Period 1861–1865, RG 109, Entry 464, Box 1, NA; *OR,* ser. 2, vol. 7, 96.

5. *OR,* ser. 2, vol. 8, 137–38; Blakey, *Winder,* 200.

6. *OR,* ser. 2, vol. 8, 138–39.

7. Blakey, *Winder,* 1–4; Forno to Cooper, 7 February 1865, Papers Relating to Confederate Camps and Other Places Where Federal Prisoners Were Confined during the Period 1861–1865, RG 109, Entry 464, Box 1, NA; *OR,* ser. 2, vol. 8, 765–66.

8. Hesseltine, *Civil War Prisons,* 171 n. 69; Futch, *Andersonville,* 117.

9. Sifakis, *Who Was Who,* 508; *OR,* ser. 2, vol. 8, 205.

10. *OR,* ser. 2, vol. 7, 582–83.

11. Morgan A. Powell, "Cotton for the Relief of Confederate Prisoners," *CWH* 9, no. 1 (March 1963): 24.

12. *OR,* ser. 2, vol. 8, 241–43.

13. Ibid., vol. 7, 1070–73, and vol. 8, 241–42.

14. Brown, *Salisbury Prison,* 168; *OR,* ser. 2, vol. 7, 168, 248–49; Blakey, *Winder,* 198.

15. John King, "Much Sickness Prevailed," in *The Illustrated Confederate Reader,* ed. Rod Gragg (New York: Gramercy Books, 1989), 145.

16. Robertson, "Scourge of Elmira," 80, 95–96. This percentage is conservative. Other historians of the prison place the mortality at between 28.5 and 32.5 percent. See Holmes, *Elmira,* 254–55.

17. *OR,* ser. 2, vol. 7, 1257.

18. For an individual listing of the documents Stanton provided, see ibid., vol. 8, 98–103.

19. Ibid., 97–98.

20. Ibid., 63.

21. McFeely, *Grant,* 196–97. To his admiring public and constituents, Butler offered a very different account of his relief. See Butler, *Butler's Book,* 609.

22. *OR,* ser. 2, vol. 8, 147–49.

23. Ibid., 170–71.

24. J. B. Stamp, "Ten Months' Experience in Northern Prisons," *Alabama Historical Quarterly* 18 (1956): 495; King, *My Experience,* 31–32; Burnham, "Andersonvilles of the North," 54.

25. Hesseltine, *Civil War Prisons,* 230; Thomas, "Prisoner of War Exchange," 288–89; Basler, ed., *Collected Works,* 7:53–56.

26. *OR,* ser. 2, vol. 8, 203, 210, 272, 237, 260.

27. Ibid., 239–40.

28. Ibid., 234.

29. G. Wayne King, "Death Camp at Florence," *CWTI* 12, no. 9 (January 1974): 42; *OR,* ser. 2, vol. 8, 206, 238.

30. *OR,* ser. 2, vol. 7, 1117, and vol. 8, 162.

31. Ibid., vol. 8, 259; Hesseltine, *Civil War Prisons,* 231–32; Hunter, "Warden for the Union," 216.

32. *OR,* ser. 2, vol. 7, 235.

33. Hunter, "Warden for the Union," 216; *OR,* ser. 2, vol. 8, 998–1001.

34. Benjamin F. Booth, *Dark Days of the Rebellion, or Life in Southern Military Prisons, Giving a Correct and Thrilling History of Unparalleled Suffering, Narrow Escapes, Heroic Encounters, Bold Achievement, Cold-Blooded Murders, Severe Tests of Loyalty, and Patriotism* (Indianola, Ia.: Booth Publishing, 1897), 180, 287–88, 337; Brown, *Salisbury Prison,* 9, 143–45.

35. Robertson, "Houses of Horror," 344–45.

36. Daniel N. Reynolds, "Memories of Libby Prison," ed. Paul H. Giddens. *Michigan History Magazine* 23 (Autumn 1939): 391, 396.

37. Ibid., 397–98.

38. General Orders No. 6, Letter of Appointment, General Records of the Government of the Confederate States of America, Records Pertaining to Prisoners of War, RG 109, Entry 445, Box 3, NA; *OR*, ser. 1, vol. 47, pt. 2, 1284, and ser. 2, vol. 8, 427–28.

39. *OR*, ser. 2, vol. 8, 427.

40. Pillow to Hoffman, 26 March 1865, General Records of the Government of the Confederate States of America, Records Pertaining to Prisoners of War, RG 109, Entry 445, Box 3, NA.

41. *OR*, ser. 2, vol. 8, 422.

42. Younger, ed., *Inside the Confederate Government*, 185, 189–90; Davis, *Man and His Hour*, 584–86; Thomas, *Confederate Nation*, 286–87.

43. *OR*, ser. 2, vol. 8, 11, 12.

44. Iverson to Winder, 31 January 1865, Secretary of War Schedule of Papers in the Archive Office Referring to the Exchange and Treatment of Prisoners of War in Southern Prisons, 1861–1865, RG 109, Vol. 245, Chap. 9, NA; *OR*, ser. 2, vol. 8, 160.

45. Northrop to Cooper, 11 February 1865, Papers Relating to Confederate Camps and Other Places Where Federal Prisoners Were Confined during the Period 1861–1865, RG 109, Entry 464, Box 1, NA; *OR*, ser. 2, vol. 8, 161.

46. Younger, ed., *Inside the Confederate Government*, 200; *OR*, ser. 1, vol. 46, pt. 2, 1209–10.

47. Moore, *Northrop*, 276–77.

48. Younger, ed., *Inside the Confederate Government*, 200; Moore, *Northrop*, 277; Davis, *Man and His Hour*, 586.

49. I. M. St. John to Jefferson Davis, 14 July 1873, in J. William Jones, ed., "Resources of the Confederacy in 1865—Report of General I. M. St. John, Commissary General," *SHSP* 3, no. 3 (March 1877): 99; *OR*, ser. 4, vol. 3, 1137.

50. *OR*, ser. 2, vol. 8, 49; Hesseltine, *Civil War Prisons*, 208–9.

51. *OR*, ser. 2, vol. 8, 337–41.

52. Ibid., 344–46.

53. Ibid., 347–53.

54. Ibid., ser. 1, vol. 46, pt. 3, 513, and ser. 2, vol. 8, 482.

55. Bryant, *Cahaba Prison*, 117, 119–20.

56. General John D. Imboden to Commanders of Military Prisons West of the Savannah River, 15 February 1865, Catalog Number 429–441, ANDE File Box 4-A, ANHS; Bryant, *Cahaba Prison*, 113, 115; General Orders No. 2, 15 February 1865, Papers Relating to Confederate Camps and Other Places Where Federal Prisoners Were Confined during the Period 1861–1865, RG 109, Entry 464, Box 1, NA.

57. Bryant, *Cahaba Prison*, 118–19, 126, 128.

58. Ibid., 129; Shelby Foote, *Civil War*, 3:1026–27.

59. *OR*, ser. 2, vol. 8, 556, 538, 709–10, 1003; Hunter, "Warden for the Union," 220–21.

60. "Roll of Prisoners of War in Confinement, October 20th 1865," Papers of General William Hoffman, 1862–1867, Records Relating to Civilian Personnel in the Office of the Commissary General of Prisoners, RG 249, NA.

61. McAdams, *Rebels at Rock Island*, 10, 59.

62. "Consolidated Statement of Prison and Parole Camp Funds during the Secession Rebellion," Papers Relating to the Office of the Commissary General of Prisoners, Ethan A. Hitchcock Papers, Box 11, Manuscript Division, LC.

63. Ibid.; "Statement of Prison and Parole Camp Funds Showing the Savings and Expenditures During Year 1864," Papers of General William Hoffman, 1862–1867, Records Relating to Civilian Personnel in the Office of the Commissary General of Prisoners, RG 249, NA; Hunter, "Warden for the Union," 160.

64. Hunter, "Warden for the Union," 221–22; Hesseltine, *Civil War Prisons,* 232; *OR,* ser. 2, vol. 8, 784.

65. Nancy A. Roberts, "The Afterlife of Civil War Prisons and Their Dead" (Ph.D. diss., University of Oregon, 1996), 323, 326; Brown, *Salisbury Prison,* 150–52, 161.

66. Roberts, "Afterlife," 322–23; Marvel, *Last Depot,* 248–49; Bearss, *Andersonville National Historical Site,* 143–50.

67. Parker, *Richmond's Prisons,* 69–70; Roberts, "Afterlife," 323, 325.

68. Roberts, "Afterlife," 323–26.

69. Ibid.

70. King, *My Experience,* 5; Ripple, *Dancing along the Deadline,* 2.

71. Chester F. Dunham, *The Attitude of Northern Clergy toward the South, 1860–1865* (Philadelphia: Porcupine Press, 1974), 177–94; David S. Chesebrough, *"God Ordained This War": Sermons on the Sectional Crisis, 1830–1865* (Columbia: University of South Carolina Press, 1991), 50–51, 143–53, 140.

72. Roberts, "Afterlife," 7–8; C. Vann Woodward, *Origins of the New South, 1877–1913* (Baton Rouge: Louisiana State University Press, 1971), 156.

73. Stuart McConnell, *Glorious Contentment: The Grand Army of the Republic, 1865–1900* (Chapel Hill: University of North Carolina Press, 1992), 15, 126, 131; Roberts, "Afterlife," 8–9.

74. See G. T. Taylor, "Prison Experience in Elmira, New York," *Confederate Veteran* 20 (September 1912): 327; Marcus B. Toney, "Our Dead at Elmira," *SHSP* 29 (1901): 193–97.

75. McConnell, *Glorious Contentment,* 94–95.

76. Roberts, "Afterlife," 28–29; Marvel, *Last Depot,* 243–45; U.S. Congress, House, *Trial of Henry Wirz,* 40th Cong., 2d sess., 1868, H. Ex. Doc. 23, 3.

77. U.S. Congress, *Reports of the Committee on the Conduct of the War,* 1865, 1:iii–iv.

78. U.S. Congress, House, *Report on the Treatment of Prisoners of War by the Rebel Authorities, during the War of the Rebellion,* 40th Cong., 3d sess., 1869, H. Rept. 45, 7.

CHAPTER 10

1. Edward Channing, *A History of the United States,* 6 vols. (New York: Macmillan, 1905–1925), 6:433, 438–39; J. G. Randall, *The Civil War and Reconstruction* (Boston: D. C. Heath, 1937), 436–43; Roland, *American Iliad,* 109; Futch, *Andersonville,* 122.

2. McPherson, *Ordeal by Fire,* 450–51; Hattaway and Beringer, *Jefferson Davis,* 246; Roland, *American Iliad,* 109.

3. Williams, "Committee on the Conduct of the War," 415–16; James P. Jones, *John A. Logan: Stalwart Republican from Illinois* (Tallahassee: University Presses of Florida, 1982), 9–10, 48; Morton Keller, *Affairs of State: Public Life in Late Nineteenth-Century America* (Cambridge, Mass.: Belknap Press, 1977), 55–56; Roberts, "Afterlife," 40.

4. "Hill–Blaine Debate on Amnesty Bill," U.S. Congress, *Congressional Record,* 44th Cong., 1st sess., 10–13 January 1876, 4:323–25.

5. Ibid., 350–51.

6. Davis, *Man and His Hour,* 663, 668–69.

7. J. William Jones, "The Treatment of Prisoners during the War between the States," *SHSP* 1, no. 3 (March 1876): 113–21, esp. 115, and no. 4 (April 1876): 225–327.

8. Jones, "Treatment of Prisoners," 115–31. The form and specifics of Jones's response to charges are evident in Davis's *Rise and Fall of the Confederate Government* and *Andersonville and Other War-Prisons* as well as in Jones's "The *Nation* on Our Discussion of the Prison Question," *SHSP* 3, no. 4 (April 1877): 197–214.

9. Blakey, *Winder,* 145; McPherson, *Ordeal by Fire,* 451.

10. Blakey, *Winder,* 188, 170.

11. "Report of the Joint Committee of the Confederate Congress Appointed to Investigate the Condition and Treatment of Prisoners of War," in *SHSP* 1, no. 3 (March 1876): 142. Italics in original.

12. Jones, "Treatment of Prisoners," 115.

13. Davis, *Rise and Fall,* 2:606–7.

14. McPherson, *Battle Cry of Freedom,* 800.

15. These depots had been fully operational since 1862. See Goff, *Confederate Supply,* 77–78.

16. Jones, ed., "Resources of the Confederacy in 1865," 99, 105.; U.S. Congress, House, *Report on the Treatment of Prisoners,* 216; Brown, *Salisbury,* 152.

17. Goff, *Confederate Supply,* 138.

18. Wiley, *Johnny Reb,* 90.

19. Ibid., 44; Davis, *Andersonville and Other War-Prisons,* 8.

20. Robert C. Black, *The Railroads of the Confederacy* (Chapel Hill: University of North Carolina Press, 1952), 294–95.

21. James F. Doster, "Were the Southern Railroads Destroyed by the Civil War?" *CWH* 7, no. 3 (September 1961): 310; Goff, *Confederate Supply,* 212.

22. For a detailed discussion of logistical support during the Petersburg campaign, see Noah Andre Trudeau, *The Last Citadel: Petersburg, Virginia, June 1864–April 1865* (Boston: Little Brown, 1991).

23. Carl L. Romanek, "The 'Inherent Logic' of Andersonville," in *Andersonville Prison: Lessons in Organizational Failure,* ed. Joseph P. Cangemi and Casimir J. Kowalski (Lanham, Md.: University Press of America, 1992), 50; Hay, "Commissary General," 20–21.

24. Jones, "Treatment of Prisoners," 115. This is also the justification offered by Varina Davis in her postwar apologia of her husband's administration. See Varina Davis, *Jefferson Davis, Ex-President of the Confederate States of America: A Memoir by His Wife,* 2 vols. (Baltimore: Nautical and Aviation Publishing Company of America, 1990), 2:536–37.

25. Brent and Richardson to General Braxton Bragg, 14 March 1864, Correspondence, Circulars, and Orders of the Confederate Military Prison at Richmond, Va., Relating to Federal Prisoners of War, 1887, RG 249, Entry 135, NA.

26. Brown, *Salisbury,* 124.

27. Jones, "Treatment of Prisoners," 115. Italics in original.

28. *OR,* ser. 1, vol. 64, pt. 1, 324; Brown, *Salisbury,* 127, 154.

29. Stewart Brooks, *Civil War Medicine* (Springfield, Ill.: Charles C. Thomas, 1966), 108–17.

30. Jones, "Treatment of Prisoners," 166–67; McPherson, *Battle Cry of Freedom,* 802; Futch, *Andersonville,* 103–7; *OR,* ser. 2, vol. 7, 1012, and vol. 8, 614–15, 618–23.

31. Jones, "Treatment of Prisoners," 115–16. Italics in original.

32. Ibid., 147.

33. *OR,* ser. 2, vol. 4, 829, 830–31; U.S. Congress, *Journal of the Congress of the Confederate States of America, 1861–1865,* 7 vols. (Washington, D.C.: GPO, 1904–1905), 5:469, 547; Hattaway and Beringer, *Jefferson Davis,* 191, 302.

34. Cooper, *Jefferson Davis,* 408; Walter L. Fleming, "Two Important Letters by Jefferson Davis Discovered," *SHSP* 36 (1908): 8–12.

35. Richardson, ed. *Messages and Papers of Jefferson Davis,* 1:445.

36. Davis to R. H. Chilton, 2 September and 9 December 1875, in Fleming, "Two Important Letters," 10–11.

37. U.S. Congress, House, *Report on the Treatment of Prisoners,* 7.

38. Jones, "Treatment of Prisoners," 326.

39. *OR,* ser. 2, vol. 6, 315.

40. Hunter, "Warden for the Union," 231.

41. An early example of this interpretation may be found in James G. Randall, *Constitutional Problems under Lincoln,* rev. ed. (Urbana: University of Illinois Press, 1964), 155. Later Lincoln biographers have also espoused this view, and Basler's edition of Lincoln's *Collected Works* is replete with examples of the president intervening on behalf of individual prisoners for either personal or political reasons.

42. Mark E. Neely Jr., *The Fate of Liberty: Abraham Lincoln and Civil Liberties* (New York: Oxford University Press, 1991), 157.

43. *Rock Island Argus,* 21 and 25 November 1864; McAdams, *Rebels at Rock Island,* 162–65.

44. Hyman and Thomas, *Stanton,* 388; Paludan, *Presidency of Abraham Lincoln,* 106.

45. Brian H. Reid, "Historians and the Joint Committee on the Conduct of the War, 1861–1865," *CWH* 38, no. 4 (December 1992): 325.

46. Hans L. Trefousse, "The Joint Committee on the Conduct of the War: A Reassessment," *CWH* 10, no. 1 (March 1964): 19.

47. Tap, *Over Lincoln's Shoulder,* 3–5, 256.

48. Paludan, *Presidency of Abraham Lincoln,* 104–5.

49. Lincoln to Stanton, 18 March 1864, Edwin M. Stanton Papers, Reel 7, Manuscript Division, LC.

50. Lincoln to Hitchcock, 10 January 1864, Abraham Lincoln Papers, Reel 97, Series 3, Manuscript Division, LC; Basler, ed., *Collected Works,* 7:257, 119–20.

51. Futch, *Andersonville,* 118–19.

52. Sabina Dismukes to Jefferson Davis, 12 October 1864, in "A Statement of the Evidence Found in the Archive Office of the War Department Relating to the Treatment of Union Prisoners," Papers Relating to Confederate Camps and Other Places Where Federal Prisoners Were Confined during the Period 1861–1865, RG 109, Entry 464, Box 1, NA.

Bibliography

PRIMARY SOURCES

Manuscript and Archival Material

Andersonville National Historic Site, Andersonville, Ga.
  Andersonville Vertical File, Section 2, American Prisoners of War, Letters
    Written by Howell Cobb and R. J. Hallett.
  Andersonville Vertical File, Section 2, American Prisoners of War, Newspaper
    Articles, Ande., Oglethorpe, Elmira (*Macon Telegraph*).
  Catalog Number 133–150, ANDE File Box 4-A.
  Catalog Number 429–441, ANDE File Box 4-A.
  Catalog Number 442–454, ANDE File Box 4-A.
  Drawer 1, Section 2, American Prisoners of War, Civil War, Confederate Sol-
    diers' Accounts, Civil War.
  Drawer 3, Folder V973.772, Camp Parole, Annapolis, Maryland.

John Hay Library, Brown University, Providence, R.I.
  Jesse W. Weik Collection of Lincoln Documents and Manuscripts

Manuscript Division, Library of Congress, Washington, D.C.
  Edward Bates Papers
  Benjamin F. Butler Papers
  Jefferson Davis Papers
  John Hay Papers
  Ethan A. Hitchcock Papers
  Abraham Lincoln Papers
  Montgomery C. Meigs Papers

John C. Nicolay Papers
Frederick L. Olmsted Papers
Edwin M. Stanton Papers
George H. Stuart Papers
Benjamin F. Wade Papers
Gideon Welles Papers

National Archives, Washington, D.C.
Record Group 109, Box 3, War Dept. Collection of Confederate Records, General Records of the Government of the Confederate States of America.
Record Group 109, Entry 1, Letterbook, Papers of Jefferson Davis.
Record Group 109, Entry 199, Box 1, Union Provost Marshal's File, Confederate Prisoners, Rolls of Confederate Prisoners, Purchased May 3, 1879.
Record Group 109, Entry 445, Box 3, General Records of the Government of the Confederate States of America, Records Pertaining to Prisoners of War.
Record Group 109, Entry 464, Box 1, Papers Relating to Confederate Camps and Other Places Where Federal Prisoners Were Confined during the Period 1861–1865.
Record Group 109, Vol. 232, Chap. 9, Secretary of War, Letters Sent, Richmond, Virginia, Relating to Prisoners, 1863–1865.
Record Group 109, Vol. 245, Chap. 9, Secretary of War, Schedule of Papers in the Archive Office Referring to the Exchange and Treatment of Prisoners in Southern Prisons, 1861–1865.
Record Group 249, Entry 107, Roll 553, Extract from the *Charleston Courier* Relating to the Killing of Federals by Confederates, December 1863.
Record Group 249, Entry 135, Correspondence, Circulars, and Orders of the Confederate Military Prison at Richmond, Virginia, Relating to Federal Prisoners of War, 1887.
Record Group 249, Entry 167, Letters, Telegrams, Orders, and Circulars Received from the Commissary General of Prisoners Relating to Paroled Federal Prisoners and to Confederate Prisoners of War, 1862–1865.
Record Group 249, Entry 181, General and Special Orders Received by Headquarters of the 5th Regiment of Paroled Prisoners, November 1862–March 1863.
Record Group 249, Entry 311, Box 1, Records of the Commissary General of Prisoners, Federal Prisoner-of-War Military Prisons and Prison Camps, 1862–1865, Johnson's Island, Ohio, Telegrams Received, November 1863–October 1864.

Record Group 249, Nos. 547–654, Box 7, Records of the Commissary General of Prisoners, Records Relating to Individual Prisoners of War, Miscellaneous Rolls and Related Records of Federal Prisoners of War, 1861–1865.

Record Group 249, Office of the Commissary General of Prisoners, Letters Sent.

Record Group 249, Records of the Office of the Commissary General of Prisoners, Papers of General William Hoffman, 1862–1867, Records Relating to Civilian Personnel in the Office of the Commissary General of Prisoners.

Southern Historical Collection, Wilson Library, University of North Carolina, Chapel Hill
    Jefferson Davis Papers
    E. Kirby Smith Papers
    John H. Winder Papers

Government Documents and Publications

Continental Congress. *Journals of the Continental Congress, 1774–1789.* 34 vols. Washington, D.C.: Government Printing Office, 1904–1937.

State of Michigan. Senate. *Resolutions of the Legislature of Michigan in Favor of the Adoption of Measures for the Exchange of Prisoners.* 34th Cong., 2d sess., 1862, Misc. Doc. 23.

U.S. Congress. *American State Papers: Foreign Relations.* 6 vols. Washington, D.C.: Government Printing Office, 1832–1859.

———. *Congressional Globe.*

———. *Congressional Record.*

———. *Journal of the Congress of the Confederate States of America, 1861–1865.* 7 vols. Washington, D.C.: Government Printing Office, 1904–1905.

———. *The New American State Papers, Naval Affairs.* 10 vols. Edited by Jack Bauer. Wilmington, Del.: Scholarly Resources, 1981.

———. *Reports of the Joint Committee on the Conduct of the War, Reports.* 8 vols. Washington, D.C.: Government Printing Office, 1863–1866.

———, comp. *A Descriptive Catalogue of the Government Publications of the United States, September 5, 1774–March 4, 1881.* Washington, D.C.: Government Printing Office, 1885.

U.S. Congress. House. *Exchange of Prisoners of War.* 37th Cong., 2d sess., 1862, H. Ex. Doc. 124.

———. *Exchange of Prisoners of War.* 38th Cong., 2d sess., 1865, H. Ex. Doc. 20.

———. *Fort Pillow Massacre*. 38th Cong., 1st sess., 1864, H. Rept. 65.

———. *Mexican War Correspondence. Message of the President of the United States, and the Correspondence Therewith Communicated, between the Secretary of War and Other Officers of the Government upon the Subject of the Mexican War*. 30th Cong., 1st sess., 1848, House Ex. Doc. No. 60.

———. *Report on the Treatment of Prisoners of War by the Rebel Authorities, During the War of the Rebellion*. 40th Cong., 3d sess., 1869, H. Rept. 45.

———. *The Trial of Henry Wirz*. 40th Cong., 2d sess., 1868, H. Ex. Doc. 23.

U.S. Congress. House. Joint Committee on the Conduct of the War. *Exchange of Prisoners*. 38th Cong., 2d sess., 1865, H. Ex. Doc. 32.

———. *Returned Prisoners*. 38th Cong., 1st sess., 1864, H. Rept. 67.

U.S. Congress. Senate. *A Digest of the International Law of the United States*. 49th Cong., 1st sess., 1886, S. Misc. Doc.162, Pt. 3.

———. *Journal of the Congress of the Confederate States of America, 1861–1865*. 7 vols. 58th Cong., 2d sess. 1903, S. Doc. 23.

U.S. Congress. Senate. Joint Committee on the Conduct of the War. *Report on Returned Prisoners*. 38th Cong., 1st sess., 1864, S. Rept. 68.

———. *Treatment of Prisoners*. 38th Cong., 2d sess., 1864, S. Rept. 142, Pt. 3.

U.S. Quartermaster General's Office. *The Martyrs Who, for Our Country, Gave up Their Lives in the Prison Pens in Andersonville, Ga*. Washington, D.C.: Government Printing Office, 1866.

U.S. Sanitary Commission. *Narrative of Privations and Sufferings of United States Officers and Soldiers in the Hands of Rebel Authorities, Being the Report of a Commission of Inquiry Appointed by the United States Sanitary Commission, With an Appendix, Containing the Testimony*. Boston: Littells Living Age, 1864.

U.S. War Department. *Bibliography of State Participation in the Civil War, 1861–1866*. 1913. Reprint, Charlottesville, Va.: Allen Publishing, 1961.

———. *Revised Regulations for the Army of the United States, 1861*. Philadelphia: J. G. L. Brown, 1861.

———. *The War of the Rebellion: A Compilation of the Official Records of the Union and Confederate Armies*. 128 vols. Washington, D.C.: Government Printing Office, 1880–1901.

Newspapers

Charleston (S. C.) Mercury, 1861–1862.
Chicago Tribune, 1864.
(St. Louis) Daily Missouri Democrat, 1864.

Frank Leslie's Illustrated Newspaper, 1862–1864.

Harper's Weekly, 1862–1864.

(Springfield) Illinois State Register, 1862.

Indianapolis (Ind.) Journal, 1862.

Indianapolis (Ind.) Sentinel, 1863–1864.

Macon (Ga.) Telegraph, 1864.

Missouri Republican, 1861.

National Intelligencer, 1862–1864.

New York Times, 1861–1865.

Richmond Daily Examiner, 1861–1864.

Richmond Dispatch, 1862–1864.

Richmond Enquirer, 1861–1865.

Richmond Sentinel, 1864.

Richmond Whig, 1862–1864.

Rock Island (Ill.) Argus, 1864.

Printed Primary Sources

Barbiere, Joe. *Scraps from the Prison Table*. Doylestown, Pa: W. W. H. Davis, 1868.

Bartleson, Frederick A. *Letters from Libby Prison*. New York: Greenwich, 1956.

Barziza, Decimus U. *The Adventures of a Prisoner of War, 1863–1864*. Edited by R. Henderson Shuffler. Austin: University of Texas Press, 1964.

Basler, Roy P., ed. *The Collected Works of Abraham Lincoln*. 8 vols. New Brunswick, N.J.: Rutgers University Press, 1953–1955.

Beale, Howard K., ed. *The Diary of Edward Bates, 1959–1866*. Washington, D.C.: Government Printing Office, 1933.

———. *The Diary of Gideon Welles, Secretary of the Navy under Lincoln*, Vol. 2, *April 1, 1864–December 31, 1866*. New York: W. W. Norton, 1960.

Booth, Benjamin F. *Dark Days of the Rebellion, or Life in Southern Military Prisons, Giving a Correct and Thrilling History of Unparalleled Suffering, Narrow Escapes, Heroic Encounters, Bold Achievement, Cold-Blooded Murders, Severe Tests of Loyalty, and Patriotism*. Indianola, Ia.: Booth Publishing, 1897.

Burdick, John M. "The Andersonville Journal of Sergeant J. M. Burdick." Edited by Ovid L. Futch. *Georgia Historical Quarterly* 45 (1961): 287–95.

Burrows, J. L. "Recollections of Libby Prison." *Southern Historical Society Papers* 11 (February–March 1883): 83–92.

Butler, Benjamin F. *Butler's Book*. Boston: A. M. Thayer, 1892.

Censer, Jane Turner, ed. *The Papers of Frederick Law Olmsted.* Vol. 4, *Defending the Union: The Civil War and the U.S. Sanitary Commission, 1861–1863.* Baltimore: Johns Hopkins University Press, 1986.

Confederate States of America. *A Digest of the Military and Naval Laws of the Confederate States, from the Commencement of the Provisional Congress to the End of the First Congress under the Permanent Constitution.* Columbia, S.C.: Evans and Cogswell, 1864.

Confederate States of America. Congress. Committee to Inquire into the Treatment of Prisoners at Castle Thunder. *Evidence Taken before the Committee of the House of Representatives to Inquire into the Treatment of Prisoners at Castle Thunder.* Richmond, Va.: n.p., 1863.

Confederate States of America. War Department. *General Orders from Adjutant and Inspector General's Office, Confederate States Army, in 1862.* Charleston, S.C.: Evans and Cogswell, 1863.

———. *General Orders from Adjutant and Inspector General's Office, Confederate States Army, from January 1862, to December 1863, Both Inclusive.* Columbia, S.C.: Evans and Cogswell, 1864.

———. *General Orders from Adjutant and Inspector General's Office, Confederate States Army, from January 1, 1864, to July 1, 1864, Inclusive.* Columbia, S.C.: Evans and Cogswell, 1864.

———. *Laws for the Army and the Navy of the Confederate States.* Richmond, Va.: Ritchie and Dunnavant, 1861.

Corcoran, Michael. *The Captivity of General Corcoran, the Only Authentic and Reliable Narrative of the Trials and Sufferings Endured during his Twelve Months' Imprisonment in Richmond and Other Southern Cities, by Brig. General Michael Corcoran, the Hero of Bull Run.* Philadelphia: Barclay, 1862.

Crist, Lynda Lasswell, ed. *The Papers of Jefferson Davis.* Vols. 7, 8, and 10. Baton Rouge: Louisiana State University Press, 1992, 1995, 1999.

Croffut, W. A., ed. *Fifty Years in Camp and Field: The Diary of Major General Ethan Allen Hitchcock, U.S.A.* New York: G. P. Putnam's Sons, 1909.

Davis, Jefferson. *Andersonville and Other War-Prisons.* New York: Belford, 1890.

———. *The Rise and Fall of the Confederate Government.* 2 vols. New York: D. Appleton, 1881.

Davis, Varina Howell. *Jefferson Davis, Ex-President of the Confederate States of America: A Memoir by his Wife.* Introd. by Craig L. Symonds. 2 vols. Baltimore: Nautical and Aviation Publishing Co. of America, 1990.

Donald, David H, ed. *Inside Lincoln's Cabinet: The Civil War Diaries of Salmon P. Chase.* New York: Longmans, Green, 1954.

Doubleday, Abner. "From Moultrie to Sumter." In *Battles and Leaders of the Civil War.* 4 vols. 1888. Reprint, Secaucus, N.J.: Castle, 1982. 40–49.

Duganne, A. J. H. *Twenty Months in the Department of the Gulf.* New York: n.p., 1865.

Eberhart, James W. "Diary of Salisbury Prison by James W. Eberhart." Edited by Florence C. McLaughlin. *Western Pennsylvania History Magazine* 56 (1973): 211–51.

Ely, Alfred. *Journal of Alfred Ely, A Prisoner of War in Richmond.* Edited by Charles Lanman. New York: D. Appleton, 1862.

Fehrenbacher, Don E., ed. *Abraham Lincoln: Speeches and Writings, 1859–1865.* New York: Library of America, 1989.

———, and Virginia Fehrenbacher, eds. *Recollected Works of Abraham Lincoln.* Stanford: Stanford University Press, 1996.

Fitzpatrick, John C., ed. *The Writings of George Washington.* 39 vols. Washington, D.C.: Government Printing Office, 1931–1944.

Froman, B. R. "An Interior View of the Camp Douglas Conspiracy." *Southern Bivouac* 1 (September 1882–August 1883): 63–69.

Frost, Griffin. *Camp and Prison Journal.* Quincy, Ill.: Quincy Herald Book and Job Office, 1867.

Gillett, Mary C. *The Army Medical Department, 1818–1865.* Washington, D.C.: U.S. Army Center for Military History, 1987.

Gorham, George C. *Life and Public Services of Edwin M. Stanton.* 2 vols. Boston: Houghton Mifflin, 1899.

Grant, Ulysses S. *Memoirs and Selected Letters: Personal Memoirs of U. S. Grant, Selected Letters 1839–1865.* Edited by John Y. Simon. New York: Library of America, 1990.

———. *The Papers of Ulysses S. Grant.* Edited by John Y. Simon. 24 vols. to date. Carbondale: Southern Illinois University Press, 1967–.

———. *Personal Memoirs of U. S. Grant.* 2 vols. New York: C. L. Webster, 1885–1886.

Gurowski, Adam. *Diary.* 3 vols. 1862–1866. Reprint, New York: Burt Franklin, 1968.

Harding, George C. "Prison Life at Camp Pratt." Edited by Author W. Bergeron Jr. *Louisiana History* 14 (1973): 386–91.

Harwell, Richard B, ed. *The Confederate Reader.* New York: Longmans, Green, 1957.

———. *The Union Reader.* New York: Longmans Green, 1958.

Hayes, John D. ed., *Samuel Francis DuPont: A Selection from His Civil War Letters.* 3 vols. Ithaca, N.Y.: Cornell University Press, 1969.

Hempstead, Junius Lackland. "How Long Will This Misery Continue?" Edited by Bess Beaty and Judy Caprio. *Civil War Times Illustrated* 19, no. 10 (February 1981): 20–23.

Howard, Francis K. *Fourteen Months in American Bastilles.* Baltimore: Kelly, Hedian, and Piet, 1863.

Hughes, Frank. "Diary of Lieutenant Frank Hughes." Edited by Norman Niccum. *Indiana Magazine of History* 45 (1949): 275–84.

James, Frederic Augustus. *Frederic Augustus James's Civil War Diary: Sumter to Andersonville.* Edited by Jefferson J. Hammer. Rutherford, N.J.: Fairleigh Dickinson University Press, 1973.

Jeffrey, William H. *Richmond Prisons, 1861–1862, Compiled from the Original Records Kept by the Confederate Government, Journals Kept by Union Prisoners of War, Together with the Name, Rank, Company, Regiment, and State of the Four Thousand Who Were Confined There.* St. Johnsbury, Vt.: Republican Press, 1893.

Jervey, Edward D., ed. *Prison Life among the Rebels: Recollections of a Union Chaplain.* Kent, Ohio: Kent State University Press, 1990.

Johnston, Joseph E. *Narrative of Military Operations.* New York: D. Appleton and Sons, 1874.

Jones, J. William, ed. "Resources of the Confederacy in 1865—Report of General I. M. St. John, Commissary General." *Southern Historical Society Papers* 3, no. 3 (March 1877): 97–111.

Jones, John B. *A Rebel War Clerk's Diary.* Edited by Earl Schenk Miers. Baton Rouge: Louisiana State University Press, 1993.

Jones, William D. *Confederate View of the Treatment of Prisoners, Compiled from Official Records and Other Documents.* Richmond, Va.: Southern Historical Society, 1876.

Julian, George W. *Political Recollections, 1840–1872.* Chicago: Jansen, McClurg, 1884.

———. *Speeches on Political Questions, 1850–1868.* Edited by Lydia Maria Child. 1872. Reprint. Westport, Conn.: Negro University Press, 1970.

Keiley, Anthony M. *Prisoner of War, or Ten Months among the Yankees.* Richmond, Va.: West and Johnston, 1865.

King, John R. *My Experience in the Confederate Army and in Northern Prisons.* Clarksburg, W.Va.: United Daughters of the Confederacy, 1917.

Libby Prison War Museum Association. *Libby Prison War Museum Catalog and Program.* Chicago: Libby Prison War Museum Association, 1890.

Lieber, Francis. *Contributions to Political Science.* Philadelphia: J. B. Lippincott, 1880.

Lossing, Benson J. *Pictorial Field Book of the Civil War: Journeys through the Battlefields in the Wake of Conflict.* Vol. 3. 1874. Reprint, Baltimore: Johns Hopkins University Press, 1997.

Marshall, John A. *American Bastille: A History of the Illegal Arrests and Imprisonment of American Citizens during the Civil War.* Philadelphia: Thomas W. Hartley, 1869.

McElroy, John. *Andersonville: A Story of Rebel Prisons.* Washington, D.C.: National Tribune, 1899.

Miller, Emily Van Dorn. *A Soldier's Honor.* New York: n.p., 1902.

Moore, Hugh. "Illinois Commentary: A Reminiscence Of Confederate Prison Life." Edited by Clifford A. Haka. *Journal of the Illinois State Historical Society* 65 (1972): 451–61.

Nevins, Allan, and Milton H. Thomas, eds. *The Diary of George Templeton Strong.* Vol. 3, *The Civil War, 1860–1865.* New York: Macmillan, 1952.

Paton, James E. "The Civil War Journal of James E. Paton." *Register of the Kentucky Historical Society* 61 (1963): 220–31.

Patterson, Edmund D. *Yankee Rebel: The Civil War Journal of Edmund DeWitt Patterson.* Edited by John G. Barrett. Chapel Hill: University of North Carolina Press, 1966.

Pettenger, William. *Daring and Suffering: A History of the Great Railroad Adventure.* Philadelphia: J. W. Daughaday, 1863.

Powell, William H. *Powell's Record of Living Officers of the United States Army.* Philadelphia: L. R. Hamersley, 1890.

Putnam, George H. "A Soldier's Narrative of Life at Libby and Danville Prisons." *The Outlook* (25 March 1911): 695–704.

Putnam, Sallie Brock. *Richmond during the War: Four Years of Personal Observation.* New York: G. W. Carlton, 1867.

Ransom, John. *John Ransom's Diary.* 1883. Reprint, New York: Berkley Books, 1963.

"Report of the Joint Committee of the Confederate Congress Appointed to Investigate the Condition and Treatment of Prisoners of War." In *Southern Historical Society Papers* 1, no. 3 (March 1876): 132–51.

Reynolds, Daniel N. "Memoirs of Libby Prison." Edited by Paul H. Giddens. *Michigan History Magazine* 23 (Autumn 1939): 391–98.

Richardson, James D., ed. *The Messages and Papers of Jefferson Davis and the Confederacy, Including Diplomatic Correspondence, 1861–1865.* 2 vols. New York: Chelsea House–Robert Hector, 1966.

Ripple, Ezra Hoyt. *Dancing along the Deadline: The Andersonville Memoir of a Prisoner of the Confederacy.* Edited by Mark A. Snell. Novato, Calif.: Persidio Press, 1996.

Ross, Charles. "Diary of Charles Ross, 1863." *Vermont History* 31 (1963): 4–64.

Sangston, Lawrence. *The Bastilles of the North.* Baltimore: Kelly, Hedian, and Piet, 1863.

Scharf, J. Thomas. *History of St. Louis City and County, from the Earliest Periods to the Present Day.* Philadelphia: Louis H. Everts, 1883.

Schmitt, Frederick E. "Prisoner of War: Experiences in Southern Prisons." Edited by John P. Hunter. *Wisconsin Magazine of History* 42 (1958–1959): 83–93.

Schwartz, Stephen. *Twenty-Two Months a Prisoner of War.* St. Louis, Mo.: F. Nelson, 1891.

Scott, Winfield. *Memoirs of Lieut.-General Scott, LL.D.* 2 vols. 1864. Reprint, Freeport, N.Y.: Books for Libraries Press, 1970.

Sedgwick, Arthur G. "Libby Prison: The Diary of Arthur G. Sedgwick." Edited by William M. Armstrong. *Virginia Magazine of History and Biography* 71 (1963): 449–60.

Shatzel, Albert H. "Imprisoned at Andersonville: The Diary of Albert Harry Shatzel." Edited by Donald F. Danker. *Nebraska History* 38 (1957): 81–125.

Sneden, Robert Knox. *Eye of the Storm: A Civil War Odyssey.* Edited by Charles F. Bryan Jr. and Nelson D. Lankford. New York: Free Press, 2000.

———. *Images from the Storm: Three Hundred Civil War Images by the Author of "Eye of the Storm."* Edited by Charles F. Bryan Jr., James C. Kelly, and Nelson D. Lankford. New York: Free Press, 2001.

Speer, William H. "A Confederate Soldier's View of Johnson's Island Prison." Edited by James B. Murphy. *Ohio History* 79 (1970): 101–11.

Spencer, Ambrose. *A Narrative of Andersonville.* New York: Harper and Brothers, 1866.

Stamp, J. B. "Ten Months' Experience in Northern Prisons." *Alabama Historical Quarterly* 18 (1956): 486–98.

Sterns, Amos E. *The Civil War Diary of Amos E. Sterns, A Prisoner at Andersonville.* Edited by Leon Basile. Rutherford, N.J.: Fairleigh Dickinson University Press, 1981.

Stevenson, R. Randolph. *The Southern Side; Or, Andersonville Prison.* Baltimore: Turnbull Brothers, 1876.

Stortz, John. "Experiences of a Prisoner during the Civil War in and out of the Hands of the Rebels." *Annals of Iowa* 37 (1964): 167–94.

Taylor, G. T. "Prison Experience in Elmira, New York." *Confederate Veteran* 20 (1912): 327.

Thompson, Holland, ed. *The Photographic History of the Civil War.* Vol. 4, *Prisons and Hospitals.* 1911. Reprint, Secaucus, N.Y.: Blue and Gray Press, 1987.

U.S. Christian Commission. *Record of the Federal Dead From Libby, Belle Isle, Danville, and Camp Lawton Prisons and at City Point, and in the Field before Petersburg and Richmond.* Philadelphia: James B. Rogers, 1866.

Welles, Gideon. *The Diary of Gideon Welles.* Edited by John T. Morse. 3 vols. Boston: Houghton Mifflin, 1911.

Welles, James M. "Tunneling out of Libby Prison." *McClure's Magazine* 22 (1902): 317–26.

Wilkins, William D. "Forgotten in the 'Black Hole': A Diary from Libby Prison." *Civil War Times Illustrated* 15, no. 3 (1976): 36–44.

Younger, Edward, ed. *Inside the Confederate Government: The Diary of Robert Garlick Hill Kean.* Baton Rouge: Louisiana State University Press, 1993.

SECONDARY SOURCES

Books

Abdill, George B. *Civil War Railroads.* Seattle: Superior Publishing, 1961.

Almund, Curtis A. *Federalism in the Southern Confederacy.* Washington, D.C.: Public Affairs Press, 1966.

Baker, Raymond, and Edwin C. Bearss. *Andersonville: The Story of A Civil War Prison.* Washington, D.C.: National Park Service, 1972.

Bauer, K. Jack. *The Mexican War, 1846–1848.* Lincoln: University of Nebraska Press, 1974.

Bearss, Edwin C. *Andersonville National Historic Site: Historic Resource Study and Historical Base Map, Sumter and Macon Counties, Georgia.* Washington, D.C.: National Park Service, 1970.

Beers, Henry Putney. *The Confederacy: A Guide to the Archives of the Government of the Confederate States of America.* Washington, D.C.: National Archives and Record Administration, 1986.

Beitzell, Edwin W. *Point Lookout Prison Camp for Confederates.* Abell, Md.: By the Author, 1972.

Bensel, Richard F. *Yankee Leviathan: The Origins of Central State Authority in America, 1859–1877.* New York: Cambridge University Press, 1990.

Benson, Berry. *Berry Benson's Civil War Book.* Edited by Susan Williams Benson. Athens: University of Georgia Press, 1962.

Black, Robert C. *The Railroads of the Confederacy.* Chapel Hill: University of North Carolina Press, 1952.

Blakey, Arch Frederic. *General John H. Winder, C.S.A.* Gainesville: University of Florida Press, 1990.

Blanco, Richard L. *The War of the American Revolution: A Selected Annotated Bibliography of Published Sources.* New York: Garland Publishing, 1984.

Boatner, Mark M., III. *The Civil War Dictionary.* New York: David McKay, 1959.

Bogue, Allan. *The Earnest Men: Republicans in the Civil War Senate.* Madison: University of Wisconsin Press, 1981.

Bowden, J. J. *The Exodus of Federal Forces from Texas, 1861.* Austin, Tex.: Eakin Press, 1986.

Bowman, Larry G. *Captive Americans: Prisoners during the American Revolution.* Athens: Ohio University Press, 1976.

Breen, Donald J., and Phillip Shriver. *Ohio's Military Prisons in the Civil War.* Columbus: Ohio State University Press, 1964.

Bremmer, Robert H. *The Public Good: Philanthropy and Welfare in the Civil War Era.* New York: Alfred Knopf, 1980.

Brooks, Stewart. *Civil War Medicine.* Springfield, Ill.: Charles C. Thomas, 1966.

Brown, Louis A. *The Salisbury Prison: A Case Study of Confederate Military Prisons, 1861–1865.* Wendell, N.C.: Broadfoots, 1980.

Bryant, William O. *Cahaba Prison and the Sultana Disaster.* Tuscaloosa: University of Alabama Press, 1990.

Catton, Bruce. *A Stillness at Appomattox.* New York: Doubleday, 1953.

Channing, Edward. *A History of the United States.* 6 vols. New York: Macmillan, 1905–1925.

Channing, Steven A. *Crisis of Fear: Secession in South Carolina.* New York: W. W. Norton, 1974.

Chesebrough, David B. *"God Ordained This War": Sermons on the Sectional Crisis, 1830–1865.* Columbia: University of South Carolina Press, 1991.

Cole, Garold L. *Civil War Eyewitnesses: An Annotated Bibliography of Books and Articles, 1855–1986.* Columbia: University of South Carolina Press, 1988.

Cooper, William J. *Jefferson Davis, American.* New York: Alfred Knopf, 2000.

Coulter, E. Merton. *Travels in the Confederate States: A Bibliography.* Norman, Okla.: University of Oklahoma Press, 1948.

Cunningham, H. H. *Doctors in Gray: The Confederate Medical Service.* Gloucester, Mass.: Peter Smith, 1970.

Davis, William C. *Battle at Bull Run: A History of the First Major Campaign of the Civil War.* Norwalk, Conn.: Easton Press, 1996.

———. *Jefferson Davis: The Man and His Hour.* New York: Harper Collins, 1991.

———. *Lincoln's Men: How President Lincoln Became Father to an Army and a Nation.* New York: Free Press, 1999.

Denney, Robert E. *Civil War Prisons and Escapes: A Day-by-Day Chronicle.* New York: Sterling Publishing, 1993.

Donald, David H. *Lincoln.* London: Jonathan Cape, 1995.

Dornbusch, C. E. *Military Bibliography of the Civil War.* Vol. 3. New York: New York Public Library, 1972.

Doyle, Robert C. *Voices from Captivity: Interpreting the American POW Narrative.* Lawrence: University Press of Kansas, 1994.

Dunham, Chester Forrester. *The Attitude of the Northern Clergy toward the South, 1860–1865.* Philadelphia: Porcupine Press, 1974.

Durden, Robert F. *The Gray and the Black: The Confederate Debate on Emancipation.* Baton Rouge: Louisiana State University Press, 1972.

Eicher, David J. *The Longest Night: A Military History of the Civil War.* New York: Simon and Schuster, 2001.

Eisenhower, John S. D. *Agent of Destiny: The Life and Times of General Winfield Scott.* New York: Free Press, 1998.

Emerson, Wilson W. *Fort Warren.* Newark: University of Delaware Press, 1960.

Fabian, Ann. *The Unvarnished Truth: Personal Narratives in Nineteenth-Century America.* Berkeley: University of California Press, 2000.

Fleming, Thomas. *Liberty! The American Revolution.* New York: Viking Books, 1997.

Flory, William E. S. *Prisoners of War: A Study in the Development of International Law.* Washington, D.C.: American Council on Public Affairs, 1942.

Fooks, Herbert C. *Prisoners of War.* Federalsburg, Md.: J. W. Stowell Printing, 1924.

Foote, Shelby. *The Civil War: A Narrative.* 3 vols. New York: Vintage Books, 1986.

Frazier, Donald S., ed. *The United States and Mexico at War: Nineteenth-Century Expansionism and Conflict.* New York: Macmillan, 1998.

Freeman, Douglas Southall. *Lee's Lieutenants.* 3 vols. New York: Charles Scribner's Sons, 1942–1944.

Friedman, Lawrence M. *Crime and Punishment in American History.* New York: Basic Books, 1993.

Frohman, Charles E. *Rebels on Lake Eire.* Columbus: Ohio Historical Society, 1965.

Futch, Ovid L. *History of Andersonville Prison.* Gainesville: University of Florida Press, 1968.

Gambee, Budd Leslie. *Frank Leslie and His Illustrated Newspaper, 1855–1860.* Ann Arbor: University of Michigan Department of Library Science, 1964.

Goff, Richard D. *Confederate Supply*. Durham, N.C.: Duke University Press, 1969.

Gragg, Rod, ed. *The Illustrated Confederate Reader*, New York: Gramercy Books, 1989.

Gray, Michael P. *The Business of Captivity: Elmira and Its Civil War Prison*. Kent, Ohio: Kent State University Press, 2001.

Green, Constance M. *Washington, Village and Capital, 1800–1878*. Princeton: Princeton University Press, 1962.

Grimsley, Mark. *The Hard Hand of War : Union Military Policy toward Southern Civilians, 1861–1865*. New York: Cambridge University Press, 1995.

Hagan, Kenneth J. *This People's Navy: The Making of American Sea Power*. New York: Free Press, 1991.

Hammerlein, Richard F. *Prisons and Prisoners of the Civil War*. Boston: Christopher Publishing House, 1934.

Hattaway, Herman, and Richard E. Beringer. *Jefferson Davis, Confederate President*. Lawrence: University Press of Kansas, 2002.

Hesseltine, William B. *Civil War Prisons: A Study in War Psychology*. Columbus: Ohio State University Press, 1930.

———, ed. *Civil War Prisons*. Kent, Ohio: Kent State University Press, 1962.

Hickey, Donald R. *The War of 1812: A Forgotten Conflict*. Urbana: University of Illinois Press, 1989.

Holmes, Clayton W. *The Elmira Prison Camp: A History of the Military Prison at Elmira, New York, July 6, 1864 to July 10, 1865*. New York: G. P. Putnam's Sons, 1912.

Horigan, Michael. *Elmira: Death Camp of the North*. Mechanicsburg, Pa.: Stackpole Books, 2002.

Hyman, Harold M. *To Try Men's Souls: Loyalty Tests in American History*. Berkeley: University of California Press, 1960.

Isham, Asa B., Henry M. Davidson, and Henry B. Furness. *Prisoners of War and Military Prisons*. Cincinnati: Lyman and Cushing, 1890.

Jones, James P. *John A. Logan: Stalwart Republican from Illinois*. Tallahassee: University Presses of Florida, 1982.

Keller, Morton. *Affairs of State: Public Life in Late Nineteenth-Century America*. Cambridge, Mass.: Belknap Press, 1977.

Lawrence, F. Lee. *Camp Ford, C.S.A.* Austin: Texas Civil War Centennial Advisory Committee, 1964.

Leckie, Robert. *From Sea to Shining Sea: From the War of 1812 to the Mexican War, The Saga of America's Expansion*. New York: Harper Perennial, 1993.

———. *George Washington's War: The Saga of the American Revolution*. New York: Harper Collins, 1992.

————. *The Wars of America.* Vol. 1, *From 1600 to 1900.* New York: Harper Perennial, 1992.

Leech, Margaret. *Reveille in Washington, 1860–1865.* New York: Harper and Brothers, 1941.

Levy, George. *To Die in Chicago: Confederate Prisoners at Camp Douglas, 1862–1865.* Gretna, La.: Pelican, 1999.

Lewis, George G., and John Mewha. *History of Prisoner of War Utilization by the United States Army, 1776–1945.* Washington, D.C.: Center of Military History, 1988.

Lynn, John W. *Eight Hundred Paces to Hell: Andersonville, A Compilation of Known Facts and Persistent Rumors.* Fredericksburg, Va.: Sergeant Kirkland's Museum and Historical Society, 1999.

Martin, Samuel J. *Kill-Cavalry: The Life of Union General Hugh Judson Kilpatrick.* Mechanicsburg, Pa.: Stackpole Books, 2000.

Marvel, William. *Andersonville: The Last Depot.* Chapel Hill: University of North Carolina Press, 1994.

Maxwell, William Quentin. *Lincoln's Fifth Wheel: The Political History of the United States Sanitary Commission.* New York: Longmans, Green, 1956.

McAdams, Benton. *Rebels at Rock Island: The Story of a Civil War Prison.* DeKalb, Ill.: Northern Illinois University Press, 2000.

McCaffrey, James M. *The Army of Manifest Destiny: The American Soldier in the Mexican War.* New York: New York University Press, 1992.

McConnell, Stuart. *Glorious Contentment: The Grand Army of the Republic, 1865–1900.* Chapel Hill: University of North Carolina Press, 1992.

McFeely, William S. *Grant: A Biography.* New York: W. W. Norton, 1981.

McPherson, James M. *Abraham Lincoln and the Second American Revolution.* New York: Oxford University Press, 1990.

————. *Battle Cry of Freedom: The Civil War Era.* New York: Oxford University Press, 1988.

————. *The Negro's Civil War: How American Blacks Felt and Acted during the War for the Union.* Urbana: University of Illinois Press, 1982.

————. *Ordeal by Fire: The Civil War and Reconstruction.* 3rd ed. New York: McGraw-Hill, 2001.

Metzger, Charles G. *The Prisoner in the American Revolution.* Chicago: Loyola University Press, 1971.

Miller, John C. *Triumph of Freedom, 1775–1783.* Boston: Little, Brown, 1948.

Millett, Alan R., and Peter Maslowski. *For the Common Defense: A Military History of the United States of America.* New York: Free Press, 1994.

Moore, Jerrold Northrop. *Confederate Commissary General: Lucius Bellinger*

Northrop and the Subsistence Bureau of the Southern Army. Shippensburg, Pa.: White Mane Publishing, 1996.

Munden, Kenneth W., and Henry Putnam Beers. *Guide to Federal Archives Relating to the Civil War.* Washington, D.C.: National Archives and Records Service, 1962.

Murray, J. Ogden. *The Immortal Six Hundred: A Story of Cruelty to Confederate Prisoners of War.* Winchester, Va.: Eddy Press, 1905.

Musicant, Ivan. *Divided Waters: The Naval History of the Civil War.* New York: Harper Collins, 1995.

Neely, Mark E., Jr. *The Abraham Lincoln Encyclopedia.* New York: McGraw-Hill, 1982.

———. *The Fate of Liberty: Abraham Lincoln and Civil Liberties.* New York: Oxford University Press, 1991.

Nichols, James L. *The Confederate Quartermaster in the Trans-Mississippi.* Austin: University of Texas Press, 1964.

Niven, John. *Gideon Welles: Lincoln's Secretary of the Navy.* New York: Oxford University Press, 1973.

Page, James M. *The True Story of Andersonville Prison; A Defense of Major Henry Wirz.* New York: Neale Publishing, 1908.

Paludan, Phillip Shaw. *The Presidency of Abraham Lincoln.* Lawrence: University Press of Kansas, 1994.

Parker, Sandra V. *Richmond's Civil War Prisons.* Lynchburg, Va.: H. E. Howard, 1990.

Randall, James G. *The Civil War and Reconstruction.* Boston: D. C. Heath, 1937.

———. *Constitutional Problems under Lincoln.* Rev. ed. Urbana: University of Illinois Press, 1964.

Reardon, Carol. *Pickett's Charge in History and Memory.* Chapel Hill: University of North Carolina Press, 1997.

Roberts, Edward F. *Andersonville Journey.* Shippensburg, Pa.: Burd Street Press, 1998.

Rock Island Arsenal. *Rock Island Prison Barracks, 1863–1865.* Rock Island, Ill.: Rock Island Arsenal, 1967.

Roland, Charles P. *An American Iliad: The Story of the Civil War.* New York: McGraw-Hill, 1991.

Royster, Charles. *The Destructive War: William Tecumseh Sherman, Stonewall Jackson, and the Americans.* New York: Vintage Books, 1993.

Sandburg, Carl. *Abraham Lincoln: The War Years.* 4 vols. New York: Harcourt Brace, 1939.

Sears, Stephen W. *To the Gates of Richmond: The Peninsula Campaign.* New York: Ticknor and Fields, 1992.

Segars, J. H., ed. *Andersonville: The Southern Perspective.* Atlanta: Southern Heritage Press, 1995.

Shriver, Phillip R., and Donald J. Breen. *Ohio's Military Prisons in the Civil War.* Columbus: Ohio State University Press, 1964.

Sifakis, Stewart. *Who Was Who in the Civil War.* New York: Facts on File Publications, 1988.

Simpson, Brooks D. *Let Us Have Peace: Ulysses S. Grant and the Politics of War and Reconstruction, 1861–1868.* Chapel Hill: University of North Carolina Press, 1991.

Smith, Justin H. *The War with Mexico.* 2 vols. New York: Macmillan, 1919.

Speer, Lonnie R. *Portals to Hell: Military Prisons of the Civil War.* Mechanicsburg, Pa.: Stackpole Books, 1997.

Sprague, Dean. *Freedom under Lincoln.* Boston: Houghton Mifflin, 1965.

Sturgis, Thomas. *Prisoners of War, 1861–1865.* New York: G. P. Putnam's Sons, 1912.

Tap, Bruce. *Over Lincoln's Shoulder: The Committee on the Conduct of the War.* Lawrence: University Press of Kansas, 1998.

Thomas, Benjamin P., and Harold M. Hyman. *Stanton: The Life and Times of Lincoln's Secretary of War.* New York: Alfred A. Knopf, 1962.

Thomas, Emory M. *The Confederate Nation, 1861–1865.* New York: History Book Club Press, 1979.

———. *The Confederate State of Richmond: A Biography of the Capital.* Austin: University of Texas Press, 1971.

Thompson, W. Fletcher, Jr. *The Image of War: The Pictorial Reporting of the American Civil War.* New York: Thomas Yoseloff, 1960.

Trefousse, Hans L. *Benjamin Franklin Wade: Radical Republican from Ohio.* New York: Twayne Publishers, 1963.

———. *The Radical Republicans: Lincoln's Vanguard for Racial Justice.* New York: Alfred A. Knopf, 1969.

Trudeau, Noah Andre. *The Last Citadel: Petersburg, Virginia, June 1864–April 1865.* Boston: Little, Brown, 1991.

Tutorow, Norman E., ed. *The Mexican-American War: An Annotated Bibliography.* Westport, Conn: Greenwood Press, 1981.

Van Tyne, Clyde H. *The Loyalist in the American Revolution.* New York: Macmillan, 1902.

Waitt, Robert W., Jr. *Confederate Military Hospitals in Richmond.* Richmond, Va.: Richmond Civil War Centennial Committee, 1964.

Ward, Geoffrey, with Ken Burns and Rick Burns. *The Civil War: An Illustrated History.* New York: Alfred A. Knopf, 1991.

Weigley, Russell F. *Quartermaster General of the Union Army: A Biography of M. C. Meigs.* New York: Columbia University Press, 1959.

Wiley, Bell I. *The Life of Billy Yank: The Common Soldier of the Union.* Baton Rouge: Louisiana State University Press, 1991.

———. *The Life of Johnny Reb: The Common Soldier of the Confederacy.* Baton Rouge: Louisiana State University Press, 1990.

Williams, T. Harry. *Lincoln and the Radicals.* Madison: University of Wisconsin Press, 1941.

Williamson, James J. *Prison Life in the Old Capitol.* West Orange, N.J.: Williamson Publishing, 1911.

Winders, Richard B. *Mr. Polk's Army: The American Military Experience in the Mexican War.* College Station: Texas A&M Press, 1997.

Winslow, Hattie Lou, and Joseph R. H. Moore. *Camp Morton, 1861–1865.* Indianapolis: Indiana Historical Society, 1940.

Woodward, C. Vann. *Origins of the New South, 1877–1913.* Baton Rouge: Louisiana State University Press, 1971.

Woodworth, Steven E., ed. *The American Civil War: A Handbook of Literature and Research.* Westport, Conn: Greenwood Press, 1996.

Yearns, Wilfred Buck. *The Confederate Congress.* Athens: University of Georgia Press, 1960.

Articles

Alabama State Department of Archives and History. "Original Interments at Cahaba Military Cemetery—Now Interred at Marietta National Cemetery." *Alabama Historical Quarterly* 25 (1963): 192–96.

Anderson, George M. "A Captured Confederate Officer: Nine Letters from Captain James Anderson to His Family." *Maryland Historical Magazine* 76, no. 1 (1971): 62–69.

Antrim, Earl. "Confederate Prison at Montgomery, Alabama." *Alabama Historical Quarterly* 25 (1963): 190–91.

Armstrong, William M. "Libby Prison: The Civil War Diary of Arthur G. Sedgwick." *Virginia Magazine of History and Biography* 71 (1963): 449–60.

Ashcraft, Allan C. "The Confederate Inspector of Railroads for Texas." *Texas Military History* 3 (1963): 32–35.

———. "Staff Functions in the Confederate District of Texas." *Texas Military History* 3 (1963): 114–19.

Baldwin, Terry E. "Clerk of the Dead: Dorance Atwater." *Civil War Times Illustrated* 10, no. 6 (1971): 12–21.

Baldwin, W. T. "In a Federal Prison: Interesting Career of Lieutenant W. W. George of Echols' Brigade." *Southern Historical Society Papers* 29 (1901): 229–39.

Baretski, Charles A. "General Albin Francis Schoepf—A Preliminary View." *Polish-American Studies* 23 (1966): 93–96.

Bensel, Richard F. "Southern Leviathan: The Development of Central State Authority in the Confederate States of America." In *Studies in American Political Development,* edited by Karen Oren and Stephen Skowronek, vol. 2, 68–136. New Haven: Yale University Press, 1987.

Blondo, Richard A. "A View of Point Lookout Prison Camp for Confederates." *Magazine of History* 8, No. 1 (Fall 1993): 30–37.

Bowman, Larry G. "The New Jersey Prisoner Exchange Conferences, 1778–1780." *New Jersey History* 97, no. 3 (1979): 149–58.

———. "The Pennsylvania Prisoner Exchange Conferences, 1778." *Pennsylvania History* 45, no. 3 (July 1978): 257–69.

Brannon, Peter A. "The Cahawba Military Prison, 1863–1865." *Alabama Review* 3, no. 3 (July 1950): 163–73.

Bray, John. "Escape From Richmond." *Civil War Times Illustrated* 5, no. 2 (1966): 28–33.

Breedon, James O. "Andersonville—A Southern Surgeon's Story." *History of Medicine Bulletin* 47 (1973): 317–43.

Bullock, Helen D. "The Papers of John G. Nicolay, Lincoln's Secretary." *Library of Congress Quarterly Journal of Current Acquisitions* 7, no. 3 (May 1950): 3–8.

———. "The Robert Todd Lincoln Collection of the Papers of Abraham Lincoln." *Library of Congress Quarterly Journal of Current Acquisitions* 5, no. 1 (November 1947): 3–8.

Burnham, Philip. "The Andersonvilles of the North." *Military History Quarterly* 10, no. 1 (Autumn 1977): 46–55.

Byrne, Frank L. "A General behind Bars: Neal Dow in Libby Prison." In *Civil War Prisons,* edited by William B. Hesseltine, 60–79. Kent, Ohio: Kent State University Press, 1962.

———. "Libby Prison: A Study in Emotions." *Journal of Southern History* 24 (1958): 430–44.

Castel, Albert. "The Fort Pillow Massacre: A Fresh Examination of the Evidence." *Civil War History* 4 (1958): 37–50.

Chance, Joseph E. "Prisoners of War: Mexican Prisoners." In *The United States and Mexico at War: Nineteenth-Century Expansionism and Conflict,* edited by Donald S. Frazier, 333–35. New York: Macmillan, 1998.

Cimprich, John, and Robert C. Manifort Jr. "The Fort Pillow Massacre: A Statistical Note." *Journal of American History* 76 (1989): 930–37.

Cleary, Ann. "Life and Death in Andersonville Prison." *Historical Journal of Western Massachusetts* 2 (1973): 27–42.

Cook, S. N. "Johnson's Island in War Days." *Ohio Magazine* 1 (1906): 226–32.

Doster, James F. "Were the Southern Railroads Destroyed by the Civil War?" *Civil War History* 7, no. 3 (September 1961): 310–20.

Felt, Jeremy P. "Lucius B. Northrop and the Confederate Subsistence Department." *Virginia Magazine of History and Biography* 69, no. 2 (1961): 181–93.

Fleming, Walter L. "Two Important Letters by Jefferson Davis Discovered." *Southern Historical Society Papers* 36 (1908): 8–12.

Foote, Morris C. "Narrative of an Escape from a Rebel Prison Camp." *American Heritage* 11, no. 4 (1960): 65–75.

Fordney, Chris, ed. "Letters from the Heart." *Civil War Times Illustrated* 34, no. 4 (October 1995): 28, 73–82.

Francis, David W. "The United States Navy and the Johnson's Island Conspiracy: The Case of John C. Carter." *Northwest Ohio Quarterly* 52 (1980): 229–43.

Gabriel, Ralph H. "American Experience with Military Government." *American Historical Review* 49 (October 1943–July 1944): 630–43.

Goldy, James. "I Have Done Nothing to Deserve This Penalty." *Civil War Times Illustrated* 25, no. 10 (1987): 17–21.

Gordon, John D., III. "The Trial of the Officers and Crew of the Schooner 'Savannah.'" *Yearbook—Supreme Court Historical Society* (1983): 31–45.

Hay, Thomas Robson. "Lucius B. Northrop, Commissary General of the Confederacy." *Civil War History* 9, no. 1 (March 1963): 5–23.

Helm, Joseph T. "Prison Life at Belle Isle." *The Cosmopolitan,* n.v. (May 1893): 47–59.

Hesseltine, William B. "Military Prisons of St. Louis." *Missouri Historical Review* 23, no. 3 (1929): 380–99.

———. "The Propaganda Literature of Confederate Prisons." *Journal of Southern History* 1 (February–November 1935): 56–66.

Hill, Louise B. "State Socialism in the Confederate States of America." In *Southern Sketches, Number 9,* ed. J. D. Eggleston, 3–31. Charlottesville, Va.: Historical Publishing, 1936.

Hollandsworth, James G., Jr. "The Execution of White Officers from Black Units by Confederate Forces during the Civil War." *Louisiana History* 35, no. 4 (Fall 1994): 475–89.

Holt, Michael F. "Abraham Lincoln and the Politics of Union." In *Abraham Lincoln and the American Political Tradition,* edited by John I. Thomas, 111–41. Amherst: University of Massachusetts Press, 1986.

Jones, J. William. "The *Nation* on Our Discussion of the Prison Question." *Southern Historical Society Papers* 3, no. 4 (April 1877): 197–214.

———. "The Treatment of Prisoners during the War Between the States." *Southern Historical Society Papers* 1, no. 3 (March 1876): 113–221.

———. "The Treatment of Prisoners during the War Between the States." *Southern Historical Society Papers* 1, no. 4 (April 1876): 225–327.

Jordan, Weymoth T., and Gerald W. Thomas. "Massacre at Plymouth: April 20, 1864." *North Carolina Historical Review* 72, no. 2 (April 1995): 125–93.

Kaufold, John. "The Elmira Observatory." *Civil War Times Illustrated* 16, no. 4 (1977): 30–35.

Keen, Nancy T. "Confederate Prisoners of War at Fort Delaware." *Delaware History* 13 (1968): 1–27.

Keller, Morton. "Much Sickness Prevailed." In *The Illustrated Confederate Reader,* edited by Rod Gragg, 144–46. New York: Gramercy Books, 1989.

King, G. Wayne. "Death Camp at Florence." *Civil War Times Illustrated* 12, no. 9 (January 1974): 34–42.

Kowaleski, John A. "Capt. Mlotkowski of Ft. Delaware." *Polish-American Studies* 23 (1966): 89–92.

Kurnat, Alan A. "Prison Life at Johnson's Island." *Western Reserve Magazine* 6 (September–October 1981): 30–34.

Long, E. B. "Camp Douglas: 'A Hellish Den'?" *Chicago History* 1 (1970): 83–95.

Mallinson, David L. "The Andersonville Raiders." *Civil War Times Illustrated* 10, no. 4 (1971): 24–31.

Marvel, William. "Johnny Ransom's Imagination." *Civil War History* 41, no. 3 (1995): 181–89.

McCaffery, James M. "The Palmyra Massacre." *Civil War Times Illustrated* 19, no. 8 (1980): 38–43.

McKelvy, Blake. "Penology in the Westward Movement." *Pacific Historical Review* 2, no. 4 (December 1933): 418–38.

McLain, Minor H. "The Military Prison at Fort Warren." In *Civil War Prisons,* edited by William B. Hesseltine, 32–47. Kent, Ohio: Kent State University Press, 1962.

Minnesota Historical Society. "A Sampling of Civil War Patriotic Covers." *Minnesota History* 38 (1925): 298–300.

Mitchell, Leon, Jr. "Camp Ford Confederate Military Prison." *Southwestern Historical Quarterly* 66 (1962–1963): 1–16.

Mitchell, Reid. "'Our Prison System, Supposing We Had Any': The Confederate and Union Prison Systems." In *On the Road to Total War: The American Civil*

War and the German Wars of Unification, 1861–1871, edited by Stig Förster and Jörg Nagler, 565–85. Washington, D.C.: German Historical Institute, 1997.

Monaghan, Jay. "How a Yankee, Mistaken for the Devil, Escaped from Andersonville Prison." *Lincoln Herald* 74 (1972): 89–91.

Morseberger, Robert E., and Katherine M. Morseberger. "After Andersonville: The First War Crimes Trial." *Civil War Times Illustrated* 13, no. 4 (1974): 30–41.

Neal, Harry E. "Rebels, Ropes, and Reprieves." *Civil War Times Illustrated* 14, no. 10 (1976): 30–35.

Parrish, T. Michael. "Taylor's Armistice." In *The United States and Mexico at War: Nineteenth-Century Expansionism and Conflict*, edited by Donald S. Frazier, 407. New York: Macmillan, 1998.

Perry-Mosher, Kate E. "The Rock Island POW Camp." *Civil War Times Illustrated* 8, no. 4 (1969): 28–36.

Powell, Morgan Allen. "Cotton for the Relief of Confederate Prisoners." *Civil War History* 9, no. 1 (March 1963): 24–35.

Quinn, Camilla A. C. "Forgotten Soldiers: The Confederate Prisoners at Camp Butler, 1862–1863." *Illinois Historical Journal* 81, no. 1 (Spring 1985): 35–44.

Ramsdell, C. W. "The Confederate Government and the Railroads." *American Historical Review* 22, no. 4 (July 1917): 794–810.

Reck, Emerson W. "Living Death on the Old *Jersey*." *American History Illustrated* 11, no. 3 (1976): 18–23.

Reid, Brian Holden. "Historians and the Joint Committee on the Conduct of the War." *Civil War History* 38, no. 4 (December 1992): 319–41.

Robertson, James I., Jr. "Houses of Horror: Danville's Civil War Prisons." *Virginia Magazine of History and Biography* 69 (1961): 329–45.

———. "Old Capital: Eminence to Infamy." *Maryland Historical Magazine* 65 (1970): 394–412.

———. "The Scourge of Elmira." In *Civil War Prisons*, edited by William B. Hesseltine, 60–79. Kent, Ohio: Kent State University Press, 1962.

Robinson, Ralph. "Retaliation for the Treatment of Prisoners in the War of 1812." *American Historical Review* 49 (October 1943–July 1944): 65–70.

Romanek, Carl. "The 'Inherent Logic' of Andersonville." In *Andersonville Prison: Lessons in Organizational Failure*, edited by Joseph P. Cangemi and Casimir J. Kowalski, 41–50. Lanham, Md.: University Press of America, 1992.

Smith, George Winston. "Propaganda in the American Civil War." *The Social Studies* 35, no. 1 (January 1944): 26–32.

Suderow, Bryce A. "The Battle of the Crater: The Civil War's Worst Massacre." *Civil War History* 43, no. 3 (1997): 219–24.

Sweet, A. Porter. "From Libby to Liberty." *Military Review* 51, no. 4 (1971): 63–70.

Taylor, Eva C. "Holmes and His Sources for 'The Elmira Prison Camp.'" *Chemung Historical Journal* 1 (1955): 59–60.

Thompson, William F., Jr. "Pictorial Propaganda and the Civil War." *Wisconsin Magazine of History* 46 (1962): 21–31.

Toney, Marcus B. "Our Dead at Elmira." *Southern Historical Society Papers* 29 (1901): 193–97.

Trefousse, Hans L. "The Joint Committee on the Conduct of the War: A Reassessment." *Civil War History* 10, no. 1 (March 1964): 5–19.

Trimble, Tony. "'A Quiet Sabbath': Reflections From Johnson's Island." *Civil War Times Illustrated* 22, no. 9 (January 1984): 20–23.

Tusken, Roger. "In the Bastille of the Rebels." *Journal of the Illinois State Historical Society* 56 (Summer 1963): 316–39.

Urwin, Gregory J. W. "'We Cannot Treat Negroes . . . As Prisoners of War': Racial Atrocities and Reprisals in Civil War Arkansas." *Civil War History* 42, no. 3 (1996): 193–210.

Virginia State Library. "Belle Isle." *Virginia Cavalcade,* n.v. (Winter 1955): 8–14.

Walker, T. R. "Rock Island Prison Barracks." In *Civil War Prisons,* edited by William B. Hesseltine, 48–59. Kent, Ohio: Kent State University Press, 1962.

Westwood, Howard C. "Captive Black Union Soldiers in Charleston—What To Do?" *Civil War History* 28, no. 1 (1982): 28–44.

White, Raymond D. "Colonel John A. Fite's Letters from Prison." *Tennessee Historical Quarterly* 32 (1973): 140–47.

Williams, T. Harry. "Benjamin F. Wade and the Atrocity Propaganda of the Civil War." *Ohio Archaeological and Historical Quarterly* 48 (1939): 33–43.

Winders, Bruce. "Prisoners of War: U.S. Prisoners." In *The United States and Mexico at War: Nineteenth-Century Expansionism and Conflict,* edited by Donald S. Frazier, 335. New York: Macmillan, 1998.

Wright, Willard E. "Some Letters of Lucius Bellinger Northrop." *Virginia Magazine of History and Biography* 68, no. 4 (1960): 456–77.

Dissertations

Dietz, Anthony G. "The Prisoner of War in the United States during the War of 1812." Ph.D. dissertation, American University, 1964.

Haffner, Gerald O. "The Treatment of Prisoners of War by the Americans during the War of Independence." Ph.D. dissertation, Indiana University, 1952.

Hunter, Leslie Gene. "Warden for the Union: General William Hoffman (1807–1884)." Ph.D. dissertation, University of Arizona, 1971.

Roberts, Nancy A. "The Afterlife of Civil War Prisons and Their Dead." Ph.D. dissertation, University of Oregon, 1996.

Thomas, Eugene Marvin, III. "Prisoner of War Exchange during the American Civil War." Ph.D. dissertation, Auburn University, 1976.

Williams, T. Harry. "The Committee on the Conduct of the War: A Study in Civil War Politics." Ph.D. dissertation, University of Wisconsin, 1937.

Internet Sites

"Camp Ford." www.texasbeyondhistory.net/ford (accessed 24 December 2004).

Ryan, Milton Asbury. "Experience of a Confederate Soldier in Camp and Prison in the Civil War, 1861–1865." www.izzy.net/~michaelg/ma-ryan.htm (accessed 24 December 2004).

Index

Bliss, Zenas R., 30

Booth, Benjamin, 278

Bragg, Braxton: warns soldiers against capture, 196

Brannock, Cyrus, 190

bread riot (Richmond), 183–84

Brent, George W., 304

Brooks, Stewart, 305

Buchanan, James: investigates Twiggs's surrender, 29

Buckner, Simon B., 90

Buell, Don Carlos, 138

Burnside, Ambrose E.: and fall of Roanoke Island, 89; and work with JCCW, 240

Butler, Benjamin F.: and the execution of Mumford, 130; unlawfully confines prisoners in New Orleans, 133; designated a felon by Davis, 145–46; proposes plan to resume general exchanges, 159–60; designated special agent for exchange, 161; inspection of Point Lookout, 176–77; negotiates and coordinates resumption of limited exchanges, 213–16; proposes resumption of general exchanges, 215–16; attempts to correspond directly with Lincoln, 216; attempts to defy Grant's order suspending exchanges, 256–57; advances plan to shift blame for suspended exchanges to the Confederacy, 258; opposes naval prisoner exchanges, 262–63; attacks Lincoln administration exchange policies, 274; relieved of command and exchange duties, 274

Cahaba Prison: establishment of, 208; unsuitability as a prison, 208–9; closed and prisoners transferred to Andersonville, 209; Winder compelled to reopen, 251; prisoners riot at, 288; postwar disposition of, 290

Cameron, Simon: arms Unionists in St. Louis, 30–31, 57, 64–65

Camp Butler: establishment of, 90; inadequacies of, 96; northern papers report on terrible conditions at, 97

Camp Chase: enlargement and designations of Prison No. 1 and Prison No. 2, 64–65; es-

tablishment and characteristics of, 64–65; addition of Prison No. 3, 99; overcrowding at, 100; selected to confine Union parolees, 134; accommodations for parolees in, 138; commander pleads for renovations, 177; postwar disposition of, 292

Camp Douglas: establishment of, 90; conditions in, 92–93; lack of security at, 94; effects of overcrowding in, 95; smallpox outbreak at, 95; selected to confine Union parolees, 143; parolee riot at, 144; designated a major confinement center, 165; Sanitary Commission recommends closing, 165; commander's request for renovations denied by Stanton, 167; torture of prisoners at, 168; inadequate medical facilities at, 169; violations of G. O. 100, 169; spiraling mortality at, 250; postwar disposition of, 292

Camp Fisk, 287

Camp Ford, 5

Camp Groce, 5

Camp Jackson, 31

Camp Morton: establishment of, 90; conditions in, 91–92; Union inspection of, 178; postwar disposition of, 292

Camp Oglethorpe: establishment of and conditions at, 209–10

Camp Parole: established for paroled prisoners, 134; inspected by Hoffman, 136; conditions at, 137, 142

Camp Sumter. *See* Andersonville Prison

Camp Verde, 29; confinement and exchange of prisoners at, 29–30

Campbell, Archibald, 11

Campbell, John A.: calls for War Department intervention at Andersonville, 233

camps of instruction: established by General Orders No. 72, 133–35

Carrington, William A.: warns of impending medical catastrophe in Richmond prisons (1863), 192; inspection of Belle Isle, 207–8

Cartel for the Exchange of Prisoners (1813): negotiation and provisions, 15–17; violations of, 19

Davis, Jefferson: issues letters of marque and general reprisal, 33; protests treatment of privateers, 34–35; threatens reprisals because of treatment of privateers, 34–35, 37; pushes for a general exchange, 76; reaction to General Orders No. 11, 128–29; orders retaliation against Hunter, Phelps, Butler, and Fitch, 129–31; refuses to relinquish control of prisoners to states, 129–31; designates Butler a felon, 145; threatens retaliation against slaves captured in arms and their officers, 147–48; blames Union for suspension of general exchanges, 218; fully aware of conditions at Andersonville, 227; forced to accede to Union conditions for exchange, 256; and calls from citizens for unilateral release of Union prisoners, 260; memoirs defend Confederate treatment of prisoners, 300, 302; degree of knowledge of conditions in Confederate prisons, 308–9

Dearborn, John, 18

DeLand, Charles V.: named commander of Camp Douglas, 166; policies increase mortality at Camp Douglas, 171

Demopolis, AL: camp for Confederate parolees, 155–56

Dennison, William, 64

Dimick, Justin E., 60–61

direct exchanges: Lee and McClellan engage in, 112; limited by Lincoln, 112

Dix, John A.: appointed to negotiate terms for a general exchange, 115

Dix–Hill Cartel (1862): revision of, 4; to be modeled on Cartel of 1813, 87; initial negotiations regarding, 87–88; provisions of, 116–17; intended to be permanent, 117; mechanics of, 118–19; rate of exchange under, 1862, 122; allows closing of prisons, 122–23; prisoners refusing exchange under, 122–23; problems concerning classification of prisoners qualified for exchange, 131–32; Union violates exchange point provisions, 149

Doster, James, 302

Dow, Neal, 193

Dykes, Ben, 198

Elmira Prison: commander protests establishment of, 246; establishment and characteristics of, 246; first prisoners arrive from Point Lookout, 246–47; scurvy and diarrhea ravage prisoners at, 248, 272; Union surgeons deplore conditions at, 250; effects of exposure at, 272; prisoners designate prison "Helmira," 272; postwar disposition of, 292

Ely, Alfred: captured at Manassas, 43; denounces rations issued in Richmond prisons, 50; prepares petition urging general exchanges, 79; calls for return of all prisoners, 114

exchange of prisoners: in Revolution, 7–9; in War of 1812, 13–20; in Mexican War, 13–23; and black prisoners, 17–18

exchange values of prisoners: in Revolution, 13; in War of 1812, 15

Fish, Hamilton: selected to arrange exchanges, 85–88

Fitch, Graham N., 130; declared a felon, 130–31

Fleming, Walter L., 309

Florence (Confederate prison at): Seddon orders filled before construction is complete, 253; postwar disposition of, 291

Fort Columbus: establishment and characteristics of, 57–58; transfer of prisoners from, 61

Fort Delaware: establishment and construction of, 101; enlargement of, 153; routine use of torture at, 181; impact of policy of systematic retaliation against prisoners on (1863), 181–82; Sanitary Commission inspection of, 182; smallpox and scurvy among prisoners at, 182; Union inspectors fault diet given at, 182–83; postwar disposition of, 292

Fort Donelson: disposition of prisoners from, 89–90

Fort Lafayette: establishment and characteristics of, 56; overcrowding in, 73; postwar disposition of, 292

Fort McHenry, 58

Fort Monroe, 83

Fort Moultrie, 25

Fort Pickens, 44

Fort Pillow, TN: massacre at, 240–41; JCCW investigation of massacre, 241

Fort Sumter: contested, 25–26; surrender of, 32

Fort Van Dorn, 30

Fort Warren: establishment and characteristics of, 59–61; overcrowding in, 73; postwar disposition of, 292

Foster, J. G.: protests shelling of prisoners on Morris Island (SC), 227–28; places Confederate officers under friendly fire, 228

Fox, Gustavus V., 262

Freedley, Henry W.: supervises delivery of captives to Vicksburg, 120

Fremont, John C.: and indirect exchanges, 82

Frost, Daniel M., 31

Frost, Griffin, 235

Fry, C. H., 138

Fuller, A. C., 94

Futch, Ovid, 297

Gage, Thomas, 9, 11

"Galvanized Yankees," 275

Gardner, William H.: assigned to command of Confederate military prisons east of the Mississippi, 228; responsibilities and authority unclear, 229; requests relief from assignment and calls for the appointment of a commissary general of prisoners, 255

Garfield, James, 298

Gee, John H.: commander of Salisbury Prison, overwhelmed by transfers (1864), 254; supervises general exchange at Salisbury, 278

general exchange of prisoners (1865): Grant's motivation for, 274–75; procedure at Salisbury regarding, 278–79; and Danville, 279; and Libby, 279–80

General Orders No. 11 (Union), 128

General Orders No. 32 (Union): increases Hoffman's authority, 104–5

General Orders No. 49 (Union), 151, 153

General Orders No. 54 (Confederate), 129

General Orders No. 59 (Confederate), 131

General Orders No. 60 (Confederate), 131

General Orders No. 67 (Union): increases Hoffman's authority, 105–6; ignored by officers in the field, 106

General Orders No. 72 (Union): rescinds paroles of Union soldiers, 133–34

General Orders No. 100 (Union): provisions of, 152–53; provisions protecting enemy prisoners violated by Stanton, 168

General Orders No. 123 (Confederate): declares Vicksburg parolees exchanged, 156

General Orders No. 190 (Union): expands Hoffman's authority over prison system, 236–37

General Orders No. 207 (Union), 154

General Orders No. 208 (Confederate): warns Confederate soldiers the Union is not abiding by the terms of the Dix-Hill Cartel, 196

Gibbs, George C., 108

Gibson, A. A., 102

Goff, Richard, 302

Goldsborough, Lawrence M.: and special exchanges, 82

Gooch, Daniel W.: participates in JCCW investigation of Fort Pillow massacre, 241

Governor's Island: prisons established on, 56; overcrowding in, 73; enlargement of, 102

Grand Army of the Republic: and use of prisoner narratives and experiences, 293–94; initiation ritual, 294

Grant, Ulysses S.: prohibits exchange, 4; favors general exchanges (1862), 80; and fall of Fort Donelson, 89; and urgency for exchanges, 1862, 89; paroles Vicksburg captives, 154; actual reason for terminating exchanges, 217; orders Butler to cease exchange negotiations, 217; professes termination of exchanges due to Confederate treatment of black prisoners, 218; ends Butler's scheme to resume exchanges, 257; rationale for suspending general exchanges, 257; and duplicity in prisoners exchange negotiations, 262; approves of plan to have each government assume responsibility for supplying its own prisoners, 270–71; moves to initiate

Stanton on condition of returned prisoners at Annapolis, 243; proposes successive reductions in ration issues to prisoners, 245; compelled to authorize rudimentary improvements (1864), 248–49; misrepresents conditions in northern prisons, 250; tightens control over exchanges, 263; moves to close prisons, 289; collects all unused money from prison funds, 289–90; duty as commissary general of prisoners ends, 290; evidence of misuse of prison funds, 290

Hood, John Bell, 281

hospital funds: established by Hoffman's orders, 125

Hough, David, 32

Houston, Sam: objects to secession of Texas, 26; condemns Twiggs's capitulation, 28

Howard's tobacco factory, 47, 77

Howe, William, 9

Huger, Benjamin: and special exchanges, 83; and exchange negotiations, 108–11

Hunter, David: accused of inciting servile insurrection, 130; declared an outlaw, 131

indirect exchanges, 82

Island No. 10, 99

Iverson, John F.: attributes high mortality at Florence to starvation, 282

James, Frederick Augustus: death at Andersonville, 252

Jeff Davis: trial of the crew of, 37, 77

Jersey, 9

Johnson, A. J., 276

Johnson, Andrew: requests control of exchanges of prisoners from Tennessee, 123

Johnson, G. K., 182

Johnson's Island: selection as a prison depot and construction, 70; inadequate size of, 73; enlargement of, 98; designated an officers' prison, 98–99

Johnston, Joseph: reports that his Army of Tennessee is well supplied even as prisoners are starving at Andersonville, 226

Joint Committee on the Conduct of the War

(JCCW): agenda and use of propaganda and, 238; pioneering use of photography for propaganda purposes, 244; releases report on returned prisoners, 244; propaganda backfires, 259; agenda, objectives, and methods survive the war, 295–96

Jones, J. William: secretary of Southern Historical Society, 299; chief author of defense of Confederate treatment of prisoners, 299–308

Jones, Sam: and shelling of prisoners on Morris Island (SC), 227–28

Julian, George: and JCCW close relationship with Stanton, 238; and attacks on Confederate treatment of prisoners, 239

Kean, Robert G. H.: reports on Richmond bread riot, 183–84; and relief of Northrop, 283

Key, Thomas M., 112

Killen's Mills, SC: Winder plans to establish a prison at, 267

Kilpatrick, Judson: leads raid on Richmond, 203

King, John: ravaged by scurvy at Elmira, 248; and oath of allegiance, 275; postwar narrative of experiences, 293

Kirkwood, Samuel J.: protests treatment of Union parolees, 135, 141

Knight, Mrs. Sylvester R., 75

L. Libby and Son, 107

Lawton, Alexander R.: Confederate quartermaster general, 186; plans for provisioning Andersonville, 199

Lazelle, H. M.: and inspection of Camp Chase, 1862, 100–101; oversees exchanges at Vicksburg, 120

Lee, Robert E.: presses for general exchange (1862), 113; urges transfer of prisoners out of Richmond to Danville (VA), 189

Lee, W. H.: capture and use as a hostage, 153

legal classification of prisoners: American Revolution, 8, 10, 12; War of 1812, 13, 17–18; Civil War, 33–34, 36, 131–33

Leighton, George E., 62

Letcher, John: requests control of captured Virginia Unionists, 129–30

letters of marque and general reprisal, 33

Libby Prison: establishment of, 107; Union rations shipped to, 157; overcrowding and deteriorating conditions in (1863), 185; escape from, 203; postwar disposition of, 291–92

Lieber, Francis: and General Orders No. 100, 152

Ligon and Company warehouse, 40–42

limited exchanges of prisoners: resumed in 1864, 213; stymied by issue of black prisoners, 215

Lincoln, Abraham: and refusal to recognize the Confederacy, 33–34, 55, 75–77; and legal status of privateers, 34–37; and suspension of the writ of habeas corpus, 56; opposes general exchanges of prisoners, 75; pressed to accede to exchanges, 78–79, 81, 112; and personal knowledge of conditions in northern prisons, 114–15, 311–15; and manipulation of exchanges for personal and political purposes, 123; supports sending Union parolees to fight the Sioux in Minnesota, 140; dissatisfied with exchanges under the cartel, 148; refuses personal meeting with Butler, 216; pressed by Radicals to retaliate after returned prisoners report, 244; political problems due to exchange termination, 245, 260; blamed by prisoners for no exchanges, 252; senior military officers advise resumption of general exchanges, 259; supporters warn he will be blamed for prisoner deaths, 259; blamed by prisoners for suspension of exchanges, 259, 264; supports plan for naval prisoner exchanges, 262

Logan, John, 298

Loomis, Gustavus, 58

"Lost Cause," 5

Ludlow, William H.: designated Union acting agent for exchange, 132; protests decision to halt exchanges, 154

Lynchburg fairgrounds: establishment of prison and conditions at, 108

Lynch's Slave Pen: conditions in, 62

Lyon, Nathaniel: appointed to command Union troops in St. Louis, 31; captures and paroles Confederate garrison at Camp Jackson, 32

Macon, GA: prison established in, 50

Macon Telegraph: and conditions at Andersonville, 221; and burden of holding prisoners at Andersonville, 229

Madison, James, 14

Manassas, Battle of (1861), 7, 39

Marston, Gilman, 173

Mason, John, 16, 66, 177

Mayo, Joseph, 45

Mayo's tobacco factory, 47

McClellan, George B.: sends prisoners to Fort Lafayette, 44; favors general exchanges (1862), 80

McCulloch, Benjamin: and capture of Union garrison in Texas, 27

McDowell, Irvin, 39

McDowell, Joseph N., 62

McDowell Medical College: selected as a Union prison, 62

McGraw, T. G., 152

McPherson, James M., 297, 300

Meade, R. K., 25

Meigs, Montgomery C.: assumes responsibility for Union prisoners, 65; recommends appointment of a commissary general of prisoners, 65–66; frugality of, 70–71, 93, 171–72, 178; refuses request for construction of additional hospital facilities at Camp Morton, 178

Mercer, Hugh, 146

Meredith, Sullivan A.: replaces Ludlow as Union agent of exchange, 155; proposes each government supply its own prisoners, 157; brokers program to send supplies to Union prisoners in Richmond, 193; and termination of the program, 194

Mexican War: lessons learned/ignored, 2, 8, 23–24; unique characteristics of, 20–21; treatment, parole, and exchange of prisoners, 22; retaliation in, 23

Millen, GA: Winder proposes prison construction at, 234; Seddon orders prison filled before construction is complete, 252; postwar disposition of, 291

Minnesota, 33

Mitchell, John, 14

Moffett, George, 181

Monroe, James, 15

Montgomery, Norris, 126

Moody, Granville, 99

Moore, A. B., 49

Morfit, Clarence: manages confiscated Union funds, 195

Morgan, John Hunt: confined at Camp Douglas, 167

Morris Island, SC: and shelling of prisoners in Charleston, 227–28

Morrison, Pitcairn, 96

Morton, Oliver P.: offers to receive prisoners, 89; protests treatment of Union parolees, 142

Mulligan, James A., 94

Mumford, William, 130

Myers, Abraham C.: denounces Lynchburg fairgrounds prison selection, 108

Myrtle Street Prison: new designation for Lynch's Slave Pen, 62

Neely, Mark E., 311

Negro prisoners: slaves captured in arms to be delivered to states of origin, 146, 151–52

New York, 256–57

New York Times: calls for implementation of forced labor for Confederate prisoners, 213–14; challenges Lincoln administration's decision to suspend exchanges, 260, 264

Newport News Prison, 289

Norman, Andrew, 57

Northrop, Lucius B.: Confederate commissary general of subsistence, 4; friendship with and sponsorship of Jefferson Davis, 186; policy of prisoner ration allocation results in starvation, 186; assumes responsibility for feeding Union prisoners and immediately proposes severe reductions in quality and quantity of food issued to prisoners, 186–88; and feud with John H.

Winder, 187; refuses to provide adequate rations for Andersonville, 225–26; and evidence that he could have provided sufficient rations for Andersonville had he wished, 226; fails to adequately provision either prisoners or Army of Northern Virginia, 281–83; allowed to resign, 283

oath of allegiance (Union): form recording, 122

Office of the Commissary General of Prisoners (War of 1812), 16–17

Old Capital Prison: establishment and characteristics of, 59

Olmstead, Frederick Law: directs and justifies Sanitary Commission inspections, 174, 176

O'Neal, Edward, 211

Ould, Robert: designated Confederate agent of exchange, 119; demands explanation of death of Mumford and unlawful confinement of Confederate prisoners, 145; blames Union for the termination of general exchanges, 151; refuses to modify Confederate position on captured ex-slaves, 155; unilaterally declares Vicksburg parolees exchanged, 155; and discipline problems with Confederate parolees, 155–56

Overland campaign: prisoners from, 219, 235

Owen, John L., 130

Owen, Richard D., 92

Palmer's tobacco factory, 47

parole of prisoners: individual paroles, 83–84; problems concerning, 133; complaints of parolees, 135; accusations of cowardice, 138

Pea Patch Island, 101

Perry, 33

Persons, Alexander: selected to command (excluding stockade) at Andersonville, 200; requests permission to enlarge Andersonville stockade, 221

Petrel, 37

Pettigrew, James J., 25

Phelan, James, 130

Phelps, John W.: accused of inciting servile insurrection, 130; declared an outlaw, 131

Pickens, Francis W., 25–26

Pierson, William S.: selected to command at Johnson's Island, 72

Pillow, Gideon J.: and indirect exchanges, 82; Davis selects to succeed Winder as commissary general of prisoners, 270; relieved of duty as commissary general, 280

Pittsfield, MA (War of 1812 prisoner-of-war camp), 16

"Plug Uglies," 46

Point Lookout Prison: establishment of, 172; Stanton refuses to allow construction of barracks at, 173; inadequate shelter at, 173–74; smallpox and scurvy ravage prisoners at, 174; Sanitary Commission inspection of, 174–76; prison fund misused at, 176–77; effects of overcrowding at (1864), 235; results of absence of fresh vegetables at, 235–36; misappropriation of prison fund at, 236; postwar disposition of, 292

Polk, James K., 21

Polk, Leonidas, 209

Pope, John: and capture of prisoners at Milford, MO, 63; issues General Orders No. 11, 128

Potter, J. A., 166

Price, Sterling: and indirect exchanges, 82

prison fund: Hoffman orders established, 125

prisoner-of-war narratives: motivations, 292–93; and use by clergy, 293; and use by veterans' groups, 293–94; and use by politicians, 294–95

prisoner-of-war system, Confederate: early development of, 50–54; effects of overcrowding in (1862), 106–7; impact of designation of Richmond as the primary point of concentration for prisoners, 183; suffers from muddled chain of command, 201; and decision to do nothing to feed starving prisoners, 269; postwar justification and rationalization for, 297–308

prisoner-of-war system, Union: early development of, 38, 55; reasons for deplorable conditions in, 1862, 103; and effects of hardening of attitudes of Stanton, Hoffman, and JCCW

toward Confederate prisoners, 310–11

prisoners of war: numbers during the war and mortality rate, 1

prisoners of war, Confederate: legal status of, 38; refusing exchange, 122–23, 275–76

prisoners of war, Union: citizens of Richmond come to resent presence of, 53; blamed for food shortages, 184

privateers, 33–34

Putnam, George, 266

Putnam, J. S., 166

Putnam, Sallie, 108

Queenstown, Battle of, 18

Radical Republicans: and dissatisfaction with Lincoln, 239; and objectives for post-war reconstruction of the South, 240; and increasing calls for retaliation, 264–65

Randall, J. G., 297

Randolph, George: and duplicity in exchange negotiations, 110–11

Ransom, John: transfer from Belle Isle to Andersonville, 204

retaliation against prisoners, Civil War: privateer case, 34–37; threats of by South lose effectiveness, 147–48

retaliation against prisoners, War of 1812, 13

Revolutionary War: lessons learned/ignored, 2, 8, 23–24; British use of prison ships in, 8; treatment of American prisoners during, 8–9; legal classification of prisoners in, 8–9, 10, 12; treatment of British prisoners during, 9–10; paroles and exchanges of prisoners in, 10–13; retaliation against prisoners in, 11–12

Reynolds, Daniel, 279

Rhodes, James Ford, 309

Richardson, T. G., 202, 304

Richmond Dispatch: calls for drastic reduction in rations issued to Union prisoners, 202

Richmond Examiner: urges population of Union prisoners be reduced by exposure and starvation, 196

CPSIA information can be obtained
at www.ICGtesting.com
Printed in the USA
LVHW101809091222
734906LV00005B/470